Does Aid Work?

THE LIBRARY OF POLITICAL ECONOMY

POLITICAL ECONOMY is the old name for economics. In the hands of the great classical economists, particularly Smith, Ricardo and Marx, economics was the study of the working and development of the economic system in which men and women lived. Its practitioners were driven by a desire to describe, to explain and to evaluate what they saw around them. No sharp distinction was drawn between economic analysis and economic policy nor between economic behaviour and its interaction with the technical, social and political framework.

The Library of Political Economy has been established to provide widely based explanations of economic behaviour in contemporary society.

In examining the way in which new patterns of social organization and behaviour influence the economic system and policies for combating problems associated with growth, inflation, poverty and the distribution of wealth, contributors stress the link between politics and economics and the importance of institutions in policy formulation.

This 'open-ended' approach to economics implies that there are few laws that can be held to with certainty and, by the same token, there is no generally established body of theory to be applied in all circumstances. Instead economics as presented in this library provides a way of ordering events which has constantly to be updated and modified as new situations develop. This, we believe, is its interest and its challenge.

Editorial Board

Andrew Graham, University of Oxford
Keith Griffin, University of Oxford
Geoffrey Harcourt, University of Cambridge
Roger Opie, University of Oxford
Hugh Stretton, University of Adelaide
Lester Thurow, Massachusetts Institute of Technology

Volumes in the Library

Dangerous Currents: The State of Economics—Lester Thurow
The Political Economy of Nationalism—Dudley Seers
Women's Claims: A Study in Political Economy—Lisa Peattie and Martin Rein
Urban Inequalities under State Socialism—Ivan Szelenyi
Social Innovation and the Division of Labour—Johnathan Gershuny
The Structuring of Labour Markets: The Steel and Construction Industries in Italy—Paola Villa
Monetarism and the Labour Market—Derek Robinson

Does Aid Work?

Report to an Intergovernmental Task Force

Robert Cassen & Associates

CLARENDON PRESS · OXFORD

Oxford University Press, Walton Street, Oxford OX2 6DP

Oxford New York Toronto
Delhi Bombay Calcutta Madras Karachi
Petaling Jaya Singapore Hong Kong Tokyo
Nairobi Dar es Salaam Cape Town
Melbourne Auckland

and associated companies in
Berlin Ibadan

Oxford is a trade mark of Oxford University Press

Published in the United States
by Oxford University Press, New York

British Library Cataloguing in Publication Data
Cassen, Robert
    Does aid work?: report to an inter-
    governmental task force.—(The Library
    of political economy)
    1. Economic assistance—Developing
    countries
    I. Title   II. Series
    338.91'1722'01724   HC 60
    ISBN 0–19–877249–1 Pbk

Printed in Great Britain by
Biddles Ltd, Guildford & King's Lynn

Preface

This study was commissioned by the Task Force on Concessional Flows set up by the Development Committee—The Joint Ministerial Committee of the Boards of Governors of the World Bank and International Monetary Fund. The following governments were members of the Task Force: Belgium, Canada, China, Costa Rica, Dominican Republic, Finland, France, Germany (Federal Republic), India, Indonesia, Italy, Japan, Kuwait, Netherlands, Saudi Arabia, Senegal, Tanzania, United Kingdom, United States. The World Bank acted as the Task Force's Secretariat. The study was funded by the donor members of the group.

It was agreed at the outset that the study would be prepared by independent consultants who would have no obligation to modify it in the light of the views of Task Force members or other agencies. A draft of the consultants' report was presented to a meeting of the Task Force in Princeton, NJ in February 1985. At that meeting it was agreed that the report could be published after revision under the consultants' editorial control. During the report's preparation, information and comments were received from a wide variety of governments—Task Force members and others—and international agencies. But the final text reflects solely the views of the consultants and the director of the study. Governments and institutions which have assisted the authors have not seen the final text, and bear no responsibility whatsoever for its contents.

In preparing the report, several contributing studies were first undertaken: country studies of Bangladesh, Colombia, India, Kenya, Malawi, Mali, and South Korea, and additional studies of Technical Cooperation, Project Aid, Comparisons of Multilateral and Bilateral Agencies, and a Literature Survey to cover materials not otherwise included. (A full list of the studies and their authors may be found in Annex A.)

Overall direction of the study was undertaken by Professor R. H. Cassen of the Institute of Development Studies, University of Sussex, England, together with Professor B. Bagley (Johns Hopkins SAIS), G. Ed. Bourgoignie (independent consultant, Ottawa), P. Chaudhuri (AFRAS, University of Sussex), P. Daniel (IDS, Sussex), A. Duncan (QEH, Oxford), S. Griffith-Jones (IDS, Sussex), C. Gulick (independent consultant, Washington, DC), A. Hewitt (ODI, London), J. Kydd (Wye College, University of London), Professor M. Lipton

(IDS, Sussex), P. Mosley (University of Bath), R. Muscat (independent consultant, Washington, DC), G. Ortona (University of Turin), J. Pell (independent consultant, Eire), E. Y. Sachse (independent consultant, Washington, DC), N. Segal (Segal, Quince, Wicksteed, Cambridge), D. Steinberg (USAID, Washington, DC), Professor J. Toye (Centre for Development Studies, Swansea), Professor B. Van Arkadie (ISS, The Hague), R. Whyte (independent consultant, Chichester), W. Wicksteed (Segal, Quince, Wicksteed, Cambridge), and K. de Wilde (ISS, The Hague).

The authors would wish to thank the many individuals who gave their time to help the preparation of the report and its component studies. Singling out any names would be invidious, but those who responded so generously will long be remembered. Lastly, the director of the study acknowledges warmly the work of 100% Word-Processing Services (London), where the text was handled with the greatest cheerfulness and efficiency.

November, 1985

Contents

List of Tables

Abbreviations

ACP	*Africa, Caribbean, and Pacific*
ADB	*Asian Development Bank*
AfDB	*African Development Bank*
BADEA	*Arab Bank for Economic Development in Africa*
CFF	*Compensatory Finance Facility*
CG	*Consultative Group*
CGIAR	*Consultative Group on International Agricultural Research*
CIDA	*Canadian International Development Agency*
CIP	*commodity import programme*
CMEA	*Council for Mutual Economic Assistance (formerly COMECON)*
DAC	*Development Assistance Committee*
DFC	*development finance corporation*
DOM/TOM	*Départements et Territoires d'Outre Mer*
EDF	*European Development Fund*
EEC	*European Economic Community*
EFF	*Extended Fund Facility*
FAO	*Food and Agriculture Organization*
FINNIDA	*Finnish International Development Agency*
FMO	*Netherlands Development Finance Co.*
IBRD	*International Bank for Reconstruction and Development*
ICOR	*incremental capital—output ratio*
IDA	*International Development Association*
IDB	*Inter-American Development Bank*
IDRC	*International Development Research Centre*
IDS	*Institute of Development Studies (University of Sussex)*
IEFR	*International Emergency Food Reserve*
IFAD	*International Fund for Agricultural Development*
IFC	*International Finance Corporation*
ILO	*International Labour Office*
IMF	*International Monetary Fund*
IPPF	*International Planned Parenthood Federation*
IRDP	*integrated rural development project*
JCGP	*Joint Consultative Group of Policy*
LIBOR	*London interbank offered rate*
LLDC	*least developed country*
MDB	*multilateral development bank*

NFS	*National Food Strategy*
NIC	*newly industrializing country*
NGO	*non-governmental organization*
ODA	*Official Development Assistance; see also UK ODA*
ODR	*Office de Développement Rurale*
OECD	*Organization for Economic Cooperation and Development*
OOF	*other official flows*
OPEC	*Organization of Petroleum Exporting Countries*
PC	*Population Council*
PRMC	*Cereals Market Restructuring Project*
SAL	*Structural Adjustment Loan*
SIDA	*Swedish International Development Authority*
TC	*technical cooperation*
TCDC	*technical cooperation among developing countries*
UK ODA	*United Kingdom Overseas Development Administration*
UMOA	*West African Monetary Union*
UMR	*usual marketing requirements*
UN	*United Nations*
UNDP	*United Nations Development Programme*
UNFPA	*United Nations Fund for Population Activities*
UNICEF	*United Nations Children's Fund*
UNIDO	*United Nations Industrial Development Organization*
UNITAR	*United Nations Institute for Training and Research*
USAID	*United States Agency for International Development*
WFC	*World Food Council*
WFP	*World Food Programme*
WHO	*World Health Organization*

Note: Throughout this report $ = US dollar, and billion = 1,000,000,000.

CHAPTER ONE
Introduction

The title of this report deliberately asks a question. The answer given here is broadly positive. But aid, like most human endeavours, is far from perfect. The report tells of aid's successes; it also focuses on its imperfections: their magnitude, their causes, how to judge them, what can be done about them.

The investigation that underlies the report has been the first attempt of its kind. Evaluations of aid typically look piecemeal at individual aid projects or other aid activities. Occasionally an aid agency or an academic undertakes a review of aid from one source to a given country or sector; a few scholars have looked at aid from all sources to a particular country, or made statistical analyses of aid across countries. There have also been desk surveys of the aid literature. But the present exercise has gone further, trying to survey a large sample of aid activities, with a number of country case studies all written to the same terms of reference, and various other papers on aid and its institutions.

Even so, the investigation has been limited. It has looked at only seven countries in detail, a small sample. And it has had to accomplish its investigative work in less than twelve months. Despite these limitations, the findings are more than suggestive. They draw on the work of many experienced and knowledgeable people—those who have worked within the project, and the many more who have written their own studies or shared their knowledge with the authors in interviews. Wider coverage and more intensive enquiries would solidify and strengthen the conclusions, modifying them here and there, perhaps modifying a few substantially. But even with much more time and resources, this report would still not have produced comprehensive and indubitable findings. A large proportion of aid has never been subjected to evaluation. The project evaluations that exist are frequently not comparable. Even without such difficulties, there are unfathomable questions about the interaction between aid activities and the milieu of policies and circumstances in which they are conducted. Clearly, the *precise* degree of the effectiveness of aid is in the end unknowable. It is the authors' hope that the issues arising here will be further examined. But it is doubtful that further examination would undermine the main conclusions of the study. The investigation, though limited, has been extensive and deep.

Of course, some writings on aid condemn the whole enterprise. But they have typically been written by people far from familiar with the enormous spectrum of aid activities, and often start from political premises which determine their conclusions even before contemplation of such evidence as they examine. There are also excessively favourable accounts of aid, whose authors are ignorant of (or choose to ignore) the evidence that a significant amount of aid has not worked well. Like everybody else, the authors of this book had their own subjective ideas about aid. They shared the view that there is nothing wrong with aid a priori, but that its virtue is not to be taken for granted. They have simply tried to assess where it has worked and where it has not.

What is aid?

First, some definitions and facts are in order. The fundamental idea of aid is a transfer of resources on concessional terms—on terms, that is, more generous or 'softer' than loans obtainable in the world's capital markets. In most of this report the word 'aid' is used in the strict sense of Official Development Assistance (ODA). The guardian of official information about aid is the Development Assistance Committee (DAC) of the OECD; its annual volume *Development Cooperation* contains the most commonly used aid statistics.

For the DAC, aid qualifies as ODA on three criteria: it has to be undertaken by official agencies; it has to have the promotion of economic development and welfare as its main objectives; and it has to have a 'grant element' of 25 per cent or more. The grant element measures the degree of concessionality of an aid transfer compared with market terms, which are normally taken to include a rate of interest of 10 per cent. Thus, an outright grant of aid has a 100 per cent grant element; a loan at 10 per cent has a zero grant element; a soft loan will lie somewhere in between. The maturity of a loan (that is, the number of years over which it is repaid) and its grace period—the interval before repayment starts—also affect the measured grant element.

This definition of aid excludes some concessional flows, namely those of the private voluntary agencies. It also excludes official flows of little or no concessionality: some of these are aid-like in purpose. Grants, soft loans, or credits for military purposes are also specifically excluded. But food aid and technical cooperation (TC) are included. The latter covers assistance (nearly all grants) for developing country individuals receiving education or training at home or abroad, and for teachers, administrators, technical experts, and the like working in developing countries. In this report, the terms 'financial aid' or 'capital aid' are sometimes used to distinguish the rest of aid from TC and food or other commodity aid. And 'aid' refers almost always to long-term development assistance, not emergency or relief aid, although official contributions for such purposes are included in overall figures for aid.

Who receives aid?

The recipients of aid are of course the developing countries. For statistical purposes, the OECD divides these into 'low-income' (1980 per capita income below $600); 'lower middle-income' (1980 per capita income between $600 and $1,200) and 'upper middle-income' (above $1,200). The low-income group includes a sub-group defined by the UN as 'least developed countries' (LLDCs). The UN definition is based on criteria of income, education, and the extent of manufacturing in national production; it is intended to identify those countries at a low level of economic development—most of them in sub-Saharan Africa, but including also Bangladesh and some smaller Asian countries, and Haiti. As the UN list contains some anomalies of inclusion and exclusion, this report speaks more loosely of the 'poorest countries', but with the same intention of referring to the most deprived countries which face particularly severe obstacles to development.

The LLDCs make up 8.6 per cent of the developing countries' population, and receive just under 24 per cent of all aid; the low-income countries (which include China and India) account for virtually 75 per cent of population and 60 per cent of aid. But, as Fig. 1.1 and Table 1.1 show, upper middle-income countries still receive nearly a quarter of all aid, mostly for political reasons.

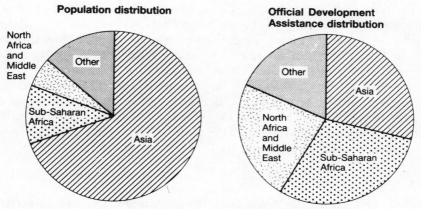

Figure 1.1. Distribution of population and ODA
Source: see Table 1.1.

TABLE 1.1.

Net receipts of Official Development Assistance by region and income groups

Region Countries	ODA (1982/3) $ billion	Percentage of total ODA 1977/8	Percentage of total ODA 1982/3	Percentage of population
Asia	7.2	27.2	28.5	69.6
(Low-income	6.2	23.3	24.6	64.4)
Sub-Saharan Africa	7.6	25.4	30.0	11.1
(Low-income	6.4	20.6	25.2	7.6)
North Africa and				
Middle East	5.9	31.9	23.1	5.6
(Low-income	1.9	14.9	7.5	1.6)
(Middle-income	3.9	16.9	15.5	4.1)
America	3.1	10.0	12.1	10.9
(Low-income	0.7	1.9	2.9	0.6)
(Middle-income	2.3	8.2	9.2	10.3)
Europe	0.6	1.9	2.4	2.6
Oceania	1.0	3.7	3.9	0.1
Total	25.4	100	100	100
Least developed	6.3	21.0	23.9	8.6
Low-income	15.3	61.0	60.5	74.2

Source: OECD, Development Assistance Committee, *Development Cooperation: 1984 Review*, Paris, November 1984. Figures in this Table are for OECD countries only.

In Asia and sub-Saharan Africa, nearly all the aid goes to low-income countries. Most of the aid for middle-income countries (upper and lower) goes to Israel, Jordan and Syria; and Egypt (low-income in the OECD's tables, lower-middle in the World Bank's) is the main recipient in North Africa. 'America' includes Central and South America and the Caribbean; a large share of the aid to the middle-income countries here is TC, and French aid to its Départements et Territoires d'Outre Mer (DOM/TOM). The European countries include Cyprus and Malta and the main aid recipient, Turkey—also an upper middle-income country.

Who gives aid?

Aid donors are for the most part the governments of the industrial countries; but OPEC members and some other developing countries also give aid. Most of the governments give their aid both directly—bilateral aid—and indirectly, via multilateral or other channels.

One of the main channels of multilateral aid is the International Development Association (IDA), the World Bank's soft loan window. The World Bank itself lends money, but this is raised on the world's capital markets (on the security of member governments' capital subscriptions) and is lent at only modestly concessional rates. The Bank's loans therefore count as 'Other Official Flows' (OOF) rather than ODA. IDA funds are contributed by donor governments in triennial 'replenishments'; its loans are highly concessional and go mostly to low-income countries.

In reality, World Bank and IDA loans are identical in everything except their financial terms. The same country may receive both types of loans, in effect borrowing on a blend of harder and softer terms. For this reason, World Bank loans are more like aid than most OOF; Bank and IDA loans together are often referred to as 'World Bank group lending'.

The other main multilateral channels are the Regional Banks and the UN 'family' of specialized agencies. The latter include the UN Development Programme (UNDP)—principally for TC—and a number of smaller UN agencies; the Food and Agriculture Organization (FAO)—also mainly for TC; and the World Health Organization (WHO). The International Fund for Agricultural Development (IFAD) has an unusual financial base, being funded jointly by DAC and OPEC countries. The Regional Banks—the African, Asian, and Inter-American Development Banks—were modelled on the World Bank, but have somewhat different funding structures. Finally there is the EEC's aid programme and its main instrument, the European Development Fund (EDF); this a multinational rather than a fully multilateral programme. (These agencies, and the differentiation of their functions from those of bilateral programmes, are discussed in Chapter 9.)

The agencies have other roles besides providing aid. They carry out wide-ranging economic analysis and reporting; and they help to coordinate aid and encourage international cooperation. Through the DAC, the main industrial country donors discuss a variety of aspects of aid, and undertake regular reviews of each others' programmes. The OPEC countries coordinate among themselves and, by participating in the multilateral organizations and liaising with the DAC, are closely involved in the aid process.

One group of donors takes a very different approach to aid: the Soviet bloc. Its aid is included in DAC statistics of total aid. But the volume of aid is reported at widely differing levels, depending on the definitions employed. On the bloc countries' own definitions, their aid is much greater than the DAC allows. The great bulk of it is confined to three countries—Cuba, Mongolia, and Vietnam—to which DAC and OPEC members give virtually no aid. Its effectiveness is not discussed in this report, which concentrates on the DAC donors and the multilateral agencies who supplied most of the material for it.

Some magnitudes

Fig. 1.2 and Table 1.2 outline the aid performance of the main official donors. The figures refer to *net* receipts, i.e. net of interest and repayments on past aid, much of which was on harder terms than current aid. The total amount of aid reached a peak in 1980, and has been roughly constant since then. In the five years to 1983, some countries—Canada, New Zealand, the United Kingdom, the OPEC donors—reduced their aid. But many others substantially increased theirs—by between 4 and 10 per cent for ten countries, and by over 10 per cent for Finland, France (excluding DOM/TOM) and Japan. Slow but positive growth of just under 2 per cent was shown by two donors: Sweden, and the largest donor, the United States. Of course, such comparisons depend on the period chosen.

Other notable facts about the pattern of aid include the large increase in the share going to sub-Saharan Africa. Correspondingly, the shares of India and Pakistan have gone down, while China, starting at a modest level, has become a major recipient of aid. (The figures in 1983 for the three countries were $1.7 billion for India, $0.7 billion for Pakistan, and $0.66 billion for China). In Africa, some twenty countries received aid of less than $100 million and another twenty between $100 and $250 million. Seven received substantially more: Kenya, Reunion, Senegal, Somalia, Sudan, Tanzania, and Zaire. The two biggest African recipients in recent years have been Sudan and Tanzania, which averaged over $740 million and $650 million a year respectively in 1980–3, though Tanzania's receipts declined a little during that period.

Other ways of breaking down the aid total include the bilateral–multilateral split—which was 75–25 per cent in 1983, reflecting some decline in the multilateral share since the late 1970s. Aid to agriculture was approximately one-fifth of total aid; so also was technical co-operation of all forms. Food aid, depending on definitions, accounted for $2–3 billion of total aid. (All figures in the above paragraphs are from the same source as for Table 1.1, except for food aid, for which see Chapter 5.)

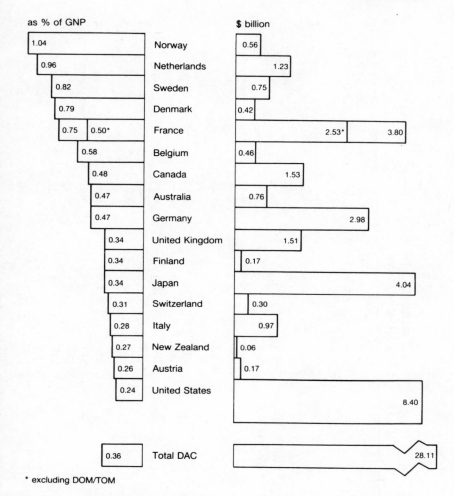

as % of GNP

$ billion

1.04	Norway	0.56
0.96	Netherlands	1.23
0.82	Sweden	0.75
0.79	Denmark	0.42
0.75	0.50*	France	2.53*	3.80
0.58	Belgium	0.46
0.48	Canada	1.53
0.47	Australia	0.76
0.47	Germany	2.98
0.34	United Kingdom	1.51
0.34	Finland	0.17
0.34	Japan	4.04
0.31	Switzerland	0.30
0.28	Italy	0.97
0.27	New Zealand	0.06
0.26	Austria	0.17
0.24	United States	8.40
0.36	Total DAC	28.11

* excluding DOM/TOM

Figure 1.2. Official Development Assistance from Development Assistance Committee countries in 1983/4.

What is effectiveness?

This study has provided its own definition of effectiveness. It is concerned with *developmental effectiveness*, not with other motives that donors or recipients may have. The questions posed by the Terms of Reference have determined this definition, as well as the shape of the component studies and of this report. Does aid contribute macroeconomically or otherwise to growth? Does it reach the poor? Is

TABLE 1.2.
Trends in aid by major donors

	ODA $ million	Share in world ODA %	ODA as per cent of GNP %	Per capita GNP[b] $
United States	7992	22.0	0.24	14120
EEC members combined[a]	11492	31.7	0.51	8680
France (incl. DOM/TOM)	3815	10.5	0.74	9460
France (excl. DOM/TOM)	2500	6.7	0.47	
Germany	3176	8.8	0.49	10650
United Kingdom	1605	4.4	0.35	8100
Netherlands	1195	3.3	1.08	9140
Italy	826	2.3	0.24	6160
Belgium	480	1.3	0.59	8270
Denmark	395	1.1	0.73	10630
Japan	3761	10.4	0.33	9700
Canada	1429	3.9	0.45	12660
Sweden	754	2.1	0.85	10650
Australia	753	2.1	0.49	10030
Norway	584	1.6	1.06	13320
Switzerland	320	0.9	0.32	15500
Austria	158	0.4	0.23	8910
Finland	153	0.4	0.33	9570
New Zealand	61	0.2	0.28	6840
Total DAC	27458	75.7	0.36	11000

Spain	70	0.2	0.05	4080
Ireland	37	0.1	0.23	5040
Luxembourg	—	—	—	—
Total OECD	27565	76.0	0.36	10610
OPEC countries				
Saudi Arabia	3916	10.8	3.53	(10680)
Kuwait	995	2.7	4.46	17240
U.A.E.	100	0.3	0.42	19610
Qatar	(22)	0.1	(0.42)	(18570)
Iraq	−3	—	—	—
Other	446	1.2	(0.14)	1860
Total OPEC	5476	15.1	1.05	2610
CMEA countries				
USSR	2449	6.7	(0.19)	(4850)
GDR	160	0.4	(0.12)	(8000)
Eastern Europe, other	330	0.9	(0.12)	(3000)
Total CMEA	2939	8.1	(0.17)	(4450)
Other donors	306	0.8	—	—
Total	36286	100.0	0.38	7800

[a]Excluding Ireland, Luxembourg, and Greece.
[b]At current prices and exchange rates.
Source: as for Table 1.1.

the policy dialogue which accompanies aid successful and valuable? How have specific types of financial and commodity aid performed? What is the contribution of technical cooperation? What are the effects of having many donors working in a single country? Does aid help or hinder an appropriate functioning of market forces? These questions define 'effectiveness in relation to what?', and underlie seven of the substantive chapters of the report. Chapter 9 discusses the relative roles of bilateral and multilateral aid and some other aspects of aid policy. The last chapter draws out the lessons for improving effectiveness.

Purposes of studying effectiveness

There are two different, if overlapping, reasons for wanting to discover the effectiveness of aid. One is for reaching judgements about how worthwhile aid is: governments, the public, and aid agencies need to know whether and how far aid succeeds and therefore deserves support. The other is to assist aid management. Because of the nature of aid evaluations—what exists, what was submitted to the consultants or kept from them, what is discoverable by other means—the search for hard evidence about what has worked and what has not has been far from fruitless, but has not yielded comprehensive answers. It has proved rather easier to propose desirable directions for change. There is no intrinsic contradiction here. It is not necessary to measure the efficiency of an operation to know that some change will improve it (though the more that is known about its efficiency, of course, the better one can prescribe the range of measures needed to raise it).

Dynamics of aid policy

One of the difficulties inherent in any assessment of aid is that the past—even where there is adequate information about it—is an imperfect guide to the future. The typical aid project may take five to seven years from start to finish. Evaluation may wait a further two years—and many would argue that that is too soon, and that five years would be more suitable. Thus it may be ten to fifteen years before one can really conclude that a project has succeeded or failed. By then, the donor agency may no longer be pursuing projects of that particular kind.

In addition, aid involves a learning process, albeit a slow one. As this report will show, there are many areas where today's aid is likely to be more effective than yesterday's because past successes and failures have been assimilated. Present aid, in other words, cannot be judged solely on its past record. By the same token, the effectiveness of present aid will only be truly apparent some years from now. Nevertheless, there are good grounds for thinking that the learning process is improving aid, not replacing old mistakes with new ones.

A basic finding

In the broadest sense, this report finds that most aid does indeed 'work'. It succeeds in achieving its developmental objectives (where those are primary), contributing positively to the recipient countries' economic performance, and not substituting for activities which would have occurred anyway. That is not to say that aid works on every count. Its performance varies by country and by sector. On the criterion of relieving poverty, even the aid which achieves its objectives cannot be considered fully satisfactory. However, this report stresses that the relief of poverty depends both on aid and on the policies of the recipient countries—a collaboration in which aid is definitely the junior partner. And there is a substantial fraction of aid which does not work—which may have a low rate of return, or become derelict shortly after completion, or never reach completion, or have positively harmful effects. Further, bilateral donors often have political and commercial motives for aid, which can interfere with developmental objectives. When these motives predominate, the results can be harmful to growth and to the poor. This report is concerned with non-developmental objectives only in so far as they interfere with the other purposes of aid.

If the evaluation of aid is imperfect, how can it be justifiable to conclude that most aid works? The answer is that that conclusion, though not a demonstrable fact, is at least a well-educated assessment. The project team (and other researchers before it) have looked at literally hundreds of evaluations or reviews of evaluations. While it is true that most aid agencies conceal some of their failures, they usually do so in cases of political or (in the case of bilateral donors) commercial sensitivity. Most evaluations are conducted by or for the agencies themselves, but this does not necessarily make them self-serving and uncritical. Some of them no doubt are. But in general, they may well be misleadingly critical, since most evaluators try to find faults—the correction of faults being one of the main purposes of evaluation.

The work done specifically for this report has broadly borne out the conclusion that most aid works. In addition, the World Bank has published reports that, for example, 80 per cent of IDA projects achieve a rate of return of 10 per cent or more. The Asian and Inter-American Development Banks have concluded that 60 per cent of samples of their loans fully met their objectives; 30 per cent partially did so, and less than 10 per cent were marginal or unsatisfactory. Five other major agencies have conducted in-house reviews of a large number of their evaluations; while three of these studies remain confidential, they all found that the great bulk of their lending had a satisfactory rate of return. Chapter 5 cites further studies with similar results, and Chapter 6 reaches a comparable conclusion about technical cooperation. Less is known about the effectiveness of the non-project part of financial aid, which is rarely measured in quantitative terms. Perhaps re-examination of some of these evaluations would reduce the proportion of successes—evaluation is by its nature open to dispute. But it is not credible that the aid agencies are concealing so many aid failures that this general conclusion about effectiveness could be contradicted.

That said, there have been a significant number of failures. The exact proportion is not known; but supposing it proved to be a quarter or a third of all aid, would that be considered 'good' or 'bad'? Certainly, if an agency's projects were all failing, it should be closed down. But if they were all succeeding, questions would be very much in order: was the agency being sufficiently innovative, or deliberately avoiding giving aid in difficult conditions? A record showing only the achievement of high rates of return would be evidence that the challenges of development were not being addressed. (It would also, of course, be impossible.)

Some failures, then, are inevitable and not objectionable. But what would be a tolerable proportion? One approach would be to compare investment under aid with other types of investment. If x per cent of aid fails, what percentage of private investment fails? Or of public investment other than aid? Unfortunately, x is unknown both in aid and in most other spheres. But the comparison may be pursued a little further, remembering that aid undertakes some investments more difficult than those normally done by the private sector or the non-aid public sector: social development in backward regions, for example.

In the private sector, investment is undertaken for profit, and profit is in part a 'reward for risk'. The risks are real, and a considerable proportion of private investment fails. Yet this is not regarded as a condemnation of private enterprise. If the Ford Edsel was a several hundred million dollar flop, or Ludwig's multi-billion dollar Amazonian empire collapsed—let alone the hundreds of less spectacular everyday bankruptcies—these are cause for comment. But they do not call into question the free enterprise system from which they originate. Nor do Lockheed's corruption scandals. Yet the British groundnuts scheme in the 1950s in Tanganyika (as it was called then) was for decades cited by the critics of aid as somehow typical, and demonstrating that aid could not succeed. 'Das goldene Bett' (the golden bed), a 1950s product of misappropriated aid to the Gold Coast (as it was then), similarly circulated for decades in German anti-aid demonology. (This report does not discuss corruption. In some notorious countries, aid activities have added costs due to corruption by officials and others. But again, this is a phenomenon affecting only a small proportion of aid; much aid is disbursed only when the equipment or construction or technical cooperation it pays for is supplied or built, which considerably reduces the scope for illicit behaviour. In countries where aid is corrupted, many other forms of public and private investment would be also.)

It would be better for all concerned if aid were more openly regarded as fallible. Most aid agencies and the 'friends of aid' consciously or unconsciously conspire in the unsatisfactory state of affairs where failures are not openly discussed. The result is that when a large aid project does go wrong and the fact becomes public, it may attract more attention than it deserves. By being more candid, the agencies have more to gain than to lose. Some already publish most of their evaluations, both critical and favourable; USAID is a notable example, but it is unusual among the major aid donors.

This report will be much concerned with the '*x* per cent' of aid that does go wrong, since it is these experiences that provide the most useful guide to doing better. It should therefore be repeated at this stage that *the great majority of aid succeeds in its developmental objectives*. The answer to the question 'Does aid work?' is 'Most of it, yes; however . . .'.

Successes and difficulties of aid

There are many ways of depicting the successes of aid. In the broadest terms, the low-income countries have achieved increases in real incomes and improved living standards to which aid has contributed. Excluding India and China, their life expectancy rose by approximately one-fifth between 1960 and 1982, and infant mortality declined by almost a third; primary school enrolments almost doubled as a percentage of the relevant age group over a similar period. The growth in per capita income has been disappointing, at 1.1 per cent a year: though another way of putting this is to say that per capita income increased by 25 per cent despite population growth of 65 per cent over the two decades. (India and China have made significantly greater progress, in China's case with little assistance from aid.)

Aid has helped not only today's low-income countries, but also some which started in the low-income group and have risen to the middle-income category. Korea is perhaps the most spectacular example, but several others—Brazil, Colombia, Thailand, for example—have also made remarkable progress. More will follow, and aid will demonstrably have helped to lay the foundations for their growth.

The contributions of aid can also be described in other ways. Sector by sector across economies, aid has built infrastructure, promoted agriculture and manufacturing, helped to extend the reach of basic services, provided skilled manpower, and promoted institution building. And today, an increasingly important part of aid is the policy dialogue which accompanies it. Here, too, both earlier and more recent experience can testify to significant successes.

Much of the world's attention is presently focused on sub-Saharan Africa. The question inevitably arises: if most aid works, why has Africa's development been so halting? Part of the answer is that aid's successes have been more common in Asia and the rest of the developing world. Sub-Saharan Africa has been the most intractable environment for development generally, and therefore for aid. It has had several major disadvantages compared with other developing regions: smaller proportions of literate and educated people, less stable political structures, less settled administrative institutions with shorter traditions. In addition, sub-Saharan Africa has faced peculiarly difficult external conditions: in particular, dependence on primary commodity exports facing highly unstable markets, and long periods of deteriorating terms of trade. All these factors have left the region without major attractions to private overseas investors, and most countries have been heavily dependent on aid for foreign capital.

Africa's agro-climatic conditions are also unfavourable. They include a proneness to long periods of drought, and vary greatly over the continent. As a result, there has been no possibility, as there was in South Asia, for a small number of high-yielding crop varieties to transform agriculture over vast areas. And the region has had the world's fastest population growth rates, close to the demographic maximum in countries such as Kenya, Mozambique, Rwanda, and Tanzania, and likely to rise in many countries where death rates still have far to fall and fertility will follow only slowly.

As if these obstacles to development were not enough, hindsight now suggests that the model followed by most developing countries was peculiarly unpromising for those of sub-Saharan Africa. African countries sought industrialization and modernization as an antidote to the colonial economic structure they inherited, in which the only developed sectors equipped with infrastructure were enclaves of mineral and export crop production, and settler agriculture. The mass of their people were in the undeveloped hinterland, engaged in subsistence agriculture. Industrializing policies led to a good deal of capital-intensive investment, uneconomic import substitution, and disadvantages for agriculture under a regime of overvalued exchange rates. Parastatal agencies expanded as part of an often burdensome public sector which, where it was engaged in marketing, did not create a price structure that would encourage investment and production.

For a long time aid donors accommodated these policies. Some of them fitted in with their own commercial interests of exporting capital goods; there was also a genuine desire to avoid neo-colonial imposition of policies on newly independent states. Today both donors and recipients can see all too clearly the failings of the old model. The current emphasis on policy-based lending is leading to a new realism on both sides. Policies have already been reformed in several African countries; others are following suit. The effectiveness of aid to sub-Saharan Africa has been inseparable from the effectiveness of development overall. The prospects are now good for a major improvement in both, provided that donors and recipients play their mutal and cooperative parts to the full.

Reasons for failure: the donors' side

When aid goes wrong, it is usually for several fairly common reasons; they are detailed in Chapters 5–7. It is not easy to generalize why these factors occur where they do, yet are absent in the much larger number of cases when all goes well. The fault may lie with the donor or the recipient, or both; sometimes misfortune or the unexpected can be the culprit. On the donors' side, one of the most common causes of failure is the excessive intrusion of commercial or political motives. When the (bilateral) donor is less interested in development than in the sale of equipment or in the political gains from supporting a regime, it is not surprising that aid may give a poor return economically. (This is not to say that all such aid is ineffective; only that these are potential causes of failure.) Many projects are *technically* poor, ill-designed for their intended purpose. But poor design, even when not the result of the donors' commercial purposes, is at least sometimes culpable, the result of inattention to local circumstances, or of failure to profit from available experience.

The last point is another reason why some aid goes wrong. This report will frequently discuss the failure to learn from mistakes, so it will not be dwelt on here. To generalize, however, donor agencies are not all that good at avoiding repetition of their own mistakes; and they are worse at avoiding each other's, since there is very little communication about failure from one agency to another. These defects, coupled with the incentives to individuals in the agencies simply to get loans made, are probably responsible for a significant share of the aid that goes wrong. There is a strong case for major efforts to improve the learning process, and for strengthening within agencies the incentives to improve the quality of lending, not just its quantity.

Much less reprehensible are the projects that go wrong because donors and recipients are trying to do ambitious things in difficult circumstances. Sometimes they may neglect to uncover information which might have forestalled failure. More generally, however, they are simply taking bigger risks. Innovative activity must be encouraged, and its occasional failure should not give grounds for abandoning the attempt. It is much easier to run infrastructure projects in South East Asia than to reach poor farmers in sub-Saharan Africa. But it is precisely where the challenge and the difficulties are greatest that aid is most needed. A safety-conscious aid programme would not promise much to poor people in the poorest countries.

Between what might be called reprehensible and virtuous failures lies a grey area, full of debatable issues: could difficulties have been anticipated, could project designers have been at fault in not acquiring knowledge which might have.saved a project, could some external event have been allowed for? Sometimes a project is seen to be going wrong in its early stages, and more money is put in to stave off failure: are these good or bad decisions? They are difficult ones, and fallible. Certainty is rarely available.

Recipient failings

Some of the reasons why some aid fails can be found on the recipients' side. Often aid activities are unsuccessful because of the policy environment in which they operate, or because of administrative deficiencies in the recipient country, or because the government does not take a keen enough interest in implementing them. (The donor too may be implicated, if it knows of these conditions and makes no attempt to circumvent them.) Recipient governments, like donors, can have political and commercial motives which are at odds with the needs of development. The recipient may have an excessive attachment to 'prestige projects' with low developmental priority, or to 'advanced' and unsuitable technology. Sometimes the recipient is at fault when he declines technical assistance that is really needed. In recent years, however, several aid projects have crumbled because the recipient government was simply unable to provide counterpart finances from its heavily constrained budget. Sometimes the constraints were exogenous, the result of world recession. Sometimes they had internal causes, because the government was spending heavily on non-development items. Sometimes aid itself was the cause, because donors were not coordinating their projects and the implications of them for financial management. Precisely who or what is at fault here? Recipient, donor, the world economy—perhaps something of all three. Another 'grey area'.

New approach to aid for the poorest countries

The things that go wrong because aid is uncoordinated and the recipient bad at administering it point to one major area of improvement for the future. Aid coordination is a problem particularly for the poorest developing countries. They also need support in other areas highlighted in this report. Greater protection from external shocks affecting the balance of payments is one of them. Greater attention to budgetary resources is another. Attempts to reduce the complexity and multiplicity of aid procedures, to lighten the recipients' administrative burdens arising from aid, to reduce the costs of aid-tying, to make longer-term commitments of aid—all these would bring real benefits as well. They are needed mainly for the poorest countries. Such measures would be helpful to other poor countries, of course, but they are less critical, and might be beyond the donors' ability to extend to all countries. This report will call for such a new approach in aid for the poorest countries.

Categorization of countries

The public discussion of aid would be enhanced if it were recognized that, in terms of their need for aid, developing countries can be classified into separate categories. At one end of the spectrum are the newly-industrializing and better-off middle-income countries, which can meet their financial needs by borrowing at market or near-market terms from private and official sources. They need many things from the international economic system; but, except perhaps for some modest technical assistance, they do not need aid. Per capita income is not the only criterion for the desirability of aid; emergencies, debt, trade problems, and other factors have to be taken into account; but given the need to ration scarce concessional funds, countries which can satisfy their borrowing needs elsewhere should not normally be candidates for long-term development aid.

A second group, the 'lower middle-income' and several low-income countries do not need aid to survive, but find it an important means of accelerating development. They may be quite poor, but they have the human resources, the administrative ability, and the development experience to make progress provided they have adequate access to concessional and official borrowing and trade. (India and China fall into this category; but because of their size and the extent of their poverty, they have to be accorded separate treatment.) Some of these intermediate countries are likely to 'graduate' into the first category in the next decades.

The third group contains the countries which this report calls the 'poorest'. For the most part they cannot survive without aid (where, at a minimum, 'survive' means having national income growing faster than population). They lack the very foundations of material development—human resources, infrastructure, strong administration. They have little capacity for generating rapid export growth from the natural resources they possess, and little resistance to external shocks. Several of them are deteriorating ecologically. Almost all have had continuous declines in real per capita income for many years; some have even had their total income shrink.

These countries will need aid for the foreseeable future. To make faster progress, they need more support—though not necessarily on the same pattern as in the recent past. There is much they must do for themselves. But they are the countries which will test the capacity of the donors to learn from experience and to rise above past performance. All the low-income countries deserve better treatment in trade and aid than they have been receiving recently. But it is these, the poorest, for whom a new effort must be made. More aid is needed to cope with emergencies and to support policy reform. But a change in the quality of aid, embracing all the respects treated in this report, is every bit as important.

The plight of the poorest countries should not distract attention and international effort from other low-income countries. The scale of these countries' problems is much greater, though their complexity is not. They have the largest number of people living in poverty; they also make the most effective use of aid; and aid to them has been declining. The trend in their aid should be halted or reversed, and any remaining shortfall made up by more non-concessional official flows.

The fundamental message of this report is clear: there is much that is already right with aid, but quite a lot to be improved. Donors and recipients have a long way to go in ensuring that the fruits of development reach the poor. And in the poorest countries, much needs to be done to ensure that development takes place at all.

CHAPTER TWO

The Macroeconomic Contribution of Aid

I Introduction

This chapter examines the effect of aid on economic performance. It concerns itself principally with the impact of aid on GNP growth and economic efficiency, not with broader aspects of development which are treated elsewhere. Has aid helped to increase the recipients' levels of output, and of output capacity, in a sustainable manner? Has aid added to investment, or merely replaced domestic savings? Have the results been roughly commensurate with the scale of the resources transferred? Has aid helped the recipient countries towards 'self-reliance' by promoting the growth of exports? Before the answers to these questions are considered, the main elements of aid should be recalled. In 1980–3, official aid from all sources averaged some $35 billion a year. Of that, over $5 billion was in the form of technical cooperation; roughly $3 billion was food aid; the rest was financial assistance, divided between project and programme aid. Some 60 per cent of all aid went to the low-income countries with which this report is principally concerned.

A simple correlation between aid and economic performance has obvious weaknesses, because aid is heterogeneous. For example, programme and project aid take effect over different periods of time. Food aid has a separate function, directly supporting consumption but potentially easing both savings and foreign exchange constraints. Technical cooperation also bears fruit over a variety of time periods, typically the longer-term. And though recorded as a 'receipt' of the developing country, much technical assistance is spent elsewhere: the Swedish forestry expert in Tanzania may be classified as $150,000 of aid, but a large part of that money remains in Sweden as the expert's savings, or as home-base support costs. Further, although aid transfers resources, it also transfers advice, institution building, and technology, items which are not measured in its financial value.

Much of the research on the macroeconomic effects of aid deals with relatively large groups of developing countries. Its results are ambiguous. The relationship between aid and growth is rather weak: it can be either positive or negative, depending on the country groupings and time period chosen. The relationship between aid and domestic savings was once thought to be stronger, and negative. But the reasons why it was found to be so remain unexplained: it is just as possible that aid fills a genuine savings gap for some countries as that it replaces some domestic savings. The result may also have been affected by national accounting practices, or by a failure to distinguish aid which is meant for consumption (e.g. food aid) from aid intended to increase investment.

There are, in addition, a number of country studies which examine the macroeconomic effects of aid. Their evidence is more selective, but in some ways stronger. They show that aid has raised growth when it has been maintained for some time and combined with sensible development policies. Aid can act either through providing extra resources to supplement domestic savings, or through the catalytic effect of easing a binding constraint. It can also help to lay a foundation for the growth of exports. Many of these relationships are not captured by cross-country statistical analysis.

All the evidence shows that the experience of aid varies enormously among countries. Some have put much aid to good use; others have done less well. Some recipient governments have learned faster than others to create an efficient policy framework for aid. Some aid has been wasted, or has had a negligible impact. Sometimes donor policies are to blame. The variety of experience suggests that blanket criticisms of aid are not convincing. Especially in the recent difficult international conditions, many developing countries have made creditable macroeconomic progress, and aid has often played a significant part.

II   Problems of interpretation

The purpose of aid is to transfer *additional* resources, beyond those that the recipient country could mobilize itself either domestically or through foreign trade. The contribution of aid can be quantitative or qualitative—more or better resources. Improvements in the quality of inputs, such as labour skills, have played an important part in growth, though qualitative changes are difficult to measure.

The nominal value of aid may differ from the real value of the resources transferred for two main reasons. First, the process of transfer itself may reduce the efficiency of a unit of aid. For example, aid-tying by donors may raise the cost of equipment or other inputs, and cumbersome disbursement procedures may cause long delays in utilizing aid. Secondly, there is the problem of 'absorptive capacity' for project aid. The recipient may be short of the infrastructure, skilled labour, or administrative capacity to generate and implement projects that are socially cost-effective. (As some of the case studies show, this is not always a question of the degree of development in the recipient country. Malawi has a good record for project implementation; Kenya's record has recently worsened.[1]) Although aid can sometimes boost absorptive capacity—through technical assistance, for example—this has not always been attempted, let alone achieved.

Fungibility

It is in order at this point to tackle the vexed question of the 'fungibility' of aid: the argument that aid really finances, not the high-priority investments it ostensibly pays for, which 'would have been carried out anyway', but the more marginal investments (or even consumption) which aid permits the recipient to finance. The model is that the recipient has a list of projects in descending order of importance, and that aid ties its label to some of those at the top of the list; but it is in fact just expanding the recipient's resources, and allowing those at the bottom of the list to be carried out. The argument is not wholly without force for some situations; but its weaknesses are so numerous as to deny it any fundamental capacity to weaken the case for aid.

In the first place the model itself is faulty. Over time, the presence of aid in significant amounts does not simply allow a country to pick more projects off a static list. It permits the list itself to be expanded and new production possibilities to be considered. This is true in particular where aid finances a large share of investment, in which case the fungibility argument scarcely applies. But the addition of resources is not the only thing. Many projects, especially large and complex ones such as major hydroelectric or irrigation schemes, would not be feasible at all in poorer countries without the technical collaboration of an experienced donor; even if they were, that collaboration and accompanying policy dialogue adds, often very potently, to their effectiveness—indeed, without aid numbers of valuable policy options might never be raised.

Second, even if the model were accurate, it does not follow that, because one thing is of lower priority than another, it is not worth doing. In most poor countries there is a fairly endless list of valuable things that cannot be done because of lack of finance. They may not be neatly packaged projects which the donor can tie to exports of capital goods, but that is another matter. If the recipient really could finance out of its own resources everything that was worth doing, aid would indeed be fungible—unnecessary, in fact. The fungibility argument assumes that all high-return investments could be financed without aid, which is clearly wrong. Third, there is of course complementarity among investments, and expanding investment possibilities may raise the productivity of the economy overall. This may also be the effect—fourth—of the large amounts of aid which do not go into investment projects: programme aid and technical cooperation in particular. And—fifth—policy reforms supported by aid cannot be put in the 'fungibility' calculus. Lastly, the argument that aid 'really' finances consumption, not investment, is considered below. It too is found wanting.

Historical causes of growth

A significant part of aid is given for capital investment. Research suggests that the quantity of investment has played a significant part in promoting economic growth, but not the major part. For developed countries in 1948–73, increases in the capital stock explain only 15 per cent of the growth of output, rising to about 23 per cent if scale effects are taken into account. Most of the increase in output came from other sources: increases in the supply of non-capital inputs, improvements in the *quality* of inputs such as labour skills, and general improvements in the ability to use resources productively.[2] In short, growth is best explained in terms of increases in 'total factor inputs' and 'total factor productivity'.[3] This does *not* mean that investment is unimportant or that aid should not be given for investment purposes. It simply means that other changes may have to be brought about simultaneously, to make investment more productive. These changes take time; 'learning by doing' implies just that.

The same point is reinforced by a recent study of different countries with similar resources and export possibilities. It argues that their natural resources, factor endowments, exports, and other variables, while important for growth, do not explain the increase in output or the widely divergent patterns of growth. The study highlights the importance of government policy and the capacity to govern—what is termed 'political organization and administrative competence'.[4]

Growth, especially 'intensive' growth (increases in per capita income or output), has historically taken a long time to achieve in most countries. For example, 'extensive' growth (expansion of GNP) and industrial development probably began in India around the late nineteenth century, whereas the rather slow and shaky 'intensive' growth began only after 1945.[5] However inadequate, India's recent growth has been much faster than before, exceeding the dire prognostications of twenty years ago.[6] Latin America's experience has been similar, although its 'intensive' growth started sooner.[7] And thirty years ago, one should recall, South Korea was regarded as a hopeless case.

Critics and supporters of aid may all have been in too much of a hurry. What has historically taken a long time to achieve is expected to come about in a couple of 'development decades'. It may do good to have expectations scaled down to more realistic levels. However, waiting for market forces alone to bring about growth may also be unrealistic. Urgency is in order because the dynamic balance between population and resources has become more unstable, requiring policy action to contain the longer-run problem of poverty. There is also considerable evidence that population policies and a decline in fertility often go hand in hand with increased prosperity and social well-being, and are more likely to bear fruit in an environment of social and economic progress.[8]

The scale of aid

The contribution that aid can make to growth depends, *inter alia*, on its size. On average, for developing countries as a whole, aid is a small proportion of total savings and investible resources. However, there are substantial inter-country differences; in recent times, aid has played a critical role in some countries. Such wide differences may also be a reason why aggregative studies of the aid/growth relationship are seldom conclusive. To take the overall GNP ratios first, in the early 1980s, aid was approximately 9 per cent of GNP of the 'least developed' countries and 3 per cent of GNP of other low-income countries. For the two largest low-income countries, China and India, the ratio was about 0.2 per cent and 1 per cent respectively. For middle-income countries, it was less than 2 per cent. For individual countries, aid varied from less than 1 per cent of GNP to over 20 per cent. Broadly, the ratio tended to be lower than 3 per cent for large developing countries, but about 20 per cent for many sub-Saharan economies; for most other low-income countries it was around 7 to 8 per cent.[9]

The same variations exist for other indicators. In 1976, for example, the gross domestic investment rate for all developing countries was 24.8 per cent of GNP, whereas net foreign resource inflows—both private and public—were only 2.9 per cent. For low-income Asian countries, which contain a large proportion of the world's poor, the rates were 16.7 and 1.3 per cent respectively.[10] However, sub-Saharan Africa is particularly dependent on aid,[11] which is the equivalent of 40 per cent of the region's imports. For the low-income African countries, net official aid constituted 50 per cent of gross domestic investment. Even for the middle-income oil importers, the ratio was as high as 24 per cent.[12] For Mali, project aid provides around 90 per cent of all investment.[13] As for public expenditure, aid financed about 80 per cent of the total in Mali in the early 1980s. The ratio for Sudan was 53 per cent, for Tanzania 36 per cent, and for Kenya 25 per cent.[14] Such countries are extremely vulnerable to any sudden contraction in aid.

As for the supply of foreign exchange, exports of goods and non-factor services from developing countries totalled $512 billion in 1980, compared to total ODA of $37.6 billion in 1981.[15] These figures show that less protectionism in developed countries against developing country exports could be as important as aid in boosting foreign exchange receipts. Incidentally, these and other figures might serve to correct the impression that is sometimes given by critics of aid, of a 'massive' hand-out from rich to poor but 'profligate' nations. For example, from 1974–6, the USA as a major donor spent 36 times as much on domestic social expenditure in the federal budget as on foreign aid. In per capita terms, it spent about $2 per head of developing country population, compared to $508 per head of US population.[16]

However, the fact that the amount of aid is small does not mean that its contribution to development is small, or that increasing its efficiency is unimportant. Even with low levels of aid, the extra output foregone or realized might make a difference between bearable and intolerable poverty. Even small changes in agricultural output can have a big effect on the poor. In addition, where aid eases a foreign exchange or savings bottleneck, it can have a large impact on output; the marginal volume of aid has a high 'shadow' value.[17] In India, relatively small amounts of non-project aid in the 1960s and early 1970s enabled a much higher level of capacity to be utilized. Similarly, aid and technical assistance for agricultural research in several South and East Asian countries made a disproportionate contribution towards increasing agricultural output, as well as reducing seasonal fluctuations.[18]

Aid and growth: a calculation

Some rough calculations can help to indicate the contribution of aid to growth. Assume that, for developing countries, the investment/income ratio lies between 15 and 25 per cent. Let the incremental capital/output ratio lie within a range of 3.0 to 5.0.[19] If aid adds 20 per cent to the *level* of investment, it will raise the investment/income ratio by 3 to 5 per cent. A 1 per cent rise in that ratio will in turn raise the growth rate of output by between 0.3 and 0.2 per cent. Assuming that population growth is exogenous in the medium run, aid will also raise per capita output by a similar amount. In other words, given a reasonable volume of aid that is used reasonably efficiently, the annual growth rate with aid would be higher by between 1.5 per cent and 0.6 per cent. These are significant increases, on plausible assumptions.

III Aid, savings, and growth

This section summarizes the main conclusions from empirical work on the macroeconomic impact of aid. Some of the more technical aspects of the empirical findings are discussed in the appendix to this chapter.[20] The main conclusions are:

1 For samples of countries, different regression studies come to quite different conclusions about the effect of aid on growth. They range from positive[21] to strongly negative effects.[22] Aid 'explains' varying proportions of growth, and its quantitative impact on growth rates appears to be weak but consistent with historical experience and theoretical expectations.[23]
2 There are sizeable regional differences, hinting at different inter-country experience. In some studies, South Asian countries seem to have used aid more effectively.[24] In others, aid has a positive impact on growth in poorer developing countries in the 1960s, and on middle-income countries in the 1970s.[25]
3 Few studies have been made of the potentially important relation between aid and the productivity of capital. Does aid increase capacity utilization, or output per unit of utilized capacity? (See appendix to this chapter.)
4 Most older studies show a negative relationship between aid and the savings ratio. But some estimates are improbably large, given that, for many countries, aid is only a small proportion of savings. The reasons for this supposed relationship between aid and savings are unexplained. Some studies show that aid and the savings ratio are negatively related even after allowing for the fact that low savings may attract aid.[26] This does not rule out the possibility that in some countries aid *is* used to bridge a savings gap.[27] Doubt is cast on much of this work, however, by a recent study which finds a positive relationship once consumption aid is allowed for.[28]
5 Few of the cross-country studies attempt to measure the effect of aid on investment. One that does finds a weak but positive effect. Some country studies point in the same direction.[29]
6 There is little evidence to support the view that aid reduces tax efforts in recipient countries, or increases budgetary deficits. One cannot argue that aid is systematically substituted for public savings by governments.[30]

7 The studies shed little light on whether aid promotes 'self-reliance'—a capacity for sustained development without aid—although evidence from individual countries suggests that some have managed to achieve it.

The studies assume a theoretical context where growth is subject to three types of constraints: absorptive capacity, savings and foreign exchange. These may operate independently, perhaps even sequentially.[31] Most of the studies tried to test some form of the hypothesis that aid stimulates growth by easing the savings constraint. Critics of aid have used some studies to argue that aid has not contributed to growth because it has supplanted rather than supplemented domestic savings, and has therefore in effect raised consumption. The implication is either that aid cannot promote growth, or that it is likely to be a never-ending commitment. While these studies might help to correct the more extravagant claims for aid as an instrument of development, their empirical bases are not solid enough to conclude that aid does supplant savings or does not promote development. The regression studies have weaknesses, and some of their conclusions conflict with the experiences of individual countries.

Measuring real aid flows

First, the volume of real resources transferred by aid must be measured correctly. Nominal values overestimate the amount of resources transferred over time; yet regression studies tend to use the nominal values of aid as an independent variable. The practice of aid-tying by donors can significantly reduce the purchasing power of aid, by 20 per cent or more in some cases.[32] As costs of tied aid vary according to donor and the ability of recipients to 'switch', the effect on the volume of resources transferred is not easy to measure. In addition, changes in international prices and exchange rates have tended to reduce the purchasing power of aid, and its 'additionality'. For 1970–8, changes in the terms of trade caused losses of 1.0 per cent of base-year GNP to the least developed and high-population Asian countries, and of 1.8 per cent to the semi-industrial South East Asian countries. During the same period, external resource flows fell by 0.8 per cent of GDP for the South Asian countries; they increased by 5.5 per cent for the least developed countries and by 0.4 per cent for the semi-industrial countries.[33]

The regression studies often ignore other significant points. For example, different donors follow different trade policies towards developing countries, thus making it unlikely that all aid would be equally 'effective' to the recipient. In practice, these differences can be substantial.[34] A donor's credit or other official lending, especially if it adds unrewardingly to the borrower's debt burden, can negate the value of its aid. On top of that, one recent study argued that the motives for bilateral and multilateral aid are different, the former being directed more towards serving donor interests.[35] The practice of tying aid directly to donor sales often reduces its value and effectiveness, according to several country studies carried out for this report.[36] If so, bilateral aid would make a smaller contribution to growth, and it would be necessary to take account of the mix between tied and untied aid in testing for aid/growth relationships. Other aspects of the aid mix could also be significant. The relations between aid and growth presumably differ depending on the relative proportions of project, programme, and food aid and technical assistance. Yet virtually all the studies lump them together as 'aid'.

This convention has other weaknesses that have already been mentioned. For example, an extra unit of aid is more valuable to the poorer countries, which cannot borrow commercially to replace that aid. This is why it is wrong to say that aid's contribution is equal to the output effect of the 'concessional element' alone. Where aid is not substitutable at the margin, as is the case for many poor countries, the opportunity cost of not receiving aid can be far greater than the difference between aid terms and the current level of LIBOR.[37] In addition, where aid does not simply supplement resources but acts to ease a 'bottleneck', its potential value-added is greater than the amount of aid received.[38]

Another point often ignored is that aid might sometimes be necessary just to ensure survival or to hold a society together. Aid to newly independent Bangladesh made a significant contribution to reconstructing the economy and resettling people. It would be difficult to argue that this was not important for the economy as a whole, or that without it, the poor would not have suffered disproportionately.[39] Aid also enabled many of the the Sahelian economies, including Mali, to survive the effects of the drought without major crises,[40] at least until 1984. A slightly different example is the construction of road and rail networks in Malawi, essential for the development of a land-locked economy.[41]

For most developing countries there are no measures of output capacity, only of output. Yet it is pertinent to ask whether aid's contribution to infrastructural development is adequately reflected in the growth of output. For various reasons, dams, irrigation facilities, power plants, roads, or even industrial capacity might not be *fully utilized*. Sometimes unused capacity is evidence of aid's inefficiency—where, for example, the wrong technology is chosen, or a plant is built without adequate assessment of demand or infrastruc-

tural support. It is therefore important to get the right balance between project and non-project aid, so that making better use of existing
capacity is not neglected in favour of expensive new investment. However, there is evidence that countries learn to make better use of
capacity once it is there. Pakistan in recent years has concentrated on
improving capacity utilization, and has significantly reduced its
capital–output ratios.

Individual country studies exhibit relationships that are ignored in
aggregate regression analysis. So do aid projects. At the project level,
there are obviously extreme examples of success or failure. However,
the average rates of return on aid projects, or the proportion that
comes near to fulfilling original expectations, compare favourably
with other investments. Average rates of return around 17 per cent (as
achieved in World Bank projects) are not particularly low, especially
if one remembers that aid often goes to difficult social sectors or
backward areas. Of IDA projects, which are of particular relevance to
poverty, 80 per cent yielded rates of return of more than 10 per cent.[42]

Aid and savings

The second set of issues concerns the negative correlation between aid
and savings found in many regression studies. Even if the global
findings are reliable, it does not follow that aid is partly 'wasted'.
Country experience varies widely, and some of it conflicts with the
results referred to above. A negative link between aid and savings has
been observed in some Latin American countries but not, for
example, in India.[43] The Bangladesh study finds that aid has largely
supplemented savings, both the ratios of aid and of savings to GNP
having risen in recent years. It is encouraging that a country with
such low per capita income and a large and growing population could
achieve this.[44] More advanced economies, like those of South Korea
and Taiwan which received substantial aid at earlier stages, also had
high rates of domestic savings. A recent survey by the IMF concludes
that, even in adverse world conditions, developing countries have
used aid to reduce balance of payments deficits, and to increase (or at
least sustain) investment rather than consumption.[45] There is some
evidence that during the 1960s, aid helped to increase investment in
India.[46]

The effect of aid on public savings seems to follow similar lines.
There is little evidence that recipient governments systematically used
aid to reduce their tax-gathering efforts. One of the few quantitative
studies on aid and public savings found that, for eleven African countries, foreign loans did not add fully to total resources. But expenditure shifted from consumption to investment, the opposite of what the

critical studies suggest would happen.[47] No doubt governments in many countries could improve their tax gathering[48]—but this is not evidence that it is aid which discourages them.

Individual countries illustrate the lack of any generalized relationship. Tunisia and the Ivory Coast score high on tax effort and have high aid/GNP ratios; Pakistan has a high ratio of aid to GNP but did poorly in tax effort in the 1970s. Brazil, which received little aid, scores well on tax effort; Mexico, also a small recipient of aid, scored badly.[49] Anyway, simple correlations can be misleading, particularly as taxes on foreign trade are a major source of revenue for many governments. If they receive more aid in times of trade recession, it may look as though they are 'substituting' aid for taxes.

Two other considerations may undermine many of these aid–savings studies. First, in most developing countries domestic savings are estimated in the national accounts as a residual. Given the level of investment and government expenditure, accounting identities may force domestic savings down if foreign savings rise. This could explain part (possibly a large part) of the alleged negative effect of aid on savings. Second, correlations should separate food and other aid intended for consumption from the rest of aid. Preliminary findings from recent World Bank research which made this distinction showed the reverse relationship: most development assistance *is* saved (and invested).

Aid and government expenditure

Undue emphasis has been put on the possible effects of aid on tax effort, while neglecting its effects on the level and composition of public expenditure. Aid accounts for a much larger proportion of government budgets than of savings or GNP, varying from about 12 per cent for India to 80 per cent for Mali.[50] A large part of aid goes to finance capital budgets. While some of this expenditure may be of questionable priority, the bulk goes to support basic infrastructure in power, transport, health, and education. Without such spending, the social structure is not likely to hold together, let alone develop. Reductions in public expenditure may bear disproportionately on poorer people.[51] Social programmes are particularly vulnerable, because the proportion of recurrent expenditure tends to be high, and the potential losers have little voice in policy decisions. Some applications of IMF or World Bank Structural Adjustment Loan (SAL) conditionality may ignore such social costs, as Chapter 3 notes.

Even if some aid goes into consumption, it must not be assumed that it is thereby 'wasted'. Much of the empirical work assumed that growth was the sole objective of aid, so it treated an increase in consumption as a 'leakage'. However, any real effort to tackle poverty directly should involve a higher share of consumption in GNP, as the increased incomes of the poor are mainly spent rather than saved. Food aid is the best example of consumption aid, and is not less valuable because of that. What matters is that the benefits of extra consumption should go to those who need them most, and that any short-term benefits should be used as far as possible to increase the capacity of the poor to maintain high levels of income and consumption.[52] Moreover, many items counted as 'consumption' in national accounts—recurrent spending on health, nutrition, education, etc.—can have substantial returns, even in terms of GNP growth.

Aid and self-reliance

Aid should, in the longer run, enable recipient countries to build up their productive capacity, so that they can finance their investment and import requirements through normal commercial channels. It is possible for aid to have a negative effect on savings in the short run and yet promote such 'self-reliance' in the long term. Theoretically, very different outcomes are possible.[53] Empirically, the question of self-reliance has not received much attention, though it can be illustrated through the contrasting experience of two countries. South Korea received a large amount of aid in the 1950s and 1960s, which then declined sharply. Its economy has grown rapidly and its domestic savings rose from 6.9 per cent of GDP in 1953–5 to 18.7 per cent in 1974–6. Its external trade deficit remains roughly constant, at around 9 per cent of GDP, while aid's share in financing it fell from 60 per cent to 17 per cent. South Korea still requires foreign capital, but obtains it through private markets.[54] It has used its aid effectively, especially after an initial realignment of policy during the Park regime.[55]

In certain respects, India has followed a similar pattern, in that its net inflow of foreign aid peaked during the early 1960s. Gross domestic savings rose from around 13 per cent of GDP in the early 1960s to around 22 per cent in the late 1970s. The net inflow of savings from abroad (not only of aid) declined from between 2.5 and 3.0 per cent of GDP to less than 1 per cent; during 1975–9, it was actually negative, at around 0.9 per cent.[56] India's ability to use aid effectively is much better than that of many countries and has improved considerably over the years, an example of the importance of 'learning by doing' for aid effectiveness.

Aid dependency is not an unchanging phenomenon. Many countries have 'graduated' from soft, IDA-type loans to hard, IBRD-type finance. Colombia decided to graduate from soft loans in 1975 on its own initiative, to achieve greater political independence. As the case of South Korea suggests, part of the 'efficiency' of aid lies in helping towards a structural transformation of the economy, to enable it to obtain foreign capital through normal commercial channels. Several countries have made considerable progress towards self-sufficiency in foodgrains, narrowly defined in terms of the ability to satisfy effective demand in normal years. Aid has obviously had a part to play in developing and disseminating higher-yielding agricultural tech-nologies. India is again a good example of where aid has given high returns in promoting agricultural research.[57] So have Mexico and the Philippines. In Pakistan, agricultural growth has been maintained at over 3 per cent a year in recent decades. It is hard to imagine that this would have been achieved without the massive investment in irriga-tion by the World Bank and other donors, and other assistance to agriculture.

These country and project experiences are not random examples. Aid is but one resource of many, and its effectiveness depends on many factors, not all of them economic or aid-related. A recent study of sub-Saharan Africa, for example, points to the influence of environmental factors (such as droughts) or exogenous factors (such as export prospects) as well as to broader changes in economic pol-icy.[58] However, much has been learned, by donors and recipients alike, about how to make better use of aid. As the India study shows, there is much for donors to learn from past experience that is relevant to current aid issues.[59] The lessons may not be dramatic, but they offer grounds for hope. At the micro-level, they include the importance of project selection, preparation, and evaluation; sensitivity to local con-ditions; and the importance of participation of the intended beneficiaries. At the macro-level, what matters is the overall policy context, especially the role of incentives and the role of government in economic activity. These points are discussed further in the next section.

IV Aid and exports

Foreign trade has a respectable record as an 'engine of growth'. It has attracted extra interest as a result of the spectacular success of those developing countries that pursued export-led growth in the 1970s. Others have arguably held back their own progress by adopting policies which restricted imports and damaged their export capacity. Not surprisingly, aid has been accused of conniving at such policies, or even of sustaining them by providing foreign exchange that coun-tries would otherwise have had to try harder to earn for themselves.

The facts are not so simple. Some countries that had been major recipients of aid became successful exporters—partly because of aid, not despite it. In many countries trade policy has long been discussed with donors, with mixed results. Much of the purpose of structural adjustment is to adjust production and policies to take account of the new realities of world trade. Many countries have started to make these adjustments. But their efforts often need to be supported by aid, rather than being an alternative to it. Lastly, it is far from obvious that countries that followed autarkic policies would have liberalized more rapidly if left to their own devices.

The importance of trade to development is beyond dispute. A recent study suggests that an increase of one percentage point in the rate of growth of exports adds on average 0.15 to 0.27 points to the growth of a developing economy.[60] However, there is some concern about the prospects for more open trade policies in low-income (and especially the poorest) countries in the 1980s. One report goes so far as to say that 'without assurances that export earnings will soon expand and barriers to external market entry will be reduced it would be foolhardy for many countries now to undertake liberalization programmes'.[61] Just what are appropriate trade policies in current conditions is discussed further in Chapter 4. Certainly many countries can improve on their past performance. But only a few are likely to achieve the success of those now classified as NICs.

Aid donors have three functions in assisting low-income countries' trade. The first is through the policy dialogue which, as Chapter 4 discusses, requires considerable sophistication. While the principal needs are often exchange rate devaluation, relaxation of controls, and removal of taxes or subsidies on exports or imports, there is no simple prescription. Protection is often needed, especially in the least adaptable economies, and ill-judged devaluations can be harmful.

The second function of aid donors is to give balance of payments support during liberalization, when imports are likely to grow faster than exports. It is especially helpful if the recipient can be confident of support over an appropriate period. (The India study describes the collapse of the post-devaluation aid package in the mid-1960s, which harmed relationships between India and its donors, and damaged the cause of trade liberalization—a cause only now coming into its own again in India.[62]) The third function is to support productive activities in the export sector, and even export promotion. A World Bank study, for example, shows the critical role of transport facilities if producers are to benefit from higher prices.[63] Another commentator notes that 'exports do not rise overnight and creation of new import-substitution capacity takes time. The same is true of the investment required . . .

delay in response can be overcome if there is assistance . . . for foreign exchange and capital goods . . . to eliminate production bottlenecks'.[64]

The quotation highlights another aspect of trade strategy. Import substitution has become a positive policy, having once been associated with over-protective and inefficient practices. It is now widely accepted as a key part of adjustment—especially in energy and food, as imports of both have become a significant drain on the balance of payments. In these fields too, of course, donors can contribute much through policy support and assistance for productive activities.

The aid community today is well apprised of all these issues. This report disputes the criticism that donors have been excessively tolerant of poor trade policies. Perhaps there are countries for which this was true; but in general, the donors have exerted their influence towards liberalizing trade policies. The results have often been striking, not just in South Korea, Taiwan, and other Asian economies, but also (if less dramatically) in such countries as the Ivory Coast and Malawi. In some countries progress has been slow—but not always because of recipient failings, as the Indian case makes clear. In others, strong pressure for change is fairly recent.

All the efforts of donors to influence trade strategy must deal with the underlying reasons for countries' restrictive policies. These have lain partly in the complex politics of the exchange rate, where vested interests have opposed competitive valuation; partly in export pessimism—not without cause when exports were mainly in weak primary commodities, and when processed goods and manufacturers face rigid trade barriers. The poorest countries are hampered by the real supply constraints that go with a lack of development. Exports may be an engine of development; but development should more often be seen as an engine for exports, for successful penetration of foreign markets requires extensive productive skills at home.

V Conclusions

Inter-country statistical analyses do not show anything conclusive—positive or negative—about the impact of aid on growth. Given the enormous variety of countries and types of aid, this is not surprising. If appropriate aid is put to good use in a satisfactory policy context, and if all the other components of growth are present, the statistical relationship between aid and growth will be positive. If such a relationship does not emerge overall, it only shows the unexciting conclusion that aid may or may not be strongly related to growth, depending on circumstances.

Studies of individual countries show something different, and more interesting. Growth requires many ingredients, financial and non-financial. Aid supplies many of them: capital, commodities, technical cooperation, policy discussion. The case studies conducted for this report offer many examples of a positive link between aid and growth. The Malawi study found the combination of financial aid, technical cooperation, and institution building in no small way responsible for the satisfactory growth of the 1970s.[65] Similarly the Colombia study showed that aid made a 'major financial contribution' to development, and was important in building up a number of essential public agencies.[66]

The Bangladesh and Mali studies[67] have something in common: in both countries, aid is a large proportion of total investment, and has also supported essential economic functions. In Bangladesh, reconstruction aid helped restore the economy after the devastation of 1971. In Mali, aid helped to finance much of the government budget over a crucial time, and assisted the economy through recent prolonged drought. Without aid, one can only wonder in what condition these two countries would have survived the last decade of turmoil in the world economy. In addition, both countries have made considerable investments in infrastructure and production, and have recently adopted significant new approaches to policy formation and reform which augur well for the future.

In Kenya,[68] the relation between aid and growth was hard to assess, partly because of the time-lags in the impact of aid, and also as aid increased in certain periods to meet economic difficulties. Nor is it easy to judge how much policies have changed under recent structural adjustment lending. In India,[69] there is less doubt. Both food and financial aid, though modest in relation to the whole economy, have at critical times eased savings and foreign exchange constraints and permitted faster growth than would otherwise have been possible. In addition, aid's contribution to India's agricultural production, particularly through the Green Revolution, has itself had major macroeconomic effects. The case of South Korea[70] demonstrates the importance of politics and policies. Under the Park regime, the combination of aid and policy dialogue helped build the foundations for the country's economic success—though under the earlier Rhee administration, neither donor nor recipient paid much attention to the necessities of development. Aid was largely political in motive, and development was a secondary consideration; not surprisingly, there was much aid and little result. In a minor way the same was true for some periods in Colombia: when the main donor was principally concerned to sustain the government in office, it refrained from pressure to promote necessary economic reforms; at other periods, however, reforms were effectively promoted.[71]

These and many other examples should make for caution in reading the results of aggregative statistical analyses. Painstaking attention to individual countries seems the only way to tell whether aid is really assisting growth; even then, answers are only partially conclusive. Aid can and does contribute to growth; so do many other things. Aid can fail as well. The record is mixed; but with current pressures for recipient-policy reform and for changes in donor practices and coordination, it should improve.

Appendix: Regression studies of aid impact: a technical note

The main conclusions that can be drawn from the empirical studies of aid's macroeconomic impact have been summarized in Chapter 2. This appendix discusses briefly some of the more technical aspects of the findings in those studies, pointing to some problems that arise in interpreting their results. It does not attempt a comprehensive review of the more theoretical aspects.[72] The following points are discussed: measurement of the variables; specifications of the models; explaining statistical relationships; problems of aggregation.

The constraints on growth—absorptive capacity, savings, and foreign exchange—may have different effects depending on a country's stage of development.[73] Though other aspects are not ignored, the main emphasis is on the role of aid as a supplier of imported inputs, especially capital goods.

The empirical studies mostly cover the period of the 1960s; more recent experiences, whether positive or negative, are not included. Mosley (1980) extends the data to 1977, and Mosley and Hudson (1984) to 1980. Aggregate data for all developing countries and for regional groups are surveyed by the authors, as are some country studies. Aid flows are measured differently, as is explained in the following section.

Measurement of the variables

Empirical investigations of the effect of aid on growth use GNP or GNP per capita as the dependent variable (and mostly real GNP). Where studies use cross-section data from many developing countries, the reliability of the statistics varies widely between countries. Even for an individual country, different sources produce widely different estimates of growth rates. In time-series data, estimates depend on whether base-year or end-year weights are used.[74] This is particularly important for the poorer economies, where growth is often accompanied by significant structural change or by the emergence of new commodities. Results also vary because of the use of widely differing prices (or, alternatively, international prices) in measuring agricultural production. This is especially significant in countries with a high degree of 'price distortion', in terms of relative commodity price ratios.[75]

More serious problems arise in measuring aid. These are of two kinds. First, some of the earlier studies used the deficit on current account as a measure of aid. This is obviously inappropriate in principle, because such deficits can be financed in several ways—official aid, private investment, suppliers' credit, or emigrants' remittances. The contribution of these different sources varies by country, the poorer ones being more dependent on aid. In practice, aid is not highly correlated with other types of capital flows, so they cannot be treated as good proxies for one another.[76]

Secondly, the significance of aid for development lies in its transfer of real resources. However, most of the studies use the nominal value of aid as an independent variable. Real values of resources transferred may be different from the nominal value of aid received, for three reasons. The first is inflation in donor countries, where most of the aid receipts are spent, and fluctuations in foreign exchange rates. The second is that the additionality conferred by a given volume of aid-financed imports depends upon the ratio of domestic to international ('dollar') prices, which varies significantly across countries.[77] The third is the practice of 'aid-tying', which can significantly reduce the purchasing power of aid.[78] Of course, this ignores the possibilities of 'switching'—which is by no means costless, as it often ties up scarce administrative resources in developing countries. Moreover, the poorer countries often find it hardest to avoid the costs of tied aid, partly due to their dependence on single donor, and partly due to a shortage of administrative capacity.

Specifications of the models

Most of the regression studies use either unlagged data or a one-year lag structure. Among the exceptions are Mosley (1980) which uses both unlagged data and a five-year lag; and Mosley and Hudson (1984) which uses both unlagged data and alternative lag structures. If aid flowed at an unchanging rate, or if all recipients were at the same stage of development, this might not matter much. As things are, it is surely unsatisfactory to use either unlagged data or an arbitrary structure of lags. For project aid, for example, the right lag to use could be the gestation period of the project plus a reasonable pay-off period, if not the discounted present value of the net project receipts.

For programme aid, short-term balance of payments assistance may sometimes have a quick impact. However, where major structural changes, or the development of indigenous skills, or substantial degrees of 'learning by doing' are required to make the most effective use of aid, much longer delays are involved. While the results obtained by the lagged and unlagged regression equations do differ, they do not substantially alter the conclusion that there seems to be no strong correlation between aid and growth.[79]

Some studies of aid impact have used the absolute volume of aid as an independent variable, while others have used the aid/GNP ratio. Some of the studies exclude food aid. Each of these approaches raises particular problems. As Chapter 2 showed, the significance of aid varies greatly between recipient countries, whether aid is measured as a proportion of GNP, or of exports, or of public expenditure. The mean value of these ratios is typically small for all developing countries, but can be very high for particular countries or groups of countries—e.g. sub-Saharan Africa.[80] For this reason, it makes no sense to use absolute levels of aid as an explanatory variable in cross-section studies. While this problem can be overcome by using some proportional measure of aid, that in turn assumes that the aid/growth relationship is linear. In reality, there is no reason to assume such linearity, either for inter-country studies or in time-series analysis for individual countries.

Aid can be effective in two distinct ways. It may supply extra resources, mainly in the form of imports or capital inputs. In such cases, the expected value of the B-coefficient of aid on growth would depend on the size of the import-coefficient or the capital/output ratio; for example, one would expect a B-coefficient of around 0.3 to 0.2 for a capital/output ratio of 3 to 5. In other cases, aid may act to remove a bottleneck or break a binding constraint. A form of 'aid multiplier' might then come into effect, yielding an expected B-coefficient exceeding unity. For example, if aid eases a foreign exchange constraint on imports, and the import-coefficient is, say, 40 per cent of value-added, the B-coefficient may be about 2.5. Neither is it surprising that the regression studies yield widely different values of R^2s and B-coefficients, nor that the mean values of B-coefficients in cross-section studies of countries in different aid circumstances are typically small.[81]

Unfortunately, few studies have tried to establish any relationship between aid and investment, or taken a total factor productivity approach that included aid's contribution aid to the development of labour skills, or assessed the significance of 'learning by doing'. The quantitative significance of the last two factors is a matter for future research. As for the link between aid and investment, there is some evidence that aid has a small but positive effect. One study found a positive correlation between inflows of public capital and increases in investment, the coefficient being large but not significant at 5 percent.[82] A study on India up to the early 1970s found a strong and significant relationship between gross aid and investment in the organized sector. The B-coefficients were in the range 1.48 to 3.15, depending on whether food aid was included.[83] The study suggested that aid has had a 'multiplier' effect on investment, by financing the import content of big projects. A more recent study found no significant effect of net aid on India's public investment, but a fairly strong positive correlation between net foreign exchange availability and public investment.[84]

Explaining statistical relationships

Most of the regression studies attempt to analyse aid's impact on growth and savings. As explained earlier, the effect on growth is not strong. However, many of the studies found a strong *negative* relationship between aid and savings which has been used to argue that aid is a substitute for domestic savings rather than a source of extra capital for development. Such results need more careful interpretation.

Some of the most influential, certainly the most talked about, findings were those of Griffin and Enos.[85] They are not, however, the most satisfactory. They found a weak positive effect of aid on growth of output, with R^2 of 0.33; and a strong negative effect of the aid/GNP ratio on savings, with R^2s in the range 0.54 to 0.90. There was a weak negative effect of aid on growth for Latin America, with R^2 of 0.62. One problem with the Griffin and Enos research is the very high values of B-coefficients. The positive aid/growth coefficient of 0.18, indicating that there is an implicit capital/output ratio of around 10, is perhaps not unreasonable. But the negative B-coefficients obtained for the aid/savings relationship, which range from -0.73 to -1.14, are on the high side. Given that aid is seldom a large proportion of domestic savings, one would not expect the average ratio to be so sensitive to aid.

Whereas Griffin and Enos use the deficit on current account as a measure of aid, Papanek's work distinguishes between different types of capital inflows—aid, private investment and others.[86] Such a distinction is important, because the various forms of capital inflows are strongly correlated and private capital inflows are concentrated among a few middle-income countries. Papanek finds that both domestic and foreign savings have a positive effect on GNP growth, together explaining about 40 per cent of the increase in output. This is roughly consistent with the results of Griffin and Enos, as well as with historical data. The effect of aid on growth is stronger than that of savings or of private investment. The latter conclusion is worth stressing, given the presumption of critics of aid that private investment is more effective in promoting growth. Papanek found aid and savings were negatively correlated, with a correlation coefficient of -0.56.[87]

Mosley and Hudson's 1984 study comes to quite different conclusions, both on the effect of aid on growth, and on the relative contributions of aid and other forms of foreign capital.[88] The authors found that the 'multiple regression coefficient of aid on growth . . . is strongly negative and almost significant in the 1960s, and positive but altogether insignificant in the 1970s . . . (These) results . . . conflict with those recorded by Papanek (1972, 1973) which suggest a positive and significant influence for aid in the 1960s, indeed that aid .'has a more significant influence . . . than . . . other forms of foreign resource flows'. The value of the B-coefficient for the total sample in the 1960s is -0.21, with an R^2 of 0.37. The same study finds both savings and the growth rate of exports to be positively correlated with growth.

For a sample of 37 poorer countries in 1960–75, a study by Bornschier finds (all) foreign capital to have a positive effect on growth, though one that is not significant statistically. The book value of the stock of capital shows a significant and negative effect on growth, but with a B-coefficient of -0.007 for the sub-sample of Asian countries. However, Bornschier does not resolve the problems of measuring the book-value of capital, so his results should be treated with caution.[89]

Some of the earlier studies that used ordinary least squares regression equations overlooked one difficulty: there is a two-way relationship between aid and savings, through possible changes in output. This tends to call into question the negative correlation found between aid and savings.[90] Models which ignore two-way links, the so-called 'open loop' models, would typically yield a larger displacement of savings.[91] However, even when such linkages are taken into account, a significant negative relationship between aid and savings still emerges. Weisskopf, who uses an *ex ante* savings function to separate the two effects, finds that for ten out of seventeen developing countries, the negative relationship was statistically significant; B-coefficients were in the range -0.27 to -0.88, with very high R^2s of 0.94 to 0.99.[92]

Such a strong negative relationship globally does not prove that aid displaces savings in every case; the direction of causality may run either way. Reflecting the limited savings capacity of the poorest developing countries, low savings might require more foreign aid to bridge a resource gap. Exogenous changes in output, caused by shocks like war or a decline in world demand, may reduce savings and increase the demand for aid.[93] By their nature, such 'shocks' are likely to be random—but it is possible for individual countries or episodes to affect the results of aggregated regression analysis. Lastly, it should be pointed out that most of these studies assumed that growth was the only objective; any diversion of aid into consumption was 'inefficient'. With a shift in policy towards tackling poverty, it cannot be assumed that any diversion of aid into consumption is a measure of its ineffectiveness, even if poor countries are expected to move towards 'self-reliance' in the medium term.

Some of the literature argues that the negative effect of aid on savings comes about partly through recipient governments reducing their tax efforts. The conclusions of two studies on this issue have been referred to in Chapter 2.[94] In addition, two studies of India found little independent evidence that aid increased the budget deficit.[95] However, where a negative correlation between aid and savings is found, there has been no attempt to study whether it is accompanied by other forms of internal or external disequilibria. A net inflow of capital mirrors an excess demand for resources—a current account deficit financed by a capital inflow. If aid substitutes for private or public domestic savings instead of adding to them, the excess demand is not absorbed to that extent. Such excess demand, in turn, will be reflected in inflation, or a worsening balance of trade or other symptoms.

It has been argued that the weak correlation between aid and growth comes about through a rise in the capital/output ratio brought about by aid.[96] The argument is intuitive—that aid influences the choice of more capital-intensive technology. Few empirical studies have tried to test such a relationship. A study of South Korea shows a decline in the ICOR, but not that it is the result of aid.[97] The argument is more complex than at first it seems. On the one hand, aid is part of total investible resources—a large part for some countries; the effect on the overall capital/output ratio of a higher ICOR in aid-financed projects will depend on their weight in total capital expenditure. If the bias, however, is a general one that is introduced by the technological monopoly of the developed countries, it would probably operate independently of aid. On the other hand, donors often favour capital-intensive technologies, such as tractors for Sri Lanka, or capital-intensive projects, such as infrastructural investment as opposed to rural development, which will operate in that direction.

Problems of aggregation

Many regression studies look at large samples of countries in heterogeneous circumstances. As the dependence on aid varies from country to country, and aid operates in different administrative, infra-structural, and policy environments, the aggregation of LDCs into single samples could be masking the phenomenon of aid effectiveness. It is therefore worth looking at the impact of aid on different regional groups and countries. By and large, Asian countries seem to have made more effective use of aid than, say, Latin American countries.[98] In his 1980 article, Mosely found that the proportion of growth explained by aid, private capital, etc. can vary from 4 to 25 per cent, according to donor (significant only for the UK). In addition, if the aid-recipient countries were divided into a 'poor' group, with per-capita income below $300 at 1977 prices, and a middle-income group above that threshold, Mosely found a strong and positive link between aid and growth for the poor countries (a B-coefficient of 0.98, with aid lagged by five years). For the middle-income group, the relationship was negative but not significant (a B-coefficient of -1.04).[99] In a later study, the relationship appears to have been reversed, showing a negative correlation for the period of the 1970s for the poorer group and a positive correlation for the middle-income group; however, neither is significant.[100] A recent study, which finds multilateral aid to be more 'effective' than bilateral aid in promoting development, was referred to in Chapter 2.[101]

Several studies have attempted to look at individual country experiences. In Latin America, negative correlations between the current account deficit and savings have been found for Colombia, and for Brazil.[102] That relationship is either insignificant or positive for India.[103] The range of possibilities is widened in a recent study of sub-Saharan Africa, which points to the influence of exogenous factors, such as drought and export prospects, as well as of broader changes in economic policy.[104] Before anything definitive can be said about the quantitative impact of aid on macroeconomic performance, detailed studies of particular countries over reasonably long periods are required. Aggregative regression studies are unlikely to resolve the issue either way.

Notes

1. Hewitt and Kydd 1984; Duncan and Mosley 1984.
2. The best 'quick' source is Dennison 1980; see also Dennison 1967.
3. Matthews *et al*. 1982.
4. Reynolds 1983.
5. See, *inter alia*, Kumar and Desai 1983.
6. Raj 1965.
7. Reynolds 1983; the terms 'intensive' and 'extensive' growth are his.
8. Cassen 1976; Steinberg 1984.
9. OECD/DAC 1983*a*.

10. World Bank 1979*b*.
11. World Bank 1981*a*.
12. *Ibid*.
13. Bourgoignie 1984.
14. OECD/DAC 1983*a*; World Bank 1984*i*.
15. World Bank 1983*e*.
16. Gordon *et al*. 1979.
17. McKinnon 1964.
18. Krueger and Ruttan 1983; Lipton *et al*. 1984*a*.
19. These are reasonable magnitudes to assume; see, for example, Wolgin 1983.
20. There are a large number of studies that have attempted to test the relationship between aid and other macroeconomic variables. The more important ones, which are considered here and in the appendix, are: Bornschier *et al*. 1978; Griffin 1970; Griffin and Enos 1970; Massell *et al*. 1972; Mosley 1980; Mosley and Hudson 1984; Papanek 1972; 1973; Weisskopf 1972. See also Grinols and Bhagwati 1976. For criticisms, other than those quoted above, see Eshag 1971; Lipton 1972; Stewart 1971. Others are referred to in the text.
21. Papanek 1973.
22. Mosley and Hudson 1984.
23. See the appendix at the end of this chapter.
24. Papanek 1973.
25. Mosley and Hudson 1984.
26. Weisskopf 1972.
27. Papanek 1973.
28. Lavy 1985.
29. Massell *et al*. 1972; Chaudhuri 1979.
30. Most regression studies do not test for such a relationship, with one exception, Heller 1975. The conclusion here is derived by comparing aid flows to indices of tax effort for recipient countries, reported in Tait *et al*. 1979.
31. Chenery and Strout 1966.
32. Bhagwati 1981; Chaudhuri 1979; Eshag 1971; Mujamoto 1973–4.
33. World Bank 1982*e*.
34. Yates 1982.
35. Maizels and Nissanke 1984; see also Chapter 9 below.
36. See, for example, Lipton *et al*. 1984*a*; Duncan and Mosley 1984.
37. For the (dubious) argument that the contribution of aid is necessarily limited to the concessional element alone, see Bauer 1981.
38. This argument is, of course, equally applicable to private capital flows. The point is that the poorer developing countries are more likely to suffer from major structural constraints, and at the same time have more limited access to forms of capital other than aid.
39. Van Arkadie and de Wilde 1984.
40. Bourgoignie 1984.
41. Hewitt and Kydd 1984.

42. World Bank 1982*b*. See further Chapter 5 below.
43. For Latin America, see Griffin 1970 and Leff 1968. For India, see Bhagwati and Srinivasan 1975 and Chaudhuri 1979.
44. Van Arkadie and de Wilde 1984.
45. IMF 1983.
46. Chaudhuri 1979; this conclusion is called into question in a recent study, which finds no significant relationship for India between *net* aid and public investment, but a strong positive effect on the latter of net foreign exchange availability (Rubin 1982).
47. Heller 1975.
48. Some were found in Kenya—see Duncan and Mosley 1984.
49. Tait *et al.* 1979.
50. Lipton *et al.* 1984*a*; Bourgoignie 1984.
51. Hewitt and Kydd 1984.
52. For a discussion of food aid, see Chapter 5 below.
53. Grinols and Bhagwati 1976.
54. Mason *et al.* 1980.
55. Fei *et al.* 1979; Franks *et al.* 1975; Mason *et al.* 1980; Steinberg 1984.
56. India, Reserve Bank of 1982.
57. Lipton *et al.* 1984*a*; Evenson 1982.
58. Wheeler 1984.
59. Lipton *et al.* 1984*a*.
60. Mosley and Hudson 1984.
61. Commonwealth Secretariat 1983, p. 99.
62. Lipton *et al.* 1984*a*.
63. World Bank, 1982*b*.
64. Diamand 1978.
65. Hewitt and Kydd 1984.
66. Bagley 1984.
67. Van Arkadie and de Wilde 1984; Bourgoignie 1984.
68. Duncan and Mosley 1984.
69. Lipton *et al.* 1984*a*.
70. Steinberg 1984.
71. Bagley 1984.
72. See note 25 above for a reference to the studies discussed. See also Chenery and Strout 1966; Papanek 1983; Tendulkar 1971; Voivodas 1973.
73. Chenery and Strout 1966.
74. World Bank 1981*e*, Technical Notes.
75. World Bank 1983*e*.
76. Papanek 1973.
77. Papanek 1983.
78. Bhagwati 1981; Chaudhuri 1979; Eshag 1967; Mujamoto 1973–4.
79. Mosley and Hudson 1984; on aid–growth correlations, see the section on interpretation of results in Section II above.
80. See p. 80 above.
81. See, for example, Papanek 1973.

82. Massell *et al.* 1972.
83. Chaudhuri 1979.
84. Rubin 1982; Lipton *et al.* 1984*a*.
85. Griffin and Enos 1970.
86. Papanek 1973.
87. *Ibid.*
88. Mosley and Hudson 1984.
89. Bornschier *et al.* 1978.
90. See, for example, Griffin and Enos 1970; Papanek 1972; for criticisms, see, for example, Eshag 1971; Stewart 1971.
91. Tendulkar 1971.
92. Weisskopf 1972.
93. Papanek 1972.
94. Heller 1975.
95. Bhagwati and Srinivasan 1975; Chaudhuri 1979.
96. Voivodas 1973.
97. Mason *et al.* 1980.
98. Papanek 1973.
99. Mosley 1980.
100. Mosley and Hudson 1984.
101. Maizels and Nissanke 1984.
102. For Colombia, see Griffin 1970; for Brazil, see Leff 1968; see also Lipton 1972 for a more detailed discussion.
103. Bhagwati and Srinivasan 1975; Chaudhuri 1979.
104. Wheeler 1984.

CHAPTER THREE
Aid and Poverty

I Introduction

Aid is often used for the immediate relief of poverty—in emergencies or Food for Work programmes. But it can also help to relieve poverty in five other ways. First, by contributing to growth, it can create the conditions for raising the incomes and consumption of the poor. Second, it can achieve those results more directly, through specific projects or sectoral activities. Third, it can improve poor people's welfare through basic services—education, health, nutrition, housing, or family planning programmes. Fourth, it can assist processes of social change which give assets to the poor. Finally, it can support policy reforms that benefit the poor. Aid has done all these things, but often in countries that have not given high priority to tackling poverty. It has not always done enough. And it can even harm the poor, if its projects involve inappropriate technology or skills, for example, or if it produces the wrong types of food.

Many people support aid because they believe that it helps to relieve poverty. That relief is most visible in famine work, such as in Africa today. Its effects are less obvious, though no less real, in many of the activities it has financed with a longer pay-off. But it would be better for all concerned if the limits of aid's capacity for the *direct* relief of poverty were clearly recognized.

Aid has generally been better at supplying hardware and undertaking major investments in construction than in developing income-raising programmes for landless labourers. The commercial pressures on bilateral aid programmes will also ensure that this bias remains. For political reasons, only 60 per cent of aid goes to low-income countries. And donors can do only a limited amount to persuade recipient governments to be more sensitive to the needs of the poor.

Aid must also contribute to countries' overall development, building up their infrastructure, skills, and productive systems. And it has to be used to finance immediate import needs, and to maintain and rehabilitate existing investment. Donors and recipients therefore need to strike a balance between these three demands on aid: long-term development, support for import needs and policy reforms, and schemes for tackling poverty. In some countries the latter should be increased at the expense of the others; but particular care is needed to ensure complementarity between various parts of the economy and to avoid the premature creation of welfare states.

II The nature of poverty

In many developing countries, the poor have not been the main beneficiaries of economic growth. However, economies such as those of South Korea and Taiwan have shown that there is no inherent contradiction between promoting growth and reducing poverty. Even some of the poorer countries (such as Sri Lanka) or some of the poorer regions in particular countries (such as Kerala in India) have managed to improve substantially the welfare of poor people, despite only modest economic growth. During the 1970s most developing countries reduced the proportions of people living in absolute poverty. The main exceptions were in sub-Saharan Africa and the least developed countries of South Asia and Latin America. But in many countries the recession of the 1980s has halted or reversed the progress against poverty.[1] With few exceptions, economic growth has proved a necessary condition for combating poverty. On its own, however, it is not sufficient. Even in most of the rich countries poverty persists after two centuries of industrial growth.

Identity of the poor

The most common definition of poverty is the condition of people below a 'poverty income threshold', determined by their ability to afford an adequate diet and other minimal necessities. In a low-income country, 40 per cent or more of the population may be below this threshold; the lowest 10 or 20 per cent are identified as the poorest. Poverty has of course non-economic dimensions, including inequalities before the law and access to public services. Such characteristics, though largely ignored in this chapter, have implications mainly for the recipients' part in the fight against poverty, but donors also need to bear them in mind.

Absolute poverty is largely a rural problem. However it is measured, the percentage of the rural population in poverty is usually at least double that of the urban population.[2] The rural poor belong to two categories: first, peasants who do not own enough land (or, more precisely, user rights over enough land) to grow food for family subsistence. Their poverty usually arises from the unequal distribution of cultivable land, which may be exacerbated by population pressure. What constitutes a 'small' farm varies according to soil, climate, and crop. As a guide, under South Asian conditions, it would be one and a half acres of owned land or over three acres of sharecropped land. Farmers who do not have enough land often have their problems compounded by inadequate access to complementary inputs, such as irrigation, fertilizer, or credit.

The second category consists of landless agricultural labourers and other non-agricultural groups who rely on employment opportunities in the countryside. This group includes some smallholders who have to supplement their farming income by some kind of job. While the problem of the landless is greatest in South and East Asia, it is starting to develop in African economies as well, largely as a result of population growth. The poverty of the landless consists not just in low agricultural wages, but also in the shortage of employment opportunities during the year.[3] Their poverty, too, has a price dimension. As the landless are net buyers of food, their real consumption is highly sensitive to food prices. They are also vulnerable to seasonal scarcities, of both jobs and food, as they typically hold no stocks and their creditworthiness is low or non-existent.

Women and rural poverty

The disadvantages suffered by women in rural life create a special dimension of poverty. Long neglect of their roles as producers, and the burdens placed on them by expectations that they will bear most of the responsibilities of the household, make them vulnerable to adversity. Subordination of women is part of the social structure of rural poverty in several countries. Where, as in many parts of Africa, they are the majority of food producers, programmes to enhance women's productive roles become virtually synonymous with action against poverty. The large family, both a cause and a consequence of poverty, is often a male rather than a female desire, and an improvement in the situation of women is an indispensable part of the 'demographic transition'—the transition from high to low mortality and fertility, from large, poor families to smaller and more prosperous ones.

Income, consumption and services

A reduction in poverty requires the poor to increase their consumption. This can be achieved either by poor people raising their output and incomes; or by governments offering them more food through food stamps or Food for Work programmes; or by governments reducing the price that the poor pay for essentials, especially foodgrains. (*Producer* prices, of course, have to be kept at remunerative levels, so the government might have to cover the difference.) Food prices are critical. Two recent studies on India have emphasized their importance in explaining the incidence of poverty and its regional variations.[4] Food prices can be reduced either as a result of increased food production or availability bringing down the market price; or through special marketing arrangements, such as public systems of grain distribution or 'fair price shops'.[5] Of equal importance is access to markets, which enables poor farmers to obtain higher or more reliable prices for their output. The rural poor can suffer when urban marketing structures are more developed than those in rural areas, as in Bangladesh.[6]

Apart from these direct methods of raising the consumption of the poor, much can be done indirectly through the provision of social services. This requires public investment in health services, sanitation, and water supply, as well as efforts to improve the access of the poor to existing services. What matters is not only the level of funding—the percentage of both public expenditure and aid spent on social expenditure is often very low—but the whole policy framework within which health and other social programmes operate, and, not least, the attention they give to women's roles and problems.

An effective assault on poverty has to start by recognizing that the concepts of 'income' and 'employment' may not apply to the poorest people. Most of them do not have a regular 'job' with a paid 'wage' so much as a repertoire of activities from which they obtain money or food. These may include 'cultivation; keeping livestock; collecting or catching, and consuming or processing and selling; common property resources (firewood, charcoal, fish, grass, medicinal plants . . .); casual labour; hawking; seasonal public relief works; seasonal migration; work as artisans . . . and many other activities'. The very poor are always vulnerable to contingencies, natural or social. In these circumstances, bettering their lot 'can involve measures quite different from the generation of conventional employment. These include improving the management and productivity of common resources and of their access to them . . .; organisation to raise casual wages or to get better prices and surer markets for produce; seasonal employment programmes which fill in slack periods; and technology to improve the productivity of whatever resources they command.' All this needs to be done in ways that reduce rather than increase their vulnerability.[7]

Urban poor

Policies for tackling urban poverty differ significantly in certain respects from those in rural areas. Creating jobs and developing skills is likely to come through encouragement of small-scale manufacturing, both formal and 'informal', through appropriate technology, and the provision of credit. Public investment in social services also brings

major benefits: better transport systems facilitate job search or travel
to work; easier access to health facilities (as in Malawi[8]) can transform
people's lives. Other obvious measures include water and sanitation,
urban slum upgrading, and 'site and service' housing policies, which
have been particularly successful.[9] The achievements of the Calcutta
Metropolitan Development Plan show what can be done even under
difficult conditions, although no single example can necessarily be
replicated elsewhere.[10]

III   The record of aid

Most aid agencies have a commitment to tackle poverty; for many, it
is written into their charters. Because poverty remains so widespread,
however, it might suggest that aid has failed in this task. Such an
impression is misleading. Directly and indirectly, aid has helped
countries to fight poverty. Broadly speaking, poverty persists despite
the achievements of aid; it would have been worse without it. When
populations are doubling in twenty to thirty years in countries where
jobs were already scarce and incomes low, even rapid and well-
distributed growth would take years to reduce mass poverty. But
growth has been slow in many countries, especially the poorest; it has
been held back by internal and external shocks, and by policy failings;
and it has seldom been evenly distributed, for reasons that have little
to do with aid.

The pattern and pace of growth is therefore a dominating influence
on poverty. Some of the fastest-growing economies have managed to
make income distribution less unequal: South Korea and Taiwan, for
example. Others have not, but their rapid growth has nevertheless
helped the poor to make some gains: Brazil and several other Latin
American countries would be cases in point. The Colombia study
carried out for this report found significant reductions in poverty, due
to successful growth and employment policies in the 1970s; but also to
the donors' povery-oriented lending.[11] In countries where rural
development has accelerated even though economic growth has been
modest, the proportion of people living in absolute poverty has been
reduced: China, India, and Pakistan are examples. In all these different groups, China alone owes little of its development successes to aid.

Most of the poorest countries have made little progress against
poverty, often despite substantial aid. Examples from this report
include Bangladesh and Mali, though Bangladesh has shown how aid
directed against poverty can be effective. In Malawi, despite many
widely applauded policy reforms, the poor have not progressed, and
may even have got poorer. Kenya, with a somewhat richer and

faster-growing economy, does not appear to have provided many benefits for its poor.

Welfare indicators

These conclusions are based on estimates of the incomes of the poor. By other measures—health and education, for example—many countries have made substantial progress in tackling poverty. Between 1965 and 1983 ten years were added to life expectancy in India and China; infant mortality more than halved in China, and fell nearly 40 per cent in India. In other low-income countries, average life expectancy rose by six to seven years over the same period, and infant mortality fell by about one-fifth. In low-income countries as a group, primary school enrolment rose from an average 62 per cent of the age group in 1965 to 85 per cent in 1982, secondary enrolment from 20 to 30 per cent.[12] Most of these achievements owe a significant debt to aid.

However, aid operates within a broader policy context set mainly by national priorities—though donors can help to shape it. And some aid has no direct relevance to poverty—for example, if it is tied to sales of high-technology equipment. But aid can help, or harm, at the margin. Even small reductions in the number of poor, or the intensity of poverty, are considerable achievements for a poor country with a rapidly growing population. That is the level of expectations against which past performance has to be judged.

Trends in aid

As Chapter 2 pointed out, aid constitutes a relatively small percentage of GNP or savings for developing countries as a whole. Sub-Saharan Africa is a notable exception, with aid providing 50 per cent of gross investment.[13] Even if every dollar of aid were without strings and were well-spent, which is not the case, there has not been enough of it to alter significantly the picture of absolute poverty in poor countries. And on present prospects, the real volume of aid is unlikely to increase significantly. Further, the conquest of poverty needs time; much aid has long-term effects whose results are not yet apparent.

However, some developments in aid programmes have been promising. Over time, aid has shifted significantly into agriculture and activities directly aimed at poverty (often the same thing). The Nordic donors have for many years devoted the bulk of their aid to the poorer countries and poor people within those countries. The International Fund for Agricultural Development (IFAD) has had particular success in reaching poor people with poverty-oriented rural projects. The World Bank group increased its poverty-oriented lending from 5 per cent of its total lending in 1968–70 to 30 per cent in 1981–3;[14] several major donors have moved in the same direction. The fact that rural lending has fallen off recently is explained partly by the diversion of aid to other things (especially programme aid), and partly by dissatisfaction with some of the results of recent agricultural projects, especially in Africa.

IV Sectoral and project impact

The conventional distinction between poverty-oriented and other aid is not entirely satisfactory. Donors tend to confine the former to rural development, the small-scale and informal sector in urban areas, and basic services. Yet aid for other purposes has major effects on the poor. As Chapter 5 argues, these are often ignored in project work; some aid agencies examine the poverty impact only in poverty-oriented projects. But it is just as important elsewhere. Irrigation projects used to be open to the criticism that big farmers benefited most; today, more trouble is taken in assessing water-management systems to try to ensure that benefits reach small farmers as well.

Similar arguments apply to a whole range of aid-financed activities. Roads may open up rural areas and provide new opportunities for local production; but they may also bring in manufactures which destroy traditional crafts and local enterprise. The case studies in this report generally reveal that donors do not pay enough attention to the poverty impact of their projects. The Kenya study finds it hard to identify any impact on the poor of aid-financed projects; many seem to lack any specific focus on poverty.[15] The Malawi study suggests that large amounts of aid have had no positive impact on either agricultural yields or the incomes of the poor.[16] The India study found that some projects, such as urban development in Calcutta or 'Operation Flood' in rural areas, have benefited the poor; but the authors point out that donors have yet to devise an overall strategy for channelling either assets or jobs directly to the poor, and have not always supported aid requests from India which would do so.[17]

Donors could do more to benefit the poor (or at least not harm them) if they paid more attention to the poverty effects of all their projects. This would involve a different approach to project evaluation. Many evaluations content themselves with a financial assessment, rather than a social cost–benefit approach. Even when the latter is used, few studies employ weights for income distribution. Most infrastructural aid has been for large power or transport projects, whose poverty impact is not systematically evaluated, although they involve large amounts of aid. This does not encourage the best use of aid. Indeed, the main contribution of cost–benefit analysis may lie in the systematic gathering of relevant project information and consideration of alternatives, before aid resources are committed to particular projects. Further, the capacity to identify suitable rural projects is a prominent aspect of the limited 'absorptive capacity' of the poor countries;[18] aid can help to build up such capacity with local skills and resources.

A full analysis of the poverty impact of projects and programmes would quickly dispel one common doubt—that poverty-oriented projects are not economically viable. Those IBRD and IDA projects that have taken social and poverty criteria into account have yielded rates of return comparable to those achieved in other sectors. The main recent exceptions have been in African rural development. In general, the Bank's Operations Evaluation Department has found no inherent conflict between helping the poor and earning satisfactory rates of return on aid funds.[19] Other donors have found much the same. But there is an important caveat: donors have found such projects difficult to mount—they are expensive in administration time, and problems abound in efforts to involve local people in participatory activities.[20]

Goods, services, and purchasing power

A poverty-oriented strategy would emphasize the production of goods and services that weigh heavily in the budgets of poor families. It would also incorporate methods for raising the purchasing power of the poor, so as to convert their needs into effective demand.[21] The sectors that supply the needs of the poor may not be those that generate income and employment opportunities for them in the most cost-effective way. However, that conflict does not seem to apply to food-grains, probably the most essential need of all poor people. There is strong evidence that a small-farmer strategy can boost both the supply of grains and the incomes of the poor. Most projects directed at small farmers have shown returns at least as high as those involving large farmers. But in the case of urban water supply, needs and purchasing power may not coincide. Donors must bear in mind that aid projects may help the poor either by increasing the supply of goods they consume or by adding to their purchasing power, and that aid agencies' comparative advantage might favour the one or the other in particular circumstances. If projects are aimed at increasing food production, for example, 'policy dialogue' may try to ensure that national policies do not neglect the issue of purchasing power. Otherwise, food 'self-sufficiency' may simply come to mean enough food for those who already have the purchasing power to satisfy their needs.[22]

Where aid is intended to increase the supply of goods and services for poor people to consume, commodity and sectoral priorities are needed. They can then be used to identify the projects which can be implemented most beneficially and cost-effectively. First, the commodity/sector choice. As an example, the Mali case study concluded that, though the country needs infrastructural facilities of all sorts, the clearest priority for the rural poor is for food and water.[23] The poor spend 70 per cent or more of their income on food, the bulk of it on locally grown staples. The most effective impact of aid might be an indirect one—increasing the supply of foodgrains so as to bring prices within the reach of the poor. This might be achieved by supplying more agricultural inputs, or by promoting agricultural research; the two strategies would of course yield results over very different time horizons.[24] However, for the poor to be able to obtain more food, physical factors would also be influential: improved marketing networks, minor roads and other infrastructural facilities are all needed, particularly in Africa. Once again, this underlies the complementarity of measures to help the poor.

In seeking to encourage the production of food, donors could concentrate more on foodstuffs that are consumed largely by the poor. Examples include millets (the price of which has risen significantly in India in recent years) and also sorghum and cassava in Africa. Cassava has the added advantage that women, who particularly need sources of income, play a large role in its production, processing, and marketing. Aid can also make an important contribution by helping to reduce seasonal fluctuations in food production: poor people are particularly vulnerable to such fluctuations, of which famines are only the most extreme examples. Greater reliability of supplies can be achieved through better storage facilities. Here again, donors should seek to encourage better use of local skills and materials rather than provide expensive, large-scale facilities that would be used mainly by the larger farmers.

Though food is the most obvious candidate for supply-boosting projects, other basic consumer goods should not be neglected. When the poor are actually asked what they want (instead of having their 'needs' assumed by planners or aid donors), items such as matches, salt, paraffin, soap, and bedding are often first on their list. In many rural areas these goods are simply unavailable. Their absence has many effects, not least in depriving producers of incentives: if they do earn money, they must have things to spend it on.

When donors are selecting projects that will increase the purchasing power of the poor, agriculture offers several effective options. For example, much aid has gone into the development of dairy farming and livestock. Although the poor are unlikely to benefit directly from these projects, simply because the food produced is too expensive for them, they can get jobs and incomes from them. Even relatively small farmers have benefited in this way, as in Maharashtra in India.[25] On the other hand, development of estates agriculture in Malawi, and various projects in Africa, have failed to do much for the incomes of the poor. They have been badly designed, and lacking the understanding of their human and social context (see Chapter 5).

It is possible to identify the obstacles that might prevent the benefits of projects from reaching the rural poor. Production of the wrong commodities might be encouraged because donors are not aware of the patterns of production and consumption of poor people.[26] For example, donors might aim to increase the availability of liquid fuels and electricity, whereas 73 per cent of demand for energy in Kenya takes the form of fuel-wood, charcoal, and crop waste.[27] Or resources might be directed at boosting the production of cash and export crops, which are largely outside the scope of peasant agriculture.[28] Another example would be to build trunk routes rather than rural roads[29] (though trunk routes can bring benefits to the poor if they open up an area for development). And some projects have conditions which, from the start, prevent the poor from sharing the benefits of projects. Some small-farmer projects, for example, simply exclude farmers below a certain size. As other projects have shown, however, it is quite possible to benefit the poor. Employment guarantee schemes, programmes for drought-prone areas in Western India, Food for Work and local self-help schemes in Bangladesh—all are examples of what can be achieved at relatively low cost.[30]

Choice of technology

Capital intensity is not always the enemy of the poor. Indeed, many capital-intensive projects are essential for development and for starting to tackle poverty. But technological decisions are sensitive, and can have a major impact (for good or ill) on poverty. Roads constructed by capital-intensive methods employ relatively few people initially, and their maintenance is less likely to create local incomes and more likely to require imported inputs. In farming, tractors have often been introduced without consideration for their effects on the poor. The choices in irrigation between shallow wells and tube-wells, between bamboo tube-wells and pump-lift methods, all affect the poor. They may deny rural workers a part in their construction, and then preclude small farmers from using them.

Basic services

Lasting improvements in the lives of the poor depend heavily on education and health. Even basic literacy increases a person's access to technology and resources. For women, it improves the way they feed and care for their children, as well as encouraging them to reduce or space their births. Health has two main components: primary health care, and (given that many infections and diseases of the poor are water-borne) water and sanitation. The physical location of health-care centres has a major bearing on whether poor people go to them, as has been the experience of Kerala; Malawi's road-building programme also helped to provide better access for the rural poor to otherwise inadequate facilities.[31] Both primary health care and primary education bring benefits to the poor and have high rates of return. So too do family-planning programmes, which are now reaching the poor in several countries (Indonesia being among the most notable examples). Many of these successes have involved aid, especially once donors learnt how to organize projects suited to the needs of poor people.

Initially, much aid for basic services had an urban or upper-income-group bias—building metropolitan hospitals or elaborate housing schemes. Now many donors have pioneered the provision of low-cost rural and urban services in health, education, water supply, slum upgrading, and family planning. Not every case has been a success, of course, and some of the old biases remain—towards elite education in some countries, for example, as Chapter 5 observes. But the failures and the biases are at least as much those of the recipients as of the donors.

The need for local finance is a characteristic of much povery-oriented investment in basic services. Though their direct import content is low, their recurring local costs tend to be high—especially if facilities are to be extended to a widely dispersed and rural population. That is one reason why bilateral donors are reluctant to expand this kind of aid. Another reason is that it may not be in the recipient's long-run interest to have services funded from abroad which are well beyond its domestic capacity to support—the 'premature welfare states' referred to earlier. This is one of development's many dilemmas: humanitarian instinct calls for every reasonable effort to meet minimum needs. There are even good economic grounds for investing heavily in basic services, since doing so can contribute to faster economic growth and slower population growth. Sri Lanka provides an instructive example: its basic services were considered too generous by many experts, but have helped to achieve economically valuable human development and much-reduced fertility. Nonetheless there are obvious dangers in trying to develop services which outstrip the productive base of an economy.

Policy dialogue

During the past dozen years, when many governments have run into financial difficulties, they have had to reduce the growth in their spending. For several reasons, they find it easier to reduce current expenditure than capital. In addition, rural social expenditure often has a low priority. Budgetary retrenchment has thus often fallen disproportionately on the rural poor.[32] There is a case for donors and international organizations such as the IMF or the World Bank to take greater note of the distributional consequences of adjustment programmes. UNICEF has held discussions with the IMF about the possibilities of protecting vulnerable groups under Fund programmes. A World Bank document, *Focus on Poverty*, included a recommendation to try to assess in advance the impact of adjustment programmes on the poorest people: it appears often to be ignored. More effort is needed to develop appropriate methodologies for such an assessment; the agencies would probably be willing to take action if they knew how to do it.

A particularly important part of the policy dialogue concerns food prices. Where government policy has kept them low, discouraging food production, raising them will bring considerable benefits. Many of the poor will benefit directly and immediately—those who are net sellers of food in particular. Employment may also increase quite rapidly. But the many poor people who are net buyers of food will suffer unless their incomes rise proportionately or the government arranges food subsidies for them. In the long run, the whole supply curve for food may shift and the relative price of food fall. That has happened with the green revolution in South Asia. Even there, however, some people suffered: tenant farmers who were evicted as landlords wanted more profits from their newly productive land; and the very poor who had depended on legumes and other crops which were displaced when land was turned over to more profitable grains. Raising food prices to incentive levels does not always help the poor. Many other things must be done to ensure that it does, and that the poor are protected in the short-run to enjoy the benefits in the long-run.[33]

Rural credit

If aid is given for rural credit, donors need to take particular care in setting interest rates and other rules of access. This chapter has already mentioned the 'ground rules' which can disqualify most of the needy from obtaining credit. For this reason, as well as for broader reasons of economic efficiency, credit schemes should charge realistic rates of interest; otherwise, low-interest rates merely subsidize the better-off farmers and reduce a government's resources for other developmental work. Similar reasoning applies to debt-recovery policies. Rural debts are larger for the better-off households, so that a high default rate has the effect of diverting resources away from the most needy.

One reason why small farmers may be disqualified from credit projects is that their holdings may be too small to serve as collateral. This problem has sometimes been overcome by lending to organized groups—women's groups in Africa being one example. Such organizations can even be creditworthy enough to borrow from commercial banks. Donors and recipients should explore such possibilities and do much more to involve the poor in credit projects.

Cost recovery

Many projects—irrigation, transport, health, and education—raise one common question: should those who use them be charged for the benefit? The issue is hard to resolve, and country experience varies widely. Malawi is an example where World Bank suggestions that the poor pay for primary education would almost certainly be detrimental to them.[34] On the other hand, both the Bangladesh and Kenya studies report the damaging consequences of failing to charge for services.[35] In Kenya, 60 per cent of the beneficiaries were paying for only 15 per cent of the cost of supplying water.[36] Charges that produce a reasonable social rate of return are important for two reasons. First, they ensure that those who can afford to pay do so. Second, a free service often leads to waste, and a soaring bill for subsidies will endanger the ability of the authorities to continue providing that service. Some studies suggest that in irrigation, for example, there is a strong positive relationship between user charges and maintenance of facilities.[37]

The issue of charging for services highlights an even broader problem: how to ensure that any subsidy remains selective, going only to the poor who need it most. A general subsidy is unnecessarily expensive, imposes a heavy fiscal burden, and leads to a misallocation of scarce resources. Nonetheless, it can bring benefits, as Sri Lanka showed with its rice ration. Sri Lanka's success in providing for basic needs—reflected in rising life expectancy, a falling infant mortality rate, and a high degree of literacy, all at relatively low per capita incomes—has been well-documented.[38] One recent study shows that if Sri Lanka had waited for the normal process of growth to achieve the same social progress, the time needed would have been anywhere between 58 and 152 years.[39] The subsidized rice ration played a big part in raising nutritional standards. Yet its fiscal cost was heavy; it was eventually abandoned under donor pressure. Almost immediately, the mortality rate rose and nutritional standards declined.[40] The rice ration was made more selective in 1978, confining the benefits to the lower half of the income distribution.[41] The results of this change have yet to be evaluated. However, the experience of a rice-rationing scheme in Kerala suggests that a selective approach can be effective in channelling benefits directly to the poor.[42]

Any discussion of user charges and subsidies can only conclude that the issues raised are delicate and of great significance for poor people. If the price elasticity of demand for education, say, is high, then charging for it would reduce access for the poor; if the elasticity is low, the poor will pay for education, but at the expense of other essentials. Donors should be aware, too, of a 'fallacy of composition' in cost recovery. If users are to be charged for education, health services, water, and so on, and all those users are the same people, poverty could well worsen (especially if food subsidies are being removed at the same time). It is essential to strike a balance between trying to make services self-financing, withholding subsidies from those who do not need them, and protecting the poor.

V   Institutional change

The institutional changes necessary for reducing rural poverty can take two forms: land reform, both distributive and tenurial; and the creation of an administrative structure capable of identifying and implementing poverty-oriented development policies. The first group of changes raises some vital but complicated issues.

The unequal distribution of land is a major cause of poverty in rural areas.[43] It is reinforced by insecurity of tenure and oppressive arrangements for crop sharing. The case for redistributive reform is strengthened by the widespread evidence that small farms are more productive than large ones.[44] Land redistribution policies are directed mainly at the small farmer who possesses some land but not enough for economic viability. It is commonly agreed that such reform cannot help the landless; indeed, it may even harm them if it reduces demand for non-family labour. In some countries, therefore, land redistribution policies may bypass a large part of the rural poor.[45]

In both South Korea and Taiwan, land reform played a vital role in promoting rapid economic growth and significantly reducing poverty. An essential complement to such reform was the creation of alternative sources of employment for a growing rural population.[46] India, on the other hand, is often cited as an example of how the failure to implement land reform has been a prime cause of the persistence of rural poverty.[47] In those regions of India where land reform has been vigorously pursued—West Bengal being an obvious case—there is evidence of a beneficial effect on poverty.[48] India's 'land ceiling' legislation may also have had some redistributive effect recently, offsetting the earlier trend back towards tenant farming.[49] In Bangladesh, land ownership has become more unequal since 1974, almost certainly with adverse effects on rural poverty.[50]

Aid and land reform

The role of aid in land reform is likely to be limited. The circumstances in which land reform was implemented in Taiwan and donor pressure exerted in South Korea were products of politics and history that will not be repeated elsewhere. Donors seldom succeed in persuading governments to adopt land reform unless the latter are anyway inclined to do so.[51] Where that is the case, however, donors can obviously help to overcome financial and other constraints on land reform. A recent study of Kenya argues that donors could encourage the government to pursue land reform policies more vigorously—and would be more likely to be listened to if their advice were combined with offers of financial assistance.[52] Years ago, the World Bank laid down specific guidelines on its lending policies on land reform. They included incentives, such as favouring countries that are willing to adopt reforms; priority for projects that have a favourable impact on poverty; and cooperation with other aid agencies. The lending guidelines also stressed that support would not be given to programmes or projects that made landholdings more unequal. Indeed, the Bank went so far as to consider excluding from aid those countries that were not willing to promote land reform policies which the Bank judged to be necessary.[53] There is little evidence, however, that the guidelines have significantly affected lending by the Bank or many other donors: few recipients have requested aid for land reform.

Aid in support of land reform could take various forms. One would provide budgetary support for compensation to large owners who were to lose land, especially if expatriates or foreign firms were involved. Another would provide technical assistance in assessing compensation levels, valuation of mining rights and royalties, etc. Another would finance agricultural investment in areas where land ownership was being reformed. One study identifies two other possible approaches: (i) extra investment in non-agricultural sectors to provide alternative employment opportunities; (ii) use of food or other aid to offset any short-term dislocation in domestic production after land was redistributed.[54] The willingness of donors to supply post-reform aid, such as inputs or rural credit to small peasant owners, could make a valuable contribution to the success of reform programmes.

Administration

The other area of institutional reform where aid may have a more direct and effective role is in building up an efficient administrative structure in rural areas. The case studies have highlighted the problems of identifying, administering, and monitoring rural development projects. These difficulties are particularly serious in Africa, even in some of the more developed economies.[55]

What are collectively referred to as 'problems of implementation' have often been the main reason why rural development strategies have failed to help the poor. Those problems take many forms. A lack of local political will is obviously one which donors cannot make good. The same is true of the failure to identify the nature of technical problems and possibilities at the grass roots, which frequently leads to the choice of an inappropriate technology for a project. However, a more general cause of failure is a weak administrative structure at the local level, because it is incapable of checking whether the poor are actually receiving the benefits intended for them. 'To use both external capital and manpower resources meaningfully to alleviate constraints on (the welfare of) rural populations one needs to create systems or mechanisms which force such resources into the services of the poor.'[56]

Three related conclusions follow from a study of the experience of rural development projects. First, success rarely depends on the form of a grand design. It comes from careful project planning, and from carrying out many detailed and related activities over a long period of time. With few exceptions, these requirements are unlikely to be met by aid-financed technical assistance through expatriate advisers. Second, therefore, aid can be used to much greater effect in developing the technical capacity of recipient countries to generate such skills themselves.[57] Lastly, projects need to involve their intended beneficiaries at as many stages as possible of decision-making and implementation.

Non-governmental organizations

Many people believe that the poor can be reached only by small-scale activities and local participation, and that governments cannot promote such things; more aid should therefore be channelled via non-governmental organizations (NGOs). This chapter does not support every part of that case. Many different activities are needed to combat poverty; some are better suited to aid agencies and governments. Nevertheless, it is true that some (though by no means all) NGOs have achieved results where governments have failed. This is particularly true where local participation and self-help schemes are needed.

A full discussion of NGOs and their role in tackling poverty is beyond the scope of this report. Nevertheless, donors and recipients should explore the possibilities of involving them more as channels for poverty-oriented aid.

While NGOs are individually small, collectively they are larger than some bilateral donors.[58] When competent they have many advantages. They are non-bureaucratic, have low manpower costs, and can penetrate directly and quickly into local conditions. They are more likely to be able to identify local needs and constraints; certainly they are better at doing so than major donor agencies, and quite often better than local government organizations. They also have particularly important parts to play in addressing women's situations—and women's own organizations are often among the key agents of social change. As this report's Bangladesh study says, NGOs can voice needs. But they can only expand up to a certain point without losing their essential virtues. If they were to become too large, they would become politicized, and not so easily permitted by governments to operate independently—or even capable of independence, if too much of their funding came from governments.

Increasing use of NGOs—including those indigenous to recipient countries—is highly desirable; but ways have to be found to fund them while preserving their integrity and smallness. Governments also do not like financing large numbers of small projects. They must therefore either lend to NGOs directly, making them accountable for projects in the first instance; or lend via institutions in the recipient country which would be responsible for monitoring the work of NGOs in the field. It should not be imagined that NGOs could without changing their character be the channels for very large sums of aid, replacing a large share of current aid activities. But those NGOs of proven ability could certainly be relied on considerably more than they are at present in efforts to reach the poor.[59]

VI Public works

Public works have many advantages as part of a policy for poverty relief.[60] They are one of the few ways of directly helping the landless poor. They are labour-intensive, with a high ratio of wages to total cost, and their size can vary according to the availability of resources. They can take advantage of seasonal unemployment, raise agricultural wages, and create rural assets. They have some potential disadvantages, however. The assets created may be used mainly by the better-off, who are thereby subsidized at public expense. Public works can increase rural inequality by raising land values. And they are not always effective in providing employment either steadily or for the most needy.[61]

Public works are thus not an easy policy option.[62] As a minimum, they need locally available supplies of food and other wage-goods to meet demand. This is one area where food aid might have a role, though the practical problems involved are formidable.[63] In addition, public works that are genuinely going to create productive assets need economic, administrative, and political resources to organize them. Nonetheless, the benefits for poor people can be considerable, not only in immediate income and employment effects but also through acquiring skills and training.[64] As an earlier report on public works concluded: 'Well-planned and executed public works programmes can indeed have a significant impact on the income levels of certain groups who are in poverty, and can create useful assets using scarce resources efficiently. In the construction phase they can provide employment for . . . groups . . . such as landless labourers, small tenant farmers and small farmers. In some circumstances they can begin to deliver benefits within a few weeks . . . .'[65] In the Food for Work programme in Bangladesh, 'the large majority of those involved in the programme (more than 70 per cent) belong to the target group of those with less than half an acre . . .. Total income of those involved was 55 per cent higher during the six weeks work period and 10 per cent higher on an annual basis.'[66] Until more effective policies can be devised for the rural poor, especially the landless, Food for Work and other programmes can make a valuable contribution.

VII Intra-family poverty

So far this chapter has been mainly concerned with the 'working poor'—small farmers and wage labourers. However, many poor people are not engaged directly in production. They include women who work in the household, and babies and young children. Even within identical income groups, women and young children suffer most from malnutrition; the same often goes for women and children from a higher income group relative to the men in the lower group.[67] Any anti-poverty programme ought to include them, but cannot easily do so when they are isolated from the formal processes of production and exchange. This is true, a fortiori, of aid-financed programmes— except in emergencies such as famines.

Aid's most promising contribution is not so much through the total numbers it can reach as in the intensity of poverty or deprivation that it can alleviate. Examples include special feeding programmes and health-care and nutrition schemes for pre-school children. Their cost-effectiveness has often been questioned, largely because they suffer from 'leakages'. For example, special feeding programmes do not always fully supplement the diets of target groups; against that, however, they might release food for other children who are undernourished. Food rations may be sold, but still provide income for the recipients which they can use for other forms of consumption.[68] And much has been learnt in recent years about how to minimize leakages, so that food really does reach the poor.[69] Thus, although special programmes cannot be seen as full substitutes for other anti-poverty programmes—such as increasing agricultural production—they can have a useful impact.

Again, all the efforts called for to improve the situation of women are especially relevant to coping with the problems of intra-family poverty. It is not just a question of organizing public services which reach women; very often the most effective methods will include participatory schemes, in which women themselves will define needs and organize and carry out services, with whatever public or private assistance is necessary.

VIII Conclusions

Despite rapid growth in many developing countries, widespread poverty remains. It has often worsened, particularly in economies with little or no growth. Although most countries have made impressive gains in education and health, in reducing mortality and fertility, in improving nutrition and welfare services, these achievements have failed to reduce significantly the number or proportion of people living in poverty. These are the grim realities against which aid's record must be judged.

It is sometimes said that aid cannot help the poor because it always reinforces the political and social status quo which engenders poverty. This—like most blanket criticisms of aid—is too simplistic. Aid may indeed do just that, depending on how it is used; or it may, even without the least intention of doing so, foster economic change which leads to political and social reform. In countries hostile to developments that favour the poor, aid is sometimes among the few forces pushing in a beneficial direction. At a more detailed level, individual aid projects can succeed in promoting the well-being of the poor, sometimes despite the prevailing policy climate.[70]

Perhaps the greatest success of aid has been in raising the consumption of the poor, mainly by assisting the growth of food production and by extending welfare services. Some of the growth supported by aid has generated jobs for poor people; and a wide variety of aid projects and programmes have benefited the poor directly. But these successes are slender when set against the burgeoning labour forces of most developing countries, and their slow growth of productive employment.

The role of aid in combating poverty is doubly constrained, first by the inevitable commercial and political pressures on bilateral aid, and also by the domestic policies of recipients. If the recipient government is not concerned with the relief of poverty, even the best aid efforts can founder. Aid's effectiveness is additionally limited by the donor's uncertainty over how to assure the widespread participation of the rural poor in development. Despite all the constraints, aid has had a significant impact on poverty. This analysis suggests a number of conclusions on how to improve it.

1. Donors could put a larger proportion of their aid into directly poverty-oriented projects. While these have not always been successful in the past, enough has been learnt to improve their effectiveness significantly in the future. But there are limits to the distance donors can go in this direction, set by competing economic needs in the recipient countries for long-term and adjustment programmes, and by the instruments available for this kind of activity.

2. Most donors attempt to tackle poverty only in certain kinds of projects—rural development schemes, urban site and service or slum upgrading, welfare programmes, etc. They could examine income-distribution effects of a far wider range of standard projects—in roads, power, and so forth—and consciously incorporate their impact on poverty into the design and evaluation of such projects.

3. More aid could be concentrated on 'self-targeting' goods and services—those consumed by the poor in particular. Certain food staples, legumes, and root vegetables are obvious examples. So are welfare services such as primary and non-academic secondary education, rural health centres (including family-planning services), and site and service housing schemes.

4. Donors should be more willing to cover local and recurrent costs. Poverty-oriented projects seldom require a large amount of imported inputs, but they do make heavy demands on recipients' budgets. As a minimum, donors should refrain from financing capital-intensive projects whose recurrent costs are so high that they strain the recipients' capacity for labour-intensive and poverty-oriented projects.[71] They should also continue to support food for work and other public works projects, provided the lessons of experience are put into practice.

5. In almost all the above, greater attention should be given to women's roles. Action against poverty is in many cases indistinguishable from action to improve the situation of women.
6. Donors could refrain from those practices which this report has found to damage the interests of the poor. For example, certain kinds of cost recovery or user charges must be sensitively chosen. Other sources of harm include using the wrong technology, particularly excessive capital intensity; failure to provide for displaced populations in large dam projects; and, in structural adjustment programmes, retrenchment which falls unnecessarily heavily on the poor and on the government services essential to them.
7. This report calls for a new approach to aid for the poorest countries, which could also be directly helpful to poor people in those countries making serious efforts to mitigate poverty. The new measures would include balance of payments protection and budgetary support, both of which can help maintain government services beneficial to the poor. Further untying of aid would also help. And even 'mixed credits' could be made less harmful to development if they were offered to poor countries with a higher grant element, and for equipment tailored to the needs of poor people, rather than being used, as such credits often are, to sell the expensive products of selected rich-country corporations, often to better-off developing countries—a complete distortion of the development purposes of aid.
8. Perhaps most controversially, aid-coordination arrangements could be used to concert anti-poverty programmes for some countries. The cooperation of the recipient is essential, but donors could do better than pursue, as they do now, a set of activities which have no cohesive focus on poverty. And they could make it clear that their public support for aid depends significantly on its being seen to improve the lot of the poor, and ask recipients, where necessary, for an appropriate response.
9. Donors could identify and make special efforts to overcome particular obstacles to poverty-oriented development, especially where these do not involve huge expense. One obvious candidate is agricultural research in Africa, which could have a huge pay-off at relatively small extra cost. It would have to stress national, adaptive research for poor people's food crops, and the development of research teams that could do on-farm work with poor smallholders.

All this said, it bears repeating that the recipient must have a commitment to reducing poverty, if aid is not merely to struggle against the tide. And donors and recipients also have to be concerned to sustain economic growth. Anti-poverty measures will not help much in economies which are running down. In recent years, donors have become heavily involved in shoring up entire economies, especially in Africa. This may have helped to create an impression that they have lost interest in tackling poverty. Other changes point in the same direction: the trend among several donors towards more mixed credits; the decade-long decline in assistance for population programmes; and, not least, cuts in overall aid budgets by some leading donors. But this report does not conclude that these trends are dominant. The aid agencies have learned much about how to help the poor with carefully directed assistance. They are not relinquishing their task, and cannot afford to do so.

Notes

1. World Bank data, from an unpublished study.
2. See, for example, Lipton 1983*c*.
3. Lipton 1983*a*; Visaria 1981.
4. Nayyar 1984; Saith 1981. The relationship is not a simple one, however; studies elsewhere show that a high food price may be correlated with higher incomes—if, for example, the price stems from strong demand for food and consequently for labour to produce it.
5. Gordon *et al.* 1979; Lipton *et al.* 1984*a*.
6. Ahmed 1979.
7. Chambers 1985. More generally, see Chambers 1983.
8. Hewitt and Kydd 1984.
9. Ayres 1983.
10. Lipton *et al.* 1984*a*.
11. Bagley 1984.
12. World Bank 1985.
13. See OECD/DAC 1985*b*.
14. World Bank, 1983*a*.
15. Duncan and Mosley 1984.
16. Hewitt and Kydd 1984.
17. Lipton *et al.* 1984*a*.
18. See, for example, van Arkadie and de Wilde 1984.
19. World Bank 1983*a*.
20. The World Bank's most recent experience bears this out; for the UK, see Morris and Gwyer 1983; for Norway, see Faaland 1984.
21. Sen 1981*b*; Streeten 1981.
22. Lipton *et al.* 1984*a*.
23. Bourgoignie 1984.
24. Lipton *et al.* 1984*a*.
25. Paul and Subramanian 1983.

26. Morris and Gwyer 1983.
27. Beijer Institute 1984; Duncan and Mosley 1984.
28. Hewitt and Kydd 1984.
29. Tendler 1979.
30. Paul and Subramanian 1983; van Arkadie and de Wilde 1984; de Vylder and Asplund 1979.
31. Hewitt and Kydd 1984; UN 1975.
32. See the March 1984 issue of *World Development*, which is wholly devoted to such matters.
33. Streeten 1985.
34. Hewitt and Kydd 1984.
35. Van Arkadie and de Wilde; Duncan and Mosley 1984.
36. Duncan and Mosley 1984.
37. Jennings 1983; the point on irrigation emerges from internal World Bank documents.
38. Isenman 1980.
39. Sen 1981*a*.
40. Isenman 1980.
41. Gavan and Chandrasekera 1979.
42. George 1979.
43. Byres 1974; Cline 1975; Griffin 1976; Lipton 1974; Minhas 1974.
44. Berry and Cline 1979.
45. Ghosh 1983.
46. Fei *et al*. 1979; Griffin 1976; Mason *et al*. 1980; Steinberg 1984.
47. For a classic statement, see Ladejinsky 1977.
48. Paul and Subramanian 1983; UN 1975; Ghosh 1983.
49. Vyas 1979.
50. Van Arkadie and de Wilde 1984.
51. See, for example, Lipton *et al*. 1984*a*; Steinberg 1984.
52. Hunt 1984.
53. World Bank 1975*b*.
54. Islam 1983. The latter was also proposed by the Bank (World Bank 1975*a*).
55. Duncan and Mosley 1984; World Bank 1981*a*.
56. Isaksen 1983.
57. Lethem and Cooper 1983.
58. OECD DAC 1984*a*.
59. For a valuable discussion of the issues touched on here, and many others, see Gorman 1985.
60. Lewis 1972; 1977.
61. Rodgers 1973.
62. Lewis 1977.
63. For some empirical studies, see Stevens 1979; see also Chapter 5 below.
64. Lewis 1977.
65. Burki *et al*. 1976, p. 74.
66. Van Arkadie and de Wilde 1984.
67. Sen 1981*a*.

68. See Chapter 5 below.
69. See World Bank 1984*c* for the lessons of successful nutrition projects.
70. Minear 1985 cites a USAID study of several rural road projects: some brought benefits to the poor, others did not; he concludes that USAID *can* design projects to reach the poor, and is not prevented from doing so by recipients' social realities.
71. Krueger and Ruttan 1983.

CHAPTER FOUR

Policy Dialogue

I Introduction

The term 'policy dialogue' describes exchanges between aid donors and recipients about the domestic policy framework, influencing the outcome of an aid transfer and the behaviour of the economy as a whole. Policy dialogue can therefore embrace anything from the exchange rate stance of a government seeking balance of payments support to the organization of the local public works department in a small, remote area destined to host a feeder road improvement project. The popularity of the concept among donors, however, has grown as donor perceptions of generalized economic malaise in a range of countries has spread and the demand for balance of payments support, rather than project aid, has increased. Some observers even claim that the most important function of aid may be to induce policy reforms engendering efficient resource allocation and economic growth, rather than to relieve scarcities of domestic savings or foreign exchange.[1]

Accordingly, the emphasis in this review of policy dialogue is on general macroeconomic, resource allocation and institutional questions, rather than upon issues which arise in project-specific exchanges and which are referred to in Chapter 5. The widening of the range of IMF facilities in the 1970s, the introduction of World Bank Structural Adjustment Loans (SALs) in 1980 (and of other 'conditional' aid mechanisms under the Bank's 'special action program'), the extension of donor–recipient Consultative Groups, and the widespread debt renegotiations of the early 1980s have all served to increase the focus upon recipient policies for long-run development and short-run economic management, while intensifying the sense among donors that they too have an interest in recipients' policy formulation. Some of this policy discussion has, of course, taken place in the past in the project context, but not with the scope it has today in several recipient countries, amounting to negotiation of major policy reform programmes.

There is no longer the reticence that once existed (most strongly with bilateral donors, but also with multilateral agencies) about seeking negotiations with recipient governments over such reforms. Recipients have, for the most part, acquiesced in procedures that might once have been considered infringements of national sovereignty. Now that it has become a prominent and overt facet of international economic relations, what does (and what could) explicit policy dialogue add to aid effectiveness? And what are the necessary conditions for the success of policy dialogue?

This chapter begins by examining the relationship between 'dialogue' and 'leverage' or 'conditionality', and reviewing the likely origin of the policies about which dialogue is conducted. It then reviews the experience of policy dialogue as practised by international financial institutions and donor agencies: the IMF, the World Bank, and bilateral donors. This is complemented by a summary of some notable recipient country experiences in policy dialogue, contrasting the long experience of India, for example, with contemporary efforts to redirect policies in sub-Saharan Africa. The chapter concludes with an evaluation of the factors constraining policy dialogue, or influencing its outcome: the coincidence of effective aid and effective dialogue; the risks of excessive use of leverage in periods of crisis; the capacity for policy analysis in the recipient country; the frankness of donors about past errors and about international conditions affecting poor countries; the problems of donor coordination; the economic context of dialogue.

The evidence clearly indicates that 'policy dialogue' will be a central feature of aid relationships for many years to come. A very large number of poor countries are already engaged in a conditional adjustment programme of some kind, commonly involving more than one donor or agency. The keys to success appear to lie in three areas: the availability of adequate resources to sustain adjustment programmes; the analytical and negotiating capacities of recipients; and the ability of donors to comprehend local circumstances and respond flexibly to changes in the assumptions or forecasts upon which programmes are based.

Some definitions and distinctions

'Leverage' refers to the capacity to impose the donor's viewpoint over the recipients, while 'dialogue' implies that either viewpoint, or both, can change to bridge an initial difference. By means of 'dialogue' the aid recipient comes to view policy changes as in the interest of its own economic progress; with 'leverage' the recipient agrees to enact certain policies in response to positive or negative incentives by the donor. Leverage, in this sense, is neither a necessary nor a sufficient condition for the success of policy dialogue.

World Bank officials offer a similar distinction between 'policy dialogue' and 'policy conditionality'. The Bank's country economic and sector work has always supported the former, but SALs and other 'policy-based loans' have introduced a much stronger element of the latter. The introduction of conditionality results in part from the view that, in success or failure at structural adjustment, vested interests count as much as the rationality of policy-making; the donor agency must therefore sometimes find a way to exert leverage. At times even governments intent on change may be inhibited by domestic vested interests; conditions 'imposed' from without can be helpful in combating those interests. Dialogue is often in fact conducted with like-minded officials in recipient countries who welcome the agencies' support.

It is doubtful whether a sharp distinction between 'dialogue' and 'conditionality' can be sustained. There is, of course, a distinction of form between aid flows governed by agreements incorporating explicit policy conditions which a recipient must meet before funds are released, and those which are not. Explicit conditionality, however, is not the only way in which leverage can be exercised. Any dialogue may contain disagreement; equally, any aid relationship implies a donor interest in resolving the disagreement, and the ultimate possibility of withdrawal of aid if the disagreement persists. 'Dialogue' and 'leverage' are not realistically separable, but there will be a continuum along which the intensity of leverage increases and the explicit use of conditions occupies a more prominent place in aid formalities. Even in the most formal example of the use of conditionality to exert leverage, the programmes of the IMF, the importance attached to a particular policy change in negotiations will not necessarily be reflected in the explicit conditions eventually incorporated in an agreement;[2] and the programmes *are* negotiated, so that measures initially proposed are not necessarily the final ones adopted.

A more workable set of distinctions concerns what can be termed the arena of dialogue: short-run economic policy, development strategy as a whole, or sector policies? The IMF traditionally confined the scope of its policy conditionality to those items necessary to ensure the repayment of its short-term loans, and those items falling within its mandate to supervise exchange rate regimes. Fund conditionality became identified largely with instruments of short-run demand management, and the Fund explicitly disclaimed any role in the determination of income distribution or the formulation of long-run development strategy. Macro-conditionality of the kind incorporated in SALs represents an extension of explicit dialogue to cover a much wider range of instruments. In parallel, the focus of donors upon the conditions of operation of individual projects has broadened into a concern with the institutional framework and individual policies which govern the sectors where projects and programmes are to take effect. The examples briefly outlined in this chapter will indicate that dialogue or leverage which can succeed at one level in one country or period will not necessarily be sustainable or appropriate elsewhere.

Is there a universal prescription? — There shouldn't be — each IST is different for Heavensakes.

If there is a disagreement on the part of the donor with the recipient's policies, there must be some source for the alternative view. A USAID paper cautions:

It is . . . salutary to keep in mind that the market for truth is a competitive one—where no monopoly survives for long—and that arrogance should be avoided.[3]

Nevertheless, concern that some universal prescription will be imposed on different countries as a result of policy decisions taken by governing bodies remote from the individual circumstances remains at the heart of doubts about conditionality and policy dialogue.

Until recently, the IMF was virtually the only international agency subject to the criticism of excessive uniformity in its policy prescriptions. The Fund has been identified with the 'three Ds' (devaluation, deflation, and decontrol), and with a short-term, demand-reducing approach to balance of payments adjustment. Whatever the merits of the criticism (see below), the Fund is able to claim that its Articles require it to emphasize stabilization, to protect the revolving nature of its resources by ensuring rapid repayment, and to stress liberalization in its approach to trade and payments practices. For other donors, such a justification for uniformity of prescription is not available; and even the Fund—since what is sought is a viable balance of payments position, and viability may only be achievable over a period of years—is increasingly concerned with the medium term.

The rise of the policy dialogue, and of the participation of agencies other than the IMF in balance of payments aid to support structural adjustment programmes, has exposed other multilateral (and to some extent bilateral) donors to similar criticisms. In part this is a consequence of a natural learning process: while policy dialogue and conditionality remain novel, donor agency personnel are bound to rely on prescriptions culled from international experience rather than the products of long experience with the policy problems of the country concerned.[4] But there is also a genuine debate between those who argue that the general thrust of 'good policy' for development is now well understood, and those who reject such a presumption.[5]

Those in the first camp assert that there is now sufficient experience of the development process to identify the kind of policy changes that are likely to pay off; in particular, donors should encourage a shift from a policy stance of 'control' over the domestic economy to one favouring a liberal trade regime and an outward-looking framework of incentives. 'Observers agree' about the benefits of uniform incentives (as between production for the home market and for export) in domestic markets and trade regimes. Perhaps the best-known espousal of this position in a prescription for a large number of countries was to be found in the World Bank's first report on the problems of sub-Saharan Africa;[6] though more recent Bank documents and Bank practice stress the movement towards improved frameworks of incentives and controls.

Those who object to a priori prescriptions point to the examples of multiple and conflicting definitions of 'good development performance' found over the years in the literature and in the pronouncements of aid agencies. They stress that many of the countries now praised for trade liberalization initially built up their industrial sectors with the help of substantial protection and state intervention. Above all, they cast doubt on the benefits for equity, efficiency, or growth of 'getting prices right' without supporting foreign aid flows, institutional change, and research into supply measures such as suitable production techniques (notably in African agriculture). In the past three or four years the extremes in the debate have to some extent yielded to more nuanced positions. A good example of the evolution of donor attitudes is afforded in the second and third reports on sub-Saharan Africa by the World Bank.[7] Although no-one would advocate 'getting prices wrong', there is now much greater emphasis on the length of time needed to achieve structural adjustment, and on the organized support for price changes and liberalization that must come from non-price measures—institutional reform; the development of markets and commerce; agricultural inputs, management and research—and the need for continued investment in social services to cope with long-term problems of education, health, and population. There is evidence (see below) that these shifts of emphasis arise from the accumulation of experience with conditional lending and the design of policy reform programmes. The World Bank is itself now completing a review of recent structural adjustment programmes, and among its major research projects are investigations of policy action relevant to them, such as the 'timing and sequencing' of trade liberalization.

While there can be few objections to a judicious transfer of the lessons of international experience, reform programmes are likely to meet with greater success when they have evolved from a process that recognizably incorporates local experience, objectives, and constraints. The atmosphere in which dialogue takes place is likely to be important to the outcome: recipient governments will probably be more responsive when not presented with a policy package developed and tested independently of their own decision-making processes and aspirations. They would presumably be interested in the results of other countries' programmes. Donor agencies routinely deny that there is uniformity in policy prescription from country to country; as agencies develop greater institutional experience with dialogue in differing circumstances, it should prove easier to demonstrate substance in this denial.

II   The International Monetary Fund

Although the IMF is not an aid-giving institution, no discussion of policy dialogue can be complete without an account of the central influence of the Fund on economic policy-making in deficit countries. Although there is no formal requirement, in practice a Fund programme is virtually a *sine qua non* for countries wishing to negotiate a SAL from the World Bank; and for debt rescheduling in the Paris Club it may be a formal requirement. Moreover, the IMF is the institution with the longest experience of the negotiation of conditional programmes; its record forms a large part of the practices by which the stance of donor institutions and governments on dialogue and conditionality has been judged.

The Fund's role is important to aid effectiveness because its programmes affect recipient countries' budgets, balances of payments, and also their domestic and external economic policies, all of which can impinge directly on the performance of project and programme aid. The Fund has not in the past seen itself, and was not seen by its founders, as a source of development capital. Indeed, IMF net purchases are not recorded in countries' balance of payments accounts as current capital flows. Nevertheless, in present circumstances, as the 1984 DAC Chairman's Report comments:

The volume of the Fund's net lending, together with the introduction of extended facilities, does raise the question whether, from a purely analytical standpoint, it is valid to treat all of the Fund's lending so differently . . . Net use of IMF resources by developing countries having reached in 1983 the entirely new dimension of $12 billion, this has clearly become a major new factor on the international financing scene.[8]

Close to sixty developing countries during 1982–4 were engaged in stabilization programmes supported by the Fund's conditional resources. Many of these were, of course, the better-off, middle-income countries; the Fund has played a major part in grappling with their debt problems. The poorer countries with which this report is concerned, though most of them were not involved heavily with commercial bank borrowing, also commonly had debt burdens resulting from official borrowing, trade credits, and import payment arrears. There was a similar need to adjust in the light of the changed conditions of—and prospects for—trade in the early 1980s. But it was combined in many countries with a perceived need for a change of course, to make corrections both for unfortunate short-term actions—such as the over-ambitious investment programmes on which several countries embarked in the wake of the short-lived commodity boom of the 1970s—and for deficiencies in their overall policy environment.

These were the events which underlay the adjustment programmes now under way, supported by the Fund and the Bank and in a number of cases by bilateral lending: programmes which give promise of overcoming some long-standing obstacles to development in the countries concerned. But the experience raises issues for discussion here, most particularly on the pace of adjustment and the relation between shorter- and longer-term measures, and Bank–Fund collaboration.

In the circumstances described, retrenchment has been inevitable in most countries—retrenchment which, as well as making for improvement in the balance of payments, has also in many cases cut into essential development expenditures. The questions asked here are whether the *degree* of retrenchment has been inevitable, and whether the Fund could do more to protect low-income countries from fluctuations in the external environment which harm long-term as well as short-term development.

The problem is principally one of resources. While the IMF's main concern is with short-term balance of payments stabilization, and its resources are of a revolving nature, its Articles do require it to show concern also for growth and employment. In the 1970s, following on the oil price increase and other upheavals in the world economy, the Fund was empowered to make a major response. The Oil and Witteveen Facilities, the Trust Fund, the Subsidy Account, and the Extended Fund Facility (EFF) were all products of this period, and played a valuable part (side by side with existing facilities) in cushioning countries against external shocks, including the provision of a concessional element for poor countries. In 1984 none of the facilities created then was operative, except the EFF, and few of the poorest countries were in a position to borrow on its conditions. But there has been a substantial increase in the use of Fund resources since 1979.

Fund resources

With the recent quota increase, the Fund's lending capacity is larger than ever before, despite the new restrictions on the proportion of quota which can be borrowed. But its resources have not expanded in proportion to need. The Compensatory Finance Facility (CFF) has not been able in some recent years to meet more than a share of the valid claims upon it, at least in some views of what constitute valid claims. Although at present the overall resource position is somewhat easier, in 1983 the IMF had to announce at one point that it could not undertake any more lending for a period (largely owing to major demands on it from heavily commercially indebted countries). The problem for some of the poorest countries is not just volume but terms; in particular cases, even if the Fund were disposed to lend larger amounts, debt profiles would caution against additional borrowing on terms close to market rates. A particularly difficult problem lies ahead in the immediate future because of the bunching of past lending: for sub-Saharan African countries alone, 'Taking the IMF loans outstanding at the end of 1983, repurchases and charges will total $0.9 billion in 1984 and $3.5 billion during 1985–87'.[9]

Adjustment capacity in the poorest countries

Some of the middle-income countries have made remarkable adjustment to the external difficulties of the 1980s. They have moved productive resources into export- and import-competing sectors, curbed excessive domestic expenditures, and—even if with greater austerity than was comfortable—have put themselves into a reasonable position to confront the future. It is precisely this that the poorest countries find so difficult. Without large manufacturing sectors, and with exports dependent usually on a small number of primary commodities, they can only slowly expand their export capacities. Imports are commonly already cut to the bone, and two large import items cannot easily be substituted by domestic production: one is energy, where increasing domestic supply is a matter of large investment, if possible at all. The other, where there is considerable scope, is food—but in a time of prolonged drought, rapid change is also problematic. This is not to say that these countries never have items to cut, be they military expenditures, 'prestige' projects, or the like. (It is increasingly the World Bank's role, where both agencies are involved in adjustment, to advise on efficient choices in public expenditure programmes.)

Part of the understanding that lay behind the establishment of the EFF in 1974, and the somewhat more flexible approach to conditionality between 1979 and 1980, was precisely this: the Fund was led 'to move toward a relatively long time-frame for adjustment effort to allow for changes in the patterns of production and demand—changes that can only be affected gradually'.[10] It is also recognized that policy reform and decontrol in areas affecting the balance of payments are not, in the short-term at least, substitutes for capital inflows but require additional assistance to support them.[11]

Performance of programmes

If EFF lending to most of the poorer countries stopped and the Fund reverted to one-year stand-bys, it was in considerable part due to experience with several of the programmes of the 1970s and early 1980s (though, it must be said, there was also pressure on the Fund from some member governments in 1981 and after to take a harder stand on conditionality).[12] A number of programmes had to be cancelled or were not working satisfactorily. The reasons for these disappointments ranged from unexpectedly adverse external conditions to a lack of commitment to the programmes on the part of some borrowing governments. It is worth bearing such facts in mind when considering the assessment of the success of IMF programmes generally in low-income countries. A recent study[13] has concluded that the record on most criteria of desired improvement has not been very favourable. But the results were obtained by international statistical analysis, of which this report is as suspicious in the present case as it was in the case of the aid–growth relationship discussed in Chapter 2.[14]

The study usefully observes, however, that 'changes in the pattern of growth ratio of program countries [i.e. countries pursuing Fund programmes] . . . follow fairly closely those of non-program countries . . . The simultaneous deterioration in both measures of the balance of payments, in the inflation rate *and* in the growth rate in 1980 point graphically to the hostage [sic] of IMF programs to the fortunes of the general world economy.' This is an important caveat, warning that the results of statistical comparisons of performance are likely to be sensitive to the period chosen, but also that external factors are likely to dominate over policy changes and modest capital inflows in the short run. If one wishes to go beyond such generalizations, there is no substitute for careful assessment of individual country programmes, their success and failure, and the reasons for positive and negative performance. The Fund is in a position to undertake and publish detailed country-by-country assessments of this kind, and should be encouraged to do so.

Adjustment within given resources

The availability of adequate Fund resources is stressed here. Nevertheless, discussions of Fund programmes have often questioned whether, even within given resources, conditionality does not sometimes impose greater contraction on countries than is absolutely necessary. This is a long-standing controversy, and one which the present report will not attempt to resolve. Suffice it to say that the few detailed country studies of Fund programmes which have been published, as well as interviews with officials outside the Fund conducted during the preparation of this report, do give grounds for the belief that, at least on some occasions, Fund programmes have pressed measures on countries that were more severe than necessary: devaluations sharper than the balance of payments required, or credit ceilings tighter than needed. Fund programmes could also have more built-in flexibilities to allow more easily for redefinition of targets and conditions in the event of changes in the economic environment affecting programmes' critical assumptions. And they could also pay more attention to supply measures and to long-term rather than short-term elasticities where new incentive-effects are introduced. (A deficiency of Bank–Fund collaboration is that the Fund has responsibility for negotiating exchange rate levels, while the conditions which may make an exchange rate change effective are the province of the Bank—not least the non-price factors which need attention if improved incentives are to lead to greater production. The two dimensions need to be brought more closely together.) [15]

When a country has an unsustainable balance of payments deficit, it must immediately export more, import less, or increase its borrowing, and then move towards a sustainable position. If raising exports is difficult, the options reduce to importing less or borrowing more. The problem for several of the poorest countries is that domestic production is already limited by import 'strangulation': agricultural production may be held back by lack of foreign exchange for fertilizers, transport by lack of imported spare parts or fuels. And production may be further constrained by domestic supply difficulties. There is a real conflict for such an economy if correction of the balance of payments can only be achieved by demand restriction or devaluation, when the export response is limited and curtailing imports may have further deleterious effects on production, and the measures taken may even hurt the fiscal balance and export production. [16]

It is not suggested that such conditions are universal, or that Fund programmes are commonly too severe. On the contrary, there are several countries even among the poorest where relations with the Fund are satisfactory and programmes successful; even the much complained-of major devaluations have been necessary and effective in some countries. Indeed, if devaluations are insufficient, the burden of adjustment falls mainly on fiscal measures which can produce unnecessary deflation. The Fund is in part the victim of its own reticence, since, in not producing its own case studies of a wide range of country programmes, which would allow a more balanced judgement, it leaves the field to others, who tend to concentrate on the really difficult and controversial cases. But the question still remains, for the poorest countries, of how more expansionary adjustment paths can be found, and what role the Fund may have in the process.

This report does not advocate any further blurring of the functions of the IMF and the World Bank. It is essential that the Fund preserve its role in relation to short-term balance of payments management, while the Bank retains its central concern with investment and development. Of course the relation between these two functions must be as close as possible, with the minimum of discordance between shorter- and longer-term adjustment measures (a subject addressed in Chapter 7). But within the traditional functions of the Fund, some movement is possible which would assist the poorest countries without relaxation of necessary disciplines; it would involve both resources and the manner of their application.

Measures for the poorest countries

One of the theses of this report is that the poorest countries face intractable developmental difficulties which require long-term investment to overcome: in education, health, population, land improvement, or reclamation, as well as provision of basic infrastructure: power, transport, and communications. Yet these long-term investment processes are frequently interrupted by short-term crises caused by external shocks or weather-induced crop failures. The development finance institutions have not really found a way to protect these countries from such hazards. As a result the long term is often sacrificed to the short, and the path which should lead to self-reliant growth seems never to shorten.

In the most recent period, many consortia or consultative groups[17] have shifted their aid into quickly disbursing forms, since the countries could not maintain or complete existing investments. This has been all to the good as a temporary measure. The current food crisis in Africa is also receiving attention—but also largely out of existing aid ceilings, not additional funds. If a steadier course for long-term investment is to be held to, the process needs thinking through. A long-term policy is required of the donors for the balance between project and programme aid (including commodity aid). Emergency situations should be met to a greater extent from contingency funds so that essential investments can continue. And greater protection from fluctuations for these countries' budgets and balance of payments is needed.

The IMF could play a part in this in a number of ways. First of all, the CFF could be enlarged and improved to give greater coverage to items affecting the balance of payments. (This report will not discuss the CFF in detail; many reasoned accounts of proposals for its extension can be found elsewhere.)[18] IMF data show that the CFF met less than one-twelfth of African countries' terms of trade deterioration in 1978–81[19]—of course it was not designed for that purpose. Coverage only extends to factors of a temporary nature and beyond a country's control; but the CFF could aim more at sustaining import capacity than protecting against export shortfalls. It is not suggested that CFF lending be unconditional. On the contrary, it is in fact already conditional if a country has already borrowed beyond a certain percentage of quota; and if additional funds are to be made available under the CFF, they will have to be similarly conditional.

Second, the Fund should examine whether conditions could now exist for a resumption of EFF lending to the poorest countries, with all the purposes for which it was intended, including its extended repayment period. This may have to be on a selective basis, if there is any concern that given countries are not committed to implementation of programmes. The relation with World Bank SALs could be important, especially where those are addressed to major programmes of policy reform.

Third, the Fund should, at least in current circumstances, join fully in efforts to assemble resources from other agencies to combine with its own resources in support of its programmes. The Fund has been open in the past to the criticism that it based its programmes on estimates of likely capital inflows rather than prepare a range of programmes related to major efforts to assemble resources; recently the Fund has been more active in cooperating with other agencies to cover a financing 'gap' collectively. It could move further in this direction. It would also be helpful if Paris Club debt negotiations were also brought increasingly into the overall framework of balance of payments management under Fund and Bank programmes (see Chapter 7).

As noted above, this report does not wish to become embroiled in controversy over the effectiveness of Fund conditionality. Suffice it to say that, at least in some countries, proposed conditions, and the way in which they were negotiated, have sometimes been counter-productive in economic effects, if implemented, or have even led to postponement of desirable reform owing to the arousal of political opposition. At the same time, in very many cases there have been highly satisfactory and salutary programmes with good relations on all sides. One can only ask that the Fund review its own experience and examine whether it too can learn from the past to achieve more understanding of conditionality in cases where it is needed. The price of greater resource mobilization must be that the agencies have confidence in their effective use. Recipient countries must share this confidence.

Finally, subsidization: for the poorest countries with difficult debt burdens, it may not make much sense to call for additional resources if they are lent on current near-market terms. If all countries are to remain subject to Fund discipline—as they should—it is important that those which need concessional terms should receive them. This implies replenishing, and using selectively, the Subsidy Account. There are various ways in which this can be done, without calling on members' budgetary funds.[20] Indeed, it is an attractive feature of making greater use of Fund resources that they can all be increased without budgetary appropriations from members.

III   The World Bank and Structural Adjustment Lending[21]

With its command of the concessional lending facilities of IDA (now much diminished), its mandate to deal with long-term development strategy, its international and country-specific capacity for research and policy analysis, and its experience of policy dialogue in donor consortia and consultative groups, the World Bank was ideally placed to establish a facility providing balance of payments lending in support of long-term adjustment programmes for low-income countries. Structural Adjustment Loans (SALs) have developed not as an alternative to Fund programmes, but as a complement to them. They are still relatively modest operations, since there is a limit of 10 per cent of annual commitments upon the Bank's SAL lending, and in 1984 that limit was not reached. Until recently, there was a concentration of SALs upon middle-income countries (and semi-industrial ones): Turkey, South Korea, Thailand, Philippines, Panama, for example. Even within Africa, middle-income and 'near middle-income' countries figure prominently in the list of SAL recipients: Ivory Coast, Kenya, Mauritius, Togo, Senegal. Conspicuously absent are low-income

South Asia (one SAL operation in Pakistan was suspended when the country's balance of payments improved), the Sahelian countries, or those populous countries in Africa suffering severe political and economic dislocation (for example Zaire, Sudan, and Ethiopia).

Not all World Bank non-project lending is channelled through SALs. Nor is policy dialogue dependent upon non-project lending. In Ghana and Zambia, for example, much the same intensity of policy dialogue has been achieved through World Bank programme or project support for rehabilitation projects in key export sectors: the operation of those sectors is sufficiently affected by macroeconomic policy and overall public investment allocation decisions to make economy-wide dialogue and conditionality a feature of what is ostensibly sector support.

A senior official of the Bank has stated that SALs are designed to:

1. support a programme of specific policy changes and institutional reforms designed to reduce the current account deficit to sustainable levels;
2. assist a country in meeting the transitional costs of structural changes in industry and agriculture by augmenting the supply of freely usable foreign exchange;
3. act as a catalyst for the inflow of other external capital to help ease the balance-of-payments situation.[22]

A further major purpose, in current circumstances especially, is to help recipient countries towards sustainable growth.

SALs[23] may originally have been designed to be preventive in character; but the realization soon dawned that, in the post-1979 international economic environment, developing countries were likely to require extensive programmes of domestic policy reform in order to respond to changed international relative prices, terms of trade deterioration, and declining net inflows of foreign finance. The postponement of such reform had left a legacy in many countries of a syndrome of severe price distortions, administrative over-regulation, public sector inefficiency, falling savings, and low-yielding capital investment. The Bank recognized the political difficulty of remedial action, and also the strong likelihood of perverse short-term economic effects from the measures required for long-term structural change. Hence the need to provide additional resources to enable a government to implement the necessary programme of reform was evident.

In principle, the distinction between Bank SALs and IMF programmes is one of time horizon and range of instruments. Whereas the Fund is primarily concerned with financing and correcting balance of payments deficits in the short-run, the Bank's SALs are intended to encourage a sustainable long-run balance of payments position. The Bank concerns itself, much more than the Fund, with resource mobilization and allocation policies directed at increasing the supply of tradeable goods. In practice, the distinction is less clear—especially where the Fund becomes involved in a series of programmes, or in an EFF. The two institutions normally complement each other well. Differences of emphasis, however, have led to occasional differences between the Bank and the Fund, particularly over programmes in East Africa. Differences, which arise in particular over the degree of retrenchment judged necessary or measures to achieve it, are partly a matter of technical judgement, and partly of political or institutional feasibility.

The key question is that of the comprehensiveness and timing of appropriate measures. The Bank's appraisals of SAL operations so far suggest that the Bank has already learned a great deal about the prerequisites for successful policy reform: comprehensiveness appears to be yielding to selectivity, while the 'short, sharp shock' is giving way to a more sensitive approach to the sequencing of critical measures such as trade liberalization, the removal of subsidies, or introduction of user charges for public services. The Fund's resource constraints, and the nature of its facilities (other than the EFF, which, as noted, is rarely available to low-income countries), make it less likely that the Fund can follow such an evolution. The tensions that may continue to arise thus need to be addressed with some urgency if the normal high degree of effective cooperation between the Bank and the Fund is to be maintained.

At 1 April 1984, twenty-eight SALs had been approved, covering sixteen countries and amounting to $4.1 billion. Four programmes had been discontinued (Bolivia, Senegal, Guyana, and Pakistan),[24] but one country (Turkey) received four consecutive loans, while eight countries received two loans each. A successful process of structural adjustment will probably take five or more years and require support from a series of SALs. For the future there may be such series of SALs, gradually effecting more difficult and detailed reforms. The programme is already a significant component of Bank lending, and represents a major extension of conditionality in aid relations. The Bank in 1985 was conducting a review of its experience with SALs; only parts of it were available to the authors of this report. The record is clearly a mixed one.

The appraisal of SALs involves four elements: the appropriateness of the policy reform package; the sequencing of programmes; the process of dialogue, including the capacity to sustain it within the recipient country; and, lastly, the accuracy of the estimates of terms of trade movements and foreign financial inflows, upon which the macroeconomic prescriptions of the programme depend.

The issue of the 'universal prescription' has already been discussed. The limited evidence so far available does *not* convict the Bank of imposing uniform policies through SALs. On the other hand, there has been vigorous attention to regularly recurring areas of desirable policy reform. The task facing the Bank is to continue to act as a catalyst for difficult domestic decisions while avoiding the elevation of disagreements to the level where they are perceived as a political or ideological challenge by the government concerned.[25] The components of SAL reform programmes tend to fall into four broad groups—not necessarily in order of priority: first, the restructuring of incentives (pricing, tariffs, taxation, subsidies, interest rates); second, the revision of public investment priorities; third, improvement in budget and debt management; fourth, the strengthening of institutions, especially public enterprises. There is widespread awareness of the complementarity between these broad groups of issues, particularly between measures to alter price incentives and the institutional reforms which might give real effect to incentive changes. The first Kenya SAL was instrumental in heightening this awareness: Bank officials, for example, now take the view that incentive reforms do not by themselves bring about the desired shifts in the structure of production; new investments are needed, together with management and labour training, suitable marketing arrangements and—in the case of public enterprise—changes in financial responsibility and management structure.

Such reforms take time. The Bank has taken the sequencing problem seriously; it has carefully reviewed the shortcomings of the Kenya and Senegal SALs in this respect. The Senegal SAL was clearly over-ambitious, covering all the main policy areas. It broke down over the pricing of rice, complications with an agricultural reform programme, and failure to finalize the public investment programme on schedule. Subsequent progress was made in all these areas (so that the SAL was not 'ineffective'), suggesting that the initial sequencing should have been made more flexible. Indeed, some have questioned whether it was wise to interrupt the loan for non-performance on one substantive issue when on four others Senegal was doing well.[26] In the Kenya SAL, the initial programme of import liberalization was curtailed by extreme foreign exchange shortage, while substantial delays occurred in other areas—'delays' from the perspective of unrealistic timetables which did not properly take into account existing administrative and staff constraints.

Now that sub-Saharan Africa has become a major focus of the structural adjustment effort, the recipient's capacity to sustain dialogue and policy reform is central to the success of SALs. With few exceptions (of which South Korea is the prime example), it seems that the initiative in SAL programme formulation often lies with the World Bank rather than with the recipient government. In present circumstances this is neither surprising nor reprehensible; but it is not as it should be, and does point to the need to strengthen recipient capacities for negotiation and policy analysis. Unless this is done, the risks remain that the programme will be regarded as an outside imposition, will fail to take root or produce lasting change, and will contain inappropriate diagnosis.

Trend estimation

Mis-estimation of trends in externally determined influences on a country's balance of payments has been a prominent cause of difficulty in SAL programmes. Export prices and capital flows, for example, are vital determinants of a country's ability to sustain trade liberalization (*vide* Kenya's first SAL). From 1979 to 1983, World Bank commodity price forecasts were persistently over-optimistic; the forecasts affected the design of programmes, and the collapse of justified expectations exacerbated programme failures (notably those in Guyana).[27] The possibility of forecasting errors does not detract from the value of SALs, but it makes a case for greater flexibility in policy reform programmes and in the volume of funds the Bank is permitted to devote to SALs. When an unexpected terms of trade deterioration makes a government unable to meet individual conditions of a programme, there should be some alternative to abandonment or renegotiation of the whole programme. Without the necessary flexibility, Bank (and IMF) adjustment programmes could become self-defeating.

The World Bank's conditional non-project lending has rapidly evolved in fruitful directions. Balance of payments support is clearly needed in a large number of low-income countries, and the new Bank schemes offer one of the most effective methods of providing it. The Bank's programmes also provide a focus for support from other donors in a framework within which recipients appear increasingly able to implement major measures of reform. There is an urgent need to expand them—learning from recent experience, bolstering them with concessional support, and improving the consistency with them of Fund operations.

IV   Other donors and policy dialogue

Policy dialogue and leverage involving bilateral donors has rarely been conducted within explicit frameworks comparable to Fund programmes or Bank SALs. Such dialogue is inevitably an extension of bilateral political and economic relations in non-aid fields; it thus raises more sensitivities, and may involve more influences extraneous to development policy, than the dialogue of multilateral agencies.[28] Some bilateral agencies—most notably USAID—have been more active than others in discussing domestic policy with recipients. The US has, for example, been successfully involved in improving agricultural policy in Egypt, Jamaica, and Zambia, and in foreign exchange liberalization in Kenya. In Bangladesh, USAID maintains a large mission and engages in continuing bilateral policy dialogue with the government. The Japanese agencies, by contrast, maintain no such representation and claim never to exert influence in bilateral discussions with the government; other donors occupy positions on the spectrum between. Some donors favour coordination of policy dialogue through the World Bank or donor consortia, others favour an independent channel.[29] The European Community, through the Lomé Convention, maintains a formal framework for dialogue with the ACP states, but such dialogue is only loosely associated with the transfer of aid. In general, bilateral donors are willing to leave macro-policy dialogue mainly in the hands of the Bank and Fund. But their capacities and experience give them roles in dialogue at sectoral or project levels on a par with the multilateral agencies.

There have been a few instances of direct use of leverage by a major bilateral donor to bring about macroeconomic policy change by a recipient government. The case of donor pressure in India in the mid-1960s is outlined below, and does not give cause for great optimism about the usefulness of the approach. The management of a long-term bilateral relationship where, for historical reasons, the recipient's reliance upon the donor's support is substantial, is a matter of great delicacy; by its nature, not much will be known about the record by non-participants. Nevertheless, the experience of France and the franc-zone countries of West Africa suggests that a close bilateral relationship can be sustained, even where issues of macroeconomic policy are involved, without disrupting the evolution of multilateral relationships (including regional ones such as the Club du Sahel) or preventing adoption of Fund/Bank programmes. In a different vein, the management of Papua New Guinea's requirement for budgetary grant aid from Australia demonstrates how sensitively organized policy dialogue (incorporating the use of independent studies and assessors) can obviate the need for highly interventionist supervision of project and programme flows. The two governments found that aid without formal 'strings', coupled with a framework for dialogue, proved more effective for development and caused less bilateral friction than conventional aid mechanisms would have done in the circumstances.

The new task for bilateral donors has been to assess the implications of the rapid spread of Bank- or Fund-organized adjustment programmes, and the counterpart need for increased flows of non-project aid. With some exceptions, bilateral agencies have traditionally been organized and staffed to cope with project aid, not with programmes of economy-wide policy reform. The World Bank has clearly invited bilateral support of SAL programmes,[31] so bilateral donors must at least be in a position to appraise them. This raises the further question of whether policy dialogue and negotiation of policy conditionality by agencies other than the Bank and the Fund will be confusing and counter-productive. Other donors, bilateral and multilateral, can also undercut conditionality if they come in with unconditional loans against the spirit of a Bank- or Fund-supported programme.

Avoidance of fragmentation in the dialogue process requires, first, strengthening of recipient negotiating capacities and of the recipient's own role in donor co-ordination. Second, greater coordination among donors is essential. Despite the well-known obstacles to donor coordination (trade interests, political competition, agency self-preservation, and so on), there could be better use of consultative groups for 'dialogue among donors', and for resolution (involving the recipient) of policy reform packages that will command wide donor support. Which, then, is to be the lead institution in the process—the Bank, the Fund, a multi-donor secretariat? The best approach will probably involve the gradual evolution of more formal procedures for consulting key bilateral donors in consultative groups, and during the process of framing Bank- or Fund-supported adjustment programmes.

There is one arena of dialogue in which stronger coordination may be urgent. A number of donors (notably the EEC, and to some extent USAID) have shown enthusiasm for the concept of sector strategies 'negotiated' between donors and recipient, and then supported by the donors' commitments. Once again, the concept has merit if the recipient is free to channel all donors' support to the sector in question in the most efficient way. But if the strategy is to be negotiated with a single donor (or grouping, such as the EEC) there are dangers to be avoided. For example, the EEC Commission has espoused both food sector strategies and mining sector strategies; not only is EEC technical assistance for strategy formulation tied to Europe, but there are strong vested interests in Europe influencing both agricultural policy and mineral trade patterns. Such interests need not affect the outcome, but multi-donor collaboration over such initiatives will at least enhance the credibility of the resulting strategy.

V Recipient experience of dialogue

India [32]

India enjoyed good relationships with aid donors up to the mid-1960s. Donors accepted India's formal planning framework and selected from among the projects it yielded; they made few noticeable attempts at intervention in the conduct of economic policy. When war, drought, and agricultural problems placed India's balance of payments under pressure from about 1965 onwards, donor attitudes quickly changed. Since then the Indian story of policy dialogue consists of three transitions: from explicit use of leverage to more relaxed dialogue; from heavy involvement of a single donor (the US) to the conduct of dialogue with a multiple donor consortium; and from macro-conditionality to a sectoral framework for dialogue.

The devaluation forced on India in 1966 was much needed, but ill-timed. It was forced as a condition of the resumption of US aid, against the wishes of the Indian Finance Minister, and it was the subject of major pressures and tensions between the donors and the Government of India. The Consortium's aid package, designed to support both devaluation and further trade liberalization measures, collapsed after one year when the US pulled out. Such a degree of leverage over macroeconomic policy was only achieved in conditions of acute economic difficulty for India, and at a cost of chronic disruption to both aid relationships and Indian economic management. In the medium-term the Indian response was to seek to diversify her sources of political and economic support; the donors who sought to promote internal changes by strong leverage in fact failed to secure the changes and, in the process, lost the capacity to influence future Indian policy.

An atmosphere of partnership in policy dialogue took considerable time to rebuild. In the past decade, major donors have shifted to a sectoral framework for dialogue and now often prefer the World Bank to mediate. Active coordination by a bilateral donor continues where the donor has special expertise (the Scandinavians in health, the UK in coal), but the general approach is multilateral.

The successful re-establishment of policy dialogue has depended greatly on India's own skills. At both sectoral and project levels, India fields a large range of capable people with accumulated skills and experience. The learning process is decidedly two-way. Moreover, Indian officials are prominent at many levels of the World Bank, so that Bank-coordinated dialogue seems far removed from bilateral leverage with its diplomatic and political overtones of an outside imposition. India's planning and budgeting systems are sophisticated, and tempered by long experience; the country has clear and project-specific priorities. Research results and capabilities are available from outside the Indian government. These circumstances are absent for the vast majority of low-income countries.

The Indian experience suggests that dialogue is most effective where aid is in any case most effective, and where the donor can persuade the recipient to go further along a path on which it already wants to go. A more radical approach—challenging prevailing vested interests or political convictions—can only be implemented when the recipient's need for aid is overwhelming. If aid constitutes more than 50 per cent of public investment, then macro-leverage is tempting, if not often successful; if aid is 25 per cent or less of public investment, donors can exert influence only if they are realistic and selective.

The influence of donors on Indian policy through dialogue is likely to diminish. First, the reduction in IDA resources and pressure to shift India from IDA or IBRD may somewhat reduce the incentive for the Indian Government to heed Bank advice—unless the volume of flows is adequate to compensate for the change in terms. Second, the perception—even if false—that the Bank has at least partially abandoned its commitment to a direct anti-poverty focus, and is increasing its stress on private sector expansion, may disengage the Bank from some of the main thrusts of Indian priorities—it is less likely to be found 'leaning on an open door'.

Given the recent success of dialogue, these developments are unfortunate. The Bank's sectoral role has been constructive, both in its impact on the general policy arena (public sector pricing, trade policy, organization of public sector systems) and on projects. A major contribution, both of the Bank and other donors, has been to fund pilot projects, to have them fully discussed over long periods with Indian officials, and then to replicate them in cost-effective ways. The successes require adequate resources, absence of suspicion that ideology is affecting the objectivity of advice, and firm control over the influence of donors' commercial interests on project and policy choice.

Colombia

The case of Colombia underlines a point made earlier, that policy dialogue had many significant forms long before the SAL; it began in

1962 as conditions proposed by the World Bank for the setting up of a Consultative Group (CG) and developed into a fairly unusual system with an annual Memorandum of Understanding on policies. This has arisen originally from conditions attaching to US programme loans, and continued as the basis for the Bank's lending and its advice to the CG, in which the major other donors were USAID and the Inter-American Development Bank. As well as the macroeconomic and sector policies in the Memorandum, sector and project-related conditions were also discussed in project lending.

The process of dialogue has been long and complex; it has gone on even after Colombia graduated out of US concessional aid in 1975. Its results have been mixed. Colombia was one of Latin America's 'success stories' in the 1970s, achieving substantial and well-distributed growth, with major increases in employment and reductions in poverty and population growth. These achievements have been attributed to successful domestic policies and management, as well as to contributions by the donors in policy dialogue and poverty-oriented lending. Assistance for institution building, and for public sector management and pricing, has also been considerable.

But donor–recipient relations have been criticized. Collaboration with Obras Publicas, a major public sector agency, has been accused of colluding with and strengthening Colombia's patronage politics; but donor attempts to avoid that by lending through more decentralized agencies have been attacked for distorting national priorities—away from rural development, for example. At times, US determination to support a government in office, rather than insist strictly on lending conditions and withdraw loans, has weakened some of the commitment to long-term development necessities. The line between appropriate firmness and recognition of realities is a narrow one. However, if today Colombia is suffering from the debt and social problems which in more virulent forms afflict much of Latin America, recession is more probably to be blamed than weaknesses of the policy dialogue.[33]

Some cases in sub-Saharan Africa

Tanzania. Until very recently, the most notorious case of the failure of dialogue in Africa was that of Tanzania. Recent policy shifts (for example, over the exchange rate and agricultural pricing) had still in 1984 to result in successful negotiation of conditional Fund and Bank programmes, despite the fact that few countries were in worse economic condition. Indeed, more than one observer subscribes to the view that Tanzanian negotiations with the Bank and the Fund

. . . have not simply failed to reach agreements that hold up but have arguably had consequences for domestic policy debate which have delayed the
pace of adjustment which would otherwise have taken place.[34]

Appraisal of the Tanzanian experience unavoidably leads to debate.
Responsibility for this débâcle of dialogue is evidently shared among
external circumstances, Tanzanian domestic mismanagement, and
donor (plus IMF) failures and mis-perceptions; but the assignment of
proportions is very much in the eye of the beholder. It is now difficult
even to quantify Tanzanian performance, since local economic data
gathering has itself fallen victim to the traumas of 1978 onwards, and
in agriculture was never very accurate.

Since 1975 agreement has been reached with the IMF only once (in
1980) on an EFF which broke down after the first drawing. Until
1984, relations with the World Bank steadily deteriorated; there was
no SAL, although there has been programme lending for rehabilitation of export sectors. While in 1978 aid inflows effectively offset the
current account deficit, the deficit subsequently widened at an alarm-
ing rate, and the increase in aid flows slowed. Even observers sym-
pathetic to the Tanzanian position agree that short-run economic
policy from 1977 to 1979 was 'fiscally reckless',[35] and some bilaterals
subsequently froze their aid; but attempts from that time forward to
redress the position have floundered in a mire of seemingly insoluble
disputes.

Where leverage is not 'leaning on an open door', and where
resources are not adequate for the task, they may fail even in the
severest economic circumstances. Fund and Bank policy advice was
perceived as an external imposition, sometimes as an ideological challenge to the Tanzanian government's chosen path, and was generally
debated in a context of fierce battles over individual instruments—usually out of all proportion to the role of the instrument in a
wider policy package. The battles were frequently over magnitudes
rather than the desirability of the measures. The exchange rate question, for example, was until 1984 debated in terms of support for or
opposition to a large-scale, single-stage devaluation; it seems likely
that this in fact prevented the adoption of a de-politicized 'crawling
peg' exchange rate adjustment mechanism that, by now, could have
had considerable effect. This phase now seems to be over, as a result
of changes in attitudes on all sides in response to Tanzania's increasingly desperate plight. It leaves an unfortunate example of how not to
conduct policy dialogue, whether as donor or recipient.

The Tanzanian case is well known, in part, because the Tanzanian
Government has been unusually willing to make public its disagree-

ments with the international finance institutions. Despite the disagreements, negotiations have continued (unsuccessfully) over a very long period; there has been no extended interruption of dialogue (as happened, for example, in Ghana and Uganda). Whereas, in other cases, agreement has been followed by failure to deliver, the Tanzanian case is distinguished by determined adherence of both sides to relatively fixed and explicit positions so that agreements have not been reached.

No other sub-Saharan examples exhibit this degree of explicit disagreement, but almost all demonstrate signs of the lack of experience of both sides in dialogue over macroeconomic and broad development policy questions, limited capacity for negotiation and policy analysis among recipient governments, and over-optimism about the extent of policy reform that can be achieved even in the most pressing of circumstances. There is debate for some about the potential efficacy of incentive reforms in conditions where net foreign resource inflows are continuing to decline (they are negative for the more heavily indebted countries); for others, domestic policies are responsible for the decline, in considerable measure. The technological or institutional support for reform in some countries is inevitably slow to develop. On the other hand, there is evidence that reform programmes are now taking hold in countries with long records of below-average performance: Tanzania has already been mentioned; Ghana, Zambia, Uganda, Mali, and Guinea have set in train major restructuring efforts. The task now is to sustain these efforts with increased resources (and also the efforts of those countries historically more favoured by the West as 'successes': Kenya, Ivory coast, Malawi), while incorporating the lessons of initial experience with macro-policy dialogue and reform.

Malawi. Malawi has received two Bank SALs to date, and is one of the very few low-income countries with a current Fund EFF. For some years Malawi has enjoyed favoured status with the international financial institutions as a result of its growth record in the 1970s, and its apparent willingness to rely more on the market and private initiative than upon state intervention. In 1979, Malawi's external position deteriorated rapidly; a Bank SAL was put together during 1980 in some haste, involving limited conditionality, but with a wide range of studies with a larger-term adjustment programme in view. There seems to have been a deliberate element of 'learning by doing'; in 1979 the Bank's country reviews of Malawi were still geared to support of project decisions. By 1983, when the second SAL was negotiated, the Bank felt confident enough to press a stronger dose of policy reform (the country's external position had further deteriorated in the meantime).

Both SALs have been disbursed with few interruptions;[36] but the extent of policy reform achieved appears to have fallen short of the World Bank's wishes, and the record has exposed the points of stress and misinterpretation in the original diagnosis of Malawi's structural difficulties. These were six: the slow growth of exports from peasant agriculture; the narrow export base (dominated by tobacco); energy shortage, especially a declining fuel-wood stock (also used for flue-cured tobacco); deterioration in the financial performance of parastatals; widening budget deficits, caused principally by rapid expenditure growth; and rigidity in government price and wage control administration. From these, the most progress has been made on improving the financial performance of parastatals, and of the large private corporation, Press Holdings, which effectively functions as a parastatal.

Progress in the other areas has been slowed down either because the structural problem was initially mis-specified (the reversion of peasant producers to subsistence cultivation was as much a function of land scarcity as of price distortions—though the latter were important), or because government played no role in the market concerned (fuel-wood pricing), or because the government resisted the Bank's approach (social service user charges, price control) and concentrated on resistance rather than compromises. It should be stressed that the government's objection, for example, to increases in school fees could be justified on distributional grounds, with the backing of independent research on the damaging effects of fees on enrolments. These shortfalls from expectations, however, are best regarded as part of the essential learning process, rather than failures of policy dialogue. The dialogue in Malawi seems set to mature, provided (once again) that there are adequate net aid flows to support it.

Mali. Bank and Fund programmes in Mali have involved more radical departures, in an excellent example of 'leaning against an open door'. Mali has no SAL, but other forms of Bank support; it reached its first IMF agreement in May 1982. Mali (following Guinea) had been one of the few former French territories to adopt an explicitly socialist path, withdrawing from the West African Monetary Union (UMOA) and from the franc zone between 1962 and 1968. Mali was seriously affected by Sahelian drought; it also accumulated over the years a vastly overgrown public sector (particularly in the civil service itself—the government guaranteed employment to secondary and higher education graduates), severe domestic price distortions, controlled grain marketing, and an unstable exchange rate. Yet, following reforms initiated in 1976 and intensified since 1980, Mali is apparently somewhat better placed to withstand environmental difficulties than some of its non-Sahelian neighbours.[37] Since 1980, Mali has responded to large increases in non-project aid flows by adopting a five-year-programme of reform. In February 1983 the automatic recruitment of graduates to the public service was abandoned, strict limits were placed on new hiring, and redundancy schemes were introduced to encourage civil servants to move into private business. There were accompanying reforms in salary determination and administration. From 1976, grain prices had been progressively increased, and more recently grain marketing has been substantially decontrolled. A Fund programme has supported debt rescheduling; it includes reforms in tax administration (evasion was running at high rates), in monetary and credit policy (including credit allocation to rural business), and the adoption of an apparently explicit target of the abolition of exchange controls on current transactions by 1985 (Mali was readmitted to the UMOA in November 1983).

The sustainability of these reforms in the exceedingly difficult conditions of a Sahelian country is clearly open to doubt. Nevertheless, this is a clear case where, after a long period of deterioration, policy dialogue associated with aid has helped to bring about wide-ranging reforms.

Zambia. The experience of Zambia is roughly intermediate between those of Malawi and Mali. Zambia has had a series of IMF programmes since 1978, and, instead of a SAL, the World Bank has lent large sums for rehabilitation of the mining sector—which still accounts for 95 per cent of foreign exchange earnings. Zambia's structural problems of excessive dependence on a single export, protected and import-intensive industry, slow agricultural growth, high relative wage costs, and an expensive public sector have since 1979 been compounded by drought, sharp falls in the purchasing power of copper exports (for reasons of both volume and price), and one of the largest debt burdens in sub-Saharan Africa—much of it contracted over 1978 to 1982, when expectations of a copper price revival encouraged fiscal laxity.[38]

Vigorous attempts at reform began in December 1982 with formal decontrol of all but four regulated consumer prices, followed by frequent devaluations of the currency, prompt increases (in real terms) in agricultural producer prices, foreign exchange retention schemes for 'non-traditional' exporters, and reductions in the budget deficit. The government has so far succeeded in avoiding compensatory wage increases, despite strong urban unions and an accelerating rate of inflation. The constraints on the success of the programme are twofold. First, the foreign exchange shortage continues to be so acute that most industries function at 30 per cent capacity or less—incentive changes alone cannot alter this position; debt service payments exceed annual export earnings, and accumulated arrears amount to more than two-thirds of export earnings—debt rescheduling is thus a chronic preoccupation. Second, it has proved far simpler to adjust prices (including the exchange rate) than to overhaul agricultural marketing, introduce user charges for public services, or cut the amount of employment in the public sector. There is a sense in which the (successful) external pressure for price changes has deflected attention from the need to reform institutions or take difficult decisions on employment. Without these reforms, and some easing of the projected net capital outflows, the effects of the price changes may well be dissipated—reducing confidence in external advice and support in the future.

These cases all indicate that dialogue- and leverage-induced reform is possible in sub-Saharan African conditions. But the experiment is still in its very early stages, and its success is still highly vulnerable. In order to sustain the momentum, three things are necessary: additional net foreign inflows; steady improvement in domestic capacities to design and negotiate reform programmes; and some reduction in expectations that incentive reforms alone will produce a 'quick fix'. Now that so many African governments have shown willingness to de-politicize exchange rate management, raise producer prices, and decontrol consumer prices, it is perhaps time to shift the emphasis to the support of other policies and institutional change that can make price changes effective.

VI Policy dialogue: the lessons so far

The effectiveness of aid and the success of policy dialogue are closely related. In the case of India (and also those of South Korea and Colombia), the policy dialogue matured over long periods during which the returns to aid-supported investments have evidently been high. But even in these cases the relationships had their critical points. Dialogue over macro-conditionality is almost always the most difficult, and cannot be sustained over long periods when there is regular use of leverage. A stable framework for dialogue in the long-term is suggested by the relationship of mutual respect which has emerged over sectoral policies in India.

Yet to reach that position requires country experience, appropriate forms of aid, and widespread confidence in the conduct of macro-economic policy or development strategy. It is clear that, in sub-Saharan Africa, reliance upon project aid had brought donors and recipients to an impasse by the late 1970s: projects provided no framework for policy dialogue, and were low-yielding (or complete failures) often because of broad failures in the policy and institutional environment. Once non-project aid forms were adopted by donors—in themselves more suited to sub-Saharan countries' contemporary needs for input support, maintenance, and rehabilitation—the way was open for the use of dialogue and leverage to engender broad macroeconomic policy changes. The recent willingness of African countries to consider and implement major reforms is doubtless in large part a product of appalling economic and social deterioration; but the design of the reforms, and the path to implementation, is predominantly the outcome of policy dialogue, conditionality, and support from non-project aid flows. In this context, the shift in the composition of aid forms has made for more effective aid, and explicit policy dialogue about macroeconomic and strategic questions has developed in tandem. If this phase is successful, the emphasis of aid, and the focus of dialogue, may shift back to sectoral support and the allocation of investment by project once economic recovery is in train. But an appropriate mix of programme and project aid will continue to be necessary, and policy dialogue will long remain in many countries as part of the apparatus of ensuring the effectiveness of aid.

The ability to exert leverage may be greatest in crisis, but the risks of failure to deliver on the donor side are also greatest. In this respect, the experience of India in the mid-1960s is salutary for donor involvement in sub-Saharan Africa today. It is essential that the reform programmes which have either been willingly adopted, or conceded under severe pressure, be supported with an adequate volume of aid in flexible forms. Otherwise programmes may not have time to take effect before the regimes which adopted them are ejected from power, or premature disillusionment with adjustment attempts sets in. In the short-run, the degree of leverage or influence is related to the volume of aid offered; this is not just because a government is offered a larger incentive; one reason why whole loans have in the past had to be made conditional on the fulfilment of all parts of an agreement is that they were too small to make withholding a part an effective means of enforcement. In the long-run, the credibility of policy dialogue in general depends on donors' ability to make and sustain long-term aid commitments.

In sub-Saharan Africa, reform programmes are currently being implemented under the pressure of extreme economic circumstances. There is no guarantee that the priority currently given to economic reform can be sustained. Past policies of discrimination against agriculture, excessive protection of import-substituting industry, and subsidization of urban consumption may have been economically irrational, but they have been entrenched by a strong political logic. Governments' political support often consisted of influential urban groups which stood to bear much of the short-run cost of structural adjustment. Reform has now become possible because economic conditions have in any case forced powerful groups to accept reductions in consumption and the rationalization of public spending, and leaderships have become aware of the costs of postponing reform. Sustaining these changes requires sufficient time (and thus external resources) to allow some of the benefits of adjustment to be realized and distributed, and to permit the groups which stand to gain substantially from reform (e.g. smallholders producing mainly for the market, or citizen businessmen) to consolidate their influence upon decision-making. It also requires technical and managerial changes which will ensure that economic matters and economic considerations remain high on any regime's agenda. Above all, it requires the political commitment of the regime, which implies in turn political sensitivity on the part of the donors.

Strengthening recipient capacities

Beyond the confines of emergencies, effective dialogue or conditional programmes also require negotiating skills and analytical capacity on the recipient side; without these, the risk that reform programmes will be seen as outside impositions, and will lapse when aid flows cease, will remain high. The task of improving negotiating skills overlaps to a considerable extent with that of strengthening decision-making capacities and economic policy-making institutions—a task which the World Bank already stresses in SAL operations—but they are not identical. There is scope for improvement of the technical assistance facilities available to governments for support in preparation for negotiation. This applies not only to negotiations with the IMF and the World Bank on adjustment programmes, but also to those with other donors and with commercial lenders.

There is a possible analogy (though by no means a precise one) with the improvement, over the late 1970s and 1980s, of governments' capacity to negotiate mutually acceptable deals with foreign private companies—particularly in minerals industries. This improvement was aided by the establishment of independent international centres of advice, research, and technical assistance upon which governments could call—not only for provision of investment appraisals, or specific technical reports, but also for regular and long-term assistance in clarifying objectives, drawing up negotiating positions, and the actual conduct of negotiations.

In the field of assistance for negotiations on debt rescheduling, and on adjustment programmes, there is at present a virtual vacuum—neatly filled at times by costly private advice from merchant banks. Technical cooperation is now beginning to be available from some aid agencies to help recipients prepare detailed action programmes for structural adjustment. This is also a valuable part of helping recipients prepare for negotiations. Multilateral agencies—and not just the main lenders—should be supported in efforts to expand advisory services for all aspects of designing and negotiating adjustment programmes.

Dialogue and technical cooperation

Increasing emphasis on policy dialogue is likely to bring changes in technical assistance practices, but there are dangers in tying technical assistance too closely to conditionality. The record of donor-financed and organized advisory projects and institutions is mixed.[39] The chief difficulty with separate structures, whether in themselves they are good or bad, is their tendency to collapse when donor personnel are withdrawn. Individual experts/advisers have often been dispatched with vague terms of reference and left to develop their tasks in response to local circumstances. Some donors (the World Bank, for example) now show signs of wishing to link technical assistance more explicitly to the implementation of policy reforms agreed in SAL-type programmes: technical assistance in support of reform programmes, with flexibility for experts to respond to changing circumstances, is certainly desirable, but such experiments should not be completely divorced from the process of programme negotiation. Moreover, such initiatives may overestimate the strength of a donor's leverage, and fail to recognize that any negotiated programme is a compromise.

In sub-Saharan Africa the present phase of dialogue involves a heavy concentration on the recipients' own macro-policies. The traffic predominantly flows one way. The Indian case suggests that dialogue becomes fully constructive and durable when there is a genuine two-way exchange. This requires recognition of past donor errors, and discussion of them in the course of dialogue. It is clear that, in Africa, many donors have a long record of preference for large infrastructure projects and capital-intensive production for which African development patterns have recently come under heavy criticism. These errors are recognized in general terms (for example, in World Bank reports on sub-Saharan Africa); it would be of greater value if the lessons of individual experiences were to be examined in country-level discussions. There is also scope for inclusion of discussion about rich-country policies which affect the performance of developing countries: trade policy and the rise of protectionism, interest rates, aid policy itself.[40]

The problem of donor coordination for policy dialogue was addressed in the above discussion of the World Bank and structural adjustment lending. There are twin dangers to be avoided. The first is that of conflict and confusion in policy advice. The second is the creation of circumstances where donors appear to 'gang up' on the individual recipient, forcing the recipient to adopt a defensive and perhaps hostile stance. The solution probably lies in the sensitive use of Consultative Group arrangements, with coordination by both the recipient and a multilateral agency, and with a strong analytical input from the recipient (see further Chapter 7).

Much has been said about the recipients' capacity for dialogue. But the donors' capacity deserves a mention also. The donors' own analytical work in support of policy prescriptions, and their ability to convince recipients of their soundness, are also key ingredients of successful dialogue. Such analysis must comprehend not only economic conditions, but the institutional and administrative constraints which may limit recipients' ability to carry out conditions, and a proper understanding of the manageability of the time-frame for desired action.[41]

The final consideration is that of the context of dialogue about recipient policies. There has to be explicit and realistic appraisal of the terms of trade outlook, of prospects for debt rescheduling, or for new capital inflows. The donor involved in dialogue, and a fortiori in the imposition of conditions, should be prepared to make clear and monitorable commitments about the aid flows that will be forthcoming if reforms are made. Moreover, an apparent donor interest in 'good domestic policy' that is in fact tempered by the commercial interest of suppliers in the donor country will breed disillusionment, and may cause serious damage.[42] (While this chapter has been mainly about *adjustment* dialogue, there is clearly an unmet need for greater dialogue over traditional developmental investment programmes. This too should include donor commercial interests, as expressed both through aid and through export credits, to try to mitigate their effects on recipients' developmental interests.)

Policy dialogue is now an integral part of international aid relations. Macro-conditionality, too, is the necessary counterpart of the volume of non-project aid that is needed in low-income countries. The record suggests that some improvements in aid effectiveness have already been achieved by these means. The tasks now are to appreciate that relationships in policy dialogue must evolve if they are to endure, that the successful exercise of leverage over macro-policies is only possible in exceptional circumstances, and that the prerequisite for consolidation of the gains already made, and for the future success of dialogue, is the strengthening of recipient capacities to make it a genuine two-way process.

The 1980s are certainly witnessing a new era in policy dialogue—so much so that past experience may only be a partial guide to the future. In Africa, many countries are undergoing sweeping policy reforms under Fund–Bank programmes, extending to macro-policy, import liberalization, greater use of market incentives, institutional reform, and reform of parastatal organizations. In particular, agriculture is receiving more determined policy attention:

At least 16 governments have lifted ceilings on farm product prices or freed them entirely. A variety of measures have been announced or proposed to reduce the role of government and of government corporations, in regulating or operating domestic marketing and to give greater scope to private and cooperative marketing. Many African governments have declared higher priority for agricultural expenditures in their national budgets.[43]

Time will be required to see if these long-needed changes will have the desired developmental impact. But aid as a vehicle for policy dialogue is certainly on the move in potentially valuable directions.

Notes

1. A view succinctly expressed by Krueger (1981): the core of her argument is not that aid flows in themselves assist capital accumulation or efficiency in resource allocation, but that 'economic growth is largely the outcome of domestic policies and incentive structures which encourage the accumulation of additional resources and their efficient utilisation' (Krueger 1981, p. 280).
2. For this (rather obvious) reason it is not possible to gauge the relative importance of different policy instruments in IMF or World Bank adjustment programmes simply by establishing the frequency of their appearance in formal agreements.
3. USAID 1982*b*.
4. Even in the case of the World Bank, which has traditionally conducted the most comprehensive reviews of overall country performance and policy, country economic work was previously carried out in support of allocation decisions about project aid rather than policy prescription at the macroeconomic level. The advent of SALs has, according to Bank

officials, significantly enhanced the importance of country and sector policy work in its own right (and of those responsible for it).

5. Contrast, for example, Krueger 1981 and Bird 1982.
6. World Bank 1981*a*.
7. World Bank 1983*d* and 1984*h*.
8. OECD DAC 1984*a*, p. 66.
9. World Bank 1984*h*.
10. Guitian 1981.
11. World Bank 1981*a*; Guitian 1981.
12. Williamson 1982.
13. Loxley 1984.
14. Though it must be said that even in a detailed analysis, conducted by Fund staff, of twenty-one African countries in 1980–1, only a fifth of the countries met growth targets, two-fifths external sector targets, and one half inflation targets—this despite the fact that in fourteen programmes 'all or a major part of the policy measures were observed' (Zulu and Nsouli 1984).
15. See, for example, Killick 1984; Green 1984; Please 1984; Williamson 1982. Please cites evidence that failure to attend to such questions has prevented several IMF-led devaluations in Africa from achieving their results.
16. For example, if ceilings on domestic credit creation deprive public- and private-sector exporters of the local currency needed to maintain adequate capacity utilization, both exports and government revenue are likely to suffer.
17. See Chapter 7 for discussion of these coordination bodies.
18. See, for example, Commonwealth Secretariat 1983; Brandt Commission 1983.
19. Williamson 1982; Stabex, the European compensatory facility, was exhausted in 1983 and could meet no further claims.
20. Some of these are outlined in Brandt Commission 1983, pp. 67–8.
21. This section draws on the Structural Adjustment Lending chapter of Cassen *et al*. 1984, the Kenya and Malawi case studies, Duncan and Mosley 1984, Hewitt and Kydd 1984, and other materials.
22. Stern 1983.
23. In what follows, World Bank policy dialogue is discussed in terms of SALs, but the points also refer to other forms of Bank conditional non-project lending.
24. See the chapter on SALs in Cassen *et al*. 1984: Pakistan's SAL became unnecessary when the country's balance of payments improved, Bolivia's collapsed as a result of political upheavals, Guyana's fell victim to the severe economic dislocation in that country; only in the case of Senegal is it possible to conclude that a different approach to policy dialogue, and greater flexibility, might have allowed the programme to be sustained—the lessons of this case seem now to be well-understood. Consequently, the Bank can fairly claim that the 'success rate' for SAL operations has been satisfactory.

25. This problem has, at different times and in markedly different ways, clouded the relations of the international financial institutions with countries as diverse as Jamaica, Nigeria, Tanzania, and India; the disputes of the IMF with Argentina, Brazil, and Peru are better known, and have recurred over many years.

26. Lewis 1985.

27. The suspended SAL in Guyana fell victim to a great deal of domestic mismanagement, but the domestic strains themselves were intensified by larger than expected deteriorations in the unit value of sugar and bauxite exports.

28. The EEC is commonly considered a multilateral agency; in this report, however, the increasingly co-ordinated foreign policy stance of EEC member states, and the relation of aid and trade under the Lomé Convention, are considered to make its role in policy dialogue more 'bilateral', or at least 'multinational'. (See Chapter 9.)

29. USAID maintains a high profile, but it is not the only agency with an independent approach. The Scandinavian donors, the Dutch, and the Canadians all maintain independent channels of dialogue—often because of their special interest in the distributional effects of aid.

30. See the account of the Papua New Guinea aid experience in Cassen *et al.* 1984. It is noteworthy that Papua New Guinea has needed recourse to neither Fund facilities nor Bank SALs despite severe external and internal balance of payments pressures in the early 1980s; the solutions lay not in the level of Australian support, but in the domestic management framework which, in part, justified the untied grant form of Australian aid.

31. Notably in its reports on sub-Saharan Africa. The EEC (European Development Fund) and the OPEC Fund both contributed in support of Kenya's first SAL reform programme.

32. See, in particular, the chapter on policy dialogue in the case study of India, Lipton *et al.* 1984a.

33. These paragraphs draw on Bagley 1984.

34. Green 1984, p. 27; similar views are expressed by van Arkadie 1983 and Payer 1982.

35. Green 1984, p. 31.

36. The second tranche of the first SAL was delayed—apparently because Malawi was in difficulty with the IMF over domestic credit ceilings; see Hewitt and Kydd 1984.

37. Bourgoignie 1984. Though in December 1984 it appeared that a famine threat had arisen again.

38. Such expectations were supported by World Bank copper price projections, and by those of the minority private shareholders in the Zambian mines.

39. See, for example, the questions about the impact on agricultural pricing policy of the donor-organized Marketing Development Bureau in Tanzania, raised in Cassen *et al.* 1984.

40. As was done in bilateral discussions between Papua New Guinea and Australia; see the case of Papua New Guinea in Cassen *et al.* 1984.
41. These points are reinforced in the Bank's own (unpublished) evaluation of its SALs to Turkey.
42. Recalling, for example, that the UK in 1969–73 could well have conducted 'policy dialogue' with Sri Lanka on how to reduce tractor imports, given: the surplus of tractors used in roadwork; rural unemployment; and lack of spare cultivable land. Instead owing in part to commercial pressures, the UK sought to *increase* tractor aid to Sri Lanka.
43. OECD DAC 1984*a*, p. 28.

CHAPTER FIVE

Performance and Evaluation: Project, Programme, and Food Aid

I Introduction

Aid is used for many purposes—humanitarian relief, services to producers, direct production, building human capital, creation of infrastructure, balance of payments support . . . The forms it takes are also diverse. One of the main distinctions is between *projects* and *programme* (also called *non-project*) aid. For years the great bulk of aid was in project form. Project aid makes a specific capital asset or piece of technical assistance available, often to specific beneficiaries; programme aid makes a cash sum available for the benefit of the entire recipient economy or a sector of it, and is normally accompanied by policy discussions; food aid is programme aid given in kind rather than in cash. But the distinction is not clear-cut: good project aid can be negated by an unfavourable policy environment, and all programme aid has sectoral ramifications. The emergence of the hybrid known as sector aid reflects this awareness.[1] For convenience, project and programme aid are discussed separately here, since they are planned and evaluated in quite different ways. But the reader should bear in mind that there are important linkages, especially between projects and policy dialogue.

II Assessing Project Aid

How are assessments made?

Definitive conclusions about the effectiveness of project aid are difficult to reach. One can compare the *ex post* assessments of capital expenditure conducted by private businesses. For the private investor, the main criteria of an investment's success will usually be the net cash flow and the profits which it generates: normally agreed, easily measurable indicators. The aid administrator must also be interested in financial performance; but, in addition, an aid project is commonly expected to deliver

a contribution to the development of the economy, measured by the economic rate of return (many infrastructure projects such as roads and sewerage may not recover costs yet have very high economic rates of return);

a contribution to the welfare of identified income (or other) groups;

a contribution to manpower development and institution building, and thus ultimately to the economic self-sufficiency of the recipient economy;

and an avoidance of a host of potential environmental, social and political problems.

One of the most important sources of overall information on how projects perform is formal evaluation. Typically, evaluation studies are carried out, jointly by the donor and recipient, or by the donor alone, at the time donor involvement ends, or at the end of each phase of a longer term programme. Such evaluation reports provide a great deal of information on the basis of which conclusions can be drawn about rates of return, institutional performance, environmental impact, and so on.

Experience with evaluation. There is now a large body of knowledge on project performance that has accrued from the experience of implementation over the years. Formal evaluation is one of the main elements of this learning process; there are thousands of evaluation studies, and a great deal of work has gone into refining the methods used. Several excellent manuals are available on evaluation practice.

Nevertheless, there are several respects in which evaluation as it is often done fails to give all the information needed. Sometimes one cannot tell what an individual project has really achieved. And it is rarely possible to take a number of evaluations and assess the overall effects of what has been done in a given sector or country.

First, and perhaps most importantly, surprisingly little is known about how projects are *sustained* after the end of the initial phase in which the donor was active. It is without question true that a number of projects which look successful at the end of, say, five years when the donor withdraws do not maintain their promise, and if reviewed five years later give much less cause for satisfaction. Inevitably the governments least able to sustain projects are those with the weakest administrations and the greatest financial difficulties—that is, typically in the poorest countries, and perhaps most acutely in Africa.

The great majority of evaluation reports are not strictly *ex post*. Typically, the report is prepared when the donor agency's disbursement obligations have been fulfilled; but how the project is going to perform in a changing environment and with fewer financial and technical resources remains an *ex ante*, and speculative, question.[2] While the cost data are bound to be better than in the original appraisal report, the data on the benefits side (which may still lie in the future) remain subject to much uncertainty. In recognition of this weakness of evaluations, donors carry out 'impact' studies on a small minority of projects some years after their involvement ends. It turns out that some projects do indeed run into later difficulties; but others improve unexpectedly. Clearly, more such studies are needed.

Second, there is no single well-developed evaluation methodology that is universally applied to an individual sector, let alone across several sectors. Even within the same aid agency, practice can vary considerably between similar projects, depending on the approach or perhaps the calibre of the individual evaluators concerned and the specificity of the guidelines provided.

Some reports tend to measure performance in terms of internal criteria such as costs and disbursement periods; others (rather fewer, because of the technical difficulties) in terms of outputs, such as impact on growth and distribution of incomes. This is particularly true of some agricultural projects which may not be themselves directly productive but rather create conditions conducive to production by farmers. Further, the distinctions are not always clearly drawn between factors controllable internally by project management and externally by others, and between those that are and those that are not controllable. Some considerations—notably market analysis and marketing, and the interconnected choices of technology, scale, and location—are seldom treated satisfactorily.

These limitations in evaluation reports as technical documents, which are well recognized by evaluation staff themselves, arise for many reasons. Two of a quite different character may be mentioned. The first is that, because of the scale and complexity of what would have to be involved in understanding everything about what makes a project tick and in assessing its development impact, the boundaries of evaluation studies are often deliberately tightly drawn. There simply may not have been available the staff resources, especially those with the breadth of experience and maturity of judgement required, to do otherwise. The second reason has to do with the time that elapses from original design and appraisal of a project to its evaluation. On the one hand, hindsight is a benefit. But on the other, it is difficult for the evaluator to identify as well as comprehend the particular circumstances, internal and external to the project, prevailing at the time of design and appraisal, and the pressures that led to the particular choices made.

The *third* difficulty of interpreting evaluation documents is that *ex post* evaluation of a project is bound to raise sensitive issues. No project can expect to have nothing go wrong; any closely involved project designer, decision-taker or manager has to exercise judgement on a large number of complex variables, and time will inevitably expose some of these judgements as having been at fault. The great majority of evaluations made available for this study appeared to be acceptably frank about errors committed, and many indeed may have over-emphasized what went wrong. But an evaluation study cannot always be totally candid—especially if it is written for wide distribution. Besides, swingeing criticisms of an aid agency's operational staff, even if technically justified, will not always be an effective way of improving their approach to similar issues in future projects. There is nevertheless a line of fine judgement which separates concealing mistakes for the right reasons and for the wrong reasons. Agencies should not entrust this judgement solely to its own operational staff but should take steps—as many now do—to ensure objectivity.

Fourth is the fact that the assumption of what would have happened without the project, an assumption that is theoretically crucial to cost–benefit analysis, can never really be ascertained. *Fifth* and last is the problem that projects may achieve useful results which yet fall short of initially over-ambitious objectives. Even with the benefit of hindsight, however, it may be difficult to distinguish such over-ambition from a justifiable element of aspiration.

Despite these difficulties, compilations of evaluation studies are a valuable contribution to arriving at sound, broadly applicable conclusions on project performance. The compilations often point to generalized findings which are hard to ignore, and have the advantage of basing management and policy recommendations on actual and often pervasive experience. Moreover, they take the focus off individual projects, thereby bypassing the sensitivities associated with each.

Reviews are becoming increasingly comprehensive. In its *Tenth Annual Review of Project Performance Audit Results* published in August 1984, the World Bank looked at over 1,000 operations. While this study is one of the most comprehensive yet undertaken, other donors have made studies since the early 1970s on a sectoral or sub-sectoral basis. One of these, by way of illustration, is an OECD-sponsored examination of several donors' experience with irrigation projects. Another involves assessment of some dozen large-scale fertilizer projects committed in the early 1970s, and which have all been running now for several years. Several donors have reviewed their integrated rural development projects. But there have not been enough of such studies. Indeed, one of the surprises for the authors of this report was to discover how little had been done by the donors *collectively* to assess their own experience. This is where a real dilemma enters. It seems that to have an optimal operational and policy impact, evaluation exercises should embrace a good number of projects and generally be wide in scope. But regularly to achieve this requires resources that evaluation departments do not ordinarily have, and cannot readily expect to have at their disposal. Moreover, few donors have sufficient projects in any one sub-sector to allow wide-ranging reviews of cross-cutting issues. Clearly this is an inter-agency matter, and a most promising development is the increasing activity of the OECD DAC as a forum for comparing the results of aid.

The above are just some of the problems inherent in the evaluation process as it has developed so far in many bilateral and multilateral agencies. Its conclusions are cautionary, especially because of the growing concern about evaluation and 'feedback'. But they are not negative: evaluation is an evolving art, a process in which accumulating experience is steadily allowing the boundaries of analysis to be pushed forward and the policy conclusions to become increasingly substantial.[3]

Institutional learning. Precisely because of all the attention focused on evaluation, it is important to remember that it is only one, albeit perhaps the most formalized, among a variety of ways in which an institution's learning process takes place. Other prominent methods of institutional learning in donor agencies include drawing evidence from monitoring and supervision, financial and management auditing analysis, and research and sector work. And an informal process of thinking about past projects and feeding the conclusions through into new projects goes on—or should go on—all the time. Review sessions of recent projects are often held when new ones are under consideration. A feature of a well-managed agency is that all its sources of information are fully employed in a continual effort to improve effectiveness.

Features of project performance

Rates of return. As development aid has multiple aims, there is no single criterion by which projects are judged. Economic rates of return are a measure of the contribution of an investment to the wider economy. They are thus one indicator, and an important one, of the performance of a project. But there are many issues that rates of return normally do not illuminate—who gains; whether just compensation has been paid to losers; environmental implications; institutional questions; economic self-reliance; and so on. There are also often difficulties in calculating rates of return, and indeed some analysts hold the view that the main value of this indicator is to focus planners and managers' minds on crucial assumptions. So in forming judgements on aid effectiveness, rates of return must be put in context alongside other considerations.

Projects *may* be making valuable contributions while having low rates of return; they can have high rates of return (as conventionally measured) and not contribute if significant aspects are omitted. But normally it should be cause for concern if the measured rate is not reasonably high, and for satisfaction if it is. The assertion earlier in this report that 'most aid works' is not wholly based on rates of return. Quantitative evaluation is important; but the broadly based evaluations made by several agencies, already briefly referred to in Chapter 1, have taken other criteria into account. Only a few donor agencies evaluate all their projects. The World Bank is rare in requiring the calculation of *ex post* rates of return as a matter of routine on virtually all projects. Its cumulated project audit results for the 1960s and 1970s suggest that *ex post* economic rates of return in projects were respectable, at 17 per cent for the twenty-year period on average.[4] Its most recent review already mentioned, of over 1000 projects completed between 1975 and 1983, found that 79 per cent had a minimum rate of return of 10 per cent, and around 90 per cent of total investments appeared to have achieved their major objectives, or were on the way to doing so. There was considerable variation among the rates of return by sector—agriculture having the highest and industry the lowest—and by year of evaluation. The highest rates of return were in Asia and the lowest in Africa, the lowest of all for any large number of projects in agriculture in Eastern Africa.[5]

The reported evaluation results of some other major donor agencies are mostly expressed in less quantitative terms than the World Bank's. The Asian Development Bank found that 97 of 139 projects completed and evaluated at the end of 1984 were judged to have been generally successful in achieving their aims and the remainder partially so. The Inter-American Development Bank reports very similar results, as do also the Canadian and Netherlands aid agencies, and three other major agencies. The common conclusion is that some 65–75 per cent of projects are found to be satisfactory or highly satisfactory, and most of the remainder problematic but not irreparably so, with a small percentage (in single figures) completely written off.[6] The overall message is that most aid projects for which data exist have, considered in themselves, made positive contributions to recipient economies. But aid performance in Africa gives cause for concern.[7] It is a disturbing fact, which emerges from evaluations, from the country studies conducted for this report, and from other materials, that the majority of cases where aid appears not to be effective arise in the poorest countries, both the African majority and the Asian minority.

Projects and poverty. The overall effects of aid on poverty were discussed in Chapter 3. Does channelling aid through particular *projects* get it effectively to poor people in recipient countries? As Chapter 3 found, the data on this subject are among the weaker parts of evaluation work. Relatively few evaluations make any serious attempt to quantify the effects of projects on low-income target groups, unless they are specifically 'poverty-oriented'.[8] This lack of usable data reflects the inherent difficulty of the exercise, and possibly the sensitivity of donors and recipients associated with determining the impact of development and aid programmes on poverty. Even when evaluations point to improvements in the lot of the poor, they often lack the baseline data for 'before and after' comparisons which would strengthen the conclusions.

Still, the findings of evaluations are consistent with the general conviction of most aid agencies, namely that a good deal of project aid (in particular the 'new-style' projects designed for the agricultural and for the urban marginal sectors during the 1970s) has a substantial direct effect through the transfer of productive assets or knowledge to the poor—the fifth to ninth deciles going down the income distribution. Very little of it, however, has been directed at, or has had any impact, positive *or* negative,[9] on the people in the bottom decile—the poorest 10 per cent. At the same time, even though the poorest may not gain much from many projects in terms of income or productive assets, they do appear to have gained indirectly from those projects which have cheapened their food; potatoes in Andean South America, fish in South-East Asia, and grains almost everywhere;[10] and also from a large number of projects in 'welfare' sectors—health, family planning, education, housing, and the like. A significant finding has been that when projects do aim to assist the poor directly, rates of return are comparable with other projects: there is no *necessary* trade-off between poverty orientation and efficiency. Very recent experience of rural projects in Africa, however, suggest that the general problems of achieving development there apply no less to efforts to reach the poor.

Projects and institution building. Increasing institutional capacity in the recipient country is a key feature of successful development, affecting both the prospects for long-term economic self-reliance and also the performance of the project itself. In a recent World Bank study,[11] 82 per cent of projects with at least partial success in institutional objectives yielded economic rates of return of 10 per cent or more, while by contrast 73 per cent of the small number of projects with poor institutional results produced low or negative returns. The contribution of projects to strengthening institutions is one of their most important functions.

Most aid donors and recipients put great stress on strengthening the capabilities of implementing institutions by means of training, technical assistance, and financial support to the organizations concerned. Progress in reaching this objective is not readily measurable, but there have been several valuable overall reviews by donor agencies of their achievements. There are notable success stories, such as the World Bank's involvement with power corporations in several countries, the contribution of both the Bank and USAID to the growth of development banks worldwide, and technical assistance to Central Banks and Statistical Offices. But the broad picture cannot be described as satisfactory.

USAID's review of its support for institutions concluded that 'the results were generally about half positive and half negative', IDB that 'the objectives of institutional development operations are seldom fully achieved', CIDA that '67 per cent of CIDA-aided host country institutions were unprepared for self-reliance at the time of CIDA withdrawal', and the World Bank that in Africa '[its] past efforts in institutional development have not been very effective'.[12]

Among the common disappointments are that successful pilot schemes have often failed to lead to successful projects because the repeat projects have not been favoured with the resources granted to the original pilot, or because the implementing institutions could not cope with the increased workload. The frustration of aid donors with implementation performance in recipient countries has often led those donors to create autonomous institutions, such as the Upper Region Development Authority in Ghana and the Project Development Unit in Southern Sudan, which, even if successful in themselves, may further weaken the planning and implementation capacity of the government. The plethora of donors and projects in some countries has exacerbated the problems. All in all, it can be said that the present concern for increasing the management capacity both of central government and of the agencies responsible for implementing development programmes, particularly in the poorest countries, is well-founded. (These issues are discussed at length in Chapters 6 and 7.)

Projects and women. A conspicuous area of concern in many, if not most, projects is connected with the role of women in development. Too often, women are little consulted and considered in the design of projects, and they may receive a disproportionately small share of the benefits. Recently, a UN agency built a training college in Ghana: its students are male; the agricultural workers whose skills it was intended to upgrade are women. All too frequently, project designers are unacquainted with women's functions as workers and in house-holds, their skills and needs, their income-earning opportunities, and the disadvantages which they have to overcome. It is evident that donors are not yet implementing the OECD DAC guiding principles for supporting the role of women in development, which enjoin donors 'to take full account of the gender composition of the population at all stages of the programming cycle'.[13]

However, a good deal of change is now going on. It is perfectly clear that involving women in development is not solely a matter of equity but, in a great range of activities, a condition for achieving develop-ment and, as far as projects are concerned, a condition for their suc-cess also. In agriculture, energy, water, sanitation, marketing, distribution, population, health, education, and nutrition—to name only some—the role of women is commonly critical. Aid agencies are now responding to the recognition of these facts. Most of them have sections responsible for bringing the relevant issues to the attention of all parts of the aid system. They have drawn up policy statements indicating their objectives and the operational means to achieve them. They report on their activities which bear on the issues.

It is impossible to do more here than illustrate the wealth of mater-ial on the subject. As a statement of policies, that of the Canadian International Development Agency (CIDA) is a model:

To support the objectives and initiatives of women in developing countries;
To achieve greater understanding of actual and potential roles for women in developing countries;
To increase participation of women in design, implementation and evalua-tion of development projects;
To include women in CIDA programs and projects in proportion to their existing participation rates in the target groups;
To work in partnership with recipient governments to close economic gaps between women and men in their countries;·
To emphasize strategies to assist women in income generation, including reduction of demands on their time and energy from household work and food production;
To support special women's programs linked to overall development where special efforts are required[14]

Many similar ones could be quoted. Evidently the donors support the DAC guidelines even if they are not yet fulfilling them to the letter.

In the field examples can now be found of positive steps being taken—in Asian Development Bank (ADB) projects in Indonesia (livestock), Nepal (rural water supply), and Pakistan (health and population); in projects in Ghana (CIDA, water) and Sri Lanka (Finnish International Development Agency (FINNIDA), income generation)—and a host of others. An International Labour Office (ILO)/ Netherlands study[15] has provided a wealth of information on energy and rural women's work, which is now being followed up in eight countries by national institutions. Many donors are working in collaboration with voluntary agencies to assist a variety of local initiatives.

There is a great deal of new activity, and the situation is changing. Yet if one looked on the ground, the picture of female disadvantage that has persisted in many places for centuries would not appear to have altered except here and there. Much remains to be done: the relative neglect of women's interests lies in the nature of society, and the complete fulfilment both of equity and productive potential requires thoroughgoing change, change which donors and recipients can and should both promote.

Projects and the environment. With large parts of developing countries under ecological pressure—and some in acute crisis—the effectiveness of aid must in part be judged by the contribution it makes to sound management of natural resources. There are three aspects to this: the support aid gives to recipients in building up their own capacity for resource planning and management; ensuring that potentially harmful ecological effects of development projects are minimized or eliminated; and giving attention to the scale and effectiveness of projects that are primarily concerned to remedy environmental problems.

Over the past decade, all major donor agencies have established procedures for taking account of environmental dimensions of aid. In the late 1970s, two reviews of their policies and practices found great differences between agencies, both in their professional strength in environmental matters and in the way environmental issues were taken into account.[16] These varied from the highly structured in USAID to the much more informal—although not necessarily less effective—in UK ODA. Documents submitted by some agencies for this report suggest that in the years since these reviews, more agencies have set up offices charged with environmental matters. This evidence of sensitivity on the environment is encouraging.

What can be said of the reality of the environmental effects of aid projects? After all, they are a part of a process of economic development which inevitably can cause ecological harm—and has in fact led to some horrifying damage, for instance, in north-east Brazil. The unsatisfying answer, inevitable with such a diversity of experience, is that the record is mixed. Many projects in rural areas are concerned, at least in part, with promoting sustainable farming practices, and many are successful. In Kenya, there is a first-rate nation wide project, supported by the Swedish International Development Authority (SIDA), introducing simple, low-cost field contouring to reduce erosion; it is highly effective. In north-west Somalia, there is an equally effective IFAD/World Bank dryland agriculture project based on soil and moisture conservation in farmers' fields. And there has been a growth in recent years of 'social forestry' projects for the provision of fuel-wood and to control erosion, although there are still too few of these projects to be effective in countering the massive fuel-wood crisis being faced by many of the poorest countries.

But if there is a great deal of solid achievement, there are also real problems. Although agencies do show concern for ecological considerations, these compete for priority with other demands—for agricultural or industrial production to meet the needs of growing populations with aspirations for higher incomes. The lead in giving greater priority to ecological issues must inevitably come from within the recipient country—donors can and should try to persuade governments of the importance of good resource management, but the extent to which they can force restraint in a country which is not prepared for it is limited. At the very minimum, donors must be more prepared to implement the policy that virtually all have explicitly adopted, namely to refuse to support projects that would lead to irreversible environmental damage. Regrettably this is not always done; some aid-funded developments appear to have foreseeable and very damaging ecological effects.[17] Such cases show up the weaknesses of standard cost–benefit analysis. A project which clears tropical rain forest for cultivation can have a high rate of return as conventionally measured, but usually only for a few years; after that it reverts to barren scrub, and the forest cover may never regenerate. Only if such issues are explicitly taken into account will the danger of ecological destruction by aid be averted.

Both environmental successes and failures underline the growing importance of integrating these issues into aid planning and management; indeed, the earlier in the project cycle they are taken into account, the more scope there is for influencing the outcome in a positive way. Here again, the OECD DAC is working to achieve an agreed approach among donors, including proposals for supporting recipients' efforts at environmental management. But a gap is likely to remain for some time between the approach, even when agreed, and actual practice.[18]

Projects and self-reliance. There is a broad and often neglected question of whether projects contribute to the economic self-reliance of the recipient country—that is, to the country's ability to do without aid in the future. At the most general level there are many countries in which the answer is affirmative. Numerous countries have experienced economic growth to which aid has contributed, and no longer require aid; and others, of which India is an important example, have invested successfully in agriculture, again with the support of aid, to the point at which large-scale food aid is not normally required. But there are also a number of countries—typically the poorest, and with African countries prominent—which have become more aid-dependent over the years, to the point at which the great majority of public investments are aid-funded.

At the level of projects, self-reliance has two main features—institutional (which has already been discussed) and financial. In some aided projects, such as public utilities or directly productive enterprises, financial self-reliance is a goal, although one that is often not achieved in practice, with the support of the Ministry of Finance or an aid donor being needed for longer than originally envisaged. (This topic is discussed below in respect of industrial projects.) For many other projects, however, such as those designed to improve infrastructure, education, or services to small-holder farmers, cost recovery from users is never intended. Rather, a growing economy is expected to generate public sector revenues adequate to provide for recurrent expenditures. In the more rapidly growing economies, this has indeed occurred and domestic revenue sources have proved adequate. But in others, and again inevitably the poorest countries, the need to provide financially for projects is one source of stress on the public sector and one reason why aid continues to be needed. This is not necessarily an argument for cutting down on project expenditures if they are contributing to economic development. But it is an argument for ensuring that the recurrent financial implications of projects are fully foreseen and incorporated in public accounts.

This chapter has not covered aid for road construction. Had it done so, the issues of sustainability, maintenance, and self-reliance and their interconnections would have been clearly illustrated. Roads are often not maintained, for lack of funds or because management is weak. But when this occurs, the fault lies at least partly with donors as well as recipients. Often the cost overruns make roads much more expensive than projected. Loan conditions which would have prevented deterioration are neglected. The donor often fails to insist on the conditions. The recipient may angle for a rehabilitation loan rather than pay for upkeep.[19] As in most other sectors, it is essential for all parties to pay much more attention to what aid is doing for long-run self-reliance.

Improving project performance

Reviews of project performance suggest that, while the majority are worthwhile, there must be a continual search for improvements. Most of the measures to be taken are specific to particular sectors of the economy, and these are discussed in the remaining sections of this chapter. But some areas for improvement are general to all sectors. They relate to the stages through which all projects should in principle pass—identification, preparation, appraisal, implementation, and evaluation, the 'project cycle'. These issues are summarized here; the full discussion is included as the appendix to this chapter, and the reader wanting an expansion of some of the terse conclusions noted below is referred there.

At the stage of project *identification* and preparation it is important that projects be tailored as closely as possible to the recipients' priorities and needs, and that the influence of donors' non-developmental concerns—commercial, political, or bureaucratic—be restrained. These influences can lead projects to being excessively capital-intensive or reliant on foreign exchange, and to neglect of low-cost options. It is important that projects be kept in line with recipients' management and financial capacity (see also Chapter 7).

At *appraisal*, which is normally carefully carried out, especially in technical and economic aspects, there has been a common tendency towards over-optimism about the time needed to complete a project, about some of the assumptions underlying the calculation of expected benefits (for example, in respect of crop yields), and about the capacity of the implementing institutions. In projects which involve a strong social element, there is often insufficient understanding of the human environment in which the project is set.

Most issues in *implementation* are specific to individual sectors, but some are general, including: the difficulty of ensuring local counterpart staff who have the right training and are in post long enough to get full benefit from an expatriate; the fact that many technical personnel do not necessarily translate into good managers; and the scarcity of recurrent funds.

And finally, it is striking how often *evaluation* findings do not effectively feed back into management decisions and project design. The remedy lies partly in making managers more aware of the value of information, partly in streamlining the process of generating the information, and partly in improving the flow, especially *between* donor agencies. Overall, donors seem to be rather good at technical and economic elements of project design and implementation, and much less good at institutional, social, and political elements—what have been called the 'soft' as opposed to the 'hard' aspects.

III Agriculture Projects

The importance of agriculture to the economies of many developing countries, and particularly the poorer ones, can hardly be overstated. Up to 90 per cent of the people in some cases derive much of their incomes from farming, agriculture is the main foreign exchange earner for many countries, and the sector provides many essential inputs for early stages of industrial development. The effectiveness of aid in promoting sustainable agriculture is therefore basic to the effectiveness of aid as a whole.

Overall evaluations

The World Bank is again the main source of quantitative evaluation. Its agricultural projects have on balance exhibited above-average rates of return. A recent review by the Bank of 221 agricultural projects started between 1961 and 1980 showed an average rate of return of 16.8 per cent, above the 10–15 per cent range conventionally considered acceptable. Since the World Bank is by far the biggest donor in agriculture, accounting for two-thirds of all multilateral and one-third of all official development assistance for agriculture, these figures are encouraging.[20] Reflecting the uncertainty of farming, however, agricultural projects have also displayed a higher failure rate than other sectors. About one-quarter of all agricultural projects in the most recent review—representing 15 per cent of investment—had not achieved their main objectives at the time of audit.[21]

The review found that performance of projects by sub-sector and by geographical area has been very variable. The credit and irrigation projects reviewed have achieved high average rates of return and low failure rates. The findings should not, however, be considered definitive; in irrigation, the favourable results should be qualified by the observation that continuing institutional and environmental problems are leading some donors to proceed cautiously in this sub-sector (see below). Area development (including integrated rural development) and especially livestock projects have performed poorly. Agricultural projects in South Asia have generally performed well, while Eastern Africa has returned the highest failure rate, followed by Latin America and the Caribbean and West Africa.

The World Bank's experience with the sector probably broadly mirrors the overall experience of other donors. The Inter-American Development Bank (IDB), for example, found 63 per cent of projects reviewed in 1981–3 were 'satisfactory', 33 per cent partially so, and the remainder unsatisfactory. But an overall conclusion is not possible, owing to the scarcity of analyses as comprehensive as those. One of the reports[23] commissioned as part of this aid effectiveness study, however, reviewed some fifty project evaluation documents of five Europe-based agencies (the EEC, French Development Cooperation, Netherlands Development Cooperation, the Swedish International Development Authority, and the UK's Overseas Development Administration). Together with the country case studies that were conducted as part of the present study, the report confirms that the record of agricultural projects is more mixed than is the case for any other sector. In particular, it found the record in Africa to be poor.

The broadly positive record of agricultural projects combined with their great variability underlines the importance of an effective learning process—which does not always take place. One study noted a 'cycling' of programme priorities and theories, that is, a tendency for particular types of lending to appear, disappear, and reappear in donors' priorities over the decades—extension and research, for example, have both come and gone in waves; and 'the failure to learn from failure' in credit programmes, for example, or in achieving integration between engineering and management in irrigation. But rates of return were high in well-conducted projects for land and water development or research. And the study emphasized that *both* technical change capable of generating new income streams at low cost *and* adequate attention to institutional design are essential if agricultural investment, surrounding infrastructure, and policy improvement are all to support each other.[24]

Some examples of sub-sectoral experience

Agricultural research. Even more than other investments in agriculture, the outcome of agricultural research is very uncertain, but can yield enormous benefits. The main sources of uncertainty are man's incomplete control over the natural conditions addressed by research, and the fact that translating the knowledge that is generated by research into economic benefits demands an appropriate framework of policies and institutions (pricing, marketing and extension, especially) which has often been lacking. The results of investments in research in developing countries reflect this uncertainty, and range from producing the highest economic rates of return of virtually any investment to failing completely. But taken as a whole, the record is very impressive.

A major review of the experience of research observes, 'In recent years there has been a proliferation of studies which indicate that returns to a great deal of investment in agricultural research have been two or three times greater than returns to other agricultural investment.'[25]

During the 1950s the received wisdom was that technology could be transferred unmodified from developed to developing countries. As the limitations of this approach became more evident, more emphasis was placed on adaptation of technology, and concessional resources were increasingly used to support agricultural research through a network of international specialized centres and regional and national research institutes. In 1971 the Consultative Group on International Agricultural Research (CGIAR) was founded, with membership of multilateral development agencies, non-profit foundations, and governments, to oversee the international institutes and to serve as the apex of the international publicly funded research structure.

The effectiveness of the research system as a whole depends on the effectiveness of each element. The essential functions of *international* institutes is to undertake costly or complex research that is beyond the capacity of most national centres. Their performance has on the whole been satisfactory, with notable successes, some of which are discussed below. The role of the *national* systems is to produce results of direct relevance to local producers, including the adaptation of the findings of the international centres. The capacity of national research institutes is one of the crucial determinants of the effectiveness of the research system as a whole, and varies very greatly from country to country. In India, one of the main influences on the diffusion of high yielding varieties has been the level of effectiveness of national and regional research capacity.[26] In many cases, however, the national research capability is the weak link in the chain linking international institutes and farmers. The World Bank has found that 'perhaps 10 per cent of developing countries already have adequate research skills, good national research programs, and effective linkages with international research institutions'.[27]

Support for research has been one of the priority concerns of some donors, notably USAID, which in 1981 allocated some 20 per cent of its appropriations for agriculture, rural development, and nutrition to agricultural research.

There have been two main thrusts to aid support for agricultural research: first, to generate the knowledge and technology to increase the production potential of farmers; and second, through training and technical assistance, to strengthen research institutional capability. In respect of the first aim of aid-supported research, the best-known results of the international institutes are the development of high-yielding varieties of wheat (CIMMYT) and rice (IRRI). By 1976/7, these varieties had come to cover a significant portion of the planted area, especially in Asia, as Table 5.1 indicates.

These varieties have led to greater production: when employed in conjunction with higher levels of fertilizer and timely and adequate water, they result in yield increases over traditional varieties, typically of 40 per cent or more and, especially with more recent high-yielding varieties, have good characteristics of disease and pest resistance. What of their impact on income distribution? While some observers have expressed concern that the new technology has led to growing inequality, the seed–fertilizer–water technology is itself neutral to scale, being infinitely divisible; the inequalities arise with respect to access to the physical resources and institutional support which are necessary to realize the full potential of the varieties. Larger farmers tend to have preferential access to credit, input supplies, and irrigation water and have thus been able to take advantage of the new technology earlier and more completely than smaller farmers. The latter, however, have generally adopted the same technology after a lag and are capable of getting even higher yields. This potential is often not fully realized, however, owing to the persistent difficulties small farmers face in getting access to vital services—credit, water, and other inputs. High-yielding varieties are also more demanding of labour and thus may benefit the landless, a large class in Asia, and one increasing in some parts of Africa, such as Kenya.

The success of the research on wheat and rice and, to some extent, maize has not generally been repeated with 'poor men's cereals' (sorghum and millets) and tropical root crops (sweet potatoes, cassava, and taro). Higher-yielding varieties of these crops would be 'self-targeting' on low-income groups, and would be likely to have a bene-

TABLE 5.1

*Proportions of planted area of wheat and rice
sown to high-yielding varieties, 1976–7*

	Wheat	Rice
Asia	73	30
Near East	17	4
Africa	23	3
Latin America	44	13
Total	44	27

Source: World Bank 1981*b*.

ficial impact on income distribution. In limited areas there has been considerable advance with all of them. But the scope for successfully transferring internationally developed varieties to other ecological zones and continents is in many cases not yet known, and sustained efforts will have to be made at the national and local levels to adapt or develop varieties that accord closely with local needs and conditions.

For the future, a major strategic question for researchers is what is to be the balance between developing varieties suitable for (i) higher potential areas with good soils and favourable moisture regimes (but perhaps with diminishing returns as levels of inputs increase) or (ii) less favoured areas with more variable moisture and poorer soils but with currently lower input levels and perhaps greater scope for addressing the welfare of very low-income groups.

The second thrust of aid for research has been institution-strengthening. USAID's research policy paper of May 1982 made a major commitment to '*develop human resources and institutional capabilities*, especially to generate, adapt and apply improved science and technology for food and agricultural development' (original emphasis). Here too, the experience has been mixed. Useful insights into institutional aspects of research supported by aid resources are provided by eight coordinated evaluations of USAID research projects and programmes in Africa (Kenya and the West Africa Rice Development Association), Guatemala and the Central America region, Asia (Nepal, Thailand, and Korea) and Tunisia.[28] In Guatemala, the Food Productivity and Nutrition Improvement Project (1975–9) worked with an existing institution with effective government commitment and was rated a success. In Korea, staff training was assessed as the most useful part of the Agricultural Research Project (1974–80) and expatriate technical assistance one of the least. In Kenya, by contrast, the evaluation reported that plant-breeding effectively stopped in 1979 after the departure of the last American.

Overall evaluations of institutional performance indicate that weakness results from an interaction of several factors, only some of which are directly addressable by donors:

(i) low government commitment;
(ii) low status of research within government and lack of credibility with farmers;
(iii) inadequate budgetary provision;
(iv) rapid staff turnover, both of national staff and expatriates;
(v) lack of information and analysis for setting consistent and appropriate research priorities;
(vi) unsuitable institutional structures and poor coordination;

(vii) the short donor project cycle, which tends to lead to short planning horizons, inappropriate phasing, and discontinuities, when what is required is sustained and logical programme development.

Effective agricultural research is crucial as population continues to press on a finite resource base, and increasing yields therefore becomes of critical importance in sustaining agricultural growth. Research should therefore be accorded a high priority in development strategies for the future. Among the major lessons from the past are the continuing great importance of support for institutions, the key role of effective commitment from the recipient government, and the need for all concerned to take the long view.

Integrated rural development and crop production projects. The integrated rural development projects (IRDPs) that have been evaluated in the early 1980s were largely planned during the early and mid-1970s. They were therefore the product of expanding aid budgets, and of an intensified commitment to distributing the benefits of aid among rural populations and low-income groups in particular. The projects represented a bold effort to attack rural poverty by addressing simultaneously the multiple obstacles in the way of rural development; they set out to improve productive services, provide infrastructure, and sometimes to provide health and education. They therefore tended to be large, multisectoral, and administratively complex.

Experience with IRDPs has been variable. For the ADB, such projects represent the main thrust of their interventions in rural areas. In a recent review of thirty-three such projects financed by the ADB up to 1982 (some of which have not yet been completed), difficulties are acknowledged—single projects have up to sixteen different executing agencies, requiring heroic coordination; procurement is slow; and counterpart funds are scarce—but the overall message is optimistic on the projects' outcome. Further, the ADB reports a steady improvement in project performance as a result of better project design which more carefully takes into account local factors. The Bank has learned that the 'blueprint' approach to rural development does not work.[29]

Overall, the experience with IRDPs in Africa has perhaps been less encouraging. The studies of Malawi and Kenya included reviews of the experience with IRDPs in both countries. In Malawi, the IRDPs did not have a well-thought-out strategy for reaching the poor, and the increases in production fell short of what was expected, especially in the earlier projects. More positively, from 1982 there is evidence that the massive increase in maize production by peasant farmers has been associated with greater use of the improved seed and fertilizer being promoted by the IRDPs. In Kenya, there were some encouraging features of IRDPs, such as the provision of veterinary artificial insemination services, but overall their results fell short of expectations. The major reasons for this were that the judgements at appraisal about the strength of implementing institutions were over-optimistic, that coordination between executing agencies was not effective, and that there was a shortage of sound technical packages for farmers to adopt. In Tanzania, four out of twelve projects have been regarded as successful. German aid has been successful with an IRDP in Togo.

These mixed results are confirmed by several overall reviews. The fourteen IRDPs supported by European agencies reviewed in a study prepared for this report had certain specific identifiable achievements in the creation of basic infrastructure such as roads and water supplies, and in provision of technical and commercial services, but most had only minor impact on food and cash crop production, and failed to strengthen either implementing organizations or the financial base for the maintenance of new infrastructure and services.[30] A review of IRDPs by the UK came to a similar conclusion,[31] as did reviews of CIDA, IDB, and USAID experience.[32]

Common reasons for IRDPs not reaching expectations were: inherently weak organization and management structures which rely in good measure on coordination *between* diverse public sector agencies, most of which gave higher priority to projects for which they were *fully* responsible; technical recommendations for farmers that were insufficiently profitable, too risky, or too demanding of labour at peak times of year; and unduly high expectations of the capacity of implementing entities to handle greatly increased funds. Few projects of the old IRDP type have been initiated in recent years. In Africa particularly, the trend is towards simpler structures based on more realistic assessments of management capacity.

There is also a class of project which aims to raise the production of a specific crop among large numbers of small-holders dependent on rain-fed agriculture. Having a smaller range of aims than IRDPs, and not calling for heavy investments in irrigation, these projects have the advantage of costing less per beneficiary and having fewer inherent organizational problems than IRDPs. Perhaps as a result there are more unambiguous successes. The Kenya Tea Development Authority, assisted by a sequence of aid-funded projects over two decades, is one; it supports well over 100,000 small-holder growers producing high-quality tea and providing one of the country's main foreign exchange earners, and it has succeeded in creating an effective organization staffed almost entirely by Kenyans. Cotton in Chad and maize in Mali are further examples.[33]

But these projects also have their problems especially in countries (often the poorer ones) where the effectiveness of the civil service as a whole is low. They rely in many cases on improving the efficiency of the extension service—often subject to constraints beyond the control of the project—and on a flow of economically and ecologically sound recommendations from the research service which may not be forthcoming. They may rely for input supplies and output marketing on public sector agencies that are themselves weak, or on a poorly developed private sector. Moreover, those that are based on rain-fed production have to allow for high levels of variability. It is not surprising, therefore, that these projects, too, often run into difficulties, again most often in Africa, less often in Asia.

Irrigation. Irrigation has played a central role in increasing food supplies in developing countries over the past two decades. Recent World Bank estimates are that 20 per cent of the harvested area in these countries is irrigated, that this land receives 60 per cent of all fertilizer applied, and that it produces 40 per cent of all crops. Food production in large parts of the South Asian sub-continent is now relatively independent of the monsoon.

(i) *Trends in aid to irrigation.* Irrigation has been one of the main users of aid to agriculture: over the years 1976–80, irrigation has taken between 16 and 22 per cent of total official bilateral and multilateral commitments to agriculture (between 22 and 30 per cent for multilateral agencies, and 11 to 14 per cent for bilateral agencies). Commitments to irrigation by bilateral and multilateral donors rose over the five years 1976–81, from $763 million to $2,193 million, but fell sharply in 1981 to $1,230 million. The World Bank group has played a leading role in support of irrigation: over the five years 1976–80, 53 per cent of all official commitments to irrigation development came from it.

Aid for irrigation development has been concentrated in South Asia and the Far East: over 1977–81, each of these regions received annually between a quarter to a third of total official commitments to irrigation. Over 1977–80, sub-Saharan Africa's share of DAC commitments to irrigation fluctuated in the range 6–13 per cent. Aid is not the only source of funds. In the Middle East, South Asia, and the Far East there has been very substantial locally financed investment in irrigation, carried out by the public and private sectors, privately financed development being mostly very small-scale.[34]

The World Bank's assessment of the irrigation projects which it has supported has come up with favourable conclusions concerning their economic viability. In a review of forty World Bank assisted irrigation projects over 1961–71, it was concluded that all but eight projects had economic rates of return of 10 per cent or better, with more than half exceeding 15 per cent.[35] Almost half of the projects undertaken exceeded their projected economic rates of return, although this was mainly due to substantially higher than anticipated prices, which were often sufficient to do more than offset physical performance below what was projected.

In a more recent World Bank survey of project performance,[36] an equally favourable view of the economic viability of investment in irrigation emerges. The eleven irrigation projects examined yielded a weighted economic rate of return of 24 per cent, slightly in excess of the average for agriculture as a whole. Irrigation projects had a higher cost per beneficiary, $394, than the average for agricultural projects of $294. However, the average is depressed by the relatively low cost per beneficiary of area development projects, although in such projects 'beneficiaries' may be no more than marginally affected. In comparison to livestock, settlement, forestry, credit, and processing projects, irrigation emerges with the lowest cost per beneficiary.

In this same review, average costs of employment creation were calculated, where data allowed, and, in this respect, irrigation came out with by far the lowest average costs. Although irrigation accounted for just 22 per cent of the costs of the agricultural projects reviewed, it was estimated to have provided 67 per cent of the total employment created by these projects. The reason for this was the high labour intensity of the improved technology promoted by irrigation projects.

The picture of irrigation projects is not universally favourable, however. Other agencies have tended to come to less positive conclusions concerning the impact of irrigation development. USAID in a major review concluded that multilateral and bilateral projects generally had not realized their potential.[37] In a recent summary of its experience, the IDB reports that three out of four evaluation exercises conducted on irrigation projects came to conclusions which were 'not very positive'; in one sample, the weighted average economic rate of return on the projects was about −1 per cent.[38] On the other hand the UK has had successful experiences—in Jordan for example; so has France in francophone Africa. Today there is some evidence of a falling-off in aid for irrigation, perhaps reflecting a mood of questioning among donors. But it continues to be a field for major aid activity.

(ii) *Current issues in irrigation development*. Certain issues feature consistently in evaluations of irrigation prospects. Three near-universal aspects of the execution of irrigation development are time delays, cost overruns, and under-funding of key components. Although the World Bank's 1983 review of project performance audits, cited earlier, came to generally favourable conclusions, it nevertheless found cost overruns and implementation delays to be, in both cases, twice the average for the agricultural sector as a whole. The basic reason appears to be the size and complexity of major irrigation projects. It is crucial that discrete activities in construction take place at the scheduled time, but this often does not happen, either because of unanticipated physical problems or because of weaknesses in the bureaucracies charged with implementation. An obvious inference from this experience is that at the appraisal stage planners should be much less sanguine in their assumptions about implementation and the immediate impact on production, especially where projects are large and complex.

There are also difficulties associated with management and maintenance. Many large surface water systems, particularly those designed to earlier standards, are now only marginally manageable. They were not designed for the flexible water supply response needed to match the varying water demand of modern agriculture. This calls for modernization well beyond simple rehabilitation, involving replanning the system to meet new performance criteria. But there is often a need for rehabilitation too. Insidious deterioration normally resulting from deferred maintenence has rendered whole systems dangerously vulnerable and segments of the canal network partially inoperative.

Maintenance is commonly deficient in part because engineers, civil servants, and donors find investing in new schemes more attractive, and in part because of the difficulty of raising funds to meet recruitment costs. This issue is closely linked with that of cost recovery. In recent years funding issues have become more pressing, for a number of reasons. First, although many schemes implemented in the 1960s and 1970s did not envisage the full recovery of capital or recurrent costs, the extent of cost-recovery has nevertheless fallen behind what was planned, as a result of a failure of governments to inflation-index charges to farmers fully. Second, the extreme constraints on government recurrent spending in many developing countries at the present time has caused both governments and aid agencies to re-examine the case for subsidizing irrigation. While it is obvious that this issue requires review, moves towards increased cost recovery should proceed cautiously, with a sensitivity to the possible production and equity effects, especially in cases where the deficiencies of marketing, pricing, and other policies and institutions unduly depress farmers' earnings. Interestingly, a recent internal World Bank document finds that good maintenance and general effectiveness of some water systems are correlated with cost recovery from users.

Management problems are often associated with the relatively low priority given to the training and motivation of irrigation managers. Solutions may lie in the reorganization of irrigation bureaucracies, with better pay, training, career structures, and safeguards against corruption. In many cases another dimension will be greater involvement in management by participant farmers. An important current development is the establishment in Sri Lanka of an International Irrigation Management Institute, mainly funded by the CGIAR.

Other concerns are that irrigation development can have damaging environmental effects, which have often been ignored in economic evaluations. The impact on health can be adverse; for example, slow-moving channels can be breeding grounds for malaria-bearing mosquitos and schistosomiasis-bearing snails. Soil salination can develop insidiously, as a result of poor drainage or waterlogging, with possibly extremely damaging long-term effects. It has become a major problem, especially in South Asia, associated with the older irrigation systems. Salination can be averted by better drainage and better designed and higher-specification water delivery systems (lining of channels and more field channels) and by the installation of sub-surface drainage. Drainage may not be necessary in the early years of the project; it is unlikely to be installed at initial implementation because of the further construction costs, land taken out of cultivation, maintenance problems, and uncertainty in predicting the extent to which salination will build up on a particular scheme. When it becomes essential to install sub-surface drainage, it often appears a rather unglamorous investment; it has no short-term impact on production, and may attract the opposition of farmers unwilling to accept disruption to their fields. Nonetheless, in numerous sites in the developing countries, installation of sub-surface drainage is an urgent priority.

As noted elsewhere, irrigation is one of the subjects where inter-agency sharing of experience is relatively advanced. Thus much current thinking in the agencies is going into the design of 'new generation' surface irrigation projects for South Asia, where timing and quantity of water has to be made more responsive to the needs of new crop varieties; rehabilitation of older systems will require major finance also. Tube-well irrigation is less problematic and will continue to be supported, but it has more limited scope. In Africa, where costs per irrigated acre are often high and the institutional base weaker, there is considerably debate about future directions, and still scope for more intensive investigation of what has worked and what has not.

Livestock projects in Africa. Accumulated evidence from project evaluations indicates that the livestock subsector has given rise to a higher degree of failure in project results than any other. The World Bank again provides much the most comprehensive experience (although USAID's knowledge is also considerable, particularly with regard to livestock production) and summarizes it in its annual reviews of project performance results. Between 1979 and 1983, thirty-five projects were reviewed: eleven—almost a third—were reckoned to have been unsatisfactory. Problem projects also had a geographical focus: seven of the eleven disappointing livestock projects were in sub-Saharan Africa.[39]

The findings of these evaluations accord with a less systematically recorded but widespread concern among those involved with the sub-sector. USAID organized a workshop on pastoralism and African livestock development in 1979 which 'was inspired by a pervasive though not well-documented sense in the planning community that livestock sector interventions in semi-arid regions had seldom achieved the expectations held for them';[40] 88 per cent of the participants in the workshop who answered a questionnaire agreed with the statement 'Livestock development projects in Africa have poor performance records'.[41] This conclusion accords with the results of the rather few livestock projects reviewed by the country case studies in the aid effectiveness study (see, for example, Kenya).

The major sources of concern that have been expressed are as follows.

1. Livestock projects have achieved low economic rates of return. The twelve livestock projects covered by the World Bank's 1983 review of project performance results had an average rate of return of 2 per cent, and 7 were actually negative.)
2. Livestock projects may be environmentally harmful if they result in increases in animal populations on an already overstocked range. There is, however, no consensus on this issue (except to agree that data are inadequate to permit a definitive conclusion). A recent work[42] contrasts the 'mainstream view' that ranges are under great pressure from grazing animals with the view that ranges are highly resilient, and that pastoralists are more capable of rational stock control than they are normally credited with. There is, however, more general agreement that provision of per-

manent water (e.g. from deep bores) in areas of low rainfall is likely to lead to localized degradation of the range.

3. Livestock projects do not adequately address the social implications of intervention and often ignore issues of inequality.

The major reasons for the frequent failure of these projects are as follows.

(a) Lack of knowledge of social factors. Planners and managers frequently have very little understanding of social structures and processes, with the consequent likelihood that intervention will be inappropriate and possibly harmful.

(b) Weakness in the technical base. In few other sectors is the margin of error so wide on key parameters, and the level of understanding among outsiders of the nature of the constraints on the existing system so low, as in the case of pastoralism. At the same time, planners often undervalue or ignore the accumulated knowledge of pastoralists.

(c) Over-complex project design. Some livestock projects, as with some integrated agricultural projects, have involved diverse components and have set out to intervene in several sectors (water, roads, etc.), and have thereby increased the complexity of the management task and the need for horizontal coordination between vertically structured agencies. It is rare, although not unknown, for this coordination to be effective.

(d) Unsatisfactory organization and management both within the project and in the parent institution, commonly a government agency. The many livestock projects that involved public sector production fared particularly badly in this respect. The normal operating problems of ministries and other public sector agencies are frequently exacerbated in the livestock sub-sector by the fact that many interventions are attempting to develop new organizations and even organizational forms, as with pastoralist associations. Institutional forms introduced by aid projects to manage common grazing lands have been almost completely ineffective, when attempted at all. Without them, raising pastoralists' herd sizes may be harmful.

(e) Some aspects of the policy environment. National and sectoral policies may undermine project viability by reducing profitability and thus militating against investment in the sector. Policies found to have this effect include overvaluation of the national currency; export bans; taxation on exporters; and controls—intended to benefit consumers—on meat prices.

(f) The political weakness of pastoral populations in the modern state. In many countries, pastoral populations have relatively poor access to the levers of political power, and are thus unable to ensure that their interests are fully taken into account in the political process.

Looking to the future, the USAID workshop reached consensus that 'if they are to have favourable and beneficial impacts on producer populations, national wealth, and environmental conditions, livestock sector programs and projects must be reoriented to make them more nearly compatible with the social, economic, and environmental realities of arid and semi-arid pastoral regions of Africa'.

Lessons from agricultural projects

Agricultural projects provide a wealth of experience of the factors that are conducive to making the most effective use of aid to the sector. All this experience is documented in donors' evaluation reports, and some actions, for example, the abandonment of many IRDPs, indicate that some lessons have been learned. It is one of the major conclusions of this study of the effectiveness of aid, however, that there is still room for improvement—not all lessons are learnt; or, if learnt, their pre-scriptions are overruled by other priorities; or they may be forgotten as time passes. The following paragraphs outline some of the often familiar lessons that donors and recipients have not always fully taken into account as they design interventions in the agricultural sector.

Where projects have run into trouble, it is often because they have attempted to persuade cultivators to abandon existing practices in favour of new ones without sufficient testing of the new ones. Insuffi-cient account is often taken of the uncertainties associated with farm-ing and hence the increased risk of loss that may be associated with higher levels of imports. The component studies describe cases where this has occurred—Nigeria, Ghana, Cameroon, India, Kenya, and Malawi.[43] Very often the introduction of new techniques has been rushed because the project staff thought that a technique which had worked well in one place would work well in a 'similar' place, only to discover at leisure that either the natural or the social environment was not similar enough. In the dry areas of Machakos, Kenya, far-mers were advised to depend on monoculture of maize, because that had substantially raised incomes in *wetter* areas of the country;[44] the Upper Region Development Project in Ghana was modelled by the World Bank on experience in dry areas of northern Nigeria (where, however, the infrastructure was a great deal more developed), leading to serious problems of input supply and marketing.[45] In other cases schemes were planned for 'modal' farmers, only for project staff to discover subsequently that very few farmers were clustered at the mode of the distribution, and that smaller farmers in particular were unable to take advantage of the recommendations offered to them.[46] In all of these cases, the outcome has been that many farmers, particularly poor ones, have concluded that compliance with the project's recommendations would impose on them a quite unacceptable increase in risk.

The tendency for agricultural projects to extend unsound recommendations has both technical and economic origins. Agricultural research, especially in Africa, although in drier areas everywhere, has generally failed to generate the flow of relevant recommendations on which a resilient and dynamic agriculture depends. Much of the strength of Indian agriculture has been based on a seed–fertilizer–water package that does not have its counterpart for most other farming systems. Providing this counterpart for other areas, tailored to local circumstances, must be a prerequisite for better project performance, and represents one of the very highest medium-term priorities for aid programmes.

The economic origins of unviable recommendations are both microeconomic—the failure fully to take account of the farmer's resource constraints; and macroeconomic—an inappropriate policy environment. The current emphasis placed on farming systems studies indicates the extent to which the former is now widely acknowledged, and these studies deserve continued support. Persistent weaknesses in the policy environment—in particular the price paid for the farmer's output—are a source of concern. The increase in recent years in aid given in programme and sector form with associated policy dialogue is in part due to a recognition of the extent to which projects are hampered by the policy context in which they operate. However, much policy dialogue has been slow to yield its intended results, for reasons discussed in Chapter 4, and studies show that in the past, agricultural projects have been hampered by inadequate prices in, for example, Mali, Malawi, and Senegal.[47] It seems, indeed, to be in Africa especially that the ability of urban political interests to overcome the combined force of technocrats and farmers is greatest; but it is encouraging that, as reported in Chapter 4, numerous African countries are now undertaking price policy reforms.

Other problems extraneous to the competence of project management also remain. The shortage of local counterpart staff, which has already been discussed above, is at its most serious in the remote rural areas of every country, and hence falls disproportionately on aid projects in the agriculture and natural resources sector. The same observation applies to other inputs financed out of local costs: building materials, diesel oil, money to finance mechanical repairs. Land reform, finally, is close to being a prerequisite of success of small farmer projects in many countries; but donors, with some exceptions, have perhaps understandably been reluctant to press this issue.

Finally, the continuing need for improved performance by implementing institutions is emphasized by many of the studies of agricultural projects that have run into trouble. Such weaknesses are often the result of a failure of the recipient's commitment, and an increase in such commitment will be necessary to future improvement. Donors, too, must play their part by taking greater care not to overload the institutions with excessive, premature, or inappropriate tasks, and by being prepared to give their support to strengthening these institutions in a more careful, consistent, precisely focused, and long-term form than has often been the case in the past.

IV   Industrial Projects

Introduction

This section discusses the lessons that can be drawn from the performance of aid in a different set of sectors: mainly manufacturing industry, including the small-scale sector. It is not difficult here, as elsewhere, to find instances of 'problem projects' and even of 'horror stories'. There is always much to be learnt from such cases—one or two are cited below to help establish the point. But there is now enough empirical evidence and broad understanding available to permit a more general assessment. It is also instructive to take a broad view of the evolution of aid practices, and to identify the key lessons that have emerged at different stages.

It is widely believed that projects in physical infrastructure and industry are easier to manage than projects in natural resources. However, the available statistical evidence does not suggest that they are always more successful; World Bank documents already cited show power and water projects as having satisfactory rates of return but, on average, lower than agricultural projects.[48] The problems are not less, but different. The difficulties associated with adapting a project to a very specific physical and social environment may appear small in the case of industry and infrastructure. But the problems of appropriate technology and of management are larger; the projects are peculiarly vulnerable to interruption or quality variation in input supplies; and there is no less vulnerability to domestic or international market conditions. In some cases, projects may be technically satisfactory but low returns are due to pricing policy—in other words, they make contributions to the economy but their distribution is affected by subsidy.

Trends in industrial lending

Until well into the 1970s there was a widespread assumption that industrialization would play a leading role in development, and would rely importantly on (large-scale) projects in sectors such as fertilizer, steel, and textiles. In most regions, of which sub-Saharan Africa would be the most prominent example, there was a natural presumption that such projects would be run by the state, or at least that the state would not hesitate to do so in the absence of a private sector capability.

There was also a general confidence that demand—in the main domestic demand, because the projects were seen as import substituting—would not be a limiting factor; and that the management capability could be developed, if it did not exist already, to handle all aspects of constructing the plant and then producing and distributing the output. In some cases, most notably the Indian fertilizer sector, there was even sufficient confidence to embark on a series of projects containing significant innovations in process technology and in the scale of operations.

With hindsight, without questioning the goals of this industrialization or whether they would be attained (or already have been), it is easy to see that there was a certain naïvety about this approach. In some if not most cases, all elements of the projects proved more difficult than had been imagined. Time and cost overruns in implementation were the rule rather than the exception; plants operated at well below break-even capacity utilization for a mixture of reasons, such as poor management capability, internal inefficiencies, input supply and power constraints, or low demand. Tariff and pricing policies were such that, combined with the poor technical performance, several projects turned out to be inefficient in terms of foreign exchange utilization; they also turned out to be financially much weaker than they should have been.

Not all these problems could have been foreseen. Many of these projects date from the 1960s. The big and prolonged impact on demand and on costs in the 1970s could not have been anticipated until the oil price increases started in 1973. Also, it must be understood that there was at the time a certain imperative about industrialization and a commitment to get on and do things, plus a confidence that things could be successfully done through the chosen route; even the World Bank in that period was drawn into being a massive investor in large-scale public sector enterprises.

Some of these investment programmes have undoubtedly been successful. Indian fertilizers are a case in point; despite formidable teething problems in some plants and a degree of overall plant utilization that remains unsatisfactorily low, there is a general feeling that the technological and management problems have been very largely overcome and that the indigenous capability exists for substantial further development of the sector. The UK, among other donors, has had broadly successful experience with its aid there, contributing to that capability as well as to investment in production. German aid has also been successful with a major fertilizer plant in Egypt.

Aid has undoubtedly played a beneficial role in many cases. Sometimes the vital contribution has been to influence the design of the projects, typically by reducing the scale. In a few cases, governments have been dissuaded from proceeding with overly ambitious schemes. More generally, transfer of technology has been facilitated because of donors' financing of technical assistance and management support. But by no means all success is due to aid: again to take Indian fertilizers, it was an independent decision by central government to break up the national corporation into smaller and more effective regional units that has now greatly enhanced the management capability of the sector.

But, despite the particular successes achieved, it remains true to say that the 1950s–1970s pattern of big industrial projects is not widely regarded as successful. There is now a lot of surplus capacity, as well as the need in many countries to rehabilitate plant—in some cases whole sectors—to make it function efficiently and competitively. Several donors are disappointed with their experience in this field. One is cited as finding that nearly all its large aid projects in industry are 'running at deficits contrary to the feasibility studies'.[49]

Further, looking to the future, a new set of issues have emerged as critical to industrialization. Big shifts in technology, both in existing and in brand-new industries, as well as in industrial and consumer demand in the industrialized countries, have left developing countries with narrow options and tighter markets. At the same time, a general deterioration of their foreign exchange position has placed a further premium on exports. Also, the public sector has become overstretched in its implementing capacity, and budgetary pressures have meant shortages of inputs as well as inadequacies in maintenance programmes.

For these and related reasons, the past few years have seen the emergence of new approaches to industrialization and the role of external aid. Over and above the need to restructure whole sectors as well as individual companies and projects (made feasible also by the fact that very few new large projects are being put forward), this approach is characterized by four principal emphases:

(i) a better appreciation of the limitations of public sector bodies as implementing agents in the industrial sector. There is correspondingly an awareness of the limitations of the influence that most individual aid agencies can bring to bear on the full range of issues that affect project performance;

(ii) a much sharper focus on management capabilities at the company and project levels, seeking wherever possible to enhance the private sector's role (the need for long-term technical back-up and training is almost always underestimated);

(iii) a corresponding focus on the sectoral and sub-sectoral context of projects. Pricing, markets, and marketing, choice of technology, stability and quality of inputs, development of management, and technical skills—these are all now better understood as issues that cannot be addressed at the level of the individual project but require a broader approach.

(iv) at a higher level of aggregation, paying attention to the overall policy environment in which the sector operates. There are several dimensions to this: the financial regime, comprising fiscal, interest rate, and overall performance considerations; economic efficiency, revolving round the concept of effective protection; institutional issues, particularly in respect of establishing the right relationships between national policy interests and narrower project and sectoral interests.

In parallel with the above approach, most highly developed in the multilateral agencies, is a renewed emphasis by many bilateral donors on the small-scale sector. Some of the same elements of thinking are evident in this too. There is, for instance, a general desire to work with non-governmental organizations in the recipient countries and to enhance the private sector role. There is more attention paid than previously to management, marketing, and choice of technology suited to the local context. There is greater awareness, too, that for maximizing developmental impact it is not just the individual project that matters but also its institutional and policy context.

Development finance corporations. Understanding development finance corporations (DFCs) helps to appreciate the approach to the small-scale sector. They have played a prominent part in aid to the industrial sector, particularly from the World Bank group, the regional development banks, and the larger bilateral donors. DFCs were originally conceived in the 1950s as institutions in the private sector whose main goals would be long-term development of domestic capital markets (in particular by introducing term lending for industrial projects) and mobilization of domestic resources for capital formation.

Over time, these objectives were widened and somewhat modified. DFCs were seen as useful vehicles both for the swift transfer of aid resources and, in some countries, provided their own performance was such as to create external confidence, potentially also for attracting resources from international capital markets. They were seen too as offering a vehicle for aid agencies' assistance to the small- and medium-sized industrial sector. Much effort was made to introduce into the institutions the concepts of economic appraisal as well as effective systems for loan processing. The 'requirement' that they be private sector institutions was relaxed. And with the increasing involvement of the public sector came a tendency in some cases for DFCs to be used as instruments of government policy in such areas as export promotion and regional development.

Until about the turn of the present decade (with the important exception of DFCs in most Latin American countries) there was little questioning of this basic model. But very poor financial performance of the corporate sector in many countries exposed the financial weakness of perhaps the majority of DFCs, and then in turn other deficiencies.

At the risk of creating an exaggerated impression, and of not allowing adequately for important exceptions to these generalizations, it is simplest to itemize the problems that have become evident:

(i) DFCs tended to remain too dependent on their relationship with donor agencies. In some cases this protected them from exchange risks and gave them no incentive to become more competitive in raising resources from elsewhere.

(ii) They tended to regard themselves as special institutions, insulated from the changes taking place elsewhere in the financial sector and hence not having to compete for clients. With the principal exception of sub-Saharan Africa, where the banking sector and other financial institutions were and still are not well-developed, this view was not justified.

(iii) As a consequence, DFCs have in only relatively few cases become more than marginal financial institutions, with a very low presence in the market.

(iv) DFCs, even those in the private sector, proved too formal and (in effect) forbidding in their style to be able to penetrate the very small-scale sector. Those in the public sector were also too bureaucratic for this purpose.

(v) Despite the efforts at institution building, some DFCs had acquired dangerously unbalanced portfolios, with excessive exposure in weak sectors, and had poor systems of financial control and a high incidence of arrears.

(vi) Interest rate and other policies in the financial sector were sometimes such as not to give DFCs the incentive to deploy their resources in an economically efficient manner.

(vii) Government intervention was rife, whether for strategic policy or narrower purposes, and few DFCs had had the chance to develop into strong institutions with the requisitely high degree of autonomy.

(viii) The aid agencies themselves tended to be too preoccupied with protecting their own portfolio in the DFCs, and lost sight of the problems facing the institutions as a totality.

Many of these problems are the findings of experience of European aid agencies. But some had become evident earlier in Latin America, where there was already a well-developed banking sector. DFCs of the 'classic' kind consequently have not generally proved popular there. Instead, maximum reliance has been placed on working with and through the commercial banking network, which of course has multiple outlets. Aid funds have been chanelled through a so-called 'apex' institution—the central bank if necessary—to the commercial banks; and associated with this has been a programme of developing the banks' appraisal and other capacities, especially in dealing with small enterprises.

A broadly similar approach is currently being evolved in aid to DFCs elsewhere (with the chief exception of much of Africa, where the earlier model is thought still to be necessary pending further development of the local banking system). This emphasis on utilizing and developing the commercial banks is being supplemented—in the World Bank group at least—by a new focus on the policies that influence the financial and industrial sectors. Interest rate, fiscal, and tariff structures; investment and export incentives; sectoral and sub-sectoral development policies; technical assistance for small firms, and management training more generally—these are among the areas of key concern for the future.

Small-scale industry. Despite the prominence given to the small-scale sector in development thinking over the past fifteen years or so, it remains fair to say that aid agencies (and recipient governments) have generally not found it easy to penetrate and have an impact on the sector. Provision of finance through DFCs (see above) has not proved especially effective. Provision of industrial estates has proved unattractive to small firms, because they are typically too expensive, 'smart', and formal for such firms, especially at their very early stages of development.

The Netherlands Development Finance Co. (FMO) has gravitated to a format for lending to small-scale enterprises which appears to be working well. It works with a local development bank, joining with it as a minority stockholder to establish a new entity devoted exclusively to such financing. It participates closely in establishing the organization, procedures, and policies of the entity, helps with training and foreign advisers if needed in the early stages, and participates actively in the deliberations of the board. The entities charge market rates. They consistently aim to draw in the commercial banks to provide normal working capital to their clients. One of the early examples (in Malawi) has elicited several hundred applicants, even though earlier studies had suggested that very little potential existed in the country.[50] SIDA's 'Sister Industry Programme', which links Swedish and recipient country firms, has also had many positive results, as have ADB and Canadian aid too.

How best to organize provision of technical assistance alongside financial assistance remains an unresolved issue in many countries. Some agencies have found, for instance, that attempting to deal with specific small-industry projects involves extremely diverse market, technological, institutional, and other circumstances which do not lend themselves to a consolidated approach, and which require expertise that cannot be readily mobilized with limited staff and other resources. There is also an extreme dearth of experts who combine a sound conceptual and practical grasp of the whole sector with the know-how and personal judgement to operate efficiently.

Because of disappointment in the effectiveness of these direct measures, there is in some quarters a trend to argue for the greater efficacy of indirect measures. In particular, it is argued that the best way of promoting small industrial firms is through accelerated development in the agricultural and rural sectors. Rising rural incomes will, on this argument, raise demand for goods and services well suited to supply by small firms; and rising agricultural output will open up new entrepreneurial opportunities on both the input and output (agro-processing) sides. (One danger to which aid agencies and recipients must be sensitive in this regard is that they may unwittingly inhibit such opportunities. One aid project involved the provision of small tools and agricultural instruments. An internal evaluation study found that to a substantial extent this was undercutting the market for small manufacturers in the country. A modified project was developed which stimulated and used the local production of such items where the potential could be found.[51])

There is clearly much validity in this argument, to which the two states of Punjab (in India and Pakistan) bear ample testimony. But there is nevertheless something to be learnt from the (continuing) efforts to assist the small-scale sector directly. Among these lessons are:

(i) There is seldom a need for financial subsidies. The critical issue facing the typical start-up or small firm is that of *access* to credit (or other facilities), and not price. In the absence of access in the formal sector, the alternative is bazaar money at very high rates.

(ii) Consequently, mechanisms must be constructed that both in style and substance are properly suited to the needs of the entrepreneur.

Issues in aid for industry

Technical choice. It is easy for an aid administrator, as for any other official, to suffer from tunnel vision. In subjecting proposals to rigorous appraisal, he or she may fail to ask: could this be done another way? The question embraces not only choice of technology but also choice of sub-sector. Thus, a poor country wishes to increase its output of energy; it makes proposals for hydro-powered generating stations to donor agencies. Some donors will subject the proposal to rigorous cost–benefit analysis. But they may not ask whether a thermal power station or a number of solar-powered units could produce a greater output per unit of input and, if so, what the implications would be for the location of the generating facilities and the transmission of power; and they will almost certainly not ask whether the aid resources should go into generating electricity or more traditional forms of energy such as wood-fuel. This is not a purely hypothetical example; it describes fairly accurately the behaviour of donor agencies in Kenya, as reported in the case study for that country.

Project disappointments probably arise as often from failure to take a broad enough view of the considerations bearing on their success as from inadequate sophistication and rigour in analysis. A power project intended to obviate the need for inefficient generators in Bali hotels, while technically sound, did not have the desired result because hotel management did not trust the utility to provide dependable supply, and because the cost of self-supply was mitigated by tax incentives. When quick action is needed to meet imminent shortages, the danger that it will not be practical to explore all relevant aspects may be particularly acute. Other similar projects looked at for this report proved ineffective because of tariff and accounting problems in some cases, excessive scale and costs in others.[52] Lack of adequate technical competence in appraisal can also lead to mis-judgements. A report on several fibre projects in Egypt found that mistaken technical assumptions rendered the economic appraisals 'meaningless'. A rubber project in Indonesia incorporated technology requiring skilled labour unavailable in the vicinity. 'Either [the tech-nology] should have been simpler or else more effort ought to have been put into technical assistance and training.'[53]

The argument that sophisticated, even if narrowly focused, appraisal techniques may have pre-empted more basic scrutiny of alternative engineering technologies and other design variables has been forcefully put:

Although the project material (from bilateral agencies) available to us was limited a number of commonalities did emerge, most notably:

(a) insufficient consideration of alternative project locations;
(b) inadequate examination of raw material supplies in terms of quantity, quality and cost;
(c) poor treatment of packaging and transportation of finished products;
(d) under-estimation of the time required to complete projects and the dura-tion and amount of technical assistance required in operation;
(e) a failure to structure project maintenance and provide spares accord-ingly . . .

. . . We found (among bilateral agencies) no internationally accepted approach to the choice of technology . . . A number of evaluation reports suggest that avoidable, poor technology has led to ineffective projects. It occurs to us that, by getting their act together so effectively, economists may unwittingly have pre-empted scarce resources, to address their professional concerns, that could have been better spent on examining other facets of projects.[54]

And one might add that most multilateral agencies do not find it easy to formulate guidelines governing technological choice. It could be argued that the World Bank took unnecessary risks in agreeing to essentially unproven technology for large fertilizer plants in the 1970s (mostly but not only in India), and that that was one of the reasons for time and cost overruns before the factories were commissioned. The International Finance Corporation (IFC) stands as possibly an excep-tion among agencies. Its approach is simple and businesslike: the chosen technology must have been *commercially* proven elsewhere, including any question of scaling-up. This has also generally been the position taken by USAID in financing major capital projects, particularly power and fertilizer plants. The review of European aid projects done for this study concluded that 'modern technologies are best fully proved in domestic commercial usage at the specific scale before being exported overseas. Scaling down or up is problematic.'

On the other hand, administrators can be excessively rigid and conservative. The same study quoted the energy specialist in the Netherlands Directorate-General for International Cooperation to the effect that:

despite growing experience elsewhere there is a ready assumption at some (country) desks that drinking water projects should use diesel fuel for pumping whereas wind or solar energy might be feasible; similarly there is a tendency to link electricity generating and transmission schemes into a national grid rather than to establish small-scale and more manageable local systems.

Of course, a manager may have legitimate concerns about the dependability or acceptability of technical alternatives; in appropriate cases, testing of alternatives in early stages of programme development may be feasible.

It is not only the choice of technology which needs prior scrutiny. Another choice is that of product among a range of substitutes. Nairobi and Lilongwe now have over-large and economically disappointing international airports financed by overseas aid,[55] not because they were built with the wrong technology, but because insufficient care was given to the relative share which air transport should occupy within the national transport budget.

Location. Another important design variable is that of location, which can so easily be a function of political rather than economic considerations. The record here too is mixed. At one extreme are projects quite evidently mis-located with respect to one or more (usually a combination) of markets, raw material, and public utilities suppliers, labour skills, and the like; some of these are noted in the supporting reports. At the other extreme are well-located projects, and also aid agencies satisfied that choice of location is always rigorously examined.

Tying. That there are certain technology and high import biases apparent in some industry and infrastructure projects is in part the result of source tying by bilateral donors who are trying to sell turbine generators, telephone exchanges, railway wagons, or other equipment made by domestic companies. The costs of tying have been demonstrated and measured for many years now;[56] further examples are recorded in the component reports of this study,[57] where cases are cited in which suppliers' commercial pressures, financed by tied aid, have resulted in profoundly unsatisfactory projects. The persistence of the practice, indeed its increase through mixed credits, is a commentary on the weight of domestic political and commercial criteria over considerations of economic effectiveness in aid ministries during the present recession.

Rectifying deficiencies. Technical deficiencies in project design of the kind noted above can often be rectified in the course of project implementation and operation. Hirschman's 'Principle of the Hiding Hand'[58] finds confirmation in the constituent studies: construction of rural access roads in Kenya and Malawi was switched to labour-intensive methods following experience of using both capital-intensive and labour-intensive methods in tandem;[59] rural water schemes in Tanzania were switched from steel to bamboo pipes, following the appearance of leaks in the plastic pipes.[60] This is effective learning. One way of encouraging it is to take advice from the right place; in particular, from people with local expertise. As an extension of this same principle, the scheme currently favoured by the German Bundesministerium für Zusammenarbeit, by which German entrepreneurs are encouraged to link up with African businessmen—in the areas of car repair, electrical contracting, steel fabrication, construction, and the use of second-hand machinery—seems highly promising.[61]

Concluding comments. One of the purposes of discussing aid to industrial projects, DFCs, and the small-scale sector has been to seek to show the ongoing nature of the learning process. That there have been mistakes in the past—strategic and project-specific—is undeniable. But that fundamental lessons have been learnt is undeniable too. And the fact that there remain unresolved questions, and that doubtless new and unexpected issues will arise in the future, does not gainsay the fact that a body of experience has been accumulated, and productive assets created, on which to build in future.

There are four general lessons. *First*, the primacy of the market must not be overlooked. There has been a persistent tendency to inflate market expectations, both on price and sales volume, and to ignore the effects of market segmentation on process and product design and quality. Insufficient attention has been paid to the strategic role and the practicalities of marketing and distribution. These will become increasingly important issues in what can be expected to be an increasingly competitive trading environment in the future.

The *second* lesson has to do with management. Given reasonable technical and market circumstances, management is commonly the weakest element of individual projects. There are both institutional and personnel aspects to this, which are most simply dealt with by discussing what generally is required to improve project management in the future. The principal need at the personnel level is for a strong, committed, and financially motivated chief executive clearly having the authority required and (save in exceptional circumstances) the assurance of continuity. He or she must have a very high degree of autonomy, be able to select and build a balanced team, and must understand the relevant markets.

At the level of organizational structure the critical need is, to put it somewhat bluntly, to be insulated from political interference and from being regarded by government as an operational tool for short-term policy purposes. In both DFCs and large industrial projects, excessive government intervention has often had a damaging impact. For public sector projects, clear financial goals and policy guidelines must be established by government; and strategic, not tactical, mechanisms used to achieve satisfactory performance. In some countries a balance may have to be struck in employment between the presence of indigenous and expatriate management personnel in order to achieve technical competence in the appropriate style.

It is interesting to ask why, given that poor management has long been understood to be a critical weakness in industrial projects, it has proved so difficult to eliminate the problem. Apart from those cases where insufficient attention has been paid to the matter, the answer probably is that it is genuinely hard in individual cases to judge who are the right people and what is the right structure. The experience of IFC is instructive: despite the fact that most of their concerned projects staff are experienced industrial managers and that they recognize in principle what critical features to look for, they know that they are prone to making errors of judgement in approving or helping select key managers for the projects they assist.

The *third* lesson is simple and, one may hope, no longer seen as controversial or ideological: the weight of experience shows the many advantages of private sector implementation for a wide range of industrial projects. This does not mean that the public sector should never get involved—there are clearly some countries and some types of investment for which such a posture would be quite unrealistic. But it is placing an enterprise in the public sector rather than the private sector that requires justification. Where domestic capability is limited, governments should not be inhibited from seeking foreign assistance to help introduce the approach and financial discipline of the private sector.

A particular facet of this issue, which also bears on the general management question, should be noted: the use of foreign consultants. Experience is mixed. There are some outstanding success stories, including some where long-term joint ventures between local and foreign firms have been created. But there is a dearth internationally of consultants having the requisite operational experience, and great care is needed in selection not just of the consulting firm but of the actual individuals who will do the work. It is also necessary in some cases to guard carefully against friction arising between local and expatriate personnel; and the consultants must have a real financial incentive to perform satisfactorily on all counts. Finally, any consultancy arrangement must be accompanied by a serious programme of management and technical training of local personnel.

The *fourth* and last general lesson concerns the policy and institutional environment surrounding individual projects and other forms of assistance. These considerations were noted before, but are so important that they are worth repeating. It is now well understood that factors technically external to an individual project can have a decisive influence not only on its performance in its own terms but also on its wider economic impact. The strong trend evident in the aid agencies to sectoral and policy analysis—whether on prices, institutional arrangements, or other aspects—in order to get the right boundary conditions and general environment for individual projects is thoroughly justified.

V   Education and Population

Education

Education is quite a substantial aid recipient—some $2.5 billion a year of DAC bilateral commitments in recent years: the World Bank and IDA approved some $700 million of loans for education in fiscal 1984. The sector probably receives in the region of 10 per cent of all aid.[62] The World Bank's 1980 *World Development Report* gave wide publicity to evidence of the importance of education in national development, as well as in individuals' lives—it has a high rate of return as a form of investment, and its value ramifies into health and family planning, into agriculture, industry, and government. But progress is slow—where countries are now in education depends on where they were twenty years ago—and hence educational development is both long-term and urgent; the later the start, the longer until satisfactory levels are reached.

Educational levels in most countries of Sub-Saharan Africa are still low: in 1980, fifteen countries had adult literacy of 25 per cent or less (in Burkina Faso it was 5 per cent). A few countries had less than 10 per cent of females aged 15–49 ever enrolled in primary education. Only a handful of countries had adult literacy levels over 60 per cent. But more than half had 60 per cent or more of the primary school age group enrolled, so that progress is being made. Drop-out rates are high, however, and there is very marginal access to education—for rural dwellers, and for families generally. Development cannot proceed satisfactorily unless there is improvement. But lack of resources, not of management capacity, is the principal constraint, 'made even more serious by the reductions in imports and the budgetary cutbacks of recent years'.[63]

The evaluation studies of aid to education examined for this report covered only North American based donors—CIDA, USAID, IBRD, IDB.[64] Typically, most projects were successful in terms of physical outputs—schools built, numbers of enrolments. Cost overruns and delays seem to be smaller than in other sectors. But evaluation studies rarely proceeded to estimate rates of return: while it would be desirable if they at least sometimes did, if only for the sake of comparability with other aid, the difficulties are well known. Knowing that there is a high return to providing education in general (and primary education in particular) is only a partial compensation.

Improving the effectiveness of educational aid seems to be a matter of solving some longstanding problems. One of the complaints in the aid projects surveyed is that those educated or trained are often later found unemployed. This may reflect unemployment levels in the recipient country; or the fact that evaluations are done too soon (commonly audits are required five years after disbursement). But it also sometimes reflects a mis-match between actual skills taught and job requirements. Observers are agreed that a much higher proportion of in-country education and training (obviously at post-school levels) is required; and on-the-job training for vocational activities. Technical colleges and schools with mechanical equipment appear to be an expensive way of achieving results, though there have been some notable successes, such as the Indian Institutes of Technology funded by several donors. Use of aid to help private sector agencies and firms to provide or improve training is one potential way out. (A variety of issues connected with training are further treated in Chapter 6.)

Another of the great problems is rural education—how to provide it, how to reduce drop-out rates, what to teach; and what sort of education will help to improve the lives and productivity of rural dwellers rather than give them motivation to head for the city? Poor teaching quality and poorly organized schools are a considerable part of the problem. Syllabuses which emphasize academic subjects and certification are really directing the child towards secondary education and urban employment. A different kind of education which teaches subjects relevant to rural self-employment and local development is relatively rare—even one which teaches in vernacular languages and supports rather than devalues indigenous culture.

There may however be difficulties with alternative types of education. Families commonly want to prepare their children for higher-earning opportunities, and see the school system as a path to them. Some families will reject 'alternative education'. Nevertheless, experiments and trials of new approaches have shown successes. In various African countries it has been found that early teaching in African languages has positive effects and few negative ones—not even on the later acquisition of a European language. Providing textbooks in African languages has been another—if infrequent—breakthrough. 'Ruralizing' early education has been attempted, with mixed results; so has non-formal education, aiming in particular at the achievement of functional literacy.

There is a great ferment of educational experiment in Africa and other low-income countries. Its results are not well collected. But even without further information, there is an enormous amount which could be done simply with more resources, which aid can supply—especially for local and recurrent costs. The need, pointed out under programme lending below (section VI), to safeguard the poorest countries' budgets by greater protection against external shocks—and internal ones, for that matter—is relevant here. Continuity of educational investment requires budgetary stability. As well as the need for more resources, the question of priority use of resources still arises. In several countries, aid is still going disproportionately to higher education, and not to basic education, where the needs are greatest. There is a need for more 'new style' educational lending directed at broadening the educational base, rather than strengthening elite education.

In the end the age-old problems of education and development have a joint solution—development (especially rural development) will help education succeed, as well as education's assisting development. The donors can help mainly by providing more of the appropriate forms of aid, and by making long-term commitments. One of the most interesting of evaluation findings comes from USAID: continued support for educational activities over ten years or longer was more successful than short-lived programmes of five years or less.[65] the World Bank's long-term commitment to a series of higher agricultural education projects in the Philippines has paid off handsomely in the emergence of a viable and dynamic institution; its assistance to primary education in Haiti has been another model of well-conceived aid. There is a moral here—one familiar from aid experience in agriculture.

Instead of increasing resources and long-term commitment, however, overall bilateral aid to education has stagnated since the 1970s, and in some of the large bilateral agencies there are pressures to go for 'quick return' activities rather than the long haul which education requires. The multilaterals have been only partially successful in filling the gap left by the bilaterals. There is an unmet need for innovation and flexibility in response to their own experience. As with other aid, the learning process has been slow, though significant. And there has been a similar cycle of shifting priorities and recurring debates about the same methodologies and analytical issues.

Appropriate assistance to education today would give greater recognition not only to long-term commitment, but to the need for involvement in countries' educational processes—not just with discrete projects but with activities in series, leaving room for continuous evaluation and adjustment. Such an involvement would imply in many cases a greater degree of willingness to spend time understanding the policies and politics of education in recipient countries, and to take greater advantage of recipients' expertise in many aspects of educational planning. A greater degree of exchange between aid agencies and academic institutions of donor and recipient countries would also be beneficial.

Population

Population assistance is one of aid's success stories: the majority of recent projects have been successful in bringing family planning services and population polices to a large range of countries, and have greatly assisted the decline in birth rates now clearly in evidence in much of the Third World. There is thus a case for stepping up aid to match the scale of the serious problems that rapid population growth causes. But it amounts only to some $500 million annually, or about 2 per cent of DAC ODA and 1.5 per cent of OPEC aid (though at its peak it equalled 2.2 per cent of DAC ODA).[66]

The effect of family planning services relative to other factors influencing birth rates used to be debated. But there is now sufficient evidence of their effectiveness to put a crucial issue more or less beyond debate: where appropriate family planning services are offered in circumstances of high fertility, the use of contraceptives will rise and fertility will fall. The pace of the effects may vary according to the setting. But it certainly can be rapid. In 1974, when Mexico adopted a new population policy, contraceptive prevalence (the proportion of eligible couples employing contraceptives) was 8–9 per cent. Within ten years it was 50 per cent and fertility had declined by 30 per cent. Very similar figures could be quoted for Indonesia and other countries.

The most rapid declines in fertility occur in countries where development has given rise to the conditions, economic and social, in which parents see the virtues of smaller families. These conditions include education, good health prospects for the survival of children, modern sector employment, opportunities for women in particular, and many others. But contraceptive acceptance has been demonstrated to be effective even in areas where some or most of these conditions are missing. Parents may still 'want' four or five children—but not necessarily eight or nine, and not at short intervals, with risks to mothers' health and the health of children already born. Thus even in sub-Saharan Africa, where it seems that conditions are least conducive to fertility decline, services offered have begun to be taken up in recent years. The more services are offered—so long as they are sensitive to local needs—the faster fertility will decline.[67]

The bulk of donor assistance—some two-thirds of it—provides supplies and training for family planning and related health programmes. It is also supports data collection, socio-economic research, information and education services, and operations research for programme management. But one of its important functions has also been in institution building and policy dialogue. Indeed, the World Bank has consciously embarked on population projects in some countries where the purpose was as much to engage in such dialogue as to conduct the projects themselves.

Today, attitudes in developing countries are changing rapidly. It was significant at the World Population Conference in 1984 how many delegations expressed concern about rates of population growth in their countries and the urgency of taking steps to redress them. Only ten years earlier, at the previous conference in Bucharest, there was far more scepticism. So the situation is now that more and more countries are calling for population assistance; a great deal is known about how to offer effective services; and population assistance has been declining in real terms since 1972.

The main donors in this field have been the US, Germany, Japan, Canada, and the Nordic countries, most notably Sweden. Multilateral agencies add a significant share. Much of the aid goes through a few organizations: the UN Fund for Population Activities (UNFPA) and the International Planned Parenthood Federation (IPPF) being the two largest. Much is channelled through the NGOs which are also supported by private funds, such as the Population Council, which offers technical assistance and also does fundamental work in contraceptive development and population related social science research. Undoubtedly USAID has been the leading donor in this field; its flexible and imaginative deployment of very considerable funds over many years has been the mainstay of much successful activity. (Recent restrictions on the direction of its funding because of Congressional sensitivity to the abortion issue are a threat to further progress—though in the end they may affect the choice of channelling agencies more than programmes in the field. There may also be a need for other donors to supply more funds, if Congress cuts into USAID funding.)

This is an area, somewhat as with education, where the principal need is for the donors to do more. Many recipients already give financial support for population activities which is greater than that contributed by aid. If donors are looking for effective aid of high priority, both population and education can absorb much more. They are of course connected: the spread of education is one of the most powerful factors in fertility decline. There is even evidence today of a significant 'diffusion effect': the more education spreads, the higher contraceptive use becomes per educated parent. And, of course, the faster fertility decline proceeds, the smaller will be the demands on education budgets—or at least, the smaller will be the number of people for whom there is no provision. (Further discussion of aid to education, as well as of population and agricultural research, will be found in Chapter 6.)

Other sectors

This chapter has inevitably been selective. Resources did not permit coverage of a wider range of sectors, including some to which donors have committed substantial funds: power, transport, and communications infrastructure generally, where the aid record has been fairly positive. Of OECD DAC members' bilateral aid 'allocable by sector' (about 90 per cent of their bilateral aid), almost a third in recent years has gone to public utilities (and 40 per cent of that for energy development). About one-sixth went to education and the same to health, social infrastructure, and welfare, and only one-twelfth to industry and mining. The sectors covered above are thus not fully representative, and include some of the more difficult areas of aid.

This has also meant that many of aid's successes have not been incorporated. A few examples can be listed here which add to those already mentioned at various places in the text. They give some idea of the range of activities in which donors are engaged: rural electrification in various countries (Finland); roads in Haiti, forestry in the Congo (France); measures against soil erosion in Brazil and Panama, improvements of the transport sector in Zaire (jointly with other donors), rehabilitation of the Tirao–Khola watershed in Nepal (Germany); remote sensing techniques for natural resource evaluation in Peru; wildlife disease control in Kenya (Canada); phosphate development in Jordan, low-cost housing in Malawi; forestry in the Solomon Islands (UK); agricultural credit in Nepal, fisheries in Sri Lanka and Burma (Asian Development Bank). . . . These cases are drawn from a selection of project reports, and illustrate both the geographical spread and some of the areas of expertise of donors. It is evident that aid can and does make headway in a great variety of enterprises, including some in the most difficult subjects and countries.

VI   Programme aid

Introduction

The case for aid in programme form, or aid money not tied to specific projects, has two elements. The first is that a balance between project and programme aid is always needed. Especially to countries undergoing balance of payments difficulties, more project aid may be of little use when they are near the limit of their capacity to absorb additional investments. The second argument is that the conditions attached to programme aid, if properly drawn up, agreed, and implemented, can help transform a badly run into a well-run sector or economy, and in the process remove a number of difficulties under which aid projects labour.

There have been two waves of support for programme aid; the first was in the late 1960s, the second in the early 1980s, as donors have recognized that the whole economy of several countries was and is in danger. Existing installations could not operate for lack of inputs, and there seemed little point in major new projects when old ones were in need of maintenance or not yet complete. Agriculture in several countries was threatened by lack of budgetary resources, foreign exchange to buy fertilizers or equipment spares—even fuel for extension workers' vehicles. Transport systems were similarly deprived of operating necessities, so that, even if crops were grown, it might not be possible to transport them to markets or ports. In these circumstances a shift to programme aid was highly desirable.

But the shift has not come about in an ideal manner; the donors have, as it were, lurched into it as a matter of urgent necessity, with a sense on the part of some agencies at least that it is temporary, and that the 'normal' preponderance of project lending will resume when circumstances are 'normal'. In fact, the dearth of programme lending has long been criticized—ever since the 1969 Pearson Report, at the very least—and the permanent place of such lending and its 'philosophy' is something the donors still have to evolve.

Increasing absorptive capacity

Countries can reach limits in absorbing aid: most commonly, limits in capacity to handle additional *project* aid because of the lack of complementary domestic resources—recurrent and local costs in the budget, foreign exchange, or manpower. And this report speaks of 'aid overload' (see Chapter 7) in a different respect, the lack of administrative capacity in a few of the poorest countries to process and manage additional aid activities. 'Absorptive capacity limitations' have sometimes been used as an argument to reduce aid. Perhaps, when administrative capacity is in question, this is a real consideration. But most commonly, limitations, if they exist, are on the ability of the recipient to absorb aid *of the kind the donors most wish to supply*, namely project aid, not on the capacity to make productive use of additional resources *per se*. A different balance between project and non-project aid (including any necessary technical cooperation) may go a long way towards increasing an economy's absorptive capacity.

Assessing programme aid

It is not easy to make any kind of rigorous comparison between the effects of project and programme aid. With project aid, the effect on income is sufficiently precisely definable for it to be possible in most cases to determine the *ex post* rate of return; for programme aid, a comparable methodology is still to evolve. 'Evaluations' of programme aid usually consist, therefore, of a discussion of trends in the recipient's balance of payments, coupled with a statement of how far the conditions insisted on by the donor have in fact been complied with by the recipient. These are useful in themselves, but they afford no basis for comparing the *relative* effectiveness of project and programme aid. In the present state of knowledge that cannot be done by science, but only by judgement.

One study states that 'the limited body of evaluation results of programme assistance shows that it has almost always been reasonably effective in rapidly transferring the intended resources'.[68] Certainly, on any count, programme aid is disbursed (paid out to the recipient) more quickly than project.[69] But this says little about the effectiveness of programme aid—about what it has achieved. For that one must turn, in the first instance, to the balance of payments statistics of the countries to whom programme aid is given. One can illustrate from trends in the balance of payments of those countries which have received some of the largest recent programme loans, namely World Bank Structural Adjustment Loans (SALs). There is an improvement in seven of the thirteen countries, and overall, countries which have received SALs were able to reduce current account deficits from 7.8 per cent of GDP in 1980 to 4.4 per cent in 1983—a somewhat greater reduction than that registered by non-oil developing countries as a whole.[70]

But how much of this improvement is due to the programme loans themselves and how much to other factors (for example, deflation, or the selected countries' greater potential for structural adjustment *before* the loans were given),[71] is not calculated. In general, the effectiveness of programme aid has been little evaluated, though this is being remedied by the OECD Export Group on Evaluation. Exceptions exist. USAID has evaluated two of its programme grants, known as CIPs (commodity import programmes), to Somalia and Zimbabwe. It found that the imports financed were 'extremely important' and that counterpart funds were generated without problems, but made no attempt to work out the incremental contribution of programme aid to the economy. Such an attempt, as the Zimbabwe report acknowledges, would involve speculation on what would have happened to the economies in the absence of the programme aid, which would require modelling the economy on the basis of alternative assumptions, a procedure which does not yield definitive results.[72]

Strictly speaking, improvement in the current account balance is only a necessary criterion of success if a deficit is unsustainable. But that is often the background for programme lending. A second yardstick for the success of programme aid, and for many people that by which it stands or falls,[73] is the extent to which it manages to elicit policy improvements (where necessary) by means of 'dialogue'. The subject of policy dialogue was covered in Chapter 4, and will not be rehearsed here.

Donor attitudes to programme aid are quite various: some have found that commercial interests are strong but distort the purposes of the aid; others, that it is not liked by domestic firms, being too hard to tie to their exports. Some donors are concerned because it is difficult to identify the tangible results as something built by the donors' aid. For some, most forms of non-project lending have one advantage—they are somewhat less consuming of donor staff time and preparation costs than project aid; others find it puts a strain on local representation, which has to monitor the uses of the aid.[74]

Maintenance and local costs

Aid for maintenance has a good deal in common with programme aid, although it is commonly supplied as part of a project: both forms are concerned to sustain the productive use of existing investments, to support necessary public services, or to provide for rehabilitation of existing capital where necessary. In recognition of the importance of achieving the right balance between making new investments and maintaining existing ones, donors have moved a long way in recent years towards providing more for maintenance, in the process having to overcome their inherent preference for normal project aid. These changing aid practices were reflected in the OECD DAC's 'Guidelines on Aid for Maintenance', issued in 1979, which recognized that budgetary problems and foreign exchange shortages were increasingly justifications for more maintenance aid.[75]

Typically projects, especially in low-income countries, now make provision for maintenance; but even so, maintenance is not always carried out by the recipient, who is often ill-organized in this respect. Roads and irrigation channels have been notorious areas of neglect in some countries. Sometimes this is due to a lack of institutional capacity, which can be improved with technical cooperation.

In parallel with increased financing of maintenance, donors have become more willing to provide for local costs.[76] Such financing is also for maintenance purposes, but refers essentially to purchases of local rather than imported goods and services. The DAC donors recognized the need to supplement the recipient's capacity to pay local costs, which became a particular problem with many 'new style' or poverty-oriented projects that often had minimal import content. Paying recurrent costs could also permit, for example, paying the salaries of teachers or health workers, which many donors now recognize is investment-like in its consequences, in so far as it contributes to forming human capital.

Perhaps the greatest concern of donors is that both maintenance and local or recurrent costs should eventually be taken over by recipients. If not, the recipient becomes more dependent and the donor may have an endless commitment. The willingness of the recipient to take them over is seen as an important and appropriate reflection of his giving adequate priority to the activity in question. For that reason, in both sets of 'Guidelines' the donors provide for the phasing out of such aid in any agreement to provide it.

One can hardly quarrel with this, though perhaps some qualification is in order. First, the donors should think more carefully about the question of the recipient's priorities. If such aid is attached to an investment which they *know* is high on the recipient's list, say in power generation, then they can give it freely, knowing the recipient *will* take it over. But some caution is needed where priorities are not so clear. If the activity is one whose urgency is seen more vividly by the donor than by the recipient government, the donor must be prepared for a possibly lengthy commitment, if he does not want to see the activity end when aid ceases; time must be allowed for the value of the programme or project to become accepted. Where the recipient does let things slide after the donor withdraws, it is often because this has not happened.

Another, perhaps more difficult, situation is where the aided activity puts in resources at a level above that normally afforded by the recipient—say, agricultural services or a primary health-care system in one area, with the aim of testing the effect of a high level of services. It may be politically embarrassing for the recipient to continue the scheme when aid ends; questions will be asked about why the aided area has such well-equipped services while others do not. In other words, the donor must think about replicability in general, and in particular in terms of *cost*, if he does not wish to see his scheme vanish after he departs. The recipient also should be encouraged to think in the same terms. Possibly willingness to assume recurrent or maintenance costs is not the ideal (or not the only desirable) expression and test of the priority recipients attach to whatever the donor has aided.

For the future

The lessons of experience from evaluating programme aid have been well summarized by the DAC Evaluation Expert Group, and can hardly be improved upon. Their findings were the following:

   (i) The objectives (including political and commercial ones) of programme aid often tend to be diffuse and need to be better focused and defined. Potential conflicts between the various objectives can also mean that none will be achieved.
  (ii) Non-project aid should be fully incorporated as part of a multi-year country programming process.
 (iii) Programme aid is most likely to be effective when it is concentrated on a sector, when it is combined with complementary inputs and when it is provided within an appropriate policy framework. Experience has shown that non-project aid without policy reform is likely to be only a short-term palliative often obscuring the need to address the underlying causes of economic deterioration.
  (iv) Procurement-tied programme aid seldom proves to be as rapid in terms of disbursements as expected. The cumbersomeness of procurement procedures may reduce the effectiveness of programme aid for dealing with urgent balance-of-payments needs. Furthermore, there is

usually a trade-off between the degree of concentration of such assistance and the rapidity of disbursements.

(v) Individual donors are rarely effective in promoting economic reform through non-project assistance. They should therefore work in concert with other donors and the international financial institutions. Decisions on the mix of project and non-project aid should also take into account the programmes of these other donors and institutions. Non-project aid should normally be provided as part of a multi-donor effort to ensure that sufficient resources are available to support objectives agreed with recipients. Consultative groups and other donor-recipient groups are necessary as constructive mechanisms for co-ordinating donors in providing non-project aid.

(vi) When urgent balance-of-payments assistance is required, tied programme aid should focus on imported recurrent inputs rather than investment goods. Rapid disbursement could be ensured by minimising restrictions, limiting bureaucratic intervention and increasing the flexibility of procedures. Sectorally oriented programme aid is more appropriate for longer-term assistance and provides a means for focusing development resources on broader sector issues which cannot be encompassed in standard project aid.

(vii) Non-project aid would considerably benefit from strengthened preparation and appraisal and a more consistent approach to implementation. There is at present considerable imbalance in these areas between project and non-project aid. Sectorally oriented non-project aid in particular, in order to be effective, requires rigorous technical and economic analysis to determine the policy, institutional and other reforms which may be required. Special studies, carefully integrated with the local agencies involved in policy-making, are often necessary to define and integrate the needed policy actions.

(viii) Sectorally oriented non-project aid would usually benefit by being associated with technical assistance for institutional strengthening. In some cases, technical assistance may even have to precede such non-project aid.[77]

The second and fifth points above, in the view of this report, touch on main concerns about programme aid. Recipient countries' balance of payments receive support in a number of different ways. But Chapter 4 raised the question of how the poorest countries could be given greater protection against the vagaries of the external environment. If long-term programmes of development are frequently interrupted by short-term stringencies imposed by external events, the path to self-reliance—and the necessity for aid—will stretch on indefinitely. Greater protection against balance of payments fluctuations would give countries a greater incentive to commit themselves to difficult policy changes. Policy change and greater macroeconomic continuity would in turn benefit long-term development.

The key point in Chapter 7 on the role of the recipient in coordination is also highly relevant here. If the recipient does a good job of budgeting for the domestic and foreign exchange costs of aid projects that he is expected to bear, aid projects are less vulnerable, and the donors have an important part of the necessary basis for judging the appropriate mix of project and programme aid. Obviously it is right for the mix to change in relation to circumstances—especially when additional project aid cannot find its complementary resources. This should however be distinguished from *emergency* assistance. A considerable admixture of programme aid (including aid for local and recurrent costs) should not be considered exceptional at any time. But if the aim is to maintain long-term programmes, then emergencies such as droughts and the like should attract additional funds from contingency budgets—as indeed they often, though far from always, do. The principle of insurance is not sufficiently present in development finance. Except for modest amounts of compensatory finance and emergency food aid, aid is mainly allocated country by country in pre-determined amounts, instead of a greater measure of special assistance when they are in trouble.

VII   Food aid

Introduction

Food aid has benefited from a large amount of both detailed and comprehensive evaluation in recent years, with the result that the record is reasonably clear, even though some issues are still unresolved. The basic finding is that food aid can satisfactorily serve most of the purposes for which it has been intended, even if it has often not done so in the past. The unfavourable aspects of food aid are well-understood and *can* now be avoided in practice, though some harmful effects continue, especially in Africa. There is, it must be said, a strand of criticism which claims that the problems are inherent and irremediable. Certainly, further adaptation is needed for this form of aid to achieve its maximum potential usefulness.

Whether at its peak at about $3 billion in 1981, or at $2.5 billion in 1983, food aid has obviously been important in magnitude. It is also important to its recipients—increasingly, the low-income countries of Africa and Asia, for whom it accounts for about one-third of food imports. It also bulks large for some donors; in 1981 it was 25 per cent of US foreign assistance (16 per cent in 1983), and 40 per cent of the EEC's Community-based assistance (25 per cent in 1983). The USA gave 94 per cent of all food aid in 1965, compared with 43 per cent in 1981 (the declining share reflecting almost a two-thirds decline in volume, and increased activity by other donors). The EEC provided 32.5 per cent in 1981, of which about two-thirds were under Community programmes, and one-third bilateral from EEC member countries; other major donors were Japan (11.8 per cent), Canada (5.5 per cent), and Australia (3.5 per cent).[78]

Effectiveness

The effectiveness of food aid can be considered under its three main uses: programme, project, and emergency aid. Under project aid the more specific purposes of food aid—as opposed to the straightforward transfer of resources—can be discussed: food security, nutritional targeting, and so forth, though in practice the distinction among the three categories is blurred. Counterpart funds from programme food aid may be directed to projects; and 'emergency' food aid in some countries acquires a semi-continuous character, and comes to resemble programme aid.

Programme food aid: macroeconomic effects and 'disincentives'. From the point of view of resource transfers, the principal contribution of food aid is through its concessionality and balance of payments support in raising the recipient country's overall availability of resources.

Are food resources *'additional'*? There are two separate questions: is food aid additional to other aid? And does it provide recipients with additional food or foreign exchange? The answer to the first question is, partially. But today, food aid resources are becoming 'fully costed'—as they were not before, when food aid was mainly surplus disposal. Three EEC member states put their support for Community food aid within their national aid ceilings, so for them food displaces other aid.

Other donors may well take account of the cost of such food aid in setting aid ceilings. Still, as long as farm support policies are pursued, allocations for food aid may face fewer legislative difficulties than equivalent amounts of financial aid, as seems to be the case for the USA. Certainly it is hard to believe that EEC and US financial aid would rise by 40 per cent and 25 per cent respectively if food aid were abolished.

There are two distinct parts to the second question. If food aid supplies imports that the recipient could not have afforded, it makes more food available. If it replaces commercial imports of food, it still gives the recipient additional foreign exchange, freeing it for other uses. Food aid is not supposed to displace normal commercial imports, but only to supply amounts in excess of Usual Marketing

Requirements (UMR). However, UMRs are applied flexibly, especially for poorer countries. For most low-income countries where a share of growing amounts of food imports is supplied by food aid, there is additionality. But this is not necessarily the universal experience.

If food aid does supply extra food resources and free foreign exchange (by substituting for imports which would otherwise have had to be paid for), then its effectiveness depends on the use made of these resources. The evaluations on this subject are inconclusive—not suprisingly, since they involve judgements about countries' entire development efforts, the contribution of external resources to them, and assumptions about what would have happened in the absence of food aid. But in so far as the debate has concentrated on the effects on recipients' agricultural production, some conclusions are possible.

There are possible disincentive effects of food aid, which can work in two ways: 'indirectly', by relieving governments of the necessity to intensify efforts to increase domestic agricultural production; or 'directly', by reducing producer prices or affecting the pattern of demand.[79] The 'indirect' disincentive is an almost impossible question; the evidence about it will be taken up in due course.

As far as production incentives are concerned, clearly a significant volume of food imports can depress the price for producers. But it need not. If food aid does substitute for imports which would have happened anyway, there need not even be a presumption that it would. The result depends on a whole range of things: the volume of imports, the use made of them, and the prevailing regime of price and other policies in the food sector. In principle, all that is necessary is to ensure that the market for food is cleared at a price that gives incentives to the growers. Imports will not reduce the price of food relative to what it would be without them, provided either that they go to people who could not have afforded to buy food (and who consume it rather than selling it), or that the government otherwise ensures that domestic production is purchased at an appropriate price—which it can do by its own procurement, or by various forms of rationing and subsidy, or both.

Wherever effective subsidies are involved, the government must cover the difference between the market clearing incentive price and the price to (poor) consumers out of budgetary funds. These funds are often large in developing country governments' finances. Ideally, the price consumers can afford should be attractive to producers. It must be said that this ideal has not been realized—even in most advanced industrial countries.

Simply looking at these aspects of the market gives, however, too limited a view to allow a judgement about the overall effects of food aid. Many early evaluations which looked only at some 'partial equilibrium' effects wrongly concluded that food aid was necessarily destructive. Of course, if governments made *no* attempt at market-clearing arrangements, as did happen in the early years of food aid, the effects could be seen as disruptive without looking much further. But only if the wider ramifications of cheaper food are considered can a balanced conclusion be reached. Suppose that the low cost of food keeps urban wages down and permits successful expansion of man-ufacturing and exporting activities—this may counterbalance some initial weakening of the agricultural sector, and lead to higher growth, higher domestic demand for food, and eventually to faster agricultural growth. If a country's export potential is weak, damage to domestic food production is more dangerous. Evidently, what is needed is a general equilibrium, dynamic analysis.

A pioneering study found that India's food imports in the 1960s did indeed weaken domestic foodgrain prices; but there were other posi-tive effects, including manufacturing growth, and a shift to commer-cial crops in agriculture with a positive overall impact on the value of agricultural production.[80] The period of faster expansion of Indian agriculture began after this, with a major reduction of food aid and food imports; the lessons of the previous period (the 1950s and early 1960s) and the role of market-clearing activities had been well absorbed. A study of Bangladesh which combined a number of partial analyses—though still short of a full general equilibrium model, for lack of data—reversed the judgement of previous studies, concluding that 'overall, the net contribution of food aid to Bangladesh, including agricultural development, has been positive and significant.'[81]

Until more general equilibirum studies have been conducted (and some are in preparation), one should be very wary of the findings of partial equilibrium studies—and even general equilibrium studies will be 'highly sensitive to the choice of model specification'.[82] It appears, therefore, that indubitable general conclusions about the macroeconomic and long-term food production impact of programme food aid are not available, positive or negative.

If that is the case for economic investigations, it is still harder to say anything about 'indirect' effects via the motivation of governments. The existence of a food aid system *must* have relieved the pressure on some governments to attend to their food production problems. How widespread or important that has been, no one can say. Some would say it has been deleterious. Others would say that governments have every incentive to solve their food problems, and that the existence of unreliable prospects of food aid does not affect them greatly.

However, the possibility of harmful effects, together with growing food and balance of payments problems, especially in Africa, has inclined donors to press more and more for conditionality on programme food aid in problem countries, or for relating it to National Food Strategies (referred to in Chapter 7).

The story does not end there, for there is one further kind of evidence. A study showed that countries which received comparatively high amounts of US food aid (relative to population) in the 1960s and early 1970s showed better growth of food production and improvement of nutritional status than other countries which received less or none at all.[83] This does not prove a great deal. But it shows that countries can use food aid successfully and graduate from it. And it certainly refutes the view that programme food aid necessarily has a negative impact.

Pattern of demand. Before leaving this topic, the question of the pattern of demand must be addressed. One of the most common accusations in the critical literature is that food aid encourages preferences for types of food which cannot be grown in the recipient countries— wheat or rice in parts of Africa, for example—and that this creates an unhealthy import dependence. Unfortunately, there appear to be no studies of this phenomenon.

While the criticism seems plausible at first glance, there are many questions which need answers before the conclusion can be reached that it is valid and of widespread importance. To the extent that food aid substitutes for imports which would have occurred anyway, the cause of the demand trends must lie elsewhere. In fact, urban populations acquire tastes for types of food using wheat and rice in preference to such staples as yams and cassava without food aid playing any part, often for reasons of 'convenience'. Further, a host of other factors affect the supply of domestically producible staples, including procurement and price policies, transport, and so forth. People are presumably allowed to change their tastes, and welfare aspects are involved—though distributional questions arise also if those who exercise their preference for imported foods do so at the expense of those who either have no such preferences or cannot afford them. Finally, it may make perfectly good economic sense to grow other things and import non-producible foods; one would have to be satisfied, though, that balance of payments and security considerations were satisfactory. In the absence of further investigation, one can only conclude that it is right to be suspicious of the pattern-of-demand effects of food aid, but not right to condemn food aid on that account without more ado.

Project food aid. The record on project food aid is also unclear, but the negative elements in the literature seem to loom rather large. Before embarking on the discussion, one should note that most food aid (over 70 per cent) is in programme form; and that current thinking is moving towards more programme and less project.

In theory many of the goals of food aid should be more easily met by channelling it through projects. There should be less 'disincentive' effect if the food is successfully directed to poor people who would not otherwise be buying food, so that farm prices are not undermined. Nutritional goals can be pursued by targeting food to groups at nutritional risk. Monitoring of the end uses of food supplied should be simpler. Physical resources, (rural) infrastructure, and human resources can be developed with project food aid. And so on. These arguments initially appealed to the World Food Programme and non-governmental organizations, which conduct the bulk of food aid projects.

In practice, all has not been well. It is probable that 'disincentive' effects have been avoided where poor people have been the main consumers. However, evaluations which conclude that the project in question has little impact on food markets may be guilty of ignoring the 'fallacy of composition'—the project-related food may be a marginal amount, but the set of all such projects in the country may give rise to non-marginal quantities. This is of course a failing typical of many single project evaluations, not confined to food aid projects. There is considerable doubt about whether many 'targeted' feeding projects really succeed in improving the nutritional status of intended beneficiaries: children fed at school, for example, may be given less food at home.

Many of the evaluations were carried out, however, before the most recent sophistication in measuring nutritional status became well-known. Thus, several relied on weight–gain measurement, ignoring energy output which may be equally important. Some very recent experiences *have* demonstrated success in nutritional projects directed at target groups (not necessarily employing food aid). The record is very diverse. Some critical arguments can be countered by others: thus, if target groups do not actually *eat* better, their incomes may nevertheless rise. Programme food aid is sometimes criticized because the food supplied is allegedly sold off or given to the army or civil service. This is deplorable if poor target groups are thereby deprived. But some of the poor may still be helped indirectly if these potential purchasers are kept out of the market, and the price of food is held down. There may also be budgetary savings to governments.

There are other 'distributional' complaints too. Thus it is claimed that the physical assets created by some Food for Work projects—feeder roads, irrigation channels, etc.—only benefit better-off rural producers. And there are complaints that projects do not create durable employment, but only for so long as the project lasts.[84] Both these criticisms ignore the benefit to the workers involved from being fed and employed at least during the projects' lifetimes. More than one author has observed that, if the proponents of project food aid made smaller claims on behalf of their projects, stressing their welfare aspects, criticism would have less to attack.[85]

There are some points that are harder to answer. Thus there is much adverse comment on the commodities supplied under food aid projects (see 'Cost issues' below), and on the administrative burdens on the recipients imposed by project management, which appear to be often beyond recipients' capacities. These, together with some of the other arguments above, put the onus of proof on the donor, to show that project food aid in a given case will not suffer from defects observed in other cases. At the same time, there are success stories, even if only of success reached after years of learning by mistakes, as is now claimed for Food for Work schemes in Bangladesh[86] and elsewhere. Nevertheless, the general presumption—at least in the better-organized countries—should be in favour of programme rather than project food aid. If the latter is sought, ways should more often be found of using food aid to support well-managed bilateral or multilateral projects which are proceeding for the sake of the designed investment, as opposed to inventing projects to make use of food aid. Latterly donors have become aware of the dangers of 'make-project' food aid, and are beginning to avoid it.

Food security. A specific purpose of some uses of food aid has been to promote food security, that is, to help iron out fluctuations in food availability, nationally or in some cases locally. The main source of insecurity is fluctuation in national food production. Economic modelling finds reliance on trade to be typically a more efficient remedy than stocking. But this often assumes away problems of information, timing of decisions, and delays, as well as the human and political importance of assuring supplies.

In the past, food aid was often pro-cyclical, largely due to the policies of the main donors (USA, Canada), who budgeted in financial, not volume, terms, and only in annual programmes for individual countries. Things have much improved since the 1980 renegotiation of the Food Aid Convention. But some programmes (e.g. Food for Peace) remain pro-cyclical. And multi-year commitments remain restricted to a few recipients. Some donors (the EEC, for example) have difficulty in meeting commitments. Further, the International Emergency Food Reserve (IEFR) is only adequate for smaller countries with acute problems: most of its limited resources go to refugees. There is no mechanism (apart from the IMF's modest financial facility) for assuring the food security of larger countries such as Bangladesh.

Food aid has been used to help build up national stocks but the experience of some countries (Kenya, Senegal, Tanzania, Burkina Faso) has discouraged donors from continuing. The problem has been the capacity of the countries concerned to use stocks for stabilization purposes, often because of inadequate transport and (local) storage facilities, or weakness of stock management institutions. A consequent need is to associate food aid with improvement of storage and marketing, and institutional capacity, and, more broadly, with National Food Strategies which take account of food security.

Some of the difficulties of achieving food security are illustrated in the experience of several countries of the Sudan–Sahel region. Most storage in these countries is done by farmers, who typically hold 80–90 per cent of national grain reserves, with fairly modest losses in store. They store unthreshed grain, which is relatively easy to keep, unlike threshed grain or, even worse, grain in plastic sacks as commonly imported. Problems arise with local storage because there is uncertainty about how much farmers will sell for cash when there is a poor harvest. But state authorities in some countries 'are not yet technically able to store cereals from one season to the next without major physical losses. Their activities are consequently confined to the distribution of current imports'.[87] Their costs are also very high. On the other hand, off-farm storage reduces the profits farmers can make by releasing stocks at peak price periods.

Three essential elements. To ensure *national* food security, in the narrow sense of year-to-year supply stability, three elements are needed: an early warning system to identify scarcity situations in advance; a safety reserve to cover the period between the determination of a need for additional imports and their arrival; and the imports themselves. Food aid is mainly useful for the latter purpose. Stocking and replenishment of the safety reserve should be carried out from locally available or imported grains, whichever are the cheaper. Aid can help with early warning systems and improving storage capacity nationally and, if necessary, locally.

Countries may need stocks for market stabilization even in non-shortage years. These stocks should ideally be operated on a different

basis from safety reserves; their management, and stocking/replen-
ishment by food aid, should be subject to the same efficiency criteria.

Meeting *local* scarcities and problems of specific at-risk groups in
acute shortage or 'normal' years is another matter. It is well-known
now that localized nutritional risk, hunger, even famines may be
unconnected with overall national food supply.[88] Thus the question,
'*Whose* food security?' is often apt. 'Food security programmes can
hardly make a direct contribution to the distribution except by assisting particularly endangered groups in the event of a disaster. Few
sub-Saharan governments satisfy the administrative requirements for
large-scale rationed distribution'.[89] There is no substitute, in other
words, for development which raises incomes *and* increases food supplies.

Improving food security requires sophisticated knowledge of marketing and storage systems and market behaviour. What is true in
semi-arid Africa is not true in humid Asia, where often the most
needed and most efficient improvements are for low-cost on-farm
storage. The role of food aid for strict food security purposes is
limited, except in the provision of emergency supplies. Of course, this
does not mean that poor countries can dispense with other forms of
food aid for other purposes: on the contrary. But the other means of
dispelling food supply fluctuations is to raise domestic production and
reduce its variability. This is a lengthy process. Because of past neglect, in Africa at least, food aid will be needed for decades just to
prevent deteriorating food situations.

The experience of Emergency Food Aid, which has often been the
subject of criticism, is not in this report. The most difficult cases arise
when those suffering food deprivation are, for some reason or another,
people whom the governments of the territories where they are living
have no desire to help, or where governments are unwilling even to
admit the existence of problems. Such political difficulties, together
with recipients' shortcomings in infrastructure or administration, are
the main problems, sometimes with inadequate donor response
thrown in. The mechanical, as opposed to political, needs are the
same as those for food security: early warning, safety reserves, and
food imports—plus the logical capacity for swift delivery by donors
and distribution at the recipient end. But in the poorest countries,
these are more easily described than put in place.[90]

Cost issues. As well as being concerned with the effectiveness of food
aid, one must also be concerned with its cost-effectiveness. The issue
arises most commonly with project food aid, especially that which has
nutritional goals or target populations. The instinct that the best way

to help hungry people is to ship food to them half-way around the world may be humane. And wrong.

An economic study[91] has promoted the notion of 'income transfer efficiency' or ' α-value' of aid-supplied commodities, which is defined as the unit value of the commodity to the recipient divided by the unit cost of delivery. The value depends on the food replaced in the recipient's diet, or, if he is a producer, on whether he is a net seller of food and at what price he sells. Suppose a kilogram of wheat costs 20 cents to buy, 20 cents to ship and 10 cents to distribute at the receiving end, or 50 cents altogether; but suppose an individual in the target group, if he did not receive the food aid, would buy sorghum at 15 cents per kilogram. Then the α-value is quite low (15/50 or 0.3); the recipient would be better off receiving the 30 cents shipping and distribution cost in cash than he is with the kilogram of wheat. (This of course assumes there are available supplies of local foods.)

The range of actual α-values in given instances is quite large. The average for US food aid as measured by the study was 0.46. Raising it to 0.8 would virtually double its value to the recipient, at modest cost to the donor. Donors are enjoined to maximize the income transfer efficiency of food aid. It may be valuable even with a low α-value. But more good could be done by other means.

Studies have also been made at a more aggregative level, with similar results. Thus the cost to the EEC of its food aid has been compared with its value to the recipient country. The EEC's food aid in dairy products especially was found be cost-ineffective. Although it may have originated as a surplus disposal programme, there are significant costs involved, over and above the costs of the dairy products themselves. Shipping subsidized dairy products to recipient countries could only benefit the latter if such products replaced commercial imports, or if there were obvious nutritional advantages to ultimate consumers (which seems rarely to be the case), or if they supported successful projects. In general, examination of dairy food aid suggests 'scope for increased cost-effectiveness through restructuring of the food aid programme'. Other forms of transfer, for example, financial transfers or export credits, could provide the same value to many recipient countries, but at lower cost to the European Community budget. A reduction in Community expenditure also implies some release of funds for other purposes through national development assistance programmes.[92]

Doing better with food aid

Some of the ways of improving food aid which the above analysis implies were set out long ago in the 'Guidelines and Criteria for Food

Aid' issued by the World Food Programme in 1978.[93] But they are rather general. The greatest opportunity for improving food aid lies in applying the detailed knowledge gained in recent studies of food aid programmes and projects. (References to these studies are to be found in the survey articles cited in this section.)

Given the problems of project food aid—especially those of administrative burdens at the recipient end, or administrative weakness—there is a presumption in favour of *programme food aid* where possible. Experience suggests that this should be linked with other aid to given recipients, as is increasingly the policy of the EDF. Coordination with other donors and integration of food aid with the Economic Support Fund was also recommended for USAID.[94] It should also relate to recipients' overall development and balance of payments needs, and to agricultural development in particular, supporting National Food Strategies where these exist. There is a need for programming of food aid on a multi-year basis, and for greater donor coordination for given countries. It has been suggested that food aid can also play a role in short-term balance of payment crises, even in debt relief, provided it substitutes for imports which would otherwise have taken place.[95]

In *project food aid*, one can only hope that the lessons of failed and successful projects will be heeded. Not only the references above but the considerable literature on nutrition are relevant to all attempts to feed target groups in a population. The delivery to these groups of special foods not normally available in local diets is quite likely to be 'an expensive way of doing the wrong thing'.[96] Perhaps the best way to improve project food aid would be to employ it in support of projects which are within countries' priority investment programmes and subject to all the normal management and evaluation conditions, rather than projects specially designed to 'absorb' food aid. Many health and nutrition or rural construction programmes being conducted by recipient country ministries could benefit from food aid resources. The trend from project to sector assistance observable in other forms of aid could be (and to some extent is being) followed in food aid also.

If efforts are going to be made to reach target populations, the lessons of past successful and unsuccessful attempts should be followed. A recent survey of the World Bank's project experience in nutrition has several relevant pointers.[97] Food supplementation aimed at severely malnourished children ('food as medicine') has been successful in a World Bank project in Tamil Nadu (Southern India); but the approach required imports normally found only in middle-income countries and may not be replicable in poorer countries. Some past nutrition projects have been 'over-designed', and simplicity both in objectives and in instruments is desirable. The World Bank has found that some countries most in need (e.g. in sub-Saharan Africa) cannot mount nutrition projects; action there should be confined to preparatory or pilot projects.

For wider distributional purposes, projects can be designed to 'enlarge the family food basket', but have to be very carefully managed to reach those in need, and at *times* of need (hunger is often seasonal). Obviously the priorities are to raise incomes, agricultural production, and food availability. But interventions are desirable to help those who lack adequate food while development to cope with fundamental problems moves forward, and the Bank (and other agencies) have experience which can guide them. This applies not least to food subsidy programmes, which can be made more efficient, confined more carefully to those really in need, designed to avoid adverse effects, and extended into other areas—such as increasing food marketing efficiency—helpful to improving nutrition among the poor.

There are some strictures in the literature on existing procedures for evaluation of (project) food aid, which have been described as 'casual' and 'neglected'. A plea is made for a comprehensive impact assessment system, in which questions are identified at an early stage of project preparation, covering at least a selection of food aid interventions, and with cooperation among major donor agencies.[98] As with other aid, evaluation of individual food aid efforts should take note of other food aid in the same country, to avoid the fallacy of composition. Enough has already been said on avoidance of 'disincentive' effects. Avoidance of *cost inefficiency* is also desirable. Donors should think seriously about whether recipients would not be better off with the additional costs of delivery of surplus foods in money form, while they themselves find other ways of eliminating surpluses (or not generating them in the first place). The various observations in the literature about the commodity composition of food aid should also be heeded. And more attention should be paid to the possibilities of local or regional procurement of food, as opposed to delivering it over long distances by sea (not that the latter is *necessarily* undesirable—far from it). The use of 'triangular transactions' in food aid deserves further expansion, i.e. the purchase with donor financial resources of food from (nearby) developing countries which have a surplus for delivery to other recipients. These transactions have a number of advantages, and avoid some disadvantages, compared with normal food aid.[99]

In the end, as with much other aid, the effectiveness of food aid is closely related to the effectiveness of overall development in the recipient countries. There are donor inefficiencies to be corrected, as noted above. For the rest, one could do worse than conclude with the words of a seasoned observer:

The food donor should not focus attention in the first place on the choice between different intervention options, but rather on the policy setting within which food is provided. An employment-oriented environment which also puts priority on food production permits virtually any kind of food aid to be effective, as it will be used as an additional resource to shape a better future for low-income people. Absence of that environment can reduce to little more than temporary relief even the most direct approach for aiding the poor.[100]

On the donors, the same author enjoins more use of the policy dialogue over food aid, directed at improving general economic policies. The donors' ability to have positive influence would be helped by continuing, multi-year commitments and short-term flexibility, by increased multilateralization of food aid, and by the existence of stocks or financial facilities to assist countries whose needs in a given year exceed those satisfied by long-term commitments. Under such conditions food aid could be used in 'much larger quantities' without threatening either commercial food exports or the recipients' proper agricultural development.

VIII   Concluding remarks

This chapter has covered a wide range of subjects, and a detailed summary is not given here. It has reflected the experience of a great deal of professional work on various stages of the project cycle, and reviewed selective sub-sector experience. The sub-sector material is mainly illustrative, and sub-sector-specific proposals are not repeated elsewhere in the report, with a few exceptions. The conclusions as far as concerns general measures to improve effectiveness will be found in Chapter 10. They lay considerable stress on improving the learning process, and on mitigating the effects of the 'fund channelling function'.

Some of the broader conclusions should be mentioned here. Much of the discussion of evaluation properly concentrates on its efficacy in assessing the performance of aid, especially project aid. There is also a wider view—the need for a mutual process of learning between donors and recipients, with a capacity to bring past experience to bear on appraising new situations, and thus to formulate better policies and projects in future.

Each side can point a finger at the other. Recipients are variously brought to book for weaknesses of the policy environment, predilections for 'advanced' technology, lack of commitment to project implementation, weaknesses in assuring the supply of complementary domestic resources for projects, administrative shortcomings. Donors are criticized for a range of failings. On both sides, commercial and political considerations often intrude to defeat or at least diminish the effectiveness of aid. Both sides, in the poorest countries especially, have a long way to go in improving aid coordination. Yet it is through the mutual involvement of both sides that progress must be made—and must continue to be made.

Once again, it will do no harm to repeat that the majority of aid functions well, and that progress is being discussed in relation to the less successful activities (or increasing the effectiveness of the already successful). Since so much has been said about the 'learning process', the points that occur through the report will also bear repetition: that a great deal of learning has gone on. In whole ranges of project types—roads, irrigation, IRDPs, health, nutrition, education, family planning—what is done by aid today has changed radically in the light of experience.

Effectiveness has also been increased by activities beyond the parts of the project cycle which are internal to donor agencies, most notably in the policy dialogue, where very considerable strides have been taken in the past five years. The policy environment has been identified as a critical factor in aid effectiveness, and there is no doubt about the weight given to it in the aid process today.

The record highlights significant differences between multilateral and bilateral project lending agencies. The former have been able to command substantial and highly professional resources for evaluation, to undertake large and ambitious projects, to engage in sustained policy analysis and dialogue with recipient countries and institutions, and by and large also to place economic development as their principal priority. Most bilaterals, by contrast, and especially the smaller ones, have been more pragmatic in their approach, and have been more affected by the overt political and commercial dimensions of their goals. They have had numerous aid successes in the areas of their particular expertise. Their resources—again, especially in the smaller countries—for evaluation and most other aspects of aid assessment are much more limited; their evaluations therefore vary between those of the highest quality and the frankly perfunctory. All the agencies have immensely valuable experience which could be more effectively shared to improve the quality of aid.

If there is a general weakness in the aid process other than those already dilated upon, it is that understanding of institutional, political, and social constraints to aid effectiveness lags very far behind economic and technical competence in virtually all agencies. The number of people skilled in the latter employed by the agencies out-number those trained and skilled in the former by several hundred to one.

Appendix: Improvements to the project cycle

What holds true for aid as a whole—that most of it is worthwhile—is also true for aid projects. Nevertheless, much goes wrong that could be improved, and in a situation of constant change, aid managers must be sensitive to the need for continual adaptation. Many of the areas in which improvements are called for relate to the stages through which most projects should pass—identification and design, appraisal, implementation, and evaluation. In discussing where improvements can be made, it is inevitable that the focus is sharpest on what has gone wrong and on the most problematic aspects of the project cycle. In what follows, it must be borne in mind that the majority of projects are not subject to most of the difficulties referred to.

Identification

To be fully effective, projects must be consistent with the recipients' priorities and needs. Consistency depends in turn on the effectiveness of the recipient government's planning and aid management process (see Chapter 7), and the extent to which donors ensure that their interventions are fully supportive of the recipient's development pro-gramme. But even when the recipient's aid management is good project quality may be threatened by non-developmental priorities—political, commercial, and bureaucratic—at all stages of the cycle, and most of all at the very outset.

Demands of the budgetary process

There is a strong incentive for the staff of donor agencies to 'get the money lent'. In part this results from a creditable wish to get things done—after all, that is what the agencies are there for; but it can also reflect a civil servant's aversion to having his budget reduced because money was unspent by a particular date. And there is a widespread belief that, during the rapid expansion of aid budgets in the 1970s, officers' promotion prospects were strongly influenced by the volume of lending they managed to initiate. The DAC gave this phenomenon a name, 'the fund-channelling function,' and identified it as a serious threat to project quality.[101] The danger from it is clear—bad projects may be identified as suitable for support, or projects may be too big to be effectively implemented.

Donors' commercial interests

Aid is just one dimension of the relationship between recipients and bilateral donors; commercial issues form another. Aid is used by most donors to stimulate their exports, either directly through aid-tying or, increasingly, through the practice of mixed credits (these are discussed in Chapter 9). In either case, aid funds are likely to be used in support of projects which are unduly complex, hard to maintain, capital-intensive, or demanding of foreign exchange for running costs.

Examples exist in large and small projects, from industrial processes to educational methods. To give just two: in both Kenya and India, rural water supply projects could have helped the poor more (and cost less in terms of foreign exchange) if they had been based on protected springs or shallow wells, rather than on deep wells and reservoirs with complicated reticulation systems depending on imported diesel pumps.[102] In India, donor money has been wasted on over-complex grain storage silos[103] when local technologies were readily available. As the OECD notes, wrong choices of this kind may reflect 'vested (i.e. commercial) interests in inappropriate technologies, which are partly reflected in the tying of aid',[104] or simply that the donor is ignorant of indigenous technologies because he has not made an adequate search. Where donors have searched, the improvement in performance is encouraging.[105]

In the case of mixed credits (when aid funds are used to soften finance terms for essentially commercial investments in order to help an exporter win a contract), the already restricted scope for aid officials to influence the project chosen is reduced by the short time that elapses between the first invitation to tender and the last moment when aid can be useful to the exporter. The case studies of India and Malawi both discuss the damage done by mixed credits to the quality of project aid.

These reasons do not exhaust the causes of poor technological specification. They may include a lack of clarity in the original formulation of a project's objectives, so that criteria for technical choice are not explicit in the first place; lack of specialized knowledge among project designers; or failure to assess in advance the consequences of particular technologies, including their economic, ecological, socio-economic, or manpower implications. Moreover, these weaknesses are not the donors' alone; recipient governments may also be at fault on many of the above counts, and not least in sometimes wanting the most 'advanced' technologies whatever their suitability. Finally, some technical devices are innovative and subject to risk—some non-reprehensible failures must be expected.

Risk aversion

The staff of donor agencies may be particularly averse to what they see as projects with uncertain outcomes, and hence to innovative approaches. A recent study of Canadian assistance to Bangladesh relates:

Just as the performance of the Agency itself is measured by its ability to spend the funds allocated to it, so too is the performance of its individual staff members. . . . There is no incentive to be innovative since innovative projects, as a rule, require more time to plan and implement than do run-of-the-mill activities. There is no pay-off for *innovation* when progress is measured by the quantity of disbursement.

CIDA officers have tended to be attached to those channels or projects where skills are minimised, rapid disbursement potential is maximised and Canadian involvement is longstanding. This contributes to the popularity of programme aid and to infrastructure projects in Bangladesh.[106]

Scarcity of professional staff in some donor agencies may exacerbate this tendency. Innovative projects are necessarily more demanding of staff time than are those whose main features are familiar from many predecessor projects.

Appraisal

By contrast with project identification, which varies from the careful to the cursory, project appraisal is generally a sophisticated process except in rare cases such as mixed credits. Aid administrators know their OECD or UNIDO manuals, and apply them with care. *Ex ante* rates of return on projects are estimated systematically and with skill. However, appraisal depends on assumptions. If these go wrong because of the unexpected—weather, the external environment, political upheaval—it is forgivable, except where experience or technique can or should allow for the unexpected. But some false assumptions to which donors seem prone are more troubling.

In respect of agricultural projects, the World Bank has found a tendency to overestimate yield increases, and participation and adoption rates. Another very common false assumption is over completion time of projects. A World Bank staff study of its aid to Bangladesh found that years of experience of project delays did not seem to instil appraisal studies with any realism about delays on new projects.[107] One reason may be that incorporation of realistic delays would increase costs and reduce *ex ante* rates of return, which project officers are loth to do. The problem is widespread among most donors. Many projects ought to be designed over much longer periods—changes which may need ten or fifteen years should not be expected in five, but they frequently are.

There are five aspects of unsatisfactory appraisal which recur with particular regularity. First, the recipient's capacity for administration and implementation is often overestimated. It is related, of course, to over-sophisticated project design about which donors *have* learned salutary lessons—classically in IRDPs. It is also coupled with a further, frequently observed design fault: the lack of proper complementarity between capital aid and technical assistance. Donors need to strengthen their own capacity for institutional analysis.

Second, the forecasting of effects on intended beneficiaries is often very imprecise.[108] Many appraisals do this, if at all, in a cursory manner, even when the agency's guidelines require it.[109] Moreover, the guidelines of some agencies are inappropriate or vague, on the lines of, for instance, 'anything which is good for small farmers is good for the poor' in circumstances where such action may fail to reach the really poor.[110] Some donors have adopted an approach of choosing to operate in poor *regions* of a recipient country, but this approach has often, for example in India and Tanzania, been thwarted by inadequate implementing institutions.[111]

Third, as the OECD notes, 'greater attention should be given in project . . . appraisal to incorporating realistic assessments regarding the time required for project self-reliance [and] the recurrent or maintenance requirements and costs which may be involved'.[112] A classic case where insufficient attention has been given to this matter is Tanzania, where the collective enthusiasm of donors and recipient to finance the development but not to finance or even foresee the recurrent component of aid projects has created a chaotic situation, in which much of the infrastructure is not properly maintained.[113] Part of the problem, of course, may arise not from the oversight of individual donors but from the collective burden which many donors impose on the recipient's recurrent budget through their combined operations, and from the recipient government's limited budgeting and management capacities. These matters are examined further in Chapter 7.

Fourth, it is a common observation of many failed projects that they betray a lack of understanding of the human, social, and physical environment in which they are set. For example, *livestock projects* aimed at benefiting nomadic pastoralists in Africa have introduced Western veterinary methods; an anthropologist familiar with the people concerned would have been aware when the pastoralists themselves had a wide knowledge of cattle disease, which might have been exploited to improve the cost-effectiveness of intervention. Most aid agencies are still reluctant to employ relevant social scientists other than economists on identification missions. In design teams for *industrial projects* economists and engineers abound, but not people with business skills who might be more familiar with the planning needs of a project, from input sources to site selection to the point of sale.

Finally, appraisal could be improved if it gave more attention to the relation of a project to other projects and programmes. As noted in Chapter 7, aid activities in a given recipient country tend to accumulate by accretion, often without much overall rationale; the main solution offered by Chapter 7 is improved coordination. But it would be possible to make progress at the project level, if projects' 'objectives and links to overall country programmes and sector objectives were clearly defined, assumptions . . . fully spelled out and clear indications established to allow performance to be checked and monitored effectively'.[114]

The disturbing feature of most of these design and appraisal faults is that they are well-known, yet the evaluation literature is replete with complaints that they keep being repeated. The DAC Expert Group on Aid Evaluation asserted that the lessons 'have frequently not been applied in practice despite the fact that they have long been recognized, with the result that mistakes recur, thereby lessening the impact of aid . . .'. Further, 'many of the problems encountered during project and programme execution, and subsequently in terms of project survival and viability, could be anticipated and to a large extent prevented through improved preparation and appraisal'.[115]

Implementation

Implementation issues are generally specific to particular sectors. Here are noted some difficulties that commonly arise.

The poor performance of implementing institutions is a frequent cause of disappointing results. In part it is related to the difficulty that can be experienced in assembling staff with the desired experience, qualifications, and incentive structure. Recipient governments may be unable to put up the number and calibre of counterparts agreed in the project document. While in some cases this may be as a result of public expenditure cuts, which have been especially frequent in the recession of 1979–82, in good measure it is the result of careless manpower planning, or of public sector salaries so low as to be incapable of attracting genuinely competent managers to work in what are often remote and unhealthy project areas.[116]

Staffing problems do not, of course, lie purely on the side of the recipient. Donors equally may be unable to recruit appropriate advisory staff to man projects; one obvious cause of this is that the majority of technical cooperation contracts are offered on a fixed-term basis by the development agency, and that the extra pay offered does not act as a sufficient inducement to counteract this insecurity of tenure.[117]

Exceptions to this principle exist, such as the UK's Corps of Specialists and the German *Entwicklungsdienst*; and it is possible to cite cases where the effectiveness of aid has been markedly improved by the availability to the recipient government of donor advisers over a long period, such as the work of the German Agricultural Team or the Harvard Technical Assistance Pool in Kenya.[118]

The giving of aid, however, is not purely a matter of technical transfer, but also of managing money, and building relationships and institutions. Excellent agronomists and doctors may be very poor administrators. As Chapter 6 notes, technical personnel are usually chosen by donor agencies on their *technical* qualifications, sometimes with little attempt being made to assess their managerial competence or their ability to work with the people and institutions of developing countries. Authoritarian and uncomprehending behaviour on the part of project staff does arise in regrettable cases, and anyone familiar with aid in practice will have personal knowledge of projects which suffer from bad human relations. (In one example the (British) team leader insisted on being treated as leader of the overall project rather than as the equal of his counterpart, and refused to allow the (Peruvian) counterpart staff to use the project's vehicles. This behaviour was so offensive to the counterparts as to make the project technically ineffective.) The moral is that effective technical assistance is made not by technical competence alone, but by technical competence well blended with the social and physical environment in which it is provided. Such blending is very much facilitated by the learning of lessons from project experience—by evaluation and feedback.

The public sector financial constraint, which results in late or inadequate government contributions to project costs, has had a particularly severe effect on the implementation of projects since the recent recession. Rather than see projects fail altogether, most donors have responded in countries where the problem has been especially acute by (i) increasing the proportion of project cost they are prepared to finance; (ii) giving more emphasis on disbursing funds through development banks and other channels into the private sector (see Chapter 8); and, in some countries, (iii) providing programme aid to both private and public sectors.

Evaluation and feedback

Evaluation's strengths and weaknesses have already been dealt with at some length, and will not be covered again here. The substantive point to make concerning the project cycle is that the findings of evaluations do not always carry enough weight in influencing what is actually done. There are two aspects to this—project management and project design. In respect of year-to-year management decisions, this is in good measure a consequence of delays in the collection, processing, and analysis of management information; but it also reflects the fact that many managers are not aware of the potential usefulness to them of such information and therefore do not ask the right questions.[119]

In respect of project design, evaluation may not affect the outcome, either because donors have other interests which carry greater weight (as discussed earlier), or because of shortcomings in the flow of information. Some agencies (for example, USAID, CIDA) are setting up computerized data bases, bringing a little closer the vision of 'a not too distant day when an aid official considering a problem will be able to call up relevant findings from the evaluation reports of all agencies from a terminal at his desk or in the next room'.[120] A recent Court of Auditors report on EEC assistance states that faults recur with 'disconcerting regularity', and recommends the setting up of such a data bank. But the vision is a long way from being realized even at the head office level; and it is the operating staff in the field who really need the data.

Data banks for individual agencies may be part of the answer. But they are not the whole of it, even within agencies, where many of the other parts of the learning and evaluation process already described are equally important. Feedback *between* agencies hardly exists in any systematic way. The recent work of the DAC Evaluation Experts group is one of the first occasions of serious dialogue on the process of evaluation itself. Possibly when individual agencies have project data banks, the organization of an inter-agency databank could be contemplated.

Notes

1. For a discussion of sector aid see Rose 1984; UK ODA 1983*b*. Sector aid is, of course, not a new concept: it dates back to the 1960s in USAID and World Bank documents.
2. Various donors do perform a modest number of 'impact evaluations' on projects several years after they have ceased to be supported by aid money. Apart from measuring long-term effects, evaluations of this sort have the merit of revealing whether aid activities have generated institutions which can survive the withdrawal of outside support. For an example of a project which looked very good when aid money was withdrawn but rather bad a few years later, see the World Bank's 'impact evaluation' of the Lake Alaotra Project in Madagascar (World Bank 1981*c*). World Bank 1984*g* (vol. 1) makes it clear that this is a serious problem with evaluation, perhaps most particularly in the agricultural sector.

3. Most of these limitations on existing evaluation material do not in any way reflect badly on evaluation staffs. Usually, they have conscientiously done what they can with the resources available. Very occasionally, lengthy studies do get as close as is humanly possible to a complete account of a project, including all its significant immediate and 'downstream' effects: see, for example, Bell *et al.* 1983, on the Muda project in Malaysia. But it would take an army of brilliant analysts to repeat such careful work for a large range of projects.

4. World Bank 1983*c*, Tables 2 and 3.

5. World Bank 1984*g*.

6. See, for example, IDB 1982*a*; 1983*a*; CIDA 1983; Netherlands 1984; and UK ODA 1984*b*. The 'three other major agencies' referred to submitted confidential studies which cannot be cited but which clearly sustain the general finding.

7. The Africa versus Asia finding is also confirmed by UK ODA 1984*b*, which refers in chapter headings to 'African Disaster' and 'Asian Promise'; and by Lele 1983. Uma Lele is currently conducting a study for the World Bank of rural development aid in Africa, which will be substantially more detailed than the present report.

8. Two valuable evaluations are the study of the Muda project in Malaysia cited in note 3 above, and the Uttar Pradesh agricultural credit project (World Bank 1980*b*). More generally, see the discussion in Chapter 3 and references cited there.

9. The second part of this statement must be addressed. There is very little statistical support for the proposition that aid projects make the poorest people worse off; technologies which appear to have this effect, such as deep tubewells in Pakistan and Bangladesh, are in general not supported by aid (see van Arkadie and de Wilde 1984). Some cases are however noted in this report, and also in World Bank 1983*a*.

10. See Lipton *et al.* 1984*a*.

11. World Bank 1982*a*.

12. See World Bank 1984*a*; USAID 1983*b*; Inter-American Development Bank 1983*c*; and CIDA 1984*a*.

13. OECD DAC 1983*b*.

14. This is quoted from a press release. For a fuller statement see CIDA 1984*b*. For other statements see FINNIDA 1984; ADB 1984*a*; UK ODA 1984*a*; etc.

15. ILO 1984.

16. Stein and Johnson 1979; Johnson and Blake 1980.

17. *The Ecologist*, vol. 15, 1/2, 1985. This journal contains much extreme and unsubstantiated criticism of aid, but some of its findings deserve attention.

18. OECD DAC 1985*c*.

19. See continuing work on transport investment in East Africa by A. Hazelwood, Queen Elizabeth House, Oxford; and Ortona 1984.

20. Yudelman 1984.

21. World Bank 1984*g*.

22. IDB 1983*a*.

23. Pell and Whyte 1984.
24. Krueger and Ruttan 1983, vol. 1.
25. Arndt *et al*. 1977.
26. Lipton *et al*. 1984*a*.
27. World Bank 1981*b*.
28. USAID 1983*e*.
29. Jha 1984.
30. Pell and Whyte 1984.
31. UK ODA 1984*b*.
32. Gulick 1984.
33. Pell and Whyte 1984.
34. All figures in these paragraphs are from Carruthers 1983.
35. F. L. Hobes, 'The experience of the World Bank' in Carruthers 1983.
36. World Bank 1983*c*.
37. USAID 1983*d*.
38. Luisi, 1983.
39. World Bank 1984*g*.
40. USAID 1980*b*, p. 1.
41. USAID 1980*b*, Appendix III, p. 1.
42. Sandford 1983.
43. For cases other than Malawi, see Pell and Whyte 1984; for Malawi, see Hewitt and Kydd 1984.
44. See Pell and Whyte 1984.
45. See Mosley 1981.
46. For cases of this in India, see Lipton *et al*. 1984*a*.
47. Bourgoignie 1984; Hewitt and Kydd 1984; World Bank 1981*a*.
48. The comparisons may be misleading in so far as they rest on financial rates of return as a proxy for economic rate of return. Because of widespread under-pricing, the former may understate the latter.
49. Segal *et al*. 1984.
50. *Ibid*.
51. *Ibid*.
52. *Ibid*.
53. *Ibid*.
54. *Ibid*.
55. For Nairobi see Duncan and Mosley 1984, Table 1; for Lilongwe see Hewitt and Kydd 1984.
56. See for example Bhagwati 1981.
57. See for example Segal *et al*. 1984; Hewitt and Kydd 1984; Duncan and Mosley 1984; Lipton *et al*. 1984*a*.
58. See Hirschman 1967.
59. Duncan and Mosley 1984 and Hewitt and Kydd 1984.
60. Elliott *et al*. 1982.
61. Segal *et al*. 1984.
62. Figures from·OECD DAC 1984*a*; World Bank 1984*f*.
63. OECD DAC 1984*a*.
64. Gulick 1984.

65. *Ibid.*
66. World Bank 1984*i*.
67. On all these issues, see Herz 1985.
68. Gulick 1984.
69. This is considered in detail in the Bangladesh case; see van Arkadie and de Wilde 1984.
70. World Bank 1984*a*, Table 5. The countries are Bolivia, Ivory Coast, Jamaica, Kenya, South Korea, Malawi, Pakistan, Panama, Philippines, Senegal, Thailand, Togo, and Turkey. Comparative country figures from World Bank 1981*e* and 1984*i*.
71. Countries concluding SAL agreements will typically have accepted the conditions of an IMF stand-by credit, which tends to exclude the 'harder cases.' None of them, except Malawi, is in the 'least developed country' group or amongst the thirty poorest countries of the world. The SAL countries in 1981–3 are estimated to have averaged GDP growth of over 4.5 per cent per year, while oil-importing developing countries as a whole managed less than 2 per cent (World Bank 1984*d*, Table 5).
72. See USAID 1984*a* and 1984*b*.
73. See, for example, Krueger 1981.
74. Bendix and Lembke 1983.
75. OECD DAC 1982*c*.
76. OECD DAC 1979.
77. OECD DAC 1984*c*.
78. See Clay 1985 for the 1981 figures; 1983 figures from UK ODA documents.
79. The *locus classicus* for discussion of 'disincentive' effects is Isenman and Singer 1977. See also Maxwell and Singer 1979, and other works cited in this section.
80. Ahluwalia 1979.
81. Reported in Nelson 1983.
82. Clay 1985.
83. Schubert 1981.
84. Jackson 1982.
85. Clay 1985; Stevens 1983.
86. Van Arkadie and de Wilde 1984.
87. Brandt 1984.
88. Sen 1981*b*.
89. Brandt 1984.
90. Shawcross 1984 contains a serious critique of emergency aid in South East Asia.
91. Reutlinger 1983.
92. Clay and Mitchell 1983.
93. The reference for the document cited in the text is WFP/CFA/21; see its Annex IV.
94. Clay and Singer 1982.
95. Singer (with Maxwell) 1983.

96. Cassen 1978.
97. World Bank 1984*c*.
98. Maxwell 1983.
99. Shaw 1983.
100. W. Tims, in World Food Programme/Government of the Netherlands 1983.
101. OECD DAC 1984*c*.
102. Duncan and Mosley 1984; Lipton *et al*. 1984*a*.
103. Lipton *et al*. 1984*a*.
104. OECD DAC 1984*c* para. 68; see also, on the same theme, Segal *et al*. 1984.
105. See, for example, Hewitt and Kydd 1984.
106. Ehrhardt 1983, pp. 112, 125–6.
107. Khan 1983.
108. This is confirmed by the OECD DAC (1984*c*, paras. 95–6).
109. One such is the UK ODA, whose appraisal documents seldom contain any assessment of the distributional consequences of projects, despite policy guideline CM 77/30, which insists that they should. CM 77/30 is reported in Gascoigne 1980, appendix.
110. Swedish SIDA has used such generic formulae on occasion: see van Arkadie and de Wilde 1984; see also, in this context, Hewitt and Kydd 1984.
111. Lipton *et al*. 1984*a*; Mosley 1981.
112. OECD DAC 1984*c*, paras. 85–6.
113. See Kleemeier 1984, especially 192–6.
114. OECD DAC 1984*c*.
115. *Ibid*.
116. The problem of low public sector salaries seemed to be having a particularly damaging effect on project success in Kenya and Bangladesh: see van Arkadie and de Wilde 1984; Duncan and Mosley 1984.
117. Muscat 1984; Duncan and Mosley 1984.
118. Duncan and Mosley 1984.
119. Deboeck and Kinsey 1980.
120. Gulick 1984.

CHAPTER SIX

Technical Cooperation

I Introduction

At well over $5 billion in the early 1980s, technical cooperation (TC) from bilateral donors constituted more than one fifth of total DAC ODA. Including multilateral TC, the proportion is still higher. Yet in the literature on aid effectiveness, TC is relatively little discussed. This chapter tries to do it justice.

The term 'technical cooperation' covers a variety of activities involving numerous financing and technical agencies in numerous and diverse countries. Its record, therefore, needs to be examined from several different perspectives: (i) pre-feasibility and feasibility studies for capital projects; (ii) engineering design and construction oversight for capital projects; (iii) research; (iv) institution building projects (which may be free-standing or combined with capital projects); (v) policy studies; (vi) individual free-standing fellowships (that is, not part of an institution building or capital project); (vii) individual expert services (consultancies; seconded expatriates); (viii) short-term training (seminars, study and observation tours, equipment familiarization). Much of the considerable TC provided by the international development banks consists of engineering and construction services for capital projects. Measured against its physical capital objectives, this TC itself has had a very high success record and will not occupy much space here. The difficulties and criticisms of TC have instead concerned the institutional and human capacity-building assistance that comprises the bulk of TC by non-bank agencies.

The difference between technical and economic assistance is clear enough in practice, although the two are often linked—for example, when technology is 'transmitted' in a piece of equipment. For present purposes the latter will not be treated as technical cooperation.

Methodology and evaluation

For convenience, the effects of TC projects are divided into the proximate and the ultimate. Proximate effects are the direct or immediate objectives (sometimes known as project 'outputs'). Ultimate effects are those that are expected to result from the project's outputs. In general, proximate effects are instrumental—that is, they are trained people, skills, institutional capabilities, etc. that are expected to have subsequent effects on production, efficiency, and growth.

The proximate effects are easier to specify and measure, so are more commonly identified in evaluations. The ultimate effects are hard to relate directly to a particular project, since they tend to become 'joint products' of many earlier activities. Some of the longer-term effects will be unintended—good and bad—while the people who have been trained will move on to affect other aspects of development. Project documentation normally deals with these consequences only very generally.

There is no ready methodology for measuring the effectiveness of TC. One obvious approach—that the effectiveness of an activity can be measured by comparing its cost with the value of its output—raises several ambiguities in practice. For example, take a project to establish a training institute for agricultural extension, designed to help increase food output. It has to pass through different stages before it can achieve its objective. Has the project deliverd its inputs as planned? Have the inputs combined with local inputs as planned? has the institutional capability been created? Has the institute gone on to function as expected? Have the planned financial arrangements for its continuity been adhered to? Have the graduates been employed as planned? Have the farmers adopted their recommendations? Did the expected increases in productivity result? Were the farmers able to sell their increased production? Are the marketing systems such that the farmers and traders are paid enough to continue their activities?

If the answer to every question is yes, the project is effective. If any answer is no, the entire sequence may collapse—even though the reasons may be outside the scope of the TC project. In planning a project, it is therefore critical to take account of this chain and all the effects it may have on the project's ultimate objectives.

Other TC activities have goals that are far more diffuse than those expected of an agricultural training institute. They are correspondingly harder to monitor. For example, in the 1950s very few developing countries had central statistical offices able to collect, process, and publish up-to-date statistics. Yet good statistical information was needed by governments to develop and manage their economies and by businesses attempting to make wise investment and trading decisions. Years of assistance played a major role in developing statistical offices in a large number of countries. As the local capacities grew, the UN and bilateral programmes started to develop new TC skills themselves, to help the national offices extend their work into (for example) household sample surveys. The results of these efforts have pervaded so many areas of official and commercial life that they cannot be assessed in a narrow framework of 'effectiveness'.

II The Evidence

A severe critic of development aid might be predisposed to suspect the evidence on TC effectiveness, since almost all of it is produced by the aid agencies themselves. This report does not find the suspicion warranted; the agencies' published evaluations contain much frank discussion of problems and failures, giving sceptics plenty of ammunition for criticism.

Evaluation of a single project can provide insights for other projects of the same type and in the same country. To draw generally applicable lessons, however, requires evaluations of many similar projects. A few development agencies have undertaken thematic studies based on a series of evaluations of individual projects. Some agencies have not been conducting evaluations long enough to have accumulated the material needed for generalization. Very few agencies have the systematic procedures for evaluating individual projects and collecting data that would allow rigorous thematic evaluation based on comparable data sets.[1] As a result, this review is not representative of all agency experience, nor is it weighted by the relative size of TC activity by sector or subject. Nevertheless, the various sources do show similar patterns.

There are thousands of evaluations of individual projects, but relatively few studies which try to draw general conclusions from many projects of a similar character or purpose. However, as far as aid effectiveness is concerned, the lessons learned from evaluations do not differ much from sector to sector. While some differences are identified between TC provided by the multilateral development banks (MDBs) compared with that of non-bank (or essentially TC) agencies, no effort has been made to compare the effectiveness of individual agencies or donors. Such an exercise would be thwarted by the lack of comparable material on their evaluations.

An important point must be made by way of introduction. By sticking as closely and soberly as possible to conclusions that can be supported by evaluation evidence, one cannot do justice to the vast creation of institutional and human capabilities throughout the Third World in the three-decade history of international development assistance. Technical cooperation played a major role in this accomplishment, and an extraordinary phase of modern economic history has yet to be properly written. When looked at in detail and very partially, the record—how could it be otherwise?—appears 'mixed'. This chapter focuses, as does the evaluation literature, on weaknesses needing correction. But the achievements of TC should not be overlooked in an excess of critical zeal.

General determinants of effectiveness and negative bias in the evidence

The subjects for TC tend to fall into two categories that partly determine the ease of achieving results. Some projects involve a small 'user community' in the recipient country; others are diffused among a large number of users. Examples of projects with small user groups are 'high-tech' subjects like remote sensing and telecommunications, or technologies for industrial processes limited to individual firms. Such activities tend to involve 'hard', science-based technologies which usually require little adaptation to local conditions.

By contrast, 'soft' subjects like rural development and agricultural extension involve huge numbers of people; their outcome is influenced by social and cultural practices; they are therefore less likely to produce unambiguous success. In addition, in contrast to engineering-based subjects, agriculture and other biological science subjects are location-specific and need local adaptation. For example, rice varieties have had to be adapted to local climatic and agronomic conditions (more so than was the case with the miracle wheats). And a recent attempt to transfer imported, fast-growing fuel-wood species to the Sahel was largely unsuccessful.[2]

Evaluation studies of TC are disproportionately focused on 'soft' activities. Those studies that draw general conclusions for whole sectors or sub-sectors, or with respect to general objectives, have concentrated on subjects like agriculture, human resources, rural development, and small-scale rural infrastructure (water, roads), rather than on subjects like meteorology, telecommunications, large-scale industry, and electronics. Although most TC is engaged in the softer subjects, the relative neglect of the hard activities in the evaluation literature gives a negative bias to the record of TC as a whole.

This highlights the importance of improving the process of diffusion in the soft TC activities. Indeed, diffusion has become a technology in its own right and a subject itself for TC. Most attention has been given to the adoption of new technology by small farmers. After many years of disappointing results from agricultural extension, some promising techniques have recently been developed, along with the recognition that the willingness of farmers to adopt new technology is closely bound up with price, marketing, and risk factors.

In family planning, TC has focused on diffusion processes, along with research and logistics management. No other subject of TC requires more sensitive adaptation to social conditions, or is more behavioural and institutional, rather than 'technical', in nature. Even here, there have been some striking successes. And in primary health care, agencies and governments now recognize that replication and management are the next priorities for TC.

The general conclusion is that TC agencies appreciate the several stages involved in the successful transfer and application of wide diffusion technologies. Their record has not been uniformly successful. But they are becoming more sophisticated, paying more attention to research and to integrating their economic, technical, and institution building skills.

Sectors and subjects

Meteorology provides a good example of a field where there is prima facie evidence of widespread impact of TC; but its record has not been systematically analysed. In an assessment of twenty years of TC, the World Meteorological Organization[3] notes the capacities created in many countries for gathering and processing meteorological and hydrological data. The data have been used in many aspects of economic development: for flood forecasting and warning services, and hurricane tracking; aeronautical meteorological services for civil aviation; and for agro-meteorological services. There is little evidence that this activity has ever been properly evaluated. For many countries, however, it would have been impossible to develop their meteorological agencies if such TC did not exist.

Forestry provides interesting illustrations of the difference between proximate and ultimate effectiveness. The relatively few sources of forestry TC have been responsible for major strategic advances in forestry development and in project approaches to the role of forests in development. Through training, development of forestry planning capabilities, research and pilot projects on renewable energy supplies and pastoral management systems, and the general concept of social forestry, TC has gone far beyond its early focus on managing watersheds and forests for large-scale exploitation.[4] At the same time, nobody has tried to assess its long-term effects. Besides the fact that forests grow slowly, forestry departments in many developing countries face demographic and economic pressures beyond their control, which are severely reducing forest cover. TC can help develop some of the skills of these departments, but that alone is not enough to ensure that forests flourish.

Agricultural research has long been an important component of TC. Much of it has been 'basic' research, conducted in central facilities. Some are in donor countries, but most of the work is done in developing countries at either regional or international centres, or at national facilities for domestic adaptation. Central research is generally linked to national bodies through international networks and coordinating groups: TC is often used to strengthen these national facilities and the role they play in international networks.

The effectiveness of research TC has been exceptional – and well-documented, because it lends itself to rate of return evaluation. Studies of eleven countries show that annual rates of return have averaged about 50 per cent, ranging over 100 per cent. [5] Apart from the work of the international centres, it is hard to draw a line between the contributions of TC and of independent domestic research. However, there is no doubt that TC has played a major role.

The powerful effects of research on agricultural production are well-known. In the words of the IBRD's 1982 *World Development Report*:

The results of the development of new grain varieties have been remarkable. In developing countries, cereal yields rose by 2 percent a year between 1961 and 1980: in the case of wheat varieties by 2.7 percent; in sorghum by 2.45 percent and in maize by 2 percent. Although rice yields increased by only 1.6 percent a year in developing countries as a whole, they rose by more than 3 percent a year in the Philippines and Indonesia, which were best suited to the new varieties.

While this has been one of the most outstanding and well-publicized experiences of international TC, it has not been uniformly effective for many reasons. As the IBRD document goes on to observe:

The Green Revolution has transformed the lives of millions of farmers; it has failed to benefit a much larger number for some or all of the following reasons:

- The technology did not fit their climate and soil
- National research systems were not available to adapt the international varieties to local conditions
- Adequate rainfall, irrigation, or flood control were not available
- Transport and marketing networks were deficient
- Prices and other incentives were inadequate

The differential impact of the institutions, funding agencies, and TC processes involved in agricultural research illustrates that effectiveness of the same TC mechanisms can vary substantially from one country to another.

USAID has conducted evaluations of many agricultural research projects. Its review[6] is instructive about the difficulties of judging the impact of TC, and about common efficiency and effectiveness problems in TC. Of almost a hundred projects for which evaluations were located, the study analysed the materials on forty-eight. Their methodologies were not uniform, nor were the standards and judgements of the evaluators. Projects placed different emphasis on their possible objectives, such as institution building, immediately tangible results, and technologies suitable for small farmers. Thus, even in a sharply defined sub-sector, the reviewers stress the difficulties of reaching general conclusions on the effectiveness of TC.

Of the thirty-nine field projects, about half of the evaluations judged overall performance to be satisfactory or better; the other half, less than satisfactory. The reviewers note that, without independent assessment of the validity of the projects' original objectives, too much cannot be read into the overall results. They focus on the common problems of implementation: phasing of activities, inadequacy of project supervision, weak links between research and extension, extent of host government support, shortages of counterpart personnel and their inadequate salaries, etc. For each of these problems, the review apparently found one-third or fewer of the projects faulted by their evaluations.

Firmer conclusions are reached in a UNDP/FAO evaluation of agriculture research projects. The study covers ninety-two projects out of the 790 supported in 1970-81, and involving $757 million of UNDP/FAO money. It concludes that 'Research findings have already demonstrated major benefits when other essential complementary inputs were available to farmers'. Of thirty-three research institutions operating for at least four years, two-thirds were 'active, on going' facilities, and the great majority of trainees had returned to their institutions. Several projects failed to apply the lessons of the past (for example focus on training needs, sufficiently long time-frame for the project), and instead concentrated on the research activities themselves. The result was 'deterioration' after the TC project ended, and the failure of the institution to attain self-reliance.[7] However, the study found it hard to connect the experience of particular projects to the very satisfactory rates of return and increases in agricultural output based on the international efforts, of which these projects were a significant part.

Researchers and practitioners generally agree that TC has had disappointing if not negative effects on *pastoralism* in Africa. This record was reviewed in 1980 by about eighty professionals, including biological and social scientists and programme adminstrators. Some of the participants were from aid agencies, others were livestock officials from countries of East and West Africa.[8] They concluded that some of the failings have been technical. TC was often based on inadequate understanding of the biological and ecological differences between Africa and other parts of the world. The problems of social and political adaption were equally daunting; the process of designing projects had seldom involved the active participation of the pastoral people themselves, although their entire way of life was to be affected.

Education, in the broadest sense, is a major objective of TC, yet projects in formal education have comprised a small fraction of total development assistance (e.g., less than 2 per cent of DAC sectorally allocated commitments in 1976–9). Education is a particularly sensitive subject for TC. It has to span huge cultural differences between the donors' school systems and those of the recipients. Among the problems encountered in educational projects are language and communications difficulties, incompatibility of personalities, poor work environment, and inadequate reporting by experts to the governments of the results of their assignments.

Evaluation in this area appears particularly limited. Researchers have great difficulty tracking the long-term effects of education on large numbers of graduates (or drop-outs), deciding how much was attributable to TC activities. They restrict their evaluations to questions of project efficiency and the most proximate effects.

The education review in the DAC Evaluation Correspondents' Report found that most of the (roughly 20) *ex post* project evaluations covered regarded the projects as successful within the limits of the objectives and available measures (e.g., enrolment), but that little could be said about their ultimate impact on development. An IBRD evaluation of fifty-five education projects (only twenty-six of which were completed at the time) also notes that conclusions are confined to initial effects.[9] The IBRD study found that (i) most borrowers felt the projects helped to provide policy continuity and discipline in implementation; (ii) the projects were largely effective in their administration strengthening objectives; (iii) the impact on educational planning was mixed; (iv) the demonstration effects of pilot innovations on educational systems were slight; (v) the impact on income distribution was generally equitable; (vi) project schools were more efficient (for example, lower rates of drop-out and grade repetition) than the system averages, and (vii) the fellowship programmes under these projects were rated as very successful.

Overall, the Bank review concluded that there was still a long-term need to build the capacity in developing countries to plan, research, and manage their educational systems. The review emphasized that, without an agreed educational strategy, government support for implementing projects was weak. And it judged that the projects had accomplished many objectives, but could have had greater impact.

An interesting contrast is provided by a UNDP/UNESCO evaluation of twenty-five projects aimed directly at major innovation and reform of national educational systems.[10] The projects fell into three groups – overall education planning, institutional reform (including 'central' institutions), and reform of rural education.

In terms of immediate outputs, two-thirds of the projects were judged successful and 13 per cent unsuccessful; the rest had mixed results. Some projects produced outputs (research studies, for example) substantially exceeding what was intended. Projects to build education planning capacity produced results similar to TC projects for developing general economic planning units in many countries: although the capacities were significantly strengthened, their impact on policy and programmes was diffuse and incremental as they were drawn into day-by-day business and decision-making. (This is not necessarily a bad outcome; annual budgets, individual projects, and the daily evolution of policy are normally more significant than formal multi-year plans.) Projects dealing with curriculum and materials were also successful in achieving their planned results, but poor at disseminating them throughout the educational system.

In terms of ultimate effects, the projects were deemed less successful. One-third of them were rated good, the rest as mixed or deficient. Projects with fewer objectives tended to be more easily achievable, although the efforts of more complex processes may emerge only over a longer period.

A highly specialized category of technical assistance is provided by the IMF to *central banks* of developing countries. A recent IMF assessment[11] concluded that, in all but a few cases, this activity had served to strengthen the central bank or improve processes of financial intermediation.

Health is a sector in which TC has played an important role and had some striking successes; smallpox eradication is the most dramatic. Similar 'functional' or 'campaign' approaches have also had a considerable impact or are in their early stages of implementation after years of development and testing. These include the development in Bangladesh of a low-cost oral rehydration technique (now being widely disseminated) to prevent infant deaths from diarrhoea; the development and introduction of vitamin A supplements in countries with severe problems of childhood blindness due to vitamin A deficiency; and iron fortification and salt iodization to reduce diseases caused by micro-nutrient deficiency.

There can be little doubt that TC in health has helped in the general improvement in health standards in developing countries; the same is true of the work of the UN agencies in creating information networks. However, policy-makers and practitioners came to recognize that previous approaches were inadequate for reaching the mass of rural poor. At the Alma Ata World Health Conference in 1978, they called for a basic shift away from urban and hospital-based curative medicine toward rural, preventive, community-based systems. In many countries TC has worked through pilot projects in villages, developing the locally appropriate technologies on which strategies for primary health care rest. In the closely associated area of *nutrition*, TC has also made a big contribution to the development of techniques for maternal and child health services, food supplementation for malnourished children, and educating people about nutrition.

It is however, difficult to demonstrate the connections between individual projects and improvements in the health of beneficiaries. This is partly because of the limits of the evaluation material; in addition, community health is a complex product of many determining factors. Despite these caveats, the DAC Effectiveness Report notes that, of thirty-nine rural health projects, about three-quarters were considered wholly or partially effective. For about two-thirds of the projects, positive assessments of their efficiency significantly outweighed negative assessments. Where effectiveness was low, common problems were reported: inappropriate technology, lack of definition of project objectives, poor project design, inadequate training and participation of the local population, poor management and decision-making capabilities, etc.

Population is an area of TC that illustrates the difficulties of drawing precise conclusions about effectiveness. TC on population has had three sorts of objectives: (i) to enhance governmental capacity to measure and recognize the relationships between population growth and economic development; (ii) to improve the planning and implementation of population programmes; and (iii) to achieve a demographic impact.

Not surprisingly, nobody has tried to demonstrate the direct effects of (i) on (iii). However, many studies have assessed the effects that TC has had on (i) and (ii), and the way that (iii) has or has not happened in different countries. In a few well-known cases, TC appears to have played a substantial role in bringing about what appears to be a demographic turnaround, probably years or decades before it would have occurred without official programmes of family planning and services.

In the judgement of one observer trying to assess the impact of population assistance, such TC aid

. . . can be said to have had a substantial impact on population policy, a marked but varying impact on family planning programs, and only an indirect effect on fertility itself. In terms of specific bilateral cases, population assistance activities can show some of the most striking successes and smashing failures to be found anywhere in the field of foreign assistance. . . . The issue of impact (is) as difficult to deal with, both conceptually and empirically, as it is for other sectoral programs. Nonetheless, we believe that a general judgement of positive impact is warranted.[12]

Comparing the successes with the failures, it is clear that the effectiveness of TC depends heavily on local conditions. The study just cited was based mainly on Asian countries, where the greatest successes have been achieved. However, considerable work is being done, even in Africa, the most problematic region – often by nongovernmental bodies. TC efforts there have not been going long enough for more than interim, operational judgements to be reached. But it is quite possible that family planning efforts will have more impact than expected, meeting some unsatisfied 'demand' among couples wishing to limit their families, as this was the result initially in several Asian countries. To achieve major demographic effects in Africa, however, population TC is only one among many influences.

High technology is an area in which TC activities exist, and are likely to increase. It was noted earlier that there is relatively little evaluation of TC activities in 'hard', science-based subjects. Scattered evidence suggests several issues that may pose novel problems of effectiveness compared with TC activities in traditional areas. Since the emerging high technologies (for example, genetic engineering and other biological techniques, communications technologies, electronic data processing, satellite remote sensing, and robotics) will grow in importance as subjects for TC, it is appropriate to anticipate some of the questions on their effectiveness.

At first sight, the process of transferring and adapting high technology for developing countries does not seem difficult. It requires only small groups of highly trained people working in only a few institutions. In practice, it may be more difficult than TC in more traditional areas, partly because of a lack of understanding between younger scientists and senior administrators. There is a danger that the attraction of modernity will result in a 'technology-driven' process, that installs a new technology but does not follow it through with education and adaptation. Thus the management of technology is at least as significant as its technical aspects, and should be treated as such in TC work.

Some developing countries are able to absorb new technologies rapidly and spread their application. Other countries can initially absorb technology without great difficulty, but lack the ability to diffuse and manage it. This may be because of shortcomings in such areas as institutional change, retraining of middle-rank staff, and adaptation of extension services.[13] For the first group of countries, TC need make only very sharply focused technical contributions. It can even be phased out entirely as a form of managed cooperation while mature institutions rely on direct linkages through 'twinning' arrangements and self-financed professional and commercial exchange. For the second group, however, the discipline and methodology of formulating TC projects will be required.

The high technologies pose special problems because they change so quickly. It is a commonplace that developing training and research institutions requires ten years or more, during which TC can play a vital role. With new technologies likely to change substantially during the life of a project, TC projects must be particularly flexible. Rapid obsolescence of equipment is another problem, especially when government budgets are pressed. A balance must be struck between making the best use of a technology that may not be state-of-the-art, and the cost of keeping abreast with the flow of new equipment. Special arrangements may be needed for almost continuous retraining of staff.

Problems such as these call for new capabilities. The multilateral TC system needs to be reviewed to see if it can recruit scientists and technicians who are at the forefront of their subjects. To identify needs, develop suitable projects, recruit the right expertise, and monitor and evaluate results, TC agencies will need to keep up with changing technologies, retrain their existing staff, and employ new blood.

Facilitating resource flows

Since TC began, one of its valuable functions has been to stimulate investment through the financing of *feasibility studies*, and the *engineering* and physical planning of capital projects. Some studies have aimed at promoting private investment, but the majority dealt with public sector projects to be financed in part by external agencies. In terms of the immediate objective of making resource transfers possible, TC has performed an effective service. In certain respects, the art of feasibility studies and project design has improved with time. Forecasting and other quantitative techniques have been refined. Appreciation of the importance of institutional aspects has begun to be recognized. Much greater emphasis is now placed on the policy and sectoral context that will have strong impact on a project's outcome. Prima facie, these technical improvements suggest that project effectiveness should be improving.

Beneficiaries: impact on poverty

Who benefits? is one of the most perplexing of aid issues. In the early 1970s, donors and developing countries agreed that benefits for the poor had earlier been taken for granted, whereas the evidence on growth and distribution showed the premises to be unwarranted.

Needless to say, the path of income distribution over time is shaped by complex forces. TC is only a small component, although it may well have a big influence in particular situations, for example, if a government is drawing on TC to help design and implement land reform. As a broad generalization, however, the content of TC shifted significantly during the 1970s towards activities designed to benefit the poor directly. These included rural development, a focus on small farmers in agricultural assistance, and increasing research and TC for primary health care and nutrition. Many of these activities were initially less effective than their predecessors, while donors and recipients were learning. Over the past few years, the learning has borne fruit: both efficiency and effectiveness have risen. TC's new emphasis has played a part in several developments: the primary health care strategy; the refinement of the sites and services approach to low-income housing; the demonstration of low-cost nutrition services for malnourished rural children; innovative methods of agricultural extension and non-formal education; the creation of diffusion processes for 'appropriate technologies', and the strengthening of programming capabilities of non-governmental organizations.

Much of the TC designed to benefit the rural poor 'directly' faces difficulties. First, the poor are numerous, often in bad health and illiterate. Second, any changes in farming techniques promoted by TC can be outweighed by the policies of the government on extension, credit, input delivery, and marketing. Third, TC agencies may come up against local power structures that want to perpetuate inequalities. For all these reasons, TC in policy, institution building and other high-leverage, indirect aspects may bring greater benefits to the poor than trying to affect their lives at first hand.

Non-governmental organizations

NGOs probably administer the bulk of TC provided directly to poor communities. Broad generalizations about the effectiveness of their work cannot be made. Some assessments[14] find their performance very varied; certainly NGOs are quite diverse. Aside from their work in relief and welfare, their development activities include health delivery, family planning, women's organizations, cooperatives, and small-scale enterprise. They have been innovators in areas shunned by governments, notably in health and population. Their commitment to community involvement and their reliance on local staff often makes them more effective agents of change than governments. On the other hand, NGOs have certain disadvantages. Many have a strong preference for welfare rather than development activities. They operate with minimal management and often without conventional financial accounting. They resist collaborating with government if that might lead to loss of their independance.

On balance, development planners see NGOs as having a respectable role in development, but a narrow one. This myopic view overlooks the fact that indigenous NGOs have become a major development force in a few countries. These NGOs have considerable potential for mobilizing and investing local savings, and for developing systems of recurrent-cost financing to supplement government budgets. Except in a few countries, the organizational problems that have stopped local NGOs from expanding have been largely – and wrongly – ignored.

Participation of women

In many TC areas, women form the bulk of the work-force. Their participation is therefore an important determinant of the programmes' effectiveness. Yet in many societies, male officials or professionals find it hard or impossible to develop training relationships with women.

Although these facts are well understood in the aid community, women's participation in TC is still the exception. On technical grounds, there is nothing to stop TC agencies insisting on greater female participation, as they should insist on other factors essential to project effectiveness. A World Bank training evaluation[15] cites a project where advertisements for training applicants specified 'preferably male'; the few women who applied were accepted, and proved as successful as their male colleagues. Other instances of prejudice are even more damaging: quite recently, training facilities were set up in a West African country to 'upgrade' male agricultural skills, although the tasks in question are performed by women.

While 'women in development' projects form an identifiable category, they are not yet very numerous and have been hard to evaluate. However, there is ample evidence that women's interests can be damaged by certain projects, especially where mechanization replaces labour-intensive technology. Project designers need to take account of the role of women in any project where their contribution is significant, quite apart from those intended to overcome women's disadvantages. (See further Chapter 5.)

TC processes

TC has had failures. More strikingly, it has had successes in most fields in at least some countries. This record suggests that aspects of the TC *process* are critical determinants of effectiveness. Where some of these aspects are absent or negative, even TC that has been effective in other circumstances is likely to fail. The reverse also holds: TC in areas of uncertain technology and in 'soft' subjects often succeeds where, for example, government commitment is strong.

Training. TC-financed training is a vast activity, although it is greatly exceeded by the numbers of trainees financed at personal expense or by their own governments. According to DAC statistics, over 10 per cent ($600 million) of bilateral TC in 1980 was devoted to individual fellowships, supporting around 110,000 students and trainees. The emphasis was on Africa and Asia, on higher-rather than mid-level training, on training in the donor country, and on men rather than women (who made up only 8 per cent of the trainees).

The cumulative effects on development of more skilled people are huge. They are also unquantifiable, because a trainee's eventual contribution to his or her country cannot be attributed with any precision to an initial period of training. Evaluations of effectiveness therefore concentrate on the near-term impact of training. A few recent studies have examined training across projects and training programmes.[16] Their conclusions are in broad agreement: the proximate objectives have generally been attained. These objectives are (in the words of one bilateral agency) 'enhanced competence' and 'capacity for professional growth' of the individual trainee. Trainees and their supervisors expressed considerable satisfaction with the training and the knowledge gained.

A recent FAO/UNDP evaluation of agricultural training in forty-eight projects in seven countries found 'generally satisfactory performance' in terms of proximate effects—i.e. 'redressing crucial personnel deficiencies' in the host institutions. To the extent that the evaluation was able to explore ultimate effects on production, it appeared that nine out of thirty-one projects had had no impact. The study concluded that impact also required 'complementary actions' from the government, outside the scope of the projects. Finally, the evaluation noted that, for projects to develop training institutions, occasional additional support was needed after the projects were completed, because 'one or two decades may be needed to establish a truly viable training institution'.

Where training was provided as part of a wider project, its results have been more mixed. Common problems include language difficulties, a poor fit between the training content and the trainee's job responsibilities, and the failure of the project agency to re-employ the trainee in the planned job.

Where big capital projects are involved, the shortcomings of training can be more serious. Some agencies have found that merely training staff does not strengthen the capacities of the recipient body to operate and maintain the facilities involved. The World Bank and IDB have reached several conclusions on how they can strengthen the planning and implementation of training and institution building activities. The details need not be discussed here, but the essential point is echoed by the conclusion of a (unique) IBRD review of all its work in one country:

The main criterion for assessing impact . . . was whether TC as a whole has helped to strengthen the institutions receiving such assistance to perform the relevant activities themselves. In general, the mission concluded that the impact of Bank TC, judged by this criterion, has not been very great, mainly because much of the TC attached to Bank projects has not pursued institutional development goals.[17]

The MDBs and the more TC-oriented agencies differ in their approach to training and the lessons they have drawn in their evaluations. Among the MDBs, training is mainly *project-driven*—intended to ensure that the design and operation of a capital project proceeds efficiently and on schedule. Other bodies prefer to concentrate on improving general skills. However, very few offer completely *free-standing fellowships*, unrelated to projects; donors want to have a more discernible impact on a country's self-reliance. Britain's attitude is particularly instructive. It has traditionally financed a large programme of fellowships, but now sees a need to rationalize its aid around 'sectoral' objectives, a change that implies lower priority for individual, non-project training.[18]

The trend towards tightening the links between overseas training and specific institution building objectives has clear implications for TC: reduced individual preference, measures to reduce trainee mobility (i.e. brain drain), etc. Although the present study appears to support such a tightening as a way of making TC more effective, the merits of free-standing training should not be ignored: (i) it allows scope for individual choice and mobility, which is economically useful for recipient countries and consistent with the values of the donors; (ii) individuals trained in business administration, accounting, engineering, information science, etc. frequently follow a varying career that is more productive than it would have been if they had been institutionally structured and constrained from the start; and (iii) the project and public sector bias in TC training means that only the children of well-off families can be trained abroad for private sector careers. These considerations suggest that the sharp decline in free-standing fellowships should be reconsidered.

Brain drain is often cited as a harmful consequence of training. It is not an unequivocal loss, of course; the individual gains, and frequently becomes a valuable source of foreign exchange remittances. (In that case, the TC training turns out as an investment in the export of services.) The immediate international competitiveness of the trainees is prima facie evidence of the effectiveness of the training. But the loss of trained staff is often a serious problem for institution-building projects. Governments can counter the loss by measures such as supplementary salaries, contractual agreements requiring a trainee to return to a specified job for a specified period, provision of research opportunities, and enhanced promotion.

Another broad training problem is the widely recognized shortage of *middle-level staff*, especially in managerial positions. While this shortage does not reflect on the effectiveness of training, it does raise a question of whether training opportunities are being properly related to manpower requirements. This in turn raises questions about the broad development of in-country public service and other training institutions, and related manpower planning to identify priorities in such development. (These could nevertheless be assisted by TC.)

Although most developing countries have improved their domestic facilities for training, the advantages of *overseas training* at certain stages of a country's development cannot be overemphasized. The benefits of such training are hard to measure. But it would be unrealistic to expect any pre-industrial society to achieve technological mastery without help from foreign institutions in creating the necessary skills. Thanks to declining school age populations, many industrial countries now have excess educational capacity and could accommodate a larger flow of TC-financed students. This appears to be a major congruence of opportunity and need that should not be overlooked.

The *expert/counterpart relationship* has been a mainstay of project training, but seems to have a lower success rate than other types of training. Complaints are familiar: the expert concentrated on getting the work done rather than the training, was good at his job but a bad trainer, upstaged the counterpart in influence, blocked the counterpart's career progress by staying too long, etc.; while the counterpart was never selected or selected late in the life of the project, was too busy with his job to spend time on the counterpart function, was inadequately trained, left for a better job, etc.

Little of this has been examined systematically. One bilateral survey found 'general dissatisfaction' among its experts over counterpart-training arrangements. An IBRD evaluation found mixed results among the projects examined; some were very effective, others very poor.[19] Effectiveness depends on how individuals are selected, the attitudes of the institutions, and good personal chemistry. When conditions are right, the results should be excellent. Although it may seem an expensive way of training, the expert also frequently performs the functions of the job until the counterpart is ready to do so unaided.

Experts

Second only to training, in terms of the numbers of people involved in TC, are the 150,000 or so external advisers, consultants, seconded expatriates, and other 'experts'. Much of the discussion about TC efficiency and effectiveness revolves around them. Seconded teachers have long been important to French TC in Africa. French aid authorities apparently aim to reduce the numbers of teachers, based on doubts as to the effects on educational self-reliance rather than on any negative findings about their effectiveness as educators. Key considerations include cost, receptivity, and quality.

Cost.   The cost of experts has risen rapidly during the past few years. Foreign experts can cost $100,000 a year (including transport, overheads, etc.); one bilateral donor now budgets for $150,000 a year. Recipients reportedly regard cost as a rising source of irritation, especially where they see aid as fungible and even more so where the expert is being financed by loans rather than grants.

Two significant alternatives have been developed: volunteer programmes, and technical cooperation among developing countries (TCDC). Where middle-ranking experts are appropriate, or where volunteer agencies can provide 'senior executives' willing to work at below-market rates, the volunteer programmes offer a useful option that should continue to be expanded. UNDP has developed a promising quasi-volunteer scheme (TOKTEN) in a couple of countries: senior consultants who had earlier emigrated are paid transport costs and expenses to return to their country of origin to provide their services voluntarily. Many volunteers under other auspices are engaged in TC activities of different kinds.

As more developing countries acquire skills and experience in different subjects, TCDC offers an increasingly attractive option for other countries. Experts from developing countries may have more relevant experience than those from the industrial countries, and may be cheaper to employ. If they could be funded by the aid budgets of the industrial countries, many more experts could go to developing countries. However, most bilateral donors regard their TC for experts as 'tied' aid, covering only their own nationals. One African country is getting round these conventions by procuring expert services internationally, under an MDB loan, using a British procurement service as executing agent.

TCDC originated in the UN system, and could take advantage of the fact that many UN staff are from developing countries. However they are paid at international salaries, so TCDC with them does not save money. Savings would be possible only if some method coune be found of hiring new UN staff seconded to developing countries at a lower rate (based on the salary scales in the country where hired), without disrupting the UN pay and pension system.

Receptivity.   Another sensitive issue is the unenthusiastic reception given to experts in some countries, questions of cost aside. The host government or institution sometimes does not agree with the aid agency that technical assistance is required. They may disagree about the recipient's ability to carry through a project without an outside adviser. In extreme cases, the host institution may feel it will be denied the project finance unless it accepts TC. On a more personal level, individual officials or professionals resent the presence of highly paid foreigners with influence over senior decision-makers – as for example, in population TC.[20]

Agencies have had a variety of reactions to TC proposals. Some report that some governments are most reluctant to see fewer seconded expatriates filling operating positions in their bureaucracies. Malawi's government, for example, makes extensive use of seconded expatriates, and judges them to be a very effective form of aid. In other cases – the Bangladesh and Korea studies, for example – foreign advisers help their local counterparts to overcome bureaucratic obstacles to projects or programmes.

Quality.   The quality of foreign experts is an issue that is more widely discussed than evaluated objectively. However, this anecdotal material is itself illustrative. It suggests that much has been learned and published on the personal characteristics required, selection criteria, preparation, backstopping, etc. It suggests that the quality of experts probably is better than average quality and effectiveness of TC projects generally. Even in fields where results are generally poor, the quality of the experts has not been at issue. Nevertheless, even minor incompetence can draw a lot of attention and disproportionately reduce confidence in experts generally. The quality or relevance of some UN experts is a recurring theme of this debate.

The personnel practices of donors vary considerably. While most bilateral agencies provide only their own nationals, the UN agencies can choose experts from any country. However, this flexibility is restricted in practice by the more or less permanent status of a large body of technical staff. As a result, the quality of UN experts is mixed, varying among agencies and among divisions within agencies. Correcting these weaknesses is no easy matter, but the best way might be for governments to improve their discrimination among sources when seeking TC for specific projects or disciplines.

Unease with the UN system highlights the possibility that donors may be providing TC services for which they are not well-equipped. For the multilateral agencies this possibility ought not to arise, since they are free, if not obliged, to undertake world-wide procurement of services. The EEC's system deserves a critical look: TC in its activities is apparently determined on a rotational basis among member states, regardless of their capacity to supply given categories of personnel. As for bilateral donors, their tying of TC may well be inefficient. However, the inefficiencies are probably substantially offset by the tendency of smaller donors to concentrate on sectors where they have a comparative advantage; by the availability of several donors in each recipient country; and by the world-wide supply of TC services under multilateral programmes.

Evaluations of TC effectiveness

Assessments of the effectiveness of TC occasionally include summary 'measurement' of success rates. Although these scores are useful indicators, they must be viewed with considerable reservations. On top of the limitations of the underlying project evaluations and the problems of generalizing across projects and subjects, the overall success rates are based on the number of projects, not on the amount of resources or time involved, or on relative project priorities. Thus the scores reveal little about cost-effectiveness or ultimate impact.

The World Bank makes the most systematic attempt to measure overall performance. The 1982 exercise concludes that, of ninety-five completed projects that had some TC aid to institutions, 36 per cent achieved 'substantial success', 51 per cent were 'partially successful', and 13 per cent had 'negligible' results. In a review of over eighty TC components of projects in one country, over half were judged 'fully or mainly' effective, about one-third 'partly effective', and 12 per cent 'wholly ineffective'. The country review notes that without data from other countries it is not possible to know if these results are better or worse than average. Prima facie, a failure rate of under 15 per cent appears quite acceptable. (The review goes on to say that the impact of the TC 'was not very great' when judged by the criterion of whether the TC helped to strengthen the institutions involved 'to perform the relevant activities themselves'. Strictly speaking, this judgement is too harsh; the TC attached to these projects was not intended to achieve institutional development, but only to facilitate implementation.)

One cross-sectoral review studied evaluations or audits of about 300 US projects containing institution building components (the majority of the projects were in food and agriculture, and development planning). It concluded that project design in two-thirds of these components had been inadequate. This was partly due to the insufficient involvement and commitment of the host government. However, half the projects were judged to have achieved their objectives and to have been adequately managed.[21]

Taking individual aspects of TC, advanced training in donor countries appears to merit a high score. Seconded expatriates appear generally effective. But long-term technical advisers present a more mixed picture; the expert–counterpart relationship seems to have provoked considerable disappointment. As for free-standing TC projects, their 'score' varies considerably from country to country and from one sector to another. Below, some conclusions are drawn about the conditions that determine the level of effectiveness, and the implications for efforts to raise that level where it is judged unacceptable.

III   Institutional perspectives

The multilateral development banks

The World Bank has become one of the largest funders of TC. It appears to have gone further than other MDBs in the proportion of financing devoted to TC, the extent of free-standing TC loans, the attention to institution building beyond the immediate needs of project implementation, and the allocation of staff time to evaluating its TC activities.

The ADB's TC has amounted to roughly 1 per cent of its annual lending. A recent staff study of future directions for ADB recommended more TC, including both project-specific TC and support 'to build up the capability of borrowers and executing agencies in project planning, evaluation and implementation on a broad-based and sustained basis'. Some of these ideas would expand ADB's TC beyond its traditional links with project lending. In a brief discussion of the implications of these ideas, the ADB study suggests changes that would strengthen and streamline TC operations. This would among other things help to develop the managerial and institutional capacity of member governments to replicate and adapt the technologies transferred. The study also notes the reliance the ADB has placed on the consultant–counterpart relationship for its TC, the paucity of evidence on its cost-effectiveness, and the criticisms of its effectiveness.

The study's most fundamental point about TC turns on the distinction between activities to facilitate individual projects, and those long-term efforts to boost institutional capacity as a foundation of development generally. The report argues that ADB limits the longer-term approach to short-term seminars and occasional placement of consultants. This approach is indequate, and when compared with alternative uses of Bank finance is not the most cost-effective opportunity for contributing to each developing member country's development process. General institution-building on a strategically selective basis offers a better alternative.

The Inter-American Development Bank (IDB) has gone further than the ADB to gear up for TC; although the bulk of its TC is also linked to capital projects, there is quite an amount which is not. In contrast with ADB (which has few field officers) and IBRD, IDB's country offices have a resident officer designated as the TC focal point in the Bank's management information and monitoring system. At the same time, TC suffers from relatively low prestige and staff interest.

This argument is reflected in other institutions as well. For example, IBRD's 1982 annual review of project performance notes that

institutional or other development objectives at the project level are increasingly linked to wider sector objectives as both the Bank and the borrowers have become aware that the effectiveness of projects and of institutions which they help to establish or to strengthen, often depends on a sector environment supportive of these objectives.

The review goes on to note the links between institution-building and the rates of return on projects. Some 82 per cent of the projects that achieved at least partial success in institutional objectives yielded returns of 10 per cent or more, while 73 per cent of the projects with poor institutional results produced low or negative returns.[22] This finding is probably the main reason why MDBs are putting more effort into institution-building and TC.

The World Bank's 1982 review draws the obvious conclusion that effective institution-building often involves remaining active *beyond the life of the individual project*, through 'a series of lending operations' that would enable the Bank to 'look for institutional and sub-sector policy improvements'. While this perspective involves more than institution-building, its implication is fundamental: *the resource transfer role* of the Bank becomes *the vehicle* for institutional strengthening. This is the opposite of the general view of the MDBs – as sources of finance and bricks and mortar, while their TC merely assists the projects that effect resource transfers.

As MDBs pay more attention to institution building and TC, so they will need to adjust their internal organization and review their relations with other bodies whose primary functions have always been technical (especially those of the UN system). The World Bank appears to have gone further in thinking about these matters, raising issues that other MDBs will also face.

A recent exercise that takes a bird's-eye view suggests several findings and conclusions pertinent to the present study:

(i) In 1982 the Bank financed $1.3 billion of TC, and estimated the amount of TC in its current total project portfolio at $4–$5 billion. For comparison, all DAC countries disbursed $5.4 billion for TC in 1982. (Financing and disbursing are not the same accounting concepts, but the importance of the World Bank for TC is clear enough.)

(ii) In contrast with earlier years, when Bank TC was primarily engineering-related, more than half is now institutional assistance and policy studies.

(iii) Engineering-related TC is considered 'generally successful'. Institutional TC is 'more difficult and demanding for both recipient and Bank staff'. Overall TC effectiveness was roughly judged by the regional and sectoral departments to be 50–70 per cent successful, and 12–15 per cent clearly unsuccessful, while the failure rate for institutional TC was judged 'considerably greater'.

(iv) The record of the Bank TC in different subjects is consistent with that of other agencies. Effectiveness is relatively good in project engineering TC, advising on management of development finance companies and on public utility accounting and auditing, promoting new engineering technologies and sector strategies, providing economic and sector advice.

(v) To increase TC effectiveness, strong borrower commitment to the TC activity is considered critical. The Bank also stresses the need to improve project design, including greater clarity on experts' terms of reference; to be more realistic about objectives and expectations about implementation; to make greater use of TC methods (for example institutional twinning) other than experts; and to strengthening the Bank's implementation method.[23]

While the Bank has begun to recognize the importance of institution-building for its lending, it appears to be in a transitional period during which (*a*) most training and institution-building TC is *ad hoc* and partial; (*b*) more comprehensive institution-building activity is added on during the course of project implementation; (*c*) TC is not yet given the recognition it warrants among Bank staff; (*d*) significant staff training and reorientation are needed, while the role of institutional development in the project cycle, in policy and in procedure, has not changed. These last two points in particular must be addressed by the Bank's senior management.

This brief review of MDB work in TC suggests certain conclusions:

(i)   As IBRD and the regional MDBs spend more time helping countries to assess and plan their overall TC requirements, they will be recognized by the developing countries as the international sources for assistance in this function.

(ii)   Unless finance for the UN agencies (especially UNDP) increases, the MDBs will see an increasing necessity to carry out TC themselves. Borrowers may then have to incur debt for TC, which many resent (though much of ADB TC is on a grant basis, financed by member countries or other agencies for which it acts. IDB has also increased funding of non-reimbursable TC in recent years.)

(iii) Between the growing conceptual and financial roles, IBRD (at least) will also be drawn deeper into operational problems. It will need to respond to the poor state of coordination in many countries, and the implications this has for project effectiveness. As the scale of Bank TC grows, so the Bank will find that the structural problems of TC delivery cannot be dealt with on a project-by-project basis.

(iv)   How will the expansion of Bank TC affect the role and responsibilities of the Bank's field offices? These offices now coordinate and support Bank field missions and provide information for headquarters. The field offices have very little authority to speak or act for their parent organizations. Tension between field office directors and their superiors at headquarters has been a recurring problem for IBRD. The more centralized operations of the MDBs generally contrast with the decentralized administration of UNDP and some of the bilaterals (Sweden is a striking example) with intensive TC programmes.

(v)   The Bank and other MDBs will need to decide how far to utilise the UN specialized agencies for TC staff and how far to go outside, in a continued reliance on competitive procurement. This will have big implications for the UN agencies – the financing of their overheads, their operations *vis-à-vis* UNDP, and the coherence of the UN system as a whole. A major related question is how the MDBs can develop satisfactory design and supervision over their TC without themselves becoming retailers, i.e. direct TC providers. Retailing would entail both duplication of other TC agency services and a very sharp rise in staff costs in relation to the volume of funds involved.

Effectiveness and field operations

This sector considers the programming processes that determine how TC resources are used, and the operational problems of TC programmes at the country level.

Programming.   UN agencies and some bilateral donors divide their TC funds between *country and inter-country programmes*. In some kinds of activities, projects involving groups of countries can be more efficient than a series of country projects attempting separately to accomplish the same objectives. Familiar examples are found in research on common ecological problems; regional educational facilities serving several small countries; or in activities where small numbers of regional advisers can serve several countries.

However, some inter-country UN projects are criticized on the grounds that (i) regional projects create bureaucracies which then try to sustain their existence after they have stopped being useful; (ii) programmes may become too responsive to regional interest groups, losing flexibility to shift to new subjects or respond to changing priorities.

An evaluation of the regional format for TC might throw light on the optimum distribution of finance between country and inter-country programmes. Examples of the issues that might be examined include: (i) improving the effectiveness of both country and inter-country TC by strengthening the relationships between programmes at both levels; (ii) strengthening the process of regional programming to ensure that objectives and projects really reflect the priorities of the governments concerned; (iii) strengthening the administration of some inter-country programmes to reduce the scope for politicization (for example, by appointing administrators who are not nationals of the areas they supervise).

The *programming processes* for allocating TC resources to the individual countries have long been seen as critical to TC effectiveness and, unfortunately, seriously deficient. For national planning authorities, the whole business of receiving and allocating external aid is a hindrance. They must cope with numerous donors that vary in how their resources are programmed and can be obtained: multi-year planning cycles vary in length and initial year, and may not coincide with the country's own planning cycle; most bilateral donors have priorities of their own that limit the subjects or goals for which their aid can be used; the procedures, information, and documentation requirements differ; donors have different practices with respect to size, authority, and capability of field staff, and the efficiency of the programming role of headquarters; the ability, or willingness, of donors to coordinate their country-level planning varies from one country to another, and from one subject to another. Just what this means is illustrated by an observation of the International Development Research Centre (IDRC). It judged the CGIAR to embody 'voluntary, informal cooperation among donors relatively unhindered by political constraints' which was a 'notable exception' in the area of agricultural research where 'rationalization and cooperation among donor agencies is not widely evident'.[24]

Developing countries also vary in their ability to develop a planning framework or efficient machinery for coordinating TC. Some governments prefer, or even require, that aid agencies do not coordinate programming among themselves. More commonly, government aid-coordinating agencies channel and administer the external inflow but do little substantive planning – especially of TC, which they find difficult to allocate among ministries without provoking complaints. Rational planning is not helped by the conflicting advice that government officials often receive from external agencies, and by the need for overburdened senior staff to devote much time to the stream of officials visiting for programming discussions. The same complaints can be made for capital projects. However, with TC, the ratio of time and effort per unit of aid is far higher.

Repeated efforts have been made to rationalize these processes. Except where governments have developed the ability to orchestrate these flows themselves, it would be difficult to demonstrate real improvements. The UN itself has long tried to grapple with the programming inefficiencies. The creation of the UNDP country-programming system in the early 1970s was the last major effort to accommodate or impose country priorities on the allocation of TC resources. For several reasons, the results have been disappointing. Many country programmes lack focus. Some UN agencies have resisted closer coordination. Donor governments have increasingly contributed funds directly to the specialized agencies, causing a steady decline in UNDP's role and influence.

Operations. The efficiency problems of TC programming have their parallel in actual operations. Coordination among agencies working in the same field is often poor. Examples include inadequate exchange of information; agency field personnel having different degrees of delegated authority for decision-making on the spot; and personal rivalries among field staff of different UN agencies.

A listing of operational woes cannot be interpreted as a full description, let alone a general indictment, of a complex system operating on several continents. Cooperation among funding agencies of the UN system, and between funding agencies and bilaterals, tends to be much closer than among technical UN agencies. Professional cooperation in the field is often excellent, and there are many cases of informal arrangements for coordination. In Bangladesh, for example, a local consultative group has set up working groups to deal with specific bottlenecks. The groups are chaired by Bangladeshi officials. They are intended to tackle operational problems, but could also be applied to planning and programming. Perhaps the commonest rule is that coordination depends heavily on local 'personalities'.

This allows the impression that the 'average' state of TC operations is 'less than satisfactory'; their efficiency could be significantly improved: a view shared by others, to judge from the recurrent debates within the UN system and the governing bodies of the operational agencies. However, problems caused by a lack of coordination become less of a hindrance to TC effectiveness as the administrative capability of a recipient government strengthens: the Korea study demonstrated this point. By the same token, they are likely to be most severe in the poorest countries. The 'less than satisfactory' rating is most applicable in these countries, and should be treated as unacceptable by the aid community. Thus the Bangladesh study found that the country's administrative structure was being over-stretched by visiting missions, project negotiations, and project paperwork.

The continuation of these problems has not been for lack of proposed remedies. UNDP has tabled a number of suggestions, to point to the most recent review (June 1984) presented to a UN governing body.[25] However, the UN system is a servant of its member governments. They have more authority to determine the effectiveness of operational processes and coordinating mechanisms within their own countries than they generally exercise. At headquarters, member governments have financial, legislative, and appointing authority to determine how the system functions. In the field the major donors in any country could assist its government to create, operate, or authorize any one of many possible arrangements for improving the administration of aid.

The world's governments voted in the General Assembly in 1977 to create the field position of Resident Coordinator of UN operational activities. But they made no change in the relations among UN agencies or the structure of authority and reporting lines between the various headquarters and their field staffs. It would be hard to find countries where the actions of the government, UN agencies, or bilateral aid agencies have given the Resident Coordinator a bigger practical role, with a discernible impact on field coordination. The problem is not what to do, but how to bring it about.

The aid process itself may be creating an overload that even better coordination among donors could not relieve. The best solution would be for governments to set priorities for institution-building; for governments and aid agencies to design TC programmes around these priorities; and for donors to combine in a limited number of projects that would drastically reduce the aid management burden on the government. Such action would require from donors rather more than the 'harmonization' of procedures that has been discussed within the DAC.

Effectiveness and the TC planning framework: self-reliance

There is a striking contrast between the economic side of development and its human aspects. Over the past thirty years, the economic dimension has been illuminated by elaborate theory, quantitative relationships, and efficiency tests. Much effort has been made to train economists, gather and process their data, and project their insights into planning and decision-making.

By comparison, the role of human capital has been neglected. Certainly its contribution to development is recognized in the literature (in the Korea study, senior government officials argued that the early stress that aid placed on human development was critical to later economic growth). Several academics have done much to highlight the contribution that education, skills, health, and experience make to the wealth of nations. In development plans, however, efforts to forecast needs and enhance the institutional framework for human development remain relatively unsystematic, if not casual. Technical needs have been studied in sectoral studies. But few go beyond short-run conclusions on the skills and institutional capabilities that are deficient at the time.

TC is an important instrument for developing human capital. However, it is part of the general planning process, and therefore often shares its short-term perspective. It is striking that the basic objective of technical assistance, especially as defined by the recipients themselves as the *raison d'être* of TC—the transition to self reliance—remains poorly defined.

Self-reliance: a point of departure

The concept of self-reliance might serve as an objective and criterion by which the process of institutional and skill development could be understood more precisely, and the medium-term objectives more sharply drawn.[25] As a policy, the notion of autarchy has little meaning or validity in science, technology and intellectual matters generally. The industrial countries considered the most self-reliant are also the biggest importers of information on science, technology, and production. They have elaborate institutional links and organized flows of information.

Seen in this light, self-reliance has three dimensions. The first is a general ability *to determine knowledge needs that cannot adequately be met domestically*, to *identify where* in other countries such needs may be met, to know *how to acquire* this knowledge, and *how to adapt and use* it at home. By this standard, there are two differences between the developed and developing countries. The developing countries range from substantial to total reliance on technical inflow, with little or no outflow; and many *depend heavily on formal inter-governmental intermediation systems* receiving technology and advice on absorbing it.

The second dimension of self-reliance is the *ability to undertake domestic research, problem-solving and policy formation*. These functions reach maturity when they can identify a country's needs for new knowledge, and react partly through indigenous technology and partly by adapting what can be acquired efficiently abroad.

Third, and most important, is the *ability to sustain these capacities*. This involves the institutional capacities for training successive generations of scientists, technicians, and managers.

In all three respects, self-reliance in any sector discipline should bear some relation to a country's population and size, its resource endowment and natural comparative economic advantages, its stage of economic development, and so on. If countries were to define realistic objectives for self-reliance, the efficiency of TC programming could be greatly enhanced. As self-reliance was achieved in particular areas, so the focus of TC could shift towards other disciplines where deficiencies were still apparent. Particularly in industrializing countries, individual TC projects (short-term experts and training schemes, transfers of specific technology and exchanges, etc.) could be used to fill discrete gaps. For less advanced countries, and those sectors or disciplines where countries rely heavily on outside expertise, both governments and TC agencies should consider individual TC proposals in the context of a strategy for achieving some level of self-reliance within a specified period. The absence of such a framework is reflected in the common complaint that TC programmes suffer from 'scatter' and a failure to achieve a 'critical mass'. With a purposeful TC strategy, planning agencies would be better placed to resist pressures to scatter TC grants across ministries.

Donors are of course aware of the need for recipient countries to develop self-reliance. They have learned the institutional damage that their aid can cause when projects ends are allowed to drive institutional means. Too often, this process has been carried to the point where special project bodies are established outside of (and in competition with) the government structure. Donors also appreciate the risks of institutional retreat, where technical capacities are built up to a commendable proficiency but then allowed to weaken or stagnate before reaching self-sustaining maturity. A case in point is maize research in one country, which stagnated partly because technical assistance had aimed at producing a high-yielding hybrid rather than developing institutional self-sufficiency. Even in this case, however, the recipient government could have changed the course of events by greater stress on the priorities and management strength of its own institutions.

Some critics cite cases where TC on a large scale hinders the development of local institutions and self-reliance. As a general proposition, this is difficult to define with clarity or substantiate with fact. The country studies prepared for this review present a mixed picture. In some instances government officials point to the harm involved in dealing with proliferating and project-driven donors. In other cases, the criticism plainly exaggerates the extent to which a country depends on outsiders (as in Malawi) or (as in Bangladesh) ignores the fact that some ministries are far better than others at implementing programmes and dealing with donors.

V. Conclusions

This chapter may be summarized by a number of points.

(i) In terms of the ultimate objectives of TC projects, effectiveness is not well-illustrated by the evaluation material, for several reasons. First, in many fields, effects develop over time. Yet no attempts were identified where completed projects had been re-evaluated twice or more over a period of years to track their impact. Second, immediate results are much easier to evaluate: the methodology for tracking and evaluating the impact of TC on ultimate objectives is less well-developed. Third, ultimate effects (for example, production increases, poverty alleviation) are the results of many factors besides the aided projects: the broader the objectives, the more they depend on the general drift of the economy and society, and the harder it is to sort out cause and effect of particular projects.

(ii) It is easy to lose sight of the wood for the trees. For example, in many countries, agricultural research and its application has had demonstrably powerful effects. Evaluating those projects at the 'front end' of such activity (for example, of local research or agricultural extension) may not elucidate the casual history between inputs and final economic change; but TC should not therefore be criticized on the grounds that effectiveness 'cannot be demonstrated'.

(iii) Many factors make it impossible to produce a single measure of the overall effectiveness of TC, among them the difficulties of setting verifiable objectives and the great variety of TC activities. However, it is probably the case that the attempts to evaluate TC have understated its effectiveness. This is because the evaluation literature concentrates disproportionately on 'soft' TC activities (where success is harder to achieve) and the tendency of evaluators to look for failure so as to improve their institutions' future perfomance.

Nevertheless, to the extent that the literature does try to measure success and failure against proximate or immediate objectives, the results are not without meaning. Evaluated projects tend to fall within the range of one-half to two-thirds judged satisfactory, of which one-third or more are projects judged fully satisfactory. Outright failures were reported in 10–15 per cent of projects. The record also suggests that critics who are inclined to make a blanket condemnation of TC projects have lacked discrimination, drawing strong conclusions from selective evidence. The more pertinent issues are what determines effectiveness in different countries, the relevance and adaptability of external technology, the ability to learn from experience, and how to overcome political and bureaucratic constraints to further improvement.

Common inadequacies

(iv) The evaluation literature amply documents inadequacies in project design; government commitment; timing and quality of project inputs (experts, training, equipment); technology; trainees back on the job; participation of users (for example, farmers) in project design and implementation; coordination with, and commitment of, domestic agencies outside the project itself; consistency of policy framework with project assumptions; coordination of related donor activities; sensitivity and adaptation to local cultural factors.

The efficiency lessons are similar from one sector to another, even from one project to another. They are generally the common-sense counsels of good management. International TC is probably harder to manage than most public activities, and can run into numerous difficulties. The Bangladesh study identified such problems as slow approval procedures, delays in customs clearance and land acquisition, slow procurement and payment, frequent personnel changes, insufficient delegation of authority. In Kenya, a World Bank rural development project was cancelled in the face of insuperable management difficulties of a complex multi-ministry programme. Evaluation could play a bigger role in rectifying these deficiencies. Feedback seldom involves systematic procedures for informing or retraining all those with a need to know, and ensuring (as does at least one donor agency) that subsequent decision-making *must* take account of previous relevant findings.

While the process of project development differs from one agency to another, it typically involves two groups – technical and programme formulators, and programme and policy reviewers and decision-makers. To ensure that evaluation lessons are being learnt and embodied in new activities, agencies should consider imposing on both these groups a mandatory review of each evaluation's relevant findings. Project formulators could be required to cite evaluation material and how the proposed new activity takes account of past lessons. The review and decision-making process could also be required to judge new activities against (*inter alia*) the relevant evaluation record. To assist this development, TC itself could help countries to build their own evaluation capabilities.

(v) The inefficiencies of the aid process do not significantly undermine the effectiveness of TC in those countries with favourable economic and social conditions. Where conditions are unfavourable, the systematic inefficiencies prevent projects from being designed and implemented with maximum efficiency. This conclusion can be illustrated by the record of the UN agencies. Few would disagree that the programming and operating processes of the UN's TC leave much to be desired. However, these problems are less serious in countries with fairly advanced administrative capabilities, and most severe in the least developed countries – where they not only compound the inherently greater difficulties of carrying out TC effectively, but also add to the administrative burden of governments with weak bureaucracies and over-taxed officials. Some specific suggestions for improving coordination are made below.

(vi) TC effectiveness is more difficult to achieve

(a) the further the country is from institutional and skill self-reliance;
(b) the greater the cultural difference between donor (of the technology, experts and training) and recipient;
(c) the greater the differences in ecology between developed and developing countries. This is because some technology then has to be adapted to local conditions. It is harder to transfer many biological technologies than those of engineering, communications, and chemicals, which can be applied more uniformly in different environments;

(d) the 'softer' the subject of the activity. TC that is directed at institution building, at activities requiring changes in social structures or behaviour, or at services like health and education, is usuallly less effective than in 'hard' areas such as physical sciences or civil works;

(e) the larger the number of users who must absorb and apply the transferred technology;

(f) the more poorly endowed the region. This is especially true within a single country where other regions are developing more dynamically and doing little to pull along the backward areas;

(g) the more dependent for its effects the individual project is on other agencies and policies, especially if the latter have to be changed.

(vii) In each sector, lessons have been learned about the particular characteristics of technology transfer and institution building. In some cases, a learning and feedback process has resulted in the development of completely new strategies.

Contextual considerations

(viii) In their different ways, the conclusions thus far have demonstrated how individual projects are affected by extraneous factors such as an unfavourable policy framework or the failure of other parties to take expected actions. Such problems pose sensitive questions. To continue to provide TC where the proximate objective of the project is attained but its fuller potential is dissipated is wasteful of TC resources and wasteful for the recipient. But if the TC agency wishes to obtain assurances that the necessary measures will be taken, outside the scope of the project itself, it may be raising issues that appear 'inappropriate' or intrusive.

Many agencies require project designers to describe the ultimate development objective of their project, and to specify the policies and/or activities of other organizations needed for the project to succeed. If the project is large enough, these assumptions may take the form of a formal understanding that the government will take the specified steps. Even though made in good faith, such undertakings often prove disappointing. If donors and recipients are sincere about aid effectiveness, however, they will spend more time on the wider framework of particular projects.

This conclusion has particular relevance for the poorest countries, especially in Africa. TC is part of the whole international effort to speed up Africa's economic development, but it has yet to show much success. Agricultural research has yet to produce results that could reverse the decline in per capita food output. The problems in nomadic pastoralism have been described. In health, much African endemic disease takes forms not found elsewhere, and for which no effective counter-measures are yet available. At independence, many African countries inherited only rudimentary educational systems and a tiny group of people with middle or high-level training. They suffer from brain drain, not offset to any significant extent by remittances. The internal drain from government and other aided institutions to the higher-paying private sector will not be alleviated for many years, making institution-building more difficult.

In the face of these shortcomings, the effectiveness of TC is bound to be relatively low for some time. The problem of how to accelerate development in Africa goes beyond an examination of TC effectiveness, but a few observations relevant to the objectives of TC can be made.

First, time and persistence have brought several countries into the middle-income category, although they were once deemed unlikely to make such progress. Korea is one example of just such a country. Some of Africa's problems are so serious simply because modern science has been addressing African problems for only a few years.

Second, the fundamental cause of many of the difficulties of TC in Africa (aside from civil disruption) is probably the lack of widespread education. This report has emphasized two points of particular relevance to Africa: the need to revive (i) aid-financed fellowship programmes in general development skills (economics, accounting, engineering, adminstration, etc.) not associated with specific projects; and (ii) large-scale overseas education programmes to take advantage of under-utilized university capacity in the industrial countries. In the long-run the poorest countries must develop their own educational systems.

Third, some countries have 'absorptive capacity' problems because they have centralized so many economic activities in the public sector. They therefore run into shortages of management skills, while neglecting the potential contribution that NGOs could make to development. The TC community needs to develop more effective ways of reaching indigenous NGOs and helping them to develop more rapidly, and to relieve bottlenecks in absorptive capacity.

Fourth, the mistakes that arise because of cultural differences can probably be reduced by greater use of (non-economist) social scientists in designing projects. This should be done through increased employment of social scientists by aid agencies (their numbers are now minuscule), and by regular use of local social scientists as consultants, especially for rural projects and activities in the 'soft' sectors.

Experts and counterparts

(ix) The evaluation literature frequently singles out the expert, and the expert–counterpart relationship, as a key element of TC in need of strengthening. The recent sharp rise in the cost of experts is particularly troublesome. More use of volunteer programmes and of local expertise is indicated, but the greatest scope for cost reduction (and for increasing the number of expert-months that can be financed by any given project) lies with recruiting developing country nationals with salaries determined by the *local*, not the international, market. For bilateral agencies this means untying their TC recruitment procedures. For the UN system, it requires developing a two-track personnel system. Neither of these changes will be easy.

For all the years of agency experience in recruiting experts, their quality is still often inadequate. This failing might be reduced if TC agencies provided mandatory training for experts in the art of cross-cultural communication and techniques for effective personal relations with local counterparts. The costs of bringing long-term experts out for interviews by the host government and their prospective counterparts would be justified by the benefits of identifying misfits or technically inappropriate people beforehand. Both governments and agencies could be much tougher in refusing to retain in the system individuals with demonstrated technical failings or an inability to work well in foreign environments.

MDBs and the UN system

(x) MDBs are devoting more resources to TC and institution building (or at least institution strengthening). At the same time, donor contributions for the TC activities of UN agencies are stagnating. There is thus a strong possibility that the traditional distinction between MDBs and capital projects, on the one hand, and UN agencies on the other will break down, and that intellectual and operational leadership in TC will drift to the MDBs, in particular IBRD. These changes pose serious issues for the internal staffing and operations of the MDBs, and for their relations with other bodies, especially in the field.

Coordination

(xi) If a country is to make effective use of aid, a prime objective should be the development of capacity to coordinate all donors and agencies. Many countries have aid coordination units, but their work is often primarily administrative rather than substantive. UNDP would be an appropriate agency to assist governments in developing such capacity. Some resident representatives have informally advised governments on coordination functions; all parties might benefit from studying the coordination experience and methods of a few successful cases. Where governments feel unable to devote staff resources to initiating coordination, they may prefer to encourage (or require) aid agencies to develop arrangements in which the government would merely participate. Such arrangements can run from exchange of information to highly structured relationships for coordinating planning and operations.

Where several agencies have projects involving the same institutions and officials, *ad hoc* coordinating committees have often proved useful, whether run by the government or a donor agency. In food and nutrition, for example, both UNDP and UNICEF have had successful experience along these lines. The Kenya study describes a good model for project-level cooperation; UNDP, IBRD, SIDA, CIDA, and USAID jointly finance a Technical Assistance Pool of twelve advisers working with the Ministries of Agriculture and Livestock Development and of Finance and Economic Planning. These arrangements tend to spring from individual initiative; more would be forthcoming if the agencies' headquarters were openly to encourage them. For the UN system, the General Assembly resolutions on this problem have apparently not been adequate.

Donors could also do much to consolidate the processing of projects in countries where administrative capacity is being over-stretched by the sheer size and variety of donor projects. Consolidation could involve settling on a narrower range of objectives, institutions, and strategies. Institution building could be enhanced by ensuring a scale of training to take account of an expected 'brain drain', and financing enough local recurrent costs to protect the institutions from unanticipated budget stringency. Donors and agencies could also agree to require only a single set of documentation covering all external inputs and descriptions of the projects, with each donor then meeting its own documentation requirements internally without involving the host government again. And of course, donors could 'specialize' more, so that fewer agencies were involved in each sector.

TC sectoral reviews

(xii) Many countries would benefit from the occasional drafting of a TC 'sectoral' review. It would perform for training and institution building the kind of function that IBRD economic memoranda serve for reviewing an economy. It could describe and assess the programmes of the donors and agencies, the relevant policies of government, coordination arrangements, regional or sectoral patterns of donor allocations, trends in the volume of TC and their relationship to requirements, operational problems, emerging areas of technical need, articulation between domestic and inter-country TC activities, TC implications of a new five-year development plan, and findings of recent TC evaluations. A review of this sort could be done each year as part of the annual Report on Development Cooperation now routinely done (but mainly limited to project information) by the Resident Coordinator. While the Resident Coordinator would be the most appropriate author (if the review were not done by the government), it could also be done under other auspices. Its preparation would require TC agencies to exchange views and information. The review should circulate widely, and could form the basis of systematic examination of findings and recommendations.

(xiii) Compared with TC in traditional subjects, high technology poses novel problems for effectiveness. They stem from the high rate of change in these technologies, the rapid obsolescence of hardware, the greater information gap between younger technicians and their senior supervisors, the attraction of modernity, and the danger of 'technology-driven' proposals. Aid agencies need to examine high-technology TC and its special requirements for effectiveness.

(xiv) There is a striking weakness in the intellectual underpinnings of institution building, human development, and associated TC compared with the theoretical and quantitative tools used to plan physical investment. Some work has been done on manpower planning and the development of individual institutions. But there is little guidance for planning institutional requirements of whole sectors, for matching institutional needs with evolving economic structures, or for systematically defining inter-sectoral institutional linkages (analogous to the economic input–output matrix). The basic TC objective of self-reliance has not been defined in terms that would aid the planning of institutional needs and facilitate rational decisions. Although this report has made some suggestions along these lines, the subject warrants a major conceptual effort.

Notes

1. OECD DAC 1982*a*.
2. Taylor and Moustapha 1983.
3. World Meteorological Organization 1972.
4. FAO 1984*a*.
5. Evenson *et al*. 1979.
6. USAID 1982*a*.
7. UNDP/FAO 1984.
8. USAID 1980*d*.

9. World Bank 1978*a*.
10. UNDP/UNESCO 1983.
11. IMF 1983.
12. Ness 1983.
13. UNDP 1984.
14. For example, USAID 1982*d*. NGOs have already been discussed in
    ` Chapter 3.
15. World Bank 1982*d*.
16. See USAID 1983*c*; FAO/UNDP 1980; World Bank 1982*d*; Laufer 1984;
    UK ODA 1979 and 1984*c*.
17. World Bank 1972.
18. UK ODA 1983*a*.
19. World Bank 1982*b*.
20. Wolfson 1983.
21. USAID 1983*b*.
22. World Bank 1982*a*.
23. World Bank 1983*c*.
24. IDRC 1981.
25. UNDP 1984.
26. *Ibid.*

CHAPTER SEVEN

The Systemic Effects of Aid and the Role of Coordination

I Introduction

One of the main characteristics of aid evaluation has been that aid agencies have commonly evaluated their own aid, whereas relatively few inquiries have been made into the composite effects of the operations of a multiplicity of donors on particular recipient economies. The studies undertaken for this report have attempted to redress the deficiency. Most of these 'composite effects' are known to aid practitioners, and are among the factors that have prompted recent intensified interest in aid coordination. But they are not often reflected upon outside the fora in which aid coordination is discussed. And even when reflected on, they have received little remedy in the past.

Systemic effects

If one were to look at a recipient country at any given time, one would see a set of aid activities that had grown by accretion over many years. Activities would be coming to an end, some to be repeated and some not; others more recent would be in progress, and under surveillance for their actual and potential contribution; and yet others, many of a new kind, would be under discussion and negotiation. Twenty-five to thirty official agencies (the average number for a recipient country) might be at work, and an even larger number of non-governmental organizations (NGOs).[1] Would they add up to a coherent set of activities? Or would they at least complement coherently the range of developmental activities undertaken within the country?

The answer, especially in the poorest countries, is likely to be 'no'; if the answer is positive, it will usually be because the recipient government has made a particular effort to establish some kind of coherence—a coherence which the uncoordinated activities of aid agencies and recipient governments often militate against. In the words of the Kenya study, if an aid programme means that provision of resources is guided by 'an identifiable and coherent set of objectives', 'there is . . . no "aid programme to Kenya"'. Similarly, the World Bank comments that in some African countries

The public investment programme has become little more than the aggregation of projects that donors wish to finance. These projects have not always been consistent with the priorities necessary for achieving national development objectives. Donors finance the projects that spending ministries and agencies want, but these wants are seldom coordinated by the core ministries.[2]

The phrase 'systemic effects' could be taken more widely to cover other aspects of the influence of aid. Political and societal influences have been little treated in this report; they would have taken the enquiry beyond manageable bounds. This chapter concentrates on features which make the impact of the whole of aid in some sense smaller than the sum of the parts. There are other features which might make it bigger: catalytic effects, whereby relatively small inputs of aid can have considerable beneficial impact—techniques of public management for example, which can spread well beyond the point of introduction; or the overall enhancement of the influence of individual aid efforts by complementarities among them. How to maximize such benefits might be the subject of further enquiry—here, the preoccupation is with reducing the lack of complementarity.

Proliferation

Some important problems lie in the area often described as 'project proliferation': aid projects are planted here and there in an almost haphazard way and in excessive numbers, with a variety of untoward consequences. One of the worst cases which has come to the notice of this study is that of Haiti—not one of the countries surveyed for this report, but one for which a multilateral agency made available a confidential report, and which has also been the subject of a published Canadian study.[3]

Both reports speak significantly of 'aid overload', of donor agencies setting up and funding projects beyond the capacity of the Haitian authorities to administer. The multilateral agency study reports that aid project proliferation has exacerbated existing manpower and administrative shortcomings. It has increased the volume of technical cooperation projects competing with investment projects for scarce local counterpart personnel, and also the number of projects being duplicated by aid agencies. In doing so, it has managed to engender a massive bureaucracy, in which the majority of local institutions are now unable to cope with the administrative and technical requirements of investment programmes. The majority of staff are described as having assignments which bear no relationship to their background or training. Attempts to substitute foreign consultants for unavailable local personnel have not had much success.

Haiti is undoubtedly an extreme case, where the combination of administrative weakness and political corruption makes the aid relationship fraught with danger. But some elements in the Haitian experience recur elsewhere. The tendency of aid agencies to negotiate in their own way with individual ministries can defeat attempts at overall control. It is remarkable how recent are the measures in some countries to achieve central direction for aid negotiations and follow-up. Thus the three African countries studied for this report, Kenya, Malawi, and Mali, all instituted central administrative control of aid *only in 1983 or 1984*. Many countries do not yet have a system at all.

And even when they do, they cannot easily prevent the excesses of project proliferation. Thus Bangladesh has, on paper, a more impressive coordinating structure than most of the poorest countries, but was unable to prevent its railways, for example, from being saddled with a considerable array of equipment types:

diesel locomotives from Japan, Canada and the US; shunting locomotives from Hungary, West Germany and the United Kingdom; and freight wagons from India, South Korea and the United Kingdom. This lack of standardised equipment compounded the training and maintenance problems of the railway.[4]

Costly proliferation of equipment types is often noted: in studies for this report, other examples are tractors in India (3,850 tractors of five different makes supplied by the UK alone), and equipment for rural water supply in Kenya—eighteen different varieties of water pump have been supplied by donors.[5]

Complementary domestic resources

A further feature of project proliferation, perhaps its most serious, is the demands that uncoordinated aid makes on complementary resources required from the recipient. As projects accrue, so do the demands they make on the recipient's budget for local and recurrent project costs, on manpower, and on foreign exchange. In many countries new projects are taken on without adequate regard for the consequences as far as these three items are concerned. Demands on the recipient's administrative capacity can also become acute.

Donor competition

In several countries the donors not only fail to coordinate, but actually compete. They are all looking for projects of a reasonable size and manageability, and go sometimes to unseemly lengths to secure them for their own aid programme rather than let them go to another agency. The aid projects themselves then compete for scarce resources in the recipient country. A common example is managerial man-power. An agency will want the best indigenous manager it can find for one of its projects. It may take the person concerned away from an important government position or a managerial post in another project. A few months later, another agency may insist on having this person manage a new project it is negotiating. A person of ability may well use his or her time sub-optimally on a series of short-term assignments as a result of aid competition.

Besides aid competition there is also aid fashion: a type of 'herd behaviour' can be seen, as the swings of intellectual analysis bring one or another type of investment to the fore as desirable. After the wave of 'basic needs' enthusiasm, most agencies wanted to get involved in, say, rural water supply. The result in Kenya was a large number of official and voluntary agencies becoming involved in the sector; not only were technological choices distorted, but donor administrative complexities and varying procedures compounded the effects of a weak Kenyan ministry. As a SIDA review noted, each individual donor sees direct involvement 'as a necessary step in successful completion of agreed goals'[6] but 'the collective effect of donors' actions is to make it more difficult for the Ministry of Water Development to administer its development budget or to forecast its recurrent implications'.[7] Aid to the sector is agreed by donors and the Kenya Government to have been a 'disaster'.[8]

A more modest but in some ways similar case of donor procedures interfering with recipient management is given in the Mali study.[9] Various of the Offices de Développement Rurales (ODR) responsible for fish hatcheries, forestry, wells, etc. are legally independent administrative and financial bodies. But once an aid operation is absorbed by them, their administration and accounting systems are disrupted. They are not consulted about all aspects of investments. The aid projects can import directly without being accounted for in the ODR's accounts; the donors' procurement and payment procedures all differ, and cause long delays. The practices of the aid agencies should be reformed to satisfy the usages of all the participants, the study concludes.[10]

Again, the Bangladesh study complains that each aid agency has its own pattern of relationships between their local representation and their head office, their own procedural systems, their own modalities for selecting and contracting experts, procurement of commodities and equipment, and financial accounting. 'This is of course a phenomenon not typical only of Bangladesh, but the multiplicity of donors aggravates the effects of such diversity in procedures'.[11]

As will be seen, some of the countries in this study have very competent aid management procedures (India, Korea), others (e.g. Kenya, Papua New Guinea, Sudan) have some valuable new features which will enhance competence. But it is precisely in the poorest countries, where administration is weak to start with, that donor practices often make the situation worse, especially when the number of donors is large. One must not exaggerate. There is simultaneously a considerable donor effort to strengthen administrative capacity in the recipient countries (see especially Chapter 6). But the donors, and their multiplicity, are part of the problem as well as part of the solution. Perhaps the best-known of the problems was one which was written up in the press recently, describing a year in which Upper Volta (now Burkina Faso) had to field 350 separate aid missions. The burden on them of arranging the missions' visits, supplying them with data, coping with the small print of the terms of agreements, following their separate practices and requirements in implementing projects, is enormous. It is difficult to expect aid to function efficiently under such conditions; and the effort of managing other government business is also disrupted.

Undoubtedly some of these 'systemic effects' of donor multiplicity are more important than others. Indeed, there may be some benefit in multiplicity when it widens the recipient's choices and permits a range of innovation which might not arise if only a few agencies were in the field—provided of course that proliferation does not go too far, as the above examples show it sometimes undoubtedly has. Perhaps the most important of the untoward effects is when no proper budget is kept of the manpower, recurrent cost and balance of payments demands of a set of projects. This can lead to an excessive number of project starts, beyond the capacity of the country to complete, and also to interruption of projects when a critical constraint is reached. This was illustrated in the Malawi case, when during the world recession of the early 1980s the squeeze on the government's recurrent budget and foreign exchange availability produced a crisis in aid project management When the IMF called for cuts in the recurrent budget, one of the largest items liable for cuts was the recurrent costs associated with aid projects—with resulting dissatisfaction among donors, as conflicts of choice arose over which projects were to be denied funds. Budgetary problems have also been a factor in Kenya's deteriorating project performance.

However, the Malawi study was also able to refute an extreme case publsihed in 1984, which actually claimed that the systemic effects of aid to Malawi were so acute that 'institutional destruction' and severe hindrance to the development process were taking place.[12] The Malawi study found, on the contrary, that while there had been cases of excessive project proliferation and some other untoward 'systemic' problems in the 1970s, coordination behind a main donor group is increasing, while the interactions of 'peripheral' donors have been helpful rather than obstructive, and technical cooperation has been highly successful in strengthening institutional capacity. Malawi, it must be said, is helped in these respects by having a relatively small number of significant donors.

Some countervailing forces

A balanced conclusion should be drawn from the above paragraphs. Examples have been given of the inefficiencies arising out of the effects of operations by a multiplicity of donors. They are there to be read as a salutary lesson. There are also more encouraging cases. But nothing has been said about how widespread the ill-effects are, nor about whether or not the lessons are being absorbed.

In fact, a number of more positive facts *can* be set against this record. In the first place, several countries, as already noted, have or are establishing reasonably satisfactory aid management systems. Some of them will be described below. Second, a number of the effects of 'donor multiplicity' have already led to corrective action.[13] Third, a new move is afoot towards enhanced coordination in the donor community, and some signs of greater willingness among recipients to accept it. Since coordination and recipient management are the main remedies for adverse systemic effects, the remainder of the chapter is devoted to such matters.

II   Coordination and Management

Country and higher-level coordination

Besides addressing the 'systemic' problems referred to above, there are other functions of aid coordination. One is to assemble resources for particular countries—to assess needs and likely flows of aid, and to provide a process for mutual encouragement among donors so that collectively their aid is well-related to the recipients' situations. A second is to provide the basic economic and technical analysis and information on which the donors can make their judgements on aid levels, project selection, needs for differing types of aid (project, programme, commodities), and aid administration for particular recipients. Another set of functions is concerned both with policy dialogue between donors and recipients *and* with the implementation and management of aid on the ground at various levels—macro, sector, project, technical cooperation.

The large array of coordinating institutions fits only loosely with these functions, and carries them out with widely varying persistence and success. There are first of all the higher-level bodies where issues of broad aid policy and practice are discussed: the DAC of the OECD, and the various regional bodies, covering the Sahel, Southern Africa, the Carribean, Central America, and (most recently) the Asian 'least developed' countries. (The present study has not examined these bodies, though a full account would include them.) The EEC and its associated African, Caribbean, and Pacific states should also be included in this list, as a mechanism for coordinating aid and trade between one quasi-multilateral agency and a group of developing countries.

In the case of some twenty-plus countries, aid is, at this higher level, organized through Consortia or Consultative Groups (CGs) most of them under the aegis of the World Bank, but many with the significant participation of the Regional Banks and other multilateral agencies. To quote the DAC Chairman's *Report:*

The World Bank . . . the participating aid donors and the IMF usually meet annually and review a presentation of the recipient government's policies, programmes and aid needs as well as the Bank's judgment of the country's development performance, opportunities for improvement, and needs. In some consultative groups a separate paper and session are devoted to a major sectoral programe such as energy in Bangladesh, population in Nepal and recently agriculture in Zaire. The Bank-led groups are oriented to macroeconomic and major sectoral issues, such as adjustment and development policies, resource mobilisation and investment strategies. The extensive preparations for the meetings provide the occasion for private discussions between senior officials of the recipient country and the Bank, and many follow-up discussions between the recipient government and other donors are based on the Bank's critiques. However, the consultative group meetings themselves do not usually entail a candid group dialogue on policies or technical issues.[14]

This was written in 1982. The conclusion in the last sentence is still generally true, though there have been some changes since the period to which it refers. CGs have in recent years grappled with the economic emergencies facing certain countries, the Sudan being one of the prime examples. Bangladesh has discussed investment priorities with its CG, developing a 'core' investment programme and ranking priority sectors, sub-sectors, and projects which should receive government and donor attention. 'The donors are quite supportive of the Bangladesh Government's rankings, and to a large extent adjusted their country programmes accordingly. As a result, the Government has used its own and donor resources more fruitfully'.[15]

Current thinking

Perhaps most important are the changes in prospect: the World Bank
has announced its intention to play a more active role in aid coordination, particularly in the poorest coutries, and particularly where policy deficiencies have been holding back development and the countries in question show willingness to undertake reform.[16] Reform programmes are not substitutes for aid; they require aid to support them,
especially in transitional phases. But donors' willingness to supply
additional assistance will be enhanced by this form of coordination.

The CG is not the only institution for country-level coordination.
As noted, only some twenty-plus countries had CGs in 1984, though
a few more came into being in 1985 and others will do thereafter. For
many countries, especially in Africa, the principal country-level coordinating forum is the 'UNDP Roundtable'. (A complete list of countries and their coordinating mechanisms is given in the appendix to
this chapter.) Unfortunately, however, these Roundtables only began
in 1982. To date they cover approximately thirty countries, and some
of them have still to meet.

These Roundtables are designed for the 'least developed countries'.
Their intended functions include reviewing a country's economic
situation and external finance; assessing progress in each country
under the UN's 'Substantial New Programme of Action' in favour of
the least developed countries; helping to secure assistance for developing programmes; reviewing aid conditions and procedures; and assisting the countries with their trade problems.

It is too soon to assess progress under these Roundtables. They
have, in many cases, provided the first opportunity for governments to
discuss aid needs and problems with donor agencies collectively. They
have so far focused more on aid programmes and projects than on the
whole economic front as do the CGs. But the UNDP has been discussing with the recipient governments concerned, and with the World
Bank, the prospect of widening their scope so as to comprehend
macro-policy aspects of coordination, as well as monitoring the workings of aid down to the field level. One must await the evidence about
the potential role of Roundtables; experience with macro-policy coordination is limited, and the UNDP's familiar staffing and institutional
problems at local representational level give grounds for initial concern. The fact that they do have local representation is, however, most
important—some forms of coordination are impractical without it.
They also command the trust of recipients. Clearly Roundtables have
potential for further development.

Coordination on the ground

At all but the highest 'levels' of coordination, the role of the recipient government is crucial. Unless the recipient has a firm grasp of the aid process, coordination will not take place, or will at best reflect only the donors' priorities. Many countries are well organized in this respect. Of those studied for this report, South Korea was perhaps exceptional—aid management was virtually impeccable by the end of the main aid period. Negotiation, implementation, and monitoring of aid were functionally integrated both with line ministries and the central authorities. Not surprisingly, the highly efficient Korean government machine was extremely efficient in the handling of aid. Today, of course, aid relationships have dwindled and the CG has been discontinued.

A case in many ways more pertinent is that of India. All aid to India is negotiated by the central Finance Ministry, so that there is no question about aid being in accordance with the Government of India's priorities. In addition, the government machine is well-equipped with skilled and knowledgeable personnel. They are capable, for example, of ascertaining competitive international prices for goods and equipment offered under aid, and can thus mitigate to a considerable extent the cost of aid-tying, by refusing aid offers when prices are excessive, or by seeking from each donor items in which the donor is competitive. (This is not to suggest that tying has no costs to India—indeed, it continues to be much complained about. But India is in a stronger position than many low-income countries to combat it.)

Indeed, few of the 'systemic effects' described above are serious problems in India. Manpower, recurrent cost and foreign exchange implications of aid are well under control, and a large country with a sophisticated central administration can cope with the multiplicity of donors with some success. The need there for additional efforts of aid coordination, therefore, is simply not comparable with the situations of the poorest countries of Africa and Asia. India is of course among the poorest in per capita income terms, but it is, in company with other South Asian countries—Pakistan, Sri Lanka—institutionally advanced. The long experience of aid in these countries has, indeed, benefited both donors and recipients, and aid to less well-endowed countries can profit from its lessons.

Other models

Even where the government machine is not so strongly set up that it can manage aid well as a part of normal business, there are many

things that can be and are being done. The present study has identified one or two models. An interesting case is that of Papua New
Guinea. Confronted in the late 1970s with the need simultaneously to
diversify its sources of aid, to ensure the conformity of aid uses to its
own development priorities, and to diminish the cost of aid-tying, it
devised a system for the purpose. The first part of it was within the
budgetary process: all forecast aid was counted on the revenue
account, and all aid-funded projects were budgeted within the same
expenditure constraints as domestically funded expenditure. Provision
was also made for adhering to a medium-term macroeconomic policy,
including foreign exchange management.

The Papua New Guinea Government sought agreement with donors
for multi-period aid commitments, for tied commitments to be 'port-
able' across a range of budgeted government activities or projects, and
for commitments to be disbursed selectively against the supply sources
to which donors expected their aid to be tied. The system would
permit aid commitments to be added to other resources available for
expediture; for expenditure programmes and projects to be selected
by normal domestic procedures and criteria; and for aid-supplied
goods and equipment to be purchased under competitive tender, while
aid was disbursed when donor-acceptable suppliers were matched with
donor-acceptable projects.

In the event, donors were not keen on conceding any formal 'porta-
bility', which they saw as possibly undermining the concept of a 'pool'
of projects supported in common by all donors; but the Government
was able to achieve its objectives by agreements with individual
donors. Each donor was able to provide multi-year commitment
(though some whose legislation precluded it formally made only
'unattributable indications'). None could complain of the incorporation of aid within the budget and planning procedures. Since most
donors did not practise procurement-tying with the country, the 'selective disbursement' provision was only established with one of the two
that did, the EEC and Japan; with the latter, a satisfactory agreement
was reached, while with the former, ways were found within Lomé
Convention provisions to minimize deflections from the chosen
course.[17]

A second case is that of Kenya, where a severe economic crisis in
the early 1980s gave rise to administrative 'reconstruction'. The
Kenya Government now prepares both a Forward Budget and a
Public Investment Programme, both of which incorporate donor-
funded projects as well as expenditure by major public agencies. Sector sub-committees have been set up, chaired by the Government with
interested donors, to harmonize aid and government activities in

agriculture and energy, as well as a new project management system within the Ministry of Agriculture, with the help of donors' technical cooperation. Further, the UNDP with USAID assistance has prepared a register of donor-supported projects, though as yet it lacks the integration with Kenya's financial management system—itself undergoing a major overhaul—to serve 'as an instrument for aid management and rationalization'.[18]

A further model is provided by the Sudan, which has experimentally added an 'in-country' mechanism to the existing CG process. The CG itself has extended its role to cover short- as well as long-term development issues, while the Government and the donors have organized a 'Joint Implementation Monitoring Committee', which meets three to four times a year in Khartoum to monitor progress under the investment programme and the donors' inputs to it; sector sub-groups are also being formed.[19]

A host of other local-level coordination activities exist in many other countries. UNDP Resident Representatives have long prepared annual reports in most countries on donor aid activities to assist development programmes. Teams from the World bank, EEC, UN agencies, Regional Banks, or bilateral donors have reviewed sectors and classes of projects. The role of the UN Resident Cordinator and its possible strengthening is under consideration by UNDP, and joint programming by the UNDP and other agencies has been undertaken in some countries. Despite all these activities, however, a great deal still remains to be done to systematize coordination and make it more effective according to the needs of each country. At recent CG meetings, besides the countries mentioned, Bangladesh, Pakistan, Ghana, Uganda, Zaire, and Zambia all undertook to strengthen in-country arrangements. UNDP Roundtables also will promote such arrangements—one can at least say there is belated recognition of past derelictions. But there is still a long way to go, not least in the data and analysis on which coordination relies. Many of the reports made by various agencies simply copy from each other, and careful checking will often discover that some crucial piece of 'information' has its source in very dubious estimates: this is particularly true in the food sector, but applies elsewhere too.

Role of coordination

What is asked of aid coordination in the 1980s? Most obviously, in the light of this chapter, that it should mitigate the 'systemic effects' arising from a multiplicity of donors operating in a given country. These are—to rehearse briefly—the ill-assortment, observed in several countries, of aid projects and programmes, whether relative to each other or to the recipient's needs and priorities; the proliferation of projects and excess of equipment types; competition among donors; the excessive number of agencies at work in particular sectors; the burden on recipient administration; and the poor relationship between aid projects and the recipient's complementary resources—recurrent costs, manpower, and foreign exchange. These problems arise to a greater or lesser degree in most low-income countries, but, as noted, are most acute in the poorest.

In addition, there are other tasks: those described under 'higher-level coordination' above, and the improvement of in-country aid management. Some arise from matters discussed in other chapters—most notably, to improve the match between types of aid provided by donors (project, programme, commodity, technical cooperation) and recipient requirements; to mitigate the effect of aid-tying and to enhance the policy dialogue.

III   Obstacles to coordination

It is clear from much that has been said already that while there is now considerable impetus behind various moves towards better aid coordination, it is very late in coming. Coordination has been the subject of lengthy deliberations in the OECD DAC over a number of years—deliberations which until recently produced a good deal of paper, but not much coordination. The reasons for this are not hard to discern.

The donor side

Both donors and recipients have had strong reservations about engaging seriously in coordination. On the donor side, there have been three main reasons: first, coordination is likely to impair the freedom with which donors can pursue their commercial and political interests through their aid programmes. Second, donors know there are subjects on which they are likely to disagree, particularly in the matter of development policies: not all donors, for example, are happy with the degree of pressure currently exerted by the USA in some parts of the world to influence recipients towards its view of the role of the private sector. Such differences are not only on a political level: they can touch on everything from ideological concerns to purely technical matters. Thirdly, coordination can be costly in administrative time and expense. The current somewhat negative attitude towards multilateralism of the USA and other donor governments may be damaging in two ways: by weakening the very multilateral agencies which play key roles in coordination; and by fostering a trend back to bilateral, and therefore less coordinated, aid.

One should not, however, underestimate the technical side of the problem—the fact that donors often do not have a common understanding of development strategy, technology, and policy in key technical areas such as agricultural research, environment, and health. Differences may be real, where technical approaches rest on differing assessments of problems and responses; or they may reflect more an absence of any attempt to harmonize views. Certainly there can be little coherence on the ground if donors pursue separate technical strategies. Within the context of the inter-agency examination of aid experience which this report suggests, as well as other coordination arrangements, such issues could well be taken up. International agencies with technical competence (WHO, UNIDO, etc.) could also play significant parts.

The recipient side

The reservation about administrative costs of coordination is shared by recipients. They have perhaps two main other reservations. They are concerned that donor coordination could result in unbearable pressures, especially in the area of policy reform. Several developing countries find such pressures hard enough to accommodate in the present, relatively uncoordinated state of aid. And in the day-to-day management of aid, some recipients have valued the freedom to play one donor off against another, to choose which donors will participate in which programmes, and to be able to influence the terms of their aid. Also, some recipients do not find it easy to resolve differences between treasuries or finance ministries bent on financial control, and sectoral ministries keen on promoting their own programmes. Donors have at times encouraged such differences, since both sides have an incentive for agreeing new project starts—an incentive which is often more potent than the desire to see projects through to a successful conclusion.[20]

If these have been the reasons which have left coordination so deplorably long in the doldrums, why is there more enthusiasm for, and more success in setting up, new coordination arrangements today? The answer appears to be that the economic and public spending crises of the early 1980s have forced both sides to try to do better. Perhaps also there is, at least in some quarters, a growing recognition that what each side has to lose through better coordination is modest compared with the potential gains. Coordination can be sensitive to most of the 'reservations'. In the end, the political and commercial objectives of the donors cannot be achieved if the development purposes of aid, which they distort, are not fulfilled. And the recipient gets saddled with an array of aid-financed activities which can make its tasks both of development and of government more difficult than it needs to be. The outside observer may be excused a certain impatience which arises from contemplating both sides of the sorry history of coordination efforts in the past. It is regrettable that only an economic crisis of unprecedented proportions has been able to start bringing them together.

IV   Coordination: what must be done

The recipients' tasks

For any recipient country, the heart of an aid coordination system must be a strong central unit in the government with a complete overview of the aid process. With such a unit the government can then link 'upwards' to the higher-level (donor) coordinating institutions, and outwards within the country to coordinating activities on the ground. The first necessity for recipient countries which do not have such a unit—and many, particularly among the poorest countries, do not—is to build up this central capacity.

Ideally, this central body or set of bodies would fulfil at least three crucial functions. It (or they) would produce a forward budget in which expected aid would take its place in both revenue and expenditure accounts, taking note of recurrent budget and foreign exchange costs associated with, but not financed by, aid. It would negotiate all major aid contracts itself, or control centrally negotiations taking place with implementing ministries. It would relate the use of aid resources to priorities in its national development programmes.

A coordination system cannot be prescribed that will serve all countries equally well. The system must be adapted to each country's capacities and administrative organization, as well as to the constellation of donor presences. But countries must move towards the ability to carry out the functions described in the previous paragraph, or strengthen the ability if it is already partially in place. It is more than a little astonishing that efforts in these directions, for so many countries, have begun only in the 1980s, or have not yet begun.

The stronger the grip a recipient country has on its aid process, the better equipped it will be to relate to higher-level coordinating mechanisms, and the easier it should be for the donors to collaborate effectively. At the CG or Roundtable level, the donors should be able to agree with the recipient, not only aid levels, but that the division among types of aid (especially between project and programme or commodity aid) is appropriate. (This will obviously be difficult to do if neither side has a clear picture of the overall demands on domestic resources made by project aid.) At this level broad support can be reached for the recipient's priorities, and a dialogue can take place over the policy environment surrounding aid and development, together with any policy reform programme that may be called for.

Strengthening consultative groups

CGs have not really performed these roles in the past. Country situations and policies were reviewed and discussed, and aid amounts pledged. But, until recently at least, donors and recipients did not even seek from the CG any kind of accord on a country's development programme and policies, and detailed donor measures to support it. As noted, this has already happened recently in the cases of Bangladesh and Sudan. The World Bank clearly wishes to see CGs take on such functions more commonly, and plans, starting with selected African countries, to try to seek accords between donors and recipients covering a priority investment programme and accompanying policy measures, and appropriate donor support.

This is all to the good, and very much a desirable direction for coordination at this level. In its latest Africa report, the Bank has even proposed a donor facility to help major policy change with a 'contingent ability to respond to countries requiring major additional assistance to support their reform programs'.[21] The Bank makes it clear that such a facility would be available to countries wishing to undertake reform, and will only be drawable as reform measures are implemented.

Programme aid and coordination

This approach of the Bank is connected with growing concerns among donors about the 'policy environment', especially in sub-Saharan Africa. But there are further reasons for intensifying coordination over policies. The recent period has seen considerable movement out of project and into programme assistance—a response to the evident fact that in this acute recessionary period, recipients' economies often cannot support additional investment or even complete or maintain existing projects. As this report stresses elsewhere, it would be better if the balance between project and programme had been more flexible in the past and remained so in the future—if the aid system is not to lurch from one mode to another. But the more programme assistance there is, to the extent that it is accompanied by conditionality, the greater the need for coordination. Donors can finance projects based on differing assumptions about the behaviour of the recipient economy and its requirements. But they cannot give programme assistance, whether for macro economic or sectoral purposes, based on contradictory policies.

The Bank and the Fund

This raises an issue about one particular part of coordination not previously discussed in this chapter but addressed in Chapters 4 and 5, namely that between the World Bank and the IMF. The IMF is not an aid agency, but it has come increasingly into the aid picture in low-income countries as World Bank SALs have become virtually conditional on the recipient's agreement with the IMF on a Fund programme; some bilateral aid in turn has become conditional on SAL programmes. There have been signs, particularly over some East African countries, of differences between the Bank and the Fund, somewhat reflecting their differences of objective: the Fund being concerned with short-term balance of payments adjustment, the Bank with longer-term developmental considerations.

Some of the differences appear to arise purely from the procedures of the two institutions and the timing of their operations. Others may be more fundamental and relate, for example, to the extent to which essential investment programmes should be cut in an immediate emergency, or different analyses of the behaviour of the economies in question leading to different views of, say, the appropriate extent of a devaluation. Despite efforts to improve their collaboration in recent years, there remains something to be desired in the coordination of Bank and Fund approaches, especially to the poorest countries. There is a need for greater harmonization between short-term and long-term measures.[22]

The principal means to improved collaboration do not lie in any alteration of legal functions, but in an intensification of cooperation over individual country programmes. Perhaps the greatest need, already commented on in Chapter 5, is for the Bank to have a greater role in exchange rate discussions. The exchange rate is strictly the province of the Fund; but given the need to relate packages of measures under Bank and Fund programmes, it is an unsatisfactory state of affairs if the Fund determines what the exchange rate change should be without much consultation and the Bank then deliberates about appropriate related measures. This appears, regrettably, to be the existing practice.

National Food Strategies

Another feature of recent coordination efforts has been the design of Natonal Food Strategies (NFSs). This has been a World Food Council initiative, arising from concerns that a variety of aid and other activities associated with food and agricultural development were not adequately integrated into a set of goals and steps to reach them. The EEC has undertaken to pursue such a programme, working initially with four countries (Kenya, Mali, Rwanda, and Zambia), evolving the NFSs, or food-sector strategies—as the EEC calls them—and then coordinating donor support. This is an admirable idea, but attempts to involve more countries in such programmes, before sufficient experience is gained with those already being tried, may be premature.

Preliminary studies suggest that there is some difficulty in achieving clarity and priority among the four main goals of NFSs—food production efficiency, national food security, food import reduction, and improvement of the population's nutritional status—which do not always point in the same direction. The state of food information systems and their relation to policy decisions is extremely weak in most of the poorest countries. There are large gaps in agricultural research and in the capacity to deliver appropriate inputs, without which the currently fashionable concentration on improved pricing policies may be too one-sided. In so far as the EEC's NFS programme is concerned, its own administrative set-up from field to headquarters is complex, not to say cumbersome, and does not make for easy management of donor–recipient relations. Altogether, there seems good reason to watch and wait a little on NFS before jumping into a major extension of the approach.[23]

CGs and Roundtables: further development

Other recent proposals for 'higher-level' coordination have focused on extending the numbers and strengthening the roles of CGs and UNDP Roundtables. There have been suggestions that CGs play a greater part in organizing co-financing of development projects; becoming involved in sector-level analysis, discussion, and coordination; analysing recipient investment programmes; and resolving programme pipeline and project implementation problems.[24] Because the World Bank is so actively involved, there have been calls for expanding Bank representation in the field to give further assistance to this work; without it, the Bank's capacity to assist coordination on the ground is severely limited. As noted above, UNDP Roundtables are still very few, and there is an ongoing process of reviewing their existing performance and inter-donor discussion of strengthening it.

V Conclusions

Mitigating the 'systemic effects'

Where there is a lack of relationship among aid activities, and between aid activities and other development priorities, the new emphasis on sectoral aid and sectoral coordination can do much to improve matters. This coordination will go on both at CG/Round-table level, and at the local level. For the latter, either the 'Kenya model' described above, where the government takes the lead in organizing a sector committee with interested donors, or a 'lead donor' organizing other donors in collaboration with the recipient, are feasible approaches. The recipient's central unit(s) already referred to, which must manage the aid process, will obviously also be important; they must also ensure a balance *among* sectoral activities—also in collaboration with CGs/Roundtables.

However, for relief from most of the remaining 'systemic effects', action must be mainly at the local level, and it is mainly for the recipient to make the running, with donor help. Proliferation of projects and equipment types and donor competition can all be mitigated most simply by sectoral specialization among donor agencies, so that the number of agencies operating in a given sector is reduced to a manageable few. (There are already signs of movement in this direction, in several countries. One need not be too discouraged by the failure of earlier efforts, such as the International Cooperation for the Development of Africa initiative in the late 1970s, which tried to find ways of dividing sectors up among donors—there is wider acceptability today of some of its ideals.)

This would in turn alleviate somewhat the burdens on recipient administrations and the problems of tying and cumbersome procedures. It is the combination of large numbers of donors with the complex procurement, contracting, and accounting procedures of each that can make aid relations trying for countries of slender administrative means.

Harmonization of procedures is one of the oldest problems on the aid coordination agenda, and one of the most intractable. Many procedures have their origins in traditions of public accountability embodied in national legislation, and are truly difficult to change. Nevertheless, there are ways forward. DAC documents report some progress recently in the streamlining of procurement and other procedures, though not a great deal of change. Other possibilities include approaches on the lines of the Papua New Guinea model (described above), or agreement among donors to channel funds through a single agency. Further relaxation of tying *at least in the poorest countries* should also be encouraged. The commercial rewards in these countries are not comparable with those elsewhere. (The switch from project to programme aid—even if the latter is tied—must also have eased these problems, a further ground for welcoming the trend, and for hoping that it will not be too drastically reversed.) In the end, to the extent that the problems do stem from traditions of accountability, the donors must ponder the fact that the accountability of each can lead to reducing the effectiveness of all. The most proper individual accounting may end up contributing to collective inefficiency.

Positive and negative signs

It is tempting to see recent progress towards intensified coordination as encouraging, as signifying some willingness of donors and recipients to limit their respective freedom of action in the interests of greater effectiveness of aid. One should perhaps not be so encouraged as to believe this virtuous trend will continue, without continuing pressure from interested parties. The DAC, after all, was only able to produce the results of recent deliberations in the form of Secretariat 'Notes', rather than as 'Guidelines', which would have signified members' formal endorsement.

Ultimately, the limits of coordination on the donors' side are set by their political and commercial interests. Here two contrasting cases can be cited. The Sudan had plans for major airfield and port constructions in which two European donors (Italy and Germany) were interested; the World Bank believed that these projects were of low priority and could not be afforded, and indeed refused to collaborate in the package recently put together by the CG except on the condition that they were removed from the budget. They were removed. In several other cases where the Bank has advised against projects, bilateral aid or export credit agencies have been only too ready to come in with finance for them, when it suited them commercially. (Export credits are not part of aid, but are much in need of being drawn into aid coordination activities.) The Bank complains about these occurrences in aid coordination fora, but usually to little effect. The Bank may not always be right, and is certainly not the unique arbiter of the worthwhileness of an investment. But the lessons of these two different types of experience are well worth pondering.

Appendix: Country-level coordination arrangements

Region	Lead agency	Type of arrangement
EUROPE:		
Turkey	OECD	Consortium
AFRICA:		
Sub-Sahara:		
Ghana, Kenya, Madagascar, Mauritius, Senegal, Somalia, Sudan, Uganda, Zaire, Zambia	IBRD	Consultative Group
Benin, Burkina Faso, Burundi, Cape Verde, Central African Republic, Chad, Comoros, Djibouti, Equatorial Guinea, Ethiopia, Gambia, Guinea, Guinea-Bissau, Lesotho, Malawi, Mali, Niger, Rwanda, Sao Tome and Principe, Sierra Leone, Togo	UNDP	Roundtable
ASIA:		
Middle East:		
Lebanon	IBRD	Donors' meeting
Yemen Democratic Republic, Yemen Arab Republic	UNDP	Roundtable
South Asia:		
Bangladesh, Burma, Nepal, Sri Lanka	IBRD	Aid group
India, Pakistan	IBRD	Consortium
Maldives	IBRD	Donors' group
Afganistan, Bhutan, Maldives	UNDP	Roundtable
East Asia:		
Indonesia	Netherlands	Inter-Governmental Group (IGGI)
Philippines, South Korea[1], Thailand	IBRD	Consultative Group
Laos	UNDP	Roundtable

Region	Lead agency	Type of arrangement
AMERICA:		
Caribbean:		
Member countries include almost all of the Caribbean countries, together with mainland Guyana and Surinam. The exceptions are Cuba and the island territories belonging to France and the USA.	IBRD	Consultative Group
Central America:		
Member countries include Costa Rica, El Salvador, Guatamala, Honduras, Nicaragua, and Panama.	IDB	Consultative Group on Economic Cooperation in the Central American Isthmus (CGECCAI)
South America:		
Colombia, Peru	IBRD	Consultative Group
OCEANIA:		
South Pacific:		
Cook Islands, Fiji, Kiribati, Nauru, Niue, Papua New Guinea, Solomon Islands, Tonga, Tuvalu, Vanuatu, and West Somoa	South Pacific Bureau for Economic Cooperation (SPEC)[2]	
West Samoa	UNDP	Roundtable

Source: OECD/DAC.

Notes:

[1]Group has been disbanded.

[2]Australia and New Zealand belong to SPEC, but there is no true aid-coordinating body for South Pacific and Papua New Guinea; a recent report has called on the World Bank and ADB to assist—see Australia, Government of, 1984.

Notes

1. In Bangladesh, thirty-five bilateral donors have given aid since 1971, six multilaterals, sixteen UN agencies and over a hundred NGOs (van Arkadie and de Wilde 1984). These figures are fairly typical.

2. Duncan and Mosley 1984; World Bank 1984*h*.
3. English 1984.
4. Ehrhardt 1983.
5. Lipton *et al.* 1984*a*; Duncan and Mosley 1984.
6. SIDA 1982.
7. Duncan and Mosley 1984.
8. *Ibid.* For some similar features in Tanzania, though a less 'disastrous' record, see USAID 1980*c*.
9. Bourgoignie 1984.
10. *Ibid.*
11. Van Arkadie and de Wilde 1984.
12. Morss 1984. But see Hewitt and Kydd 1984.
13. For example, in Kenya rural water supply, several agencies have quit the field leaving it to a more sensible number.
14. OECD DAC 1982*a*.
15. USAID 1983*a*.
16. World Bank 1984*e* and 1984*h*.
17. The Papua New Guinea system is described in greater detail in Cassen, Chaudhuri and Daniel 1984.
18. Duncan and Mosley 1984.
19. OECD DAC 1983*a*.
20. The Kenya study (Duncan and Mosley 1984) makes it clear that two previous attempts to promote coordination in the 1970s foundered on just such donor and recipient reservations. The same points arise in the multilateral–bilateral comparison study made for this report (Sachse 1984).
21. World Bank 1984*h*.
22. Members of the OECD DAC were recently asked for consideration of measures which will permit 'the design of adjustment programmes more supportive of medium-term development', including improved collaboration between the Bank, the Fund, and DAC members. ˜
23. See Lipton *et al.* 1984*b*.
24. USAID 1983*a*.

CHAPTER EIGHT
Aid and Market Forces

I Introduction

Any discussion of the effectiveness of aid must examine the relations between aid and market forces. Market forces have two separate aspects. One is the use of price signals in the allocation of resources, in consumption and in production. The proper uses of prices and incentives are conditions for efficiency in any type of economy, be it centrally planned, free enterprise, or somewhere in between. The other aspect is the form of economic organization, and whether private enterprise is dominant in an economy, with a minimal role for government.

When aid first began in most countries, the production and ownership structure and important features of economic organization were already in place, often inherited from a recent colonial past. In many countries, especially the poorer ones, the public sector dominated, and commercial activities were little developed apart from trading in basic goods and some exports and imports. African economies in particular lacked, and still commonly lack, commercial development with markets, competing firms, and a flow of commercial information. Very often government does things because there is no competitive private sector which could do it.

Economic history does not yield any simple truths about the relations between economic organization and economic performance. In recent times, some of the most successful economies have been those which skilfully combined a good deal of governmental direction in finance, investment, and overall policy with active use of the price mechanism among privately owned corporations, in a mixture of large oligopolistic firms and small and very competitive ones: Japan, South Korea, and other South East Asian countries are prime examples. These countries were also highly protectionist at critical stages of development, and in some sectors still are. The forms that the mixed economy can take are very numerous. Of course, the private enterprise system has shown tremendous productive power. Perhaps the most notable feature of the privately oriented economies is their capacity for innovation, with all that implies for economic progress—something noticeably missing in the command economies.

Though today, even conservative writers ask whether modern technological developments do not require a partnership between government and business.[1]

The debate about what form of organization is best for development does not have to be resolved before one can point very clearly to features which are obviously harmful in some developing countries today: inefficient parastatal organizations and government purchasing agencies offering disincentive prices; tax, interest, and exchange rate levels which distort production and investment decisions; trade regimes which go far beyond infant industry protection and preserve uncompetitive industries at home and even harm exports by excessive curbs on imports; lack of encouragement to beneficial private foreign investment; investment licensing which throttles the expansion of domestic enterprise. The domination of production by state intervention and controls has been a clear source of poor economic performance in many cases. Countries exhibiting such a 'control syndrome' could well be said to be making insufficient use of market forces, simply on grounds of efficiency.

Aid has been accused of fostering just such inefficiencies. This report accepts the justice of the criticism in certain cases, many of them a decade or more ago, but not as a matter of generality. In fact, if asked whether aid has been a friend or foe of market forces, one would have to answer, on balance, a friend. A significant part of aid goes directly to the private sector; a large part goes to public sector infrastructure without which the private sector could not function; and a considerable part of the policy dialogue has been occupied with questions of the efficiency of specific forms of economic organization, and has commonly intervened to promote increased use of incentive prices, competitive exchange rates, trade liberalization, reform of parastatals, reduction of industrial controls, and even the conditions for the operation of foreign private companies.

One of the critics of aid has made an extreme case of the opposite view:

Aid . . . enables governments to pursue policies which patently retard growth and exacerbate poverty . . . [including] persecution of the most productive groups . . . restraints on the activities of traders . . . restriction of the inflow of foreign capital, enterprise and skills; voluntary or compulsory purchase of foreign enterprises . . . forced collectivization; price policies which discourage food production; and, generally, the imposition of economic controls which restrict external contacts and domestic mobility and so retard the spread of new ideas and methods.[2]

This blanket critique is overdone. It lumps together instances which have occurred in one country or another, suggesting they are true in the general case; it implies that aid has been responsible for these things, and that they would not have happened in the absence of aid. But what would have happened otherwise cannot be proved. The least convincing claim of this position is that, in the absence of Western aid, the things complained of would not have happened, and market forces in particular would be flourishing more than they do throughout the developing world. (It is worth pointing out that commercial bank lending has gone to many developing country governments, often in much larger amounts than aid, and often to support public sector enterprises.) The case studies conducted for this report, together with much other experience, support a position completely different from the critique quoted above.

Countries following the sort of policies referred to above as the 'control syndrome' are sometimes described as *dirigiste*. The latter term is a convenient if somewhat misleading shorthand; misleading because it is used to describe a great variety of economies, often ones with very substantial private sectors. It is employed here with that caveat. If aid were systematically biased towards countries pursuing dirigiste policies, or if there were causal links in a large number of countries between the receipt of aid and the flourishing of such policies, aid would have a case to answer.

Aid assists a variety of governments, some of which pursue price policies and policies towards the private sector which are inimical to growth and to poverty reduction. Should donors avoid all contact with such countries? Would these countries' policies change if they did? An aid agency can either refuse aid on the assumption that defective policies will not be changed, thus losing the opportunity of making any other aid-financed improvement meanwhile. Or it can give aid, take the opportunity of actively pursuing other improvements, and hope to persuade the recipient government to change its defective policies—and possibly fail. This is clearly a difficult judgement

This chapter acquits aid of being biased towards countries with dirigiste policies; there is no evidence that it has been. Nor, when aid has assisted such countries, has it accepted all the policies it found in place. This chapter also finds that, in recent years at least, aid has not been complacent about the role of market forces in the first sense defined above, the use of prices. It certainly should do everything it can to encourage efficient allocation of resources where possible by market signals. But there is another question to answer: could and should aid do more to promote market forces in the second sense, the development of private enterprise? First, the actual destination of aid must be described.

II   The destination of aid

It tends to be assumed by some aid critics that, if a relatively small share of aid is directed to final uses in the private sector and a larger one to final uses in the public sector, the aid inflow must be damaging to the interests of the private sector. (Some of the cruder critics even try to argue that, because all ODA goes *in the first instance* to the government of a developing country, it must damage the interests of the private sector, an obvious *non sequitur*.) But the assumption that the public–private split of aid in final uses is crucial for the well-being of the private sector lacks a sound basis in logic. If the recipient country has a mixed economy (and few do not) the public sector will consist of three elements. The first comprises the minimum functions of government—justice, police, revenue, and arms; the second comprises utilities for the provision of infrastructure—water, electricity, gas, roads, public transport, education and training and public health; the third comprises production of goods and services which could, given the availability of private capital and competitive conditions, be produced in the private sector. Aid which goes to finance the first two categories of public activities will benefit the private sector because better services will be provided per unit of tax and non-tax revenue levied on the population. Aid which goes to the third category of activity may potentially conflict with private development, but only if it makes a difference to the amount of such activity and if private capital *is* available to provide it instead.

What is crucial is the extent to which aid is financing activities in the public sector which *would not be* in the public sector in a privately dominated mixed economy. For the purposes of this discussion, it is usually assumed that in such a mixed economy the public sector should perform the 'minimum' plus the 'infrastructural' functions, i.e. the first two elements identified in the previous paragraph, but not the third. This comes quite close to the private/public boundaries of functions that actually exist in the United States. It may or may not be an ideal situation, but it is the situation which some aid critics have at the back of their minds when referring to the 'desirable' mixed economy. It so happens that, on this criterion, a study by the US Department of the Treasury[3] showed that only between 6 and 8 per cent of multilateral development bank lending went to final uses that were actually in the public sector but would have been in the private sector if the US definition of boundaries of public and private activities had applied. The remainder either went to the private sector, or to joint ventures between government and private enterprises, or to usual public sector functions in the US definition of 'usual'. The

6–8 per cent that was 'reversed', that is, which went to public sector activities in recipient countries which would have been private in the USA, will have done so in many cases either because the government insisted on this as a priority project, with aid or without, or because no competitive private capital was available in the amounts or at the time required.

Where the same calculations can be done for individual countries, a similar conclusion emerges. The India study, for example, looks at this problem during the period of the Second and Third Plans, that is, up to 1966. It shows that during this period, a period when aid was least disposed to question recipients' public–private 'mix', less than 8 per cent of World Bank loans were 'reversed' in the above sense. Even that figure is calculated by assuming that all lending to ports, civil aviation, and agriculture went to public sector enterprises, but should have gone to private sector enterprises in those sectors.[4]

The increase in on-lending to the private sector

Unfortunately, comparable figures are not available for bilateral aid. But it does seem to be generally true that, from about 1970 onwards, a rising share of that aid has been directed to private sector final users via different types of national financial intermediaries. There are a number of reasons for this. Although the use of aid for private sector credit is a venerable practice, being at least as old as the IBRD foundation loan to the new Industrial Credit and Investment Corporation of India in 1955, it was initially limited by two restrictions. On the one hand, the IBRD at that time refused to lend to the private sector if the financial intermediaries involved were themselves in the public sector. This considerably reduced the size of the flows that could be properly administered, until this restriction was abandoned in 1968. Since then, development banks have received aid finance in a number of countries. On the other hand, it was private enterprise in the industrial sector which was the major recipient of such on-lending. The 1970s brought a changed emphasis in development priorities, putting a new and urgent weight on the technological transformation of agriculture. Leaving aside fertilizer plants and research institutes, which could still be in the public sector, the switch to rural development opened up a large additional area of aid absorption—rural credit—which has been taken up with vigour by multilateral and bilateral agencies alike in the last fifteen years.

As well as lending through intermediaries, a variety of direct on-lending has been seen or is in prospect. Data on such lending are not generally available; indeed even qualitative accounts of what aid agencies are doing directly for the private sector are rarely available.

The picture of the 'publicness' of aid might well look somewhat different if they were. For IDA, the bulk of agricultural lending has gone to private farmers, and the overwhelming majority of its lending to DFCs has supported private sector manufacturing. Lending through DFCs is practised by several donors, and is an important means of support for private enterprise in development. In addition, there are institutions which make major contributions to promoting foreign direct investment and the development of indigenous private sectors with technical assistance and/or modest infusions of capital—the World Bank's IFC, the Commonwealth Development Corporation and several others. UNDP has its Capital Development Fund and UNIDO the Investment Cooperation Programme, both of which perform related functions. In the absence of quantitative data—one which aid agencies would do well to correct—one can list a number of aid's activities.

Promotion of private sector development. As noted above, in many parts of the developing world there is no private sector to speak of, especially in large parts of Africa, and in remote rural regions elsewhere. Aid has on occasion been directly used to help establish it. An example cited in the 'Berg Report' on sub-Saharan Africa was in Ghana, where the World Bank supported a five-year project to develop a competitive road construction industry.[5] Such development has also occurred as an indirect, but deliberate, by-product of project aid in the public sector. For example, public sector construction loans often stipulate that construction be undertaken by private companies. Such a stipulation in an early road construction project in Thailand brought into existence a myriad of construction firms doing work which was previously handled by the Department of Public Works. A very large proportion of aid projects in the public sector today enforce the strong donor preference, commonly a legal requirement, for procurement by competitive bidding: there is thus a powerful 'implementation' effect on (and flow of resources to) the private sector resulting from public sector aid projects.

Development of marketing. Aid and technical cooperation frequently go into the development of agricultural markets, including activities ancillary to marketing such as storage, distribution, and the promotion of commercial information networks. The same is true of export marketing and trade promotion, now frequently donor-assisted in poorer countries.

Aid for industrial complexes. Aid or IFC-type agencies have financed critical components of large investment complexes, often supporting the central investments where scale economies or elements of risk exist, while the remainder of the complex is taken up by the private sector. Petrochemical installations where the cracker is supported in this way while downstream units are financed privately are examples; so are tourism complexes.

Programme lending. The magnitude of the shift from project to programme aid, while uncertain, has been considerable in several countries recently. A great deal of programme lending directly assists the private sector. The foreign exchange permits higher levels of capacity utilization, and sector loans or general purpose bilateral aid is made available for spare parts and inputs required by private enterprise. It is sometimes argued that the shift from project to programme lending in recent years has reduced the possibility of 'crowding out' of private by public investment. The argument is obscure, however; it is not clear whether there is any great deal of 'crowding out', since so much aid goes into activities that the private sector would not enter at all, or would not enter in specific countries because of political risk. Aid projects in the public sector can complement private investment as well as possibly compete with it.

Not all uses of programme-type assistance are helpful to private activity, however. Chapter 5 discusses the role of food aid in this critical light, though it suggests that past mistakes are to a considerable extent being remedied, or are certainly remediable. The Kenya study also gives an instance of aid in the form of fertilizers, which has had some unhappy results. With physical commodities, it is the government's responsibility to organize the terms on which they are sold or otherwise distributed to end-users in the private sector. It may be in the government's interest to maximize the proceeds of the sales, often leading it to wait for a better price. This might not matter for commodities whose use is not sensitive to timing; but fertilizers and food are sensitive to the time of their consumption. Bad timing in their release by the government can actually lead to worse outcomes than if they did not exist at all. One option here is to try and find ways of distribution which rely on the government less directly.[6]

(Both project and programme or commodity assistance affect the relative scarcity of inputs and outputs in the private sector, and the final incentive effects depend on the working out of all the aid's direct and indirect ramifications—something which could only be computed in a general equilibrium model. In the end, the main practical consequences go back to appropriate pricing (including interest rate) policies in the public sector—the 'crowding out' question effectively reduces mainly to this, rather than being a major separate issue, given the small proportion of aid which is actually 'reversed').

Other direct assistance to private sector activity includes business management training, policy analysis, joint venture promotion, access to technology, and executive assistance. Both UN and Commonwealth organizations offer assistance to developing countries in negotiating with multinational corporations, which has been helpful in smoothing the path for private foreign investment in many instances. (See also Chapter 6 on these topics.)

An important contribution of aid has been in introducing a market element into the provision of basic services. Some areas, such as health or education, have for so long been thought of as the domain of public provision that no alternatives were ever tried. But where resources are limited and supply often inefficient, the result is often a subsidized service reaching only the better-off. Aid has supported a variety of self-help and private schemes in service sectors, often with the help of NGOs; and it has encouraged the extension of user charges and other means to try to ensure that subsidized benefits reach those who need them most. In health, education, housing, and a variety of productive activities—including power supply or irrigation—there is much to be done with a greater use of market forces to achieve both efficiency and equity, provided the interests of the poor are treated with care.

It would be desirable if some quantification were available of the volumes of financial aid and technical cooperation going directly or indirectly to support or promote private sector development. Such aid is clearly substantial already; and, coupled with the elements of the policy dialogue which are instrumental in bringing forward increased incentive pricing, competitive exchange rates, and other desirable aspects of the use of the market-place, it adds up to a respectable record of aid in fostering market forces which only someone unfamiliar with aid practice over recent years could describe as hostile to those forces. A review of some case histories bears out many of these points.

III Some case histories

India

India is a country which has been criticized for its dirigiste policies.[7] India has also received official aid continuously, though with varying sizes of flow in real dollar terms, since the 1950s. It would therefore seem to be an ideal example to clinch the aid critics' argument. But does it really do so? There are various reasons for believing that it does not. One important reason concerns the chronology of events. In India, the institutional apparatus of economic dirigisme was all in place before the Aid-India Consortium began to organize large-scale aid inflows from 1957–8 onwards. The controls on foreign trade and on industrial investment were in a direct line of descent from those established and operated by the British Imperial government during the Second World War. They had been retained, re-enacted and in some instances strengthened for a mixture of nationalistic and socialistic motives. The nationalization of the central bank and the life insurance companies had taken place in 1955, and was the last act of its kind of any significance apart from the nationalization of the domestic commercial banks in 1969.

Thus there is no justification for saying that aid agencies *created* economic dirigisme in India. They found it established and in possession in the political field, although just past its high-water mark. The agencies had to decide whether to aid India at the moment when its planning strategy, operating in a dirigiste context, proved to be too ambitious for the available foreign exchange reserves. They decided to do so, in the hope that many projects that would otherwise have been indefinitely postponed could be salvaged, and that aid would confer some influence over the future evolution of economic policy.

Unfortunately, the Aid-India Consortium not only failed to exert its influence successfully, it set back its chances of doing so for almost a decade. In 1965 and early 1966, it pressed India to undertake extensive liberalization of foreign trade, including a substantial devaluation of the rupee.[8] Devaluation took place in June, 1966, but the process of trade liberalization quickly petered out, as the timing proved to be wrong and the Consortium failed to provide the aid required to see the sequence of liberalization measures through to a successful conclusion. This episode created a strong wave of nationalistic resentment of foreign interference in India. The attempt to exert leverage against an important component of India's economic controls had been badly misjudged. It was done incompetently, in that it misjudged the foreign exchange consequences of the devaluation and the future availability of supporting aid. Finally, it was done too crudely, with political pressure, rather than with dialogue and full-hearted mutual agreement. After this fiasco, and the ill will created by aid withdrawals at the height of India–Pakistan conflicts in the late 1960s and early 1970s, it proved difficult for aid agencies in India to regain an influence which could be used in favour of the relaxation and dismantling of economic controls. It must be said that both before and during this period, aid was acquiescent in India's public–private mix. Public sector manufacturing enterprises were established in fertilizers or cement, sometimes with aid support, bilateral and multilateral. Donors lectured the Government of India on the need to decontrol industrial investment; business and diplomatic missions came and went, seeking greater freedom for private foreign investment. But there was little willingness to make aid conditional on India's taking such action; nor was there much chance that the threat of withdrawing aid would have changed policies. 'Congress socialism' combined with nationalism harboured a pervasive suspicion of private enterprise, domestic or foreign, and was deeply entrenched.

In the last ten years, a number of useful measures of liberalization have occurred. They include the relaxation, rather than the dismantling, of controls over imports and industrial investment. Many more categories of imports are now available on open general licence, and the apparatus of quantitative restrictions on imports, though still in being, is used much more sparingly. Industrial investors still require licences, but they are now available to private firms in a larger number of economic sectors than was the case after 1956, when certain activities were reserved exclusively for the public sector by the Industrial Policy Resolution. Price controls have been ended for key intermediate products in recent years, for steel, and for certain types of cement. Where administered prices remain in force, as for energy products such as coal and oil derivatives, they have been brought closely into line with world market prices. These changes are consistent with the general tenor of policy advice given over the years by the World Bank and other members of the Consortium. The Indian government has moved more slowly than suggested by the aid agencies, but it has moved in the right direction, the slowness itself ensuring that the transitions do not out-run available supporting resources or generate undesirable resentment. It has acquired freedom of manoeuvre by the gradual improvement of the balance of payments and considerable independence from the uncertainties of aid. But the policy dialogue, as well as forceful domestic debate, have been important in the gradual liberalization process. Aid may have 'buttressed economic dirigisme' in India in the 1960s and early 1970s, although it is doubtful that dirigisme would have diminished in the absence of aid. Over the more recent period, aid and political change have combined to assist in weakening 'the control syndrome'. Had there been more confidence in India that market access for exports to the industrial countries would improve, the trade regime might have been relaxed much further and sooner.

South Korea

The more simple-minded advocates of free market economics often contrast South Korea with India in the following way: 'South Korea's economy is less dirigiste than Indian, therefore it has enjoyed much faster economic growth.' But not only does the conclusion not necessarily follow from the premise, it may also be that the premise is false. In popular discussion, an important distinction is usually glossed over—that between a closely controlled economy and an economy with many controls. Korea is an example of the former while India is an example of the latter. Following the distribution of a large portion of Japanese assets to the public sector after the Second World War, Korea has experienced a long and unbroken tradition of centralization and government control over the economy. This control is exercised through credit allocation, veto power over corporate appointments, and policies of administered pricing of foodgains, fertilizers, consumer goods, labour, and many other goods and services. Government involvement in regulating and influence the business community occurs through both formal and informal mechanisms and is profound. It is evident in both industrial and agricultural sectors, and in relation to both domestic and foreign investment.[9] For most of its history to date, the government in South Korea has been both markedly authoritarian and intelligently interventionist in economic policy towards the private sector, features which give it in some ways a stronger claim than India's government to the label 'dirigiste'.

How has official aid influenced the degree of dirigisme in South Korea? In the 1950s, the primary aid donor to South Korea was the USA. During that period, the overall impact of government intervention was *not* well co-ordinated, and, in particular, the management of the foreign trade sector showed many of the defects of indiscriminate import substitution policies. But this was an inherently temporary situation, because the USA had no desire to remain a sole donor, or to continue indefinitely giving aid at the extraordinarily high per capita level that had been necessary to sustain the country in the immediate aftermath of the Korean war. The USA saw that two things were needed. The first was to prepare South Korea to receive aid from other donors who imposed somewhat stricter qualifying conditions. The second was to find a way of stimulating such rapid economic growth that aid from *all* sources could quickly become of diminishing importance for the success of the economy, and thus for the long-term survival prospects of the country. A reform of the foreign trade sector, centred around the move to a realistic foreign exchange rate, could serve both purposes and was carried out in the early 1960s. South Korea thus became more aidable, receiving its first World Bank loan, for the railway sector, in 1962. It was also well placed to embark on a long period of export-led growth, not uniquely in response to market signals, but in response to intelligent anticipation by the government of what export markets would probably be demanding in a year or two's time. The dedication and thoroughness with which this strategy was executed was rewarded by the early 1970s with a virtual escape from aid dependence, and a steady inflow of funds on commercial terms. In South Korea there is an initial period when aid does buttress dirigisme, but it is followed by one in which as aid diminishes, dirigisme does also—but the donors were active in promoting liberalization policies.[10]

During the first period (the 1950s), complaints were raised in the USA that US aid was doing too little to assist the private sector. It was noted then, and later, that US funds were channelled to government-controlled industries, and often to large and well-established enterprises as well.[11] But if such complaints had been taken seriously at that time, aid directed to the private sector might well have been ineffective, given the prevalence of excess capacity and an unfavourable policy context, especially in the foreign trade area. The attempt by donors to persuade the government to relax its controls over the private sector only began in earnest as economy was becoming decreasingly aid-dependent. Apart from the liberalization of trade and the admission of private foreign investment, the most visible achievement of donor pressure in this direction has been some reform of banking practice to alleviate what has been termed 'financial repression'.[12]

The key change in Korea between these two periods was the advent of the Park Government in 1961, bent on reform and a greater degree of national self-reliance. There was thus a greater congruence between the policy changes desired by donors and those desired by the government. An important role was also played by officials trained in (mainly) US universities able to articulate the new lines of policy within the government. Both the desire to reduce dependence on aid, and the legacy of aid in investment, personnel, and policy advice, played their parts: but the policy advice was only accepted by a government wishing to move in the directions indicated.[13] Korea's rapid growth began just as aid declined, but not *because* aid declined. And its economy has both benefited from its past period of import substitution and remained somewhat dirigiste—certainly not the private enterprise model some have claimed. Indeed, Korea's development has been quite idiosyncratic. It possesses some transferable lessons; but perhaps the main ones could be summed up paradoxically as being that a dirigiste economy can succeed if, after a period of protection, it makes skilful use of the price mechanism and maintains a competitive exchange rate.

Bangladesh

Bangladesh might appear at first glance to be a classic instance of aid buttressing dirigisme. That case has certainly been argued.[14] It is claimed that aid has created a powerful group of intermediaries in both the private and public sectors whose wealth and power are maintained by aid. It is in the interest of this group to continue to postpone difficult political decisions on structural adjustment. Such development as does occur is biased in favour of reliance on imports, and the potential growth of local capacity (in either public or private sectors, presumably) is frustrated. Although this case is explicitly argued from a leftist position and a Bangladeshi nationalist perspective, the substance of it is similar to that of free market aid critics who complain of 'the politicization of economic life' as a result of aid-giving.[15]

The case study carried out for this report[16] sees the situation differently. In the first place, as in the Indian context, the chronology of the argument is wrong. Bangladesh has only been independent of Pakistan for twelve years, and thus an aid recipient for a much shorter period than either India or South Korea. Many of the features of the 'intermediary group', on whose existence the argument turns, were already present at the birth of Bangladesh, particularly the rural inequalities and the elite from which the intermediary group has been recruited. In addition, there is little evidence of any interaction between aid inflows and the political changes (often quite dramatic) that have occurred in the short life of the state. This second objection is sustained if donor attitudes are consulted. They would like to see more successful aid influence. Their deep frustration is thus a rather telling point against the view which implies that donors bear the responsibility for the existing socio-political situation in Bangladesh. Finally, it is far from clear how powerful the existing intermediary group would prove to be in resisting indigenous pressures for social and political change, were these to arise at some future date.

One could make an alternative assumption, such as is favoured by free-market critics of aid, that the withdrawal of aid would produce a smaller public sector and the convergence of actual key prices on shadow prices that reflect the true underlying scarcities. The Bangladesh study finds that this assumption, too, is unconvincing. Aid withdrawal would only lead to 'a messier, less effective and poorer version of the existing system'. Like India, Bangladesh has carried through in recent years a number of reforms in the economic sphere.[17] Successive World Bank reviews of the Bangladesh economy have rec-

ognized as improvements such changes as privatization in the industrial sector and in the distribution network for agricultural inputs.
Public sector prices have been brought into a better relation to industrial costs, and the over-valuation of the currency has been reduced by
exchange rate adjustments. Although aid donors have been pressing
for such change, it is not clear that it was such pressure which actually
produced them. In Bangladesh politics, a conservative trend has been
strong in recent years, and this has coincided with the very adverse
macroeconomic conjuncture of 1981–2. At most, donor persuasion
has been a third prong of the trident of reform, ideological commitment and the external environment being the other two. In Bangladesh, as in India, there is some evidence for the view that, if aid fails to
bring spectacular Korean-style growth, it may nonetheless eventually
begin to help dismantle the apparatus of dirigisme.

Malawi

The example of Malawi provides a final warning against the easy
acceptance of the claims that aid encourages dirigisme. Malawi has a
private sector—albeit not a highly competitive one—which plays a
significant and independent role in the economy. The steady and
balanced economic growth which it had enjoyed, with the help of
UK-led aid (much devoted to technical assistance) did not outlast the
1970s. After 1979, external shocks to the balance of payments made
structural adjustment urgent, a need met by lending from the IMF,
the EDF, and the World Bank. These resources have been accompanied by policy advice designed to strengthen the private sector,
both in agriculture and in industry and commerce. The Malawi study
advises that this process could be taken further, with encouragement
of a more central role in investment decisions for the private commercial banks. But in Malawi, aid could hardly be more distant from the
accusation that it 'politicizes economic life' at the expense of the
private sector, which is well entrenched in the country's political
outlook.[18]

These examples could be supplemented with many more. As noted
at the end of Chapter 4, a large number of countries are currently
undergoing policy reforms stressing incentive pricing, competitive
exchange rates, and trade liberalization, undoubtedly in many cases
at the instigation of the aid donors. This reflects a combination of
increasing perception by recipient countries of the need for reform,
and a diminishing enthusiasm among donors for giving aid to countries where, whatever may be the fate of an individual aid activity, the
policy climate for overall economic progress strikes them as adverse.

It may also reflect a more deep-seated historical trend: in the 1960s, aid had a considerably stronger political and specifically Cold War element. The donors were more willing to finance the kinds of development the recipient wanted. They competed, for example, to supply India with public sector steel plants—something that would be unimaginable today. Such force as the free market criticism of aid ever had was most applicable to the aid of twenty years ago; some of these critics are still repeating what they were saying then, and sound increasingly like the prisoners of history.

The future

Some aid agencies—perhaps most notably those of the USA and West Germany—are keen to see a higher proportion of aid directed to the private sector. Others do not see this as a high priority. But the dangers of excessive state intervention and controls are becoming more and more clearly recognized among aid recipients, many of whom show increasing willingness to move away from them. This chapter has already noted several areas where aid has assisted private sector development and improved the role of price and other incentives. Wherever this leads to greater economic efficiency, it is to be welcomed, and an increasing trend is desirable. An area referred to which could benefit greatly from increased aid—especially in Africa—is the *promotion* of commercial networks, firms, markets, and institutions where these are weak or non-existent. There is not much point in improving price signals if the signals are not received by individuals and firms capable of responding in an efficient and competitive framework.

A business task force in the USA has recently produced a report recommending increased USAID assistance for private enterprise activities.[19] Its detailed proposals include support for agribusiness in recipient countries, and for agribusiness development corporations to promote that activity; and for lending US executive managerial personnel to assist recipient country agricultural entrepreneurs. It also proposed support for venture capital, intermediate credit institutions, business management training, prototype private enterprise projects with potential for replication, co-financing, trading companies and other business-brokering institutions, and joint undertakings between business and private voluntary organizations. (Additional proposals for aid to private sector development were made in 1982 by USAID itself.[20])

Aid already does many of these things, and undoubtedly development would benefit if such activities received additional support. The report in question recommends a substantial reorientation of US aid in such directions. Each donor will have his own view of how far to go down this path, and which activities in particular of his own and of the recipients' he is in the best position to assist and promote. There is no question that aid has not given the highest priority to private sector development in the past, and that much good can come from raising its priority in future.

But the fact must not be lost sight of that a key purpose of aid is to do things that the private sector will not do or cannot do efficiently—the first two functions of the public sector referred to above. Indeed, if the public sector provides the conditions in which private activity can flourish—which include infrastructure, public services, and the legal and regulatory framework, all of which can be assisted and encouraged in appropriate directions by aid and the policy dialogue—private activity should become more prominent of its own accord. Foreign investors avoid some countries because of the policy climate towards them, but they will not enter many others because of risks of all kinds and the lack of infrastructure. In fact, large corporations, wishing to invest in the Third World, lobby aid agencies to provide the power or transport facilities and other conditions without which private investments cannot function.

Public subsidies

In the past there has been an opposite criticism: public sector facilities supported by aid have systematically benefited the private sector by under-pricing output or services beyond the point where, on social efficiency grounds, there is a case for doing so. Under-pricing of public goods has been progressively reduced in recent years, partly under donor pressure. If an output is administratively under-priced, some other allocation mechanism must be at work to balance supply and demand, eliminating excess demand. If this works badly, high-priority users may be unable to get the supplies they need—for them the price subsidy will be of academic interest only. This is indeed one of the reasons why aid agencies have argued for liberalization packages: administrative under-pricing is a mixed blessing for the private sector. (A common case in point is subsidized credit and artificially low interest rates, which often end up in the hands of large firms or farmers, effectively restricting the access to credit of small businesses and farms.)

Another, if indirect, effect can also sometimes be observed: an aid-supported project can indirectly compete with the private sector by driving up the prices of local goods and services which could have been used for other, different projects that private investors wanted to undertake in the area The effect may help explain why many of the large-scale aid projects started in remote areas did not induce a rush of additional private investment, but remained as giant enclaves. Such projects today are viewed with caution for a variety of reasons. Indirect effects of this kind have been little studied, but they add to the list of reasons why existing agency policies of urging economic liberalization while engaging in extensive dialogue over detailed sectoral policies are moves in the right direction.

Two qualifications

Chapter 4, on policy dialogue, has already noted that there are limits beyond which liberalization should not be pushed—not least in the field of trade liberalization in the poorer countries, the pace of which must be sensitive to each country's capacity to adjust to and benefit from an opening up of the economy to international market forces. Similarly, the pendulum must not swing so far towards the private sector that the desirable functions of the public sector are neglected. Nor should donors attempt to push recipients on private sector issues so far as to infringe on their social philosophies, going beyond any evidence that economic efficiency, rather than ideological preference, is at stake. Enthusiasm for the virtues of the private sector should not overwhelm recollection of its well-documented deficiencies, in particular that the public sector has to correct market imperfections and to intervene when there are major discrepancies between private and social costs.

Dispute can be avoided with the recognition that what is sought is an appropriate balance between the private and public sectors. This is true both of the broad division of investment and of activities in particular sectors. No one denies the traditional roles of government in the economy. But in many developing countries some government activities have become an impediment to development. Limiting their scope need not compete with social goals—it may accelerate their achievement. There is much scope for increasing the role of prices and markets in the 'mix' of public and private activities—in almost every sphere, including some of those normally thought of as mainly in the public domain—forestry, resettlement schemes, even health and family planning. Much greater involvement of non-governmental, voluntary organizations is also called for; the good ones have numerous advantages, particularly where participatory involvement of project beneficiaries is a priority. Their drive, commitment, and understanding often contrast all too vividly with the dead hand of government.

A second qualification is what might be termed 'asymmetrical liberalism'. This refers to the success which aid agencies can have and are having in persuading recipient countries to adopt economic liberalization packages, while liberal aid practices in donor countries retreat. Bilateral donors are actively furthering that retreat by devising new methods of formal tying of aid, such as mixed credits, even new forms of invisible, informal tying arrangements. Similarly, lectures on the virtues of import liberalization come somewhat ill from the platforms of industrial countries which follow fairly illiberal trade policies themselves. As noted earlier, improved access for developing countries' products in industrial countries' markets would do wonders for developing countries' 'outward orientation'.

Adam Smith's vision of a decentralized economy guided by price signals has been extensively and often acrimoniously debated. Yet, curiously, the central question of whether the failures of the market are grosser and more heinous than the failures of government intervention has still neither been settled nor abandoned from exhaustion of interest. It may well be that, in the early days of aid-giving, it was assumed much too readily that governments could channel aid through bureaucratic conduits effectively to achieve the desired developmental results. In the present state of economic knowledge, it is justified to diversify the aid effort, pushing an increasing share of aid through non-governmental mechanisms (whether profit-seeking or not). Such diversifications are to be welcomed, but not because public channels and public sector recipients necessarily misuse aid, while private channels and recipients do not. Mixed strategies tend to be more successful than pure strategies (whether purely public or purely private). Diversification should broaden the range of aid management experience still further, and from greater competition it is more likely that good solutions to particular aid management problems will emerge. The doctrine of competition need not be interpreted in a narrow way to mean exclusively competition within the sphere of private economic activity. Competition in which both private and public sectors play their part can be expected to be even more fruitful. Indeed, it is essential.

Notes

1. Phillips 1984; see also Scott *et al.* 1984.
2. Bauer 1984, p. 46. Compare USAID's findings on, for example Cameroon: 'As a broad generalization, aid to Cameroon has on balance helped the development and effectiveness of private markets' (USAID 1983*g*).
3. United States, Government of 1982. The figures for the IDB and ADB are almost identical.
4. The calculation is set in the Indian country study (Lipton *et al.* 1984*a*).

5. World Bank 1981*a*. Further information—by no means comprehensive—on World Bank assistance to the private sector can be found in IMF/World Bank 1981.
6. For a fuller discussion, see Duncan and Mosley 1984.
7. For example, Lal 1983.
8. For an account of this episode, see particularly Bhagwati and Srinivasan 1975, Part III, 'The Liberalisation Episode'.
9. Cf. Luedde-Neurath 1984; Moore 1984; Steinberg 1984; White and Wade 1984.
10. Steinberg 1984.
11. The complaints were embodied in reports submitted by the Comptroller General of the United States dated 1957 and 1972 (see Bibliography, under Comptroller General . . .).
12. McKinnon 1981.
13. See the Korean country study, Steinberg 1984.
14. By Sobhan 1982, for example.
15. See Bauer 1984, though not specifically on Bangladesh.
16. Van Arkadie and de Wilde 1984.
17. Perhaps the centrepiece of these reforms has been the introduction of the so-called New Marketing System, in place of a distribution system for agricultural inputs run exclusively by the public sector Bangladesh Agricultural Development Corportation. Under the NMS, most of the BADC's local marketing and distribution functions will be transferred to private and co-operative retail dealers. Additionally, prices of agricultural inputs will be decontrolled and the licensing requirements for private dealers will be liberalized. This reform was negotiated through USAID's dialogue with the Bangladesh Ministry of Agriculture. One study predicts that price decontrol will adversely affect small farmers, especially in remote and inaccessible areas (Ahmad and Hassain 1983: p. 57).
18. As the Malawi study puts it: 'Malawi has placed greater reliance on the market . . ., has shown restraint in expanding its public sector . . . and has taken a positive view of international trade . . . Thus most of the policy changes which the Bank advocated for Malawi were not alien or unacceptable in terms of the government's general approach to development' (Hewitt and Kydd 1984).
19. See Andreas 1984.
20. USAID 1982*c*.

CHAPTER NINE

Multilateral–Bilateral Comparisons

I Introduction

This chapter compares the roles of the multilateral and bilateral agencies. Several of the major issues in such an assessment—policy dialogue, aid coordination, and technical cooperation—have already been considered in this report. The focus here is first on the aid record of the multilateral and bilateral institutions, and then on the factors influencing governments' decisions on allocating aid. Finally, the chapter turns to another issue—aid-tying, and its increasingly complex variants—which illustrates the different concerns of donors and recipients.

A historical note

At the end of the 1960s, the Pearson Commission commented that development assistance had once had a relatively simple structure, dominated by the bilateral aid of the United States. But by 1969, its Report said:

Making aid effective is not simply a question of procedures and techniques. Even more important is overall organization and purpose. As the aid system has grown, its channels have multiplied and tangled. Unless this machinery acquires greater coherence, aid cannot be used to best advantage.[1]

The same report outlined the shortcomings in the international system of development assistance. The processes established for joint, authoritative monitoring and review were inadequate. There was unnecessary duplication in economic reporting and feasibility studies. The links between policies on aid and those in related areas—trade and capital flows—were largely ignored. These inadequacies implied a lack of purpose and direction in development assistance, which meant there was no rallying point for public support.

To remedy these deficiencies, the Pearson Commission advocated many changes—among them, the strengthening of multilateral agencies. It saw those agencies as a way of internationalizing the sensitive aspects of aid; they represented neither charity nor geopolitical intervention. The multilaterals could offset the biases in bilateral aid, which then accounted for 90 per cent of ODA. At the same time, they could make bilateral aid more effective by their coordinating role and their assessment of recipients' economic performance. There were also technical grounds for strengthening the multilaterals, since many of the problems that aid recipients faced were global in scope. Multilateral agencies already had expertise in selecting and implementing projects. And, where appropriate, they could facilitate regional integration among developing countries.

Since the Pearson Report—and partly as a result of its recommendations—aid's effectiveness has improved considerably. The work of the multilateral institutions has become even more important, both for the reasons that the report advocated, and for others that were not then so clearly foreseen.

II Donors and Recipients

The DAC members provide the bulk of ODA, although others—particularly countries belonging to OPEC—are also major contributors (see Table 9.1). However, this table also makes it clear that *non-*

TABLE 9.1

Composition of external financial receipts of developing countries: 1971–3, 1976–8, and 1981–3 (percentages)

	1971–3	1976–8	1981–3
ODA	40.1	32.3	34.5
Bilateral	34.3	25.3	26.9
DAC	25.6	15.4	18.1
OPEC	3.6	7.7	5.3
Other	5.1	2.2	3.5
Multilateral	5.8	6.9	7.5
Other resource flows	60.0	67.6	65.6
Private grants	4.2	2.1	2.2
Non-concessional flows	55.8	65.5	63.4
Direct investment	15.5	14.1	11.9
Bank sector and bond lending	22.9	28.8	30.6
Private export credits	7.2	12.0	7.7
Other[a]	10.1	10.6	13.2

Source: OECD DAC 1984*a*, Table II.A.2.

Note: All figures are simple averages for years indicated; details may not sum to totals due to rounding.

[a] Includes official export credits, multilateral agencies, and other.

TABLE 9.2

Net external financial receipts of developing countries by type and income group, 1981–2 average[a]

(percentages)

	LLDCs	India China	OLICs	LMICs	UMICs	All LDCs
ODA	92.3	67.9	53.4	35.4	13.5	35.6
Bilateral	62.2	26.7	40.8	29.6	12.4	27.9
Multilateral	30.1	41.1	12.6	5.8	1.1	7.7
Non-concessional flows	7.7	32.1	44.6	64.6	86.5	62.2
Bilateral	6.3	24.3	39.1	52.0	78.8	56.0
Multilateral	1.4	7.8	5.5	12.6	7.7	6.2
Total	100.0	100.0	100.0	100.0	100.0	100.0
Memo: Shares[b]						
ODA	18.7	6.4	22.9	14.5	15.3	100.0
Non-concessional	0.9	1.7	11.3	14.9	55.5	100.0

Source: OECD DAC, 1984a, Table II.A.3.

[a] Recipient country groups as defined by the DAC; see OECD DAC 1984a, Table II.I.13. DAC notation is used here: LLDC = least developed countries; OLICs = other low-income countries; LMICs = lower-middle income countries; UMICs = upper-middle income countries.

[b] More than 22 per cent of ODA and almost 16 per cent of non-concessional flows are unallocated or unspecified, hence shares sum to less than total.

concessional flows have consistently accounted for a larger proportion of the external financial receipts of developing countries.

Taking DAC members as a group, in 1970 their private flows and ODA each accounted for 44 per cent of their total net disbursements to developing countries.[2] In current dollars, net disbursements of private capital rose nearly ninefold over the 1970s, largely due to the big increase in commercial bank lending; those of ODA 'merely' trebled, with the biggest growth being in contributions to multilateral institutions. By 1981, ODA accounted for only 28 per cent of net disbursements, while the share of private flows had reached 63 per cent. Then direct investment and bilateral portfolio flows declined abruptly, so by 1983 private flows were only 50 per cent of net disbursements. ODA's share had recovered to 40 per cent, although in current dollars ODA from DAC countries was little more than it had been in 1980.

The changing pattern of financial flows in the early 1980s reflects, first, the debt difficulties of several big developing countries, which have slowed the net disbursements of private capital. In addition, policy reforms in some recipient countries have elicited an increase in ODA, and donors have also increased their emergency relief, especially food aid for Africa. The same factors appear likely to sustain increased flows of ODA from DAC members in the mid-1980s.

As Table 9.2 shows, the poorer the country group,[3] the higher the share of ODA in its external finance; non-concessional flows to the very poorest countries were minimal in 1981–2. While the multilaterals accounted for less than 22 per cent of all ODA, they provided about one-third of the ODA receipts of the lowest income group, and some 60 per cent of those for India and China.[4]

However, the data also suggest that some of the lower-income group are unhealthily dependent on non-concessional resources, while concessional aid may be going disproportionately to countries that need it less. Table 9.3 gives examples of countries in the various income groups defined in Table 9.2. Four of the major recipients of ODA—Jordan, Syria, Turkey, and Israel—are outside the lower-income group. The ODA they obtain is from bilateral donors, whereas none of the main recipients of multilateral ODA is outside the lower-income group. Yet, by often reiterated international agreement, ODA is intended to be for the poorest, or poorer, countries—certainly not for the upper-middle income group.

Multilateral—bilateral shares of ODA

Until 1970, roughly 90 per cent of all ODA had been bilateral. By 1971–3, that share had dropped to 80 per cent; a decade later, it was less than 70 per cent (see Table 9.4). The multilateral share doubled

TABLE 9.3
Major ODA recipients and their sources, 1980–1[a]

| | | ODA sources | | | |
| | | Bilateral | | | |
ODA recipients	Total	DAC	OPEC	CMEA	Multilateral
LLDCs	Bangladesh Sudan Tanzania	Bangladesh Sudan Tanzania	Somalia Sudan Yemen	Afghanistan Laos	Bangladesh Sudan Tanzania Ethiopia Somalia
China India	India	India	India	India	China India

OLICs	Egypt Pakistan Indonesia Vietnam	Egypt Pakistan Indonesia Kenya	Egypt Pakistan Mauritania	Egypt Pakistan Vietnam Kampuchea	Egypt Pakistan Indonesia Kampuchea Zaire
LMICs	Jordan	Thailand	Jordan Morocco	Cuba	
UMICs	Syria Turkey Israel	Turkey Israel Korea Rep.	Syria Lebanon Oman Bahrain	Syria Turkey Algeria Argentina Iraq	
Memo: $ million	14 785	8 291	4 515	2 375	3 484
%	45	46	81	92	50

Source: OEDC DAC 1983a, Tables III-6 and J. 13.
[a]For notation, see Table 9.2.

TABLE 9.4

Net disbursements of ODA by all DAC members, 1971–3 and 1981–3 (period averages)

	1971–3				1981–3			
	Total	Bilateral (US $ million)	Multilateral	(% of total)	Total	Bilateral (US $ million)	Multilateral	(% of total)
EEC-DAC[a]	3 547	2 705	843	23.7	12 125	8 434	3 691	30.4
Other DAC	5 609	3 977	1 092	22.4	14 783	9 950	4 833	32.7
Australia	266	236	30	11.3	762	549	213	28.0
Austria	23	6	17	73.9	205	151	54	26.3
Canada	458	327	130	28.4	1 271	807	464	36.5
Finland	21	8	12	57.1	144	86	58	40.3
Japan	711	558	153	21.5	3 318	2 351	967	29.1
New Zealand	21	16	5	23.8	65	49	16	24.6
Norway	64	30	34	53.1	536	307	229	42.7
Sweden	211	109	101	47.9	887	572	315	35.5
Switzerland	53	28	25	47.2	269	188	81	30.1
United States	3 242	2 658	584	18.0	7 325	4 890	2 435	33.2
All DAC	8 616	6 682	1 682	22.4	26 908	18 385	8 524	31.7
Memo: Growth factors								
EEC-DAC					3.4	3.1	4.4	
Other DAC					2.9	2.5	4.4	
ALL DAC					3.1	2.8	4.4	

Source: OECD DAC 1948a, Tables II.1.3–8.
[a]See Table 9.5 for country detail.

TABLE 9.5

Net disbursements of ODA by EEC DAC members, 1971–3 and 1981–3 (period averages)

	1971–3				1981–3			
	Total	Bilateral	EEC	Other multilateral	Total	Bilateral	EEC	Other multilateral
US $ millions								
Belgium	191	140	25	27	518	317	85	116
Denmark	100	51	1	48	404	218	31	155
France	1 285	1 114	89	82	4 009	3 334	347	328
Germany	882	641	92	149	3 169	2 203	400	566
Italy	159	102	44	13	768	308	184	276
Netherlands	282	192	26	64	1 392	1 006	108	278
United Kingdom	648	465	4	179	1 866	1048	302	516
EEC total	3 547	2 705	280	563	12 125	8 434	1 457	2 234
Growth factors					3.4	3.1	5.2	4.0
Shares (%)								
Belgium		72.9	13.0	14.1		61.2	16.4	22.4
Denmark		51.0	1.0	48.0		54.0	7.7	38.4
France		86.7	6.9	6.4		83.2	8.6	8.2
Germany		72.7	10.4	16.9		69.5	12.6	17.9
Italy		64.2	27.7	8.2		40.1	24.0	35.9
Netherlands		68.1	9.2	22.7		72.3	7.8	19.9
United Kingdom		71.8	0.6	27.6		56.2	16.2	27.6
EEC total		76.2	7.9	15.9		69.6	12.0	18.4
Change						-6.6	4.1	2.5

Source: OECD DAC 1948a, Tables II.I.3–8.

between 1970 and 1975. The shift continued until 1977–8, before swinging back slightly towards bilateral aid. Although the multilateral share did decline slightly in 1983 and (according to preliminary estimates) 1984, these figures alone are not strong enough to confirm what some perceive as a firm and lasting preference among donors for bilateral aid. Such a preference was, however, indicated in some donors' actions and policy statements in the early 1980s.

As Table 9.4 makes clear, ODA from the EEC countries grew more rapidly in the 1970s than that from other DAC members. While some of the growth in the EEC's contribution was in multilateral ODA, however, more came from bilateral programmes. On the face of it, that seems a false conclusion, since the share of bilateral ODA from the EEC countries fell over the decade. However, only one-third of the percentage by which it fell was taken over by the other multilaterals, two-thirds by the EEC development agencies (see Table 9.5). For the EEC countries, the shifts in aid differ in character from seemingly similar shifts by other donors.

II   A Spectrum of Official Institutions

The previous section's distinction between bilateral and multilateral agencies follows convention. But that convention could result in misleading inferences. For example, it suggests that the expansion of the EDF is part of a shift toward multilateral aid. In fact, as the main aid agency of the EEC, the EDF has numerous features more appropriately categorized as bilateral than multilateral. The EDF is itself an agency of a multi*national* but nonetheless governmental entity that has obvious independent status. As such, EEC assistance reflects the political and commercial interests of EEC members in a far more direct way than any 'true' multilateral body would do. The fact suggests, not a dichotomy, but a spectrum of development institutions ranging from clearly bilateral to almost purely multilateral. This section discusses that spectrum.

Bilateral agencies

National aid agencies and programmes have evolved considerably since their beginnings in the 1950s and 1960s. Their early history has been fairly well documented.[5] But similarly independent assessments of their more recent experience are scarce.

Motives for providing development assistance vary, not only among countries, but within one country over time. The first and most obvious is national interest. Donors support countries with which they have, or hope to have, strong ties. Those ties may be cultural, economic, political, or strategic. Britain and France give much of their aid to their former colonies; Japan concentrates its aid in the Asian region; political and cultural relations are evident in OPEC's aid allocations; so are the strategic aspects in the United States' bilateral programme. Donors may also expect straightforward economic benefits—through more trade, obtaining supplies of needed resources, and so on. Or they may look for global and strategic benefits—such as the recipient's political or military support for its position. These motives do not necessarily reflect the condition or the needs of the recipients. Nonetheless, some recipients feel that special links at least provide a sustained inflow of bilateral aid.[6] That position needs to be tempered by the reality that views and alliances do change, both in donors and recipients; politically motivated aid can be as fickle as politics itself.

Domestic politics may determine the character of bilateral aid programmes; but it is not always easy to see how the balance between national self-interest and developmental concern has been struck—in so far as they do not point in the same direction. For some donors, notably the Nordic countries, developmental and humanitarian motives have almost invariably been in the ascendant. For others, national interest has predominated; without it they might never have had aid programmes, certainly not such large ones—although without the more altruistic motives their programmes would undoubtedly have been smaller and very different in character. The various bilateral programmes show how such differences work out in practice.

The USA. The US aid programme, though below average as a share of its GNP, is still by far the biggest in absolute terms. Not only in quantity but also in quality, the USA was for long a pioneer in aid. It has made major contributions to most aspects of the development of the Asian sub-continent, of East Asia and Latin America, and more recently of Africa. US aid has had many strengths, as other parts of this report make clear. Perhaps its greatest achievements have been in the development of agriculture and the setting up of agricultural research institutions and training of developing country researchers. It has also been a leader in population assistance and many other fields, and a major supporter of the multilateral system. It is the only bilateral agency whose aid, like that of the World Bank, has covered more or less the whole range of development activities, and whose economic and analytical work makes a major contribution to the aid process as a whole.

Today, the US aid effort is changing. While the country has always been aware of the geo-political dimensions of aid, in the 1980s much of the growth in its aid has been under the heading of security assistance rather than development assistance: their respective proportions of total US aid are now two-thirds to one-third, compared with 55 to 45 per cent only four years ago.[7] This has inevitably reduced the developmental impact of aid. The desire to use aid more specifically for national purposes has also led to a questioning of multilateral aid. The USA has made it clear that it values the multilateral system and will continue to support it, but more selectively than in the past. Other developments—a greater emphasis on the private sector, doubts about the ethical basis of some aspects of population pro-grammes—are also changing the focus of US assistance. But the size of the US programme, the sophistication of its analytical and evalua-tion work, and the experience of USAID will continue to make the USA a potent force in development assistance.

Japan and Germany.   The next two largest OECD donors (if France's aid to its DOM/TOM is excluded) are Japan and Germany. They have some things in common—an absence of significant post-imperial connections and a strong economic and commercial orientation to their aid. They have also both had traditional strengths in giving aid for infrastructural development and for industry. In the early years of their aid programmes, both made extensive use not only of grants, but of loans on relatively hard terms, primarily for projects. Neither country wished to allow the mix of commercial and political motives inherent in 'soft' lending, or the economic distractions that can thereby be caused.

Germany viewed private capital as the most desirable form of assis-tance, and sought 'multilateral measures as much as necessary, bi-lateral measures as much as possible'[8] But although German aid policies were not articulated in detail until 1971, their social and humanitarian objectives had been evident much earlier.[9] Shifting in response to domestic concerns, German aid has continued to concen-trate on the poorest countries. The government's policy is to favour untied aid, except for projects in the railroad and ship-building sec-tors. The country allocation of German assistance tends now to reflect foreign policy interests that often have no strong commercial aspects.

The thrust of Japanese aid in the 1960s has been characterized as national:[10] Japan wanted to regain international respectability, and to develop its influence in Asia. Like Germany's, Japan's bilateral aid initially sought to strengthen economic ties with recipient countries. Later, it began putting more emphasis on the needs of the recipient. The allocation of Japanese aid is motivated by regional strategic sec-urity and the goal of self-help for recipients. The Asian emphasis, although still strong, is declining. Although the programme is still set and run by multiple decentralized aid agencies within the government, its total size has been increased substantially, as has the proportion devoted to multilateral ODA.

France and the UK. The next biggest OECD donors have aid programmes obviously connected with their colonial past. About a third of French aid goes to the DOM/TOM, Departments and Territories with small populations, which are considered to be part of metropolitan France. Aid to them is akin to regional assistance within a European country. The rest of French aid is weighted towards francophone Africa and other countries with which France has had historical associations. About a third of it, also, is devoted to education, reflecting—as well as developmental motives—the strong French desire to promote their language and culture.

British aid is similarly influenced by history, most of it going to former colonies that are now independent members of the Commonwealth. Britain's aid, like that of France, is available for many purposes in agriculture and industry in which its present and past give it relevant expertise. Both Britain and France have always sought commercial benefits from their aid. They have joined with others in international efforts to reduce tying and other distortions; but lately—in common with several other donors—Britain in particular has been under pressure to increase employment at home by tying aid to British-made goods. Despite this, it has a higher proportion of its bilateral aid going to the least developed countries than any other major donor.

Canada and the Netherlands. These two countries qualify as 'major' donors, in that they gave aid of more than $1 billion in 1983. Canada's aid as a percentage of GNP has been above average; the country has traditionally been among the strongest supporters of multilateral assistance (up to 50 per cent of its aid in 1977) and the readiest to use aid for unselfish purposes. Yet in recent years domestic political pressures have forced the aid programme to seek greater commercial gains, taking it further away from its liberal policy goals. The Netherlands has a significant colonial past; but its aid programme is in general more like that of the Nordic countries, in terms of relative size, untying, and the share going to the poorest countries. India receives more aid from the Netherlands than do any of the former Dutch dependencies (though the latter do take about a quarter of the country's aid budget).

The smaller donors.   These vary greatly in their use of aid for 'unselfish' purposes. On the aid-to-GNP criterion, the Scandinavian countries are particularly generous; the same applies to their untying practices, and their support for the poorest countries and the multilateral agencies. They have also been more willing than most donors to support some of the socialistically inclined low-income countries. After Sweden, the two biggest programmes are those of Australia and Italy. The former is notable for dividing two-thirds of its aid between the multilateral agencies and one country, Papua New Guinea, with which it has a special relationship;[11] the latter, for the big increase in its aid in very recent years, combined with 'unselfish' policies at a time of domestic economic difficulty.

Bilateral advantages

These brief notes on individual bilateral programmes do no more than illustrate their diversity. Each one is vastly richer in its character and functions than can be described here. But some important features of bilateral aid are apparent. The fact that it does serve national interests means that it appeals to significant political constituencies and commands public support. This is indispensable, and makes the bilateral part of aid in any democratic country its principal *raison d'être*.

But bilateral programmes also have developmental advantages. Countries often are peculiarly well placed to assist others with which they have long-standing relationships. They have specific technical skills often developed in, or because of their association with, the countries concerned. They have linguistic and personal affinities which may facilitate relationships, and, not least, the ability to render appropriate technical assistance. Their institutional structures are often derived one from the other and—where the transplants are satisfactory—this may also assist reciprocal comprehension. Lengthy histories of commercial interaction can make the aid relationship one of mutual advantage. At the same time, there are opposite sides to many of these coins. Such problems were among the considerations which gave rise to the need for multilateral assistance—a need which the bilateral donors recognized in setting up the multilateral agencies. But they do not diminish the importance of bilateral aid.

The middle of the spectrum

EEC development assistance agencies.   At much the same time as the DAC and IDA were being set up, the EEC established the European Investment Bank and the European Development Fund. The notion of 'associated states' was that non-European countries having special relationships with EEC members would be helped in promoting their economic and social development, and establish close economic relations with the EEC. The creation of these associations was the first step towards later agreements—first at Yaoundé in 1963 and 1969, and still more significantly at Lomé in 1974 and 1979—between the enlarged EEC and a broader group of states (including many of the British Commonwealth territories) in Africa, the Carribbean, and the Pacific—the ACP.

A review of the negotiations for successive Lomé agreements shows the relatively bilateral character of both the EEC and its aid agencies.[12] Initially, the EDF did not boost the overall aid-giving of any EEC members: if the associated states recieved more, others received less. The first Lomé Agreement did produce a substantial growth in both numbers of aid recipients and aid volumes, along with improvements in trading arrangements and lending policies. But by Lomé II, morale on both sides had worsened: the innovative, consultative spirit of Lomé I had moved towards a preponderance of Community influence.[13] Lomé II gave the recipients a little more than its predecessor on trade, but a lot less in aid. The nominal increase approved for the Fifth EDF masked a real decline of some 20 per cent on a per capita basis. The Sixth EDF, approved in 1984, when Lomé III was negotiated, was essentially the same as the Fifth in real terms.

Nonetheless, these institutions have channelled an increasing amount of EEC capital for development—both on concessional and non-concessional terms.[14] Fundamental questions remain unanswered: about the effectiveness of the EEC development agencies; about the internal political, rather than developmental, character of some of their lending criteria, and about the impact of the growth of EEC aid on the receipts of the non-associated states. Perhaps the most vexed question has been that of the conditionality of EEC assistance. In principle, the aid relations with the ACP are contractual, something they much appreciate. In recent years, however, concern about effectiveness has led to efforts to include in agreements a greater element of conditionality.

Arab development assistance.   Arab countries have been concerned about the economic development of their own region since long before the OPEC surpluses of the mid-1970s.[15] The League of Arab States was founded in 1945; agreement to establish the Arab Financial Institution for Economic Development was reached in June 1957. Kuwait, in 1961, and Abu Dhabi, in 1972, set up their own bilateral aid agencies. And, although actual disbursements did not start until 1974, The

Arab Fund for Social and Economic Development had commenced formal operation in early 1972.

Since 1973–4, the number of Arab aid institutions has grown. Saudi Arabia and, on a much smaller scale, Iraq established bilateral agencies. Three major 'multilateral' agencies—the Arab Bank for Economic Development in Africa (BADEA), the Islamic Development ment Bank, and the OPEC Fund for International Development—joined the Arab Fund as significant donors to developing countries. Saudi Arabia is the fourth largest donor after the United States, Japan, and France. Net disbursements of ODA from OPEC amounted to almost $5.4 billion in 1983; preliminary data show a decline of nearly $1 billion in 1984. Even so, ODA from OPEC members was then 0.86 per cent of their combined GNPs. It is on somewhat harder terms than DAC aid, but mostly untied, which probably more than compensates. And much of it is available in non-project form. In contrast to the EDF, the OPEC and Arab Funds both contribute to multilateral agencies and are genuinely multilateral themselves:

The political set-up in the Arab Fund differs from that found in national aid agencies . . . . There is no monolithic political interest to be served. Rather, politics . . . is manifest in the need to balance the interest of the various members.[16]

In that respect, the Arab agencies are more like the regional development banks (discussed below) than the EDF.

Multilateral official institutions

The major multilateral development agencies have grown in number and size over nearly forty years. The first group, the United Nations and the sister institutions created at Bretton Woods, commenced operations after the war; but it was several years before the UN and the World Bank concentrated exclusively on development. The IMF was not then—and is not now—a development institution, although its work in many spheres, national and international, has a considerable impact on developing countries. A second group, the regional development banks, began to grow in the late 1950s; from the start, their objectives were developmental.

In 1970, UN development agencies accounted for more multilateral ODA than any other channel. By 1977/8, however, they have been overtaken by the World Bank Group, while the regional development banks had almost doubled their share of multilateral ODA (see Table 9.6). Since then, the World Bank Group's share has fallen; the size of

TABLE 9.6

Percentage distribution of multilateral and EEC ODA by agency grouping, 1970, 1977–8, and 1979–83

	1970	1977–8	1979–83
United Nations	33	23	26
World Bank Group	26	46	36
Regional Banks	7	13	14
EEC	14	14	18
Other	20	4	6

Source: World Bank data, 1985.

the Seventh Replenishment of IDA, the concessional window of the Bank, implied that the decline would continue.[17]

The evolution of UN agencies, particularly from the late 1950s, has reflected changes in thinking about development magnified by the international assertion of political sovereignty by the developing countries themselves. The UN Special Fund, established in 1959, was intended to provide technical assistance, thereby facilitating rapid growth in public works and private investment. In 1965, the Special Fund and the Expanded Program for Technical Assistance were combined into the UN Development Programme (UNDP). Working closely with national and regional authorities, the UNDP was to specialize in pre-investment work. Other UN agencies—such as UNITAR, in research, and UNIDO, in industry—were established to complement UNDP activities. The UN's role in technical assistance extends to areas of human resource development; agencies like UNICEF, WFP, and UNFPA share this aspect of UNDP's work. Still other members of the 'UN family', such as FAO, specialize in particular forms of technical cooperation.

However, the UN agencies have functioned less than effectively. The Jackson report on the UN development system in 1969 proposed sweeping reform. Its implementation has been extremely slow, with only recent signs of progress.[18] The UNDP is, for example, concentrating on its organizational and manpower constraints, enhancing the quality and role of its Resident Representatives (whose weaknesses have been particularly apparent) and developing its support for improved administration and management in developing countries. As another example, UNICEF, UNDP, WFP, and UNFPA formed the Joint Consultative Group on Policy (JCGP) in 1984[19] The purpose of the JCGP is to implement practical measures of coordination among its members, rather than altering institutions or procedures.

Given the overlapping priorities of the JCGP agencies, their collaboration from the early stages of projects would provide mutual support and avoid needless duplication. The success of the JCGP's efforts will depend largely on convincing the field staff that the central office is serious about reform; only with their full participation can effective collaboration come about among these UN agencies, and between them and others—the World Bank, regional development banks, and non-governmental organizations.

Duplication and inefficiency in parts of the UN system should not be allowed to blacken the reputation of its better parts, or indeed—as seems sometimes to occur—of multilateral assistance in general. IFAD deserves special mention in this context. Established relatively recently, with majority funding from OPEC members, it has promoted rural development projects directed to the poorest people. It has a good and imaginative record in this difficult endeavour, which is high on the list of donors' proclaimed priorities. Its recent difficulties in replenishing its budget cast an unflattering light on some donors' willingness to practise what their policy statements preach.

The multilateralization of technical cooperation also has important advantages. In particular, when UNDP, FAO, and other agencies provide experts for pre-investment studies or project preparation for projects which they are not going to execute, it minimizes the possibility that the work is designed to favour a particular country's suppliers.

The World Bank Group. The establishment of the International Finance Corporation (IFC) and the International Development Association (IDA) altered the capacity and character of the World Bank. Each had a distinct purpose: IFC was to facilitate the private sector in all developing countries; IDA was to finance long-term development projects in the low-income countries on highly concessional terms. IDA was thus intended to reach those countries that could not satisfy the traditional criteria of credit-worthiness in private markets, criteria that the IBRD itself had to meet in order to borrow successfully from the markets. Indeed, some would argue that IDA was created only because many countries were either not credit-worthy for Bank loans, or were capable of servicing less in Bank loans than their needs and adsorptive capacity suggested was appropriate; in all other respects, Bank and IDA lending policies remained identical. Both have expanded into the sectors implied by a concern for distributional aspects of development, and into structural adjustment loans (SALs) which deal with macroeconomic and sectoral policies.

Enough has been said about the World Bank Group throughout this report to make further description unnecessary. For the purposes of this chapter, it suffices to say that the Group is the corner-stone of multilateral aid. It is not just that its lending is the largest part of multilateral assistance; its functions make it a key reference point for the whole system. Its country reports are widely used as the basis of statistical and economic knowledge for all donors. Its policy analysis similarly guides many donors' lending. It has provided intellectual leadership in development thinking. Its chairmanship of Consortia and Consultative Groups, as well as the size of its operations, make it a focal point for donor relations with numerous countries.

The World Bank is neither all-powerful nor infallible. Many other agencies rightly take pride in their independent work, and are often critical of the Bank's approaches to development. But the Bank's professionalism is outstanding among development agencies, most of which depend on it in numerous ways. Western aid in its present form could not function without it.

The World Bank has recently been aiming to encourage cooperation among the multilateral agencies. It has participated in many Cooperative Programmes with UN agencies. It seeks closer collaboration with the IMF, particularly in work on countries where both are active. And it has identified major areas of common interest with the regional banks: in projects where the regional bank has the comparative advantage, in joint economic and sector work, and in technical assistance for some of the regional bank's activities.

Despite these efforts, cooperation among multilateral agencies has been slow to develop. Opportunities for collaboration have too often been missed, mired in debate over the effectiveness of different institutions in particular spheres, or stifled by perceptions of arrogance on the one hand and reticence on the other.

The regional development banks.   Had the World Bank decentralized, establishing its own regional branches, the regional development banks might not have been needed. But the World Bank kept the bulk of its operations in Washington. The Inter-American Development Bank (IADB) was established in 1960; the African Development Bank (AfDB) in 1964 (although it was a decade before its soft loan window, the African Development Fund, became operational); and the Asian Development Bank (ADB) in 1966.

Although the regional banks lend much less than the World Bank (see Table 9.7), they have expanded rapidly. Each of the banks has financed projects to stimulate development in the countries of its region. All three see policy dialogue on the macroeconomy as being the province of the World Bank and the Fund. But the ADB is increasingly emphasizing policy dialogue on the sectoral and project-related

TABLE 9.7
Selected indicators of sizes of multilateral development institutions[a],
1973 *and* 1982

	Disbursements ($ million)		Commitments/ disbursements (%)	
	1973	1982	1973	1982
Regional banks	713	2 738	52.9	52.2
Non-concessional	364	1 848	45.6	53.2
Concessional	349	890	63.5	50.4
African	20	280	46.5	36.1
Ordinary Capital	20	147	46.5	36.8
AFDF	–	124	–	34.6
Nigerian Trust	–	9	–	100.0
Asian	146	795	34.7	45.9
Ordinary Capital	120	620	39.6	52.3
ASDF	26	175	22.0	32.0
Inter-American	547	1 663	61.9	60.6
Ordinary Capital	224	1 081	49.4	57.1
Fund for Special Operations	312	485	73.1	61.7
Other	11	97	275.0	147.0
The World Bank Group	1 637	8 393	49.1	64.5
IBRD	1 180	6 326	57.5	61.2
IDA	493	2 067	36.3	77.0

Source: World Bank.
[a]Excludes Caribbean Development Bank.

issues in its operations. Its recent study of its own future highlights its potential as a catalyst, cooperating with other regional institutions and building its own capacity in economic planning, analysis, and management.[20] It has launched Development Roundtables to encourage an exchange of views among Asia's policy-makers and has begun sponsoring seminars and financing research and training activities. It arranged a Roundtable on Industrial Development and Trade in late 1984, and a Conference of Privatization Policies in January 1985. The latter has helped the ADB to develop its own strategy for providing more assistance to the private sector.[21]

The IDB is the main development agency in Latin America. By 1983 it had disbursed over $15 billion, some 35 per cent on highly concessional terms. Its size could make it more vulnerable to external pressures than other regional banks—because of changing attitudes in the United States, its biggest backer, and also because of broader changes in Latin America. Its Sixth General Increase in 1983 included a small reduction in support for the Fund for Special Operations, its primary concessional window.

Perhaps in consequence, the IDB has since changed some of its operations significantly. It has put more emphasis on cooperation with the private sector, setting up the Inter-American Investment Corporation (which is modelled on the World Bank's IFC). The IDB is also helping five Central American countries to coordinate their receipts of development assistance. And it has adopted a flexible operating programme to promote the timely completion of projects, and to encourage new projects in member countries that are economically hard-pressed.

The AfDB, the smallest of the three regional banks accepted no external support in its early years. Even in 1982, its relatively new (and externally backed) concessional window, the African Development Fund, disbursed only 15 per cent of the regional banks' soft lending. But the AfDB's resources were increased by 50 per cent in its 1984–6 replenishment, and virtually all the main providers of development finance are expanding their work in sub-Saharan Africa. The World Bank will provide technical assistance and advice to the AfDB, and has sought its participation in the Action Program recently adopted for Africa. Properly supported, the AfDB could make a growing contribution to Africa's development.

Despite having many sources of finance, the regional banks do not fit neatly into the multilateral category. Each has a leading backer: the USA in the case of the IDB, Japan for the ADB,[22] and the EEC countries for the AfDB. The relationship between donors and agencies affects the nature of the changes that the regional banks are making to their operations. Handling these changes requires some strategic sense and considerable tactical diplomacy, the more so as an agency moves to the multilateral end of the bilateral–multilateral spectrum.

IV The pressures on ODA

Two developments—the slow-down in the world economy since the early 1970s, and negative attitudes of some donors towards aid—underlie recent trends in the size and allocation of ODA. When economic growth is rapid, aid grows rapidly too. Its multilateral component can expand without seeming to pre-empt bilateral activities.

But when economic growth slows, part of the pressure for cuts in government spending falls on development assistance. In those circumstances, any increase in multilateral aid is often achieved only by reducing bilateral programmes. This pressure on the multilateral agencies has been reinforced by the rapid expansion of the EDF.

The other reasons for the constraints on some aid budgets are less clear. Public support for aid, at least as measured by opinion polls, has risen rather than fallen.[23] However, people may have become more sceptical about particular aspects of aid—its capacity to reach the poor, for example, or the performance of official as opposed to private agencies.[24] But are governments which cut aid reflecting public opinion on these specific issues? Or do their decisions on ODA have a stronger administrative and ideological base?

These and other broader influences have certainly played a role in the way some donors have approached their aid budgets. Some national governments have sought more direct control over aid, biasing it towards bilateral programmes. They may also have wanted to emphasize the role of the private sector in promoting development: again, that has inclined them to bilateral programmes. The obvious example of these tendencies is the USA.

In 1981, President Reagan emphasized his belief that trade, the free market, and private investment would stimulate economic development.[25] In 1982, the US Treasury prepared a policy paper; *US Participation in the Multilateral Development Banks in the 1980s*; while acclaiming the contributions of those agencies to development, it nonetheless recommended that the USA should reduce its support for their soft lending windows. It did so for two reasons: first, the administration's desire to reduce most types of public spending; and second, the argument that India should no longer be eligible for IDA funding, which would allow IDA to be smaller. A year later, the Carlucci Report strongly reasserted the links between security and economic aid, echoing the views of the 1963 Clay Report.[26] The Carlucci Report also stressed promotion of the private sector. So did the Andreas Report, published in December 1984. Although it asserted rather than substantiated its view that the multilateral institutions 'have followed the easy path of supporting state-owned or managed activities', it did conclude that they have made a major contribution to development and should be supported.[27]

The change in official attitudes to development was not confined to the USA. In the UK, similar preoccupations tended to downgrade somewhat the developmental objectives of the aid programme. In Canada, the government formally adopted the 0.7 per cent ODA target in 1980, but planned to achieve it only in 1990–1; that date has since been postponed by five years, and the ODA target reduced. Among the major donors, Japan has been a notable exception, since it substantially exceeded its target of doubling ODA between 1977 and 1980. It has a further plan to double the average ODA contribution of 1976–80 during 1981–5. If achieved, this would be a substantial increase. Should budget stringencies continue, however, the plan may be in jeopardy.[28] Italy has also made a very substantial increase in its programme.

The attitudes of the major donors that had emerged in the early 1980s were illustrated in the Economic Declaration following the Bonn summit in May 1985:

Flows of resources, including official development assistance, should be maintained and wherever possible, increased, especially to the poorer countries. In particular, more stable long-term finance, such as direct investment from industrial countries, should be encouraged.[29]

The statement offered only weak support for a larger volume of aid. And its assertion that direct investment provides a stable source of finance is not borne out by the facts: for example, private investment flows to Africa fell from $2 billion in 1982 to $200 million in 1983.[30] Further, the effective defining—implicitly for *all* developing countries—of direct investment as a key source of 'stable long-term finance' raised disturbing questions about the role left for concessional aid, bilateral or multilateral. However, by the time of the Seoul meeting of the World Bank and IMF in October 1985 there were clear signs of a return to international recognition of the importance of the two institutions, and willingness to increase their resources.

V Comparative advantages

Multilateral agencies have several advantages:

they are largely apolitical, a fact much appreciated by recipients;
their bidding procedures for procurement are relatively transparent and internationally competitive;
the pooling of resources increases the power to borrow from the capital markets and widens the range of feasible activities; the capital base also provides backing for co-financing operations;
the multilaterals' size gives them the competence to handle large projects;
the experience of their personnel and the wide range of their economic and technical work are of value to all agencies;
smaller donors with limited overseas experience or administrative capacity use the multilaterals as a channel for their aid.

These advantages have produced particular strength in two increasingly important areas—policy dialogue and aid coordination. Both are discussed elsewhere in this report. But the others merit further consideration here.

For any borrowers, the multilateral institutions have special appeal. A bilateral donor's geo-political concerns can change, so its financial support is not necessarily reliable. Further, the bilateral donor's emphasis on its own security needs, while doubtless ensuring some aid, may well not serve the developmental priorities of the recipient. Nor are the historical and geo-political concerns of bilateral donors such as to guarantee that aid will go where the need is greatest. By contrast, multilaterals are relatively apolitical, and more exclusively concerned with development. The multilateral agencies can and do channel more ODA to the poorest countries, partially compensating for the bias in bilateral programmes towards the middle-income group. Recipients also derive significant benefits from competitive procurement procedures, as the final section of this chapter makes clear.

As for donors, many of them see considerable attractions in the multilateral institutions. This is particularly true of donors whose geo-political role has been minor, or who cannot afford the administrative costs of a big bilateral programme. The effectiveness of development assistance depends to a large extent on intimate knowledge of the recipient countries. Most donors lack the resources to build and maintain such knowledge; even the larger donors can do so for only a few recipients. The multilaterals have accumulated years of experience on a whole range of development issues, and have established close relations with their borrowers.

Donors can obtain other financial advantages from supporting multilateral bodies. The impact of a single donor's limited resources can be greatly enhanced by becoming part of the bigger pool of funds available to a multilateral agency. More and larger projects can be financed. And donors' capital subscriptions provide the collateral for some multilateral agencies to borrow in the international capital market, thus multiplying the resources available for lending. The authority of the multilaterals is also important in cooperating with public and private bodies in co-financing operations.

From the viewpoint of both donors and recipients, therefore, the multilateral agencies offer real advantages. Their very existence, and their rapid growth over the past twenty-five years, is testimony to a demand for what they offer. The donors themselves chose to support multilateral channels as a way of redressing imbalances which their own bilateral programmes necessarily (and in many ways quite properly) fostered. And both they and the recipients appreciate that the entire aid system is guided and coordinated largely by multilateral intervention.

Competition among aid channels

There are many aid agencies, and they compete in two ways: attracting donors' resources, and serving recipients' needs. The competition for resources affects the UN family and the World Bank Group. Where donors are seeking to reduce public spending, the size of the UN and World Bank Group make them a ready target for cuts. In contrast, the regional development banks usually make only small demands on donors' budgets, so have been able to grow. Because the development agencies of the EEC, particularly the EDF, have claimed increasing shares of Community members' aid budgets, less remains for the larger multilaterals.

As for serving the needs of the recipients, some aspects of the increased competition in country lending operations can be beneficial, if only because they offer more options to borrowers. But two aspects of lending policy—the severity of the appraisal process and the policy conditions imposed—raise potential problems. On the one hand, the more demanding the lender (irrespective of whether its demands are appropriate), the less attractive it appears to the recipient. On the other hand, assuming the lender's demands are appropriate, the impact of its loans will be greater the more demanding it is. In those circumstances, competition between lenders is unobjectionable *only* if they all impose broadly similar conditions. Otherwise, the more lenient lenders will undercut the rest, and the quality of development will suffer.

This analysis provides a strong argument for aid coordination and policy dialogue. These issues in turn naturally focus attention on the World Bank and the IMF.[31] But other multilateral institutions have a role to play and, as Section II of this chapter made clear, they are improving their effectiveness in a variety of ways.

These developments underline the changing character of multilateral aid. Yet it is not clear whether those changes are being viewed from a broad enough perspective. As the 1984 DAC Chairman's Report argued:

If donors are not to enter a debate on the future of multilateral aid, they need to take a view of its long-term evolution within the totality of development cooperation efforts. It is no longer enough just to preach the virtues of multilateralism as a general principle. There is a need for discussion of the specific and complementary roles of individual agencies.[32]

The subject could certainly benefit from an international review in which governments could express their views.

The future

To what extent do the functions of multilateral agencies depend on their being a particular size? Could the multilaterals still be effective if they were smaller? These questions are prompted by the present stringency of finance for development, which has already forced the multilaterals to change their operating methods. They have designed, or are considering, new financing vehicles, and are restricting access to scarce concessional funds. The search for greater efficiency in resource use, and for greater productivity in operations, has been undertaken intensively within most of the multilateral agencies.

These steps imply that the multilaterals can make more efficient use of their existing resources. But improved efficiency with existing resources is one thing, reduced resources quite another. Those experienced in the operational work of development at the country level argue that the multilaterals would be less effective if they were smaller, and for three main reasons. First, the volume and nature of development assistance strongly influences the character of policy dialogue—its form, its scope, its time-frame. Hence, second, *continuity* of operation and exposure, especially in small countries, has an important bearing on the capacity for dialogue. Unless lending is regular, contact with the agencies, institutions, and government of the recipient is lost, and the multilateral 'loses its seat at the policy table'. Third, for the poorest recipients, aid must be highly concessional if it is not to impose financial burdens that will constrain future development

There is a fourth sense in which fewer resources would mean less effective work by the multilaterals. Project quality would suffer if agencies spent less on appraisal, monitoring, and supervision. A key suggestion of this report is that inter-agency sharing of aid experience should be strengthened. For that purpose, the institutions' evaluative and analytical capacity needs reinforcing not—as current stringencies require—undermining.

Much of this section can be summarized by saying that the parts of the multilateral system predominantly engaged in technical co-operation must have adequate resources; but they could be streamlined and the effectiveness of their various parts carefully scrutinized. The mainly capital-lending institutions, while not faultless, are by and large not only highly effective themselves, but important to the effectiveness of aid and development overall. They should be firmly supported, and not allowed to rest in uncertainty about long-term future levels of funding.

In a broader sense, of course, two multilateral agencies—the IMF and the World Bank—have roles in the world economy that go far beyond aid. The two institutions act within and maintain surveillance over key parts of the world's financial flows. Even before the indebtedness of developing countries grew to today's proportions, it was argued that a dangerous situation could arise if an excessive share of their overseas borrowing were carried by commercial banks. The necessity for the multilaterals' intermediation in capital flows is not going to diminish. Nor will their roles in monitoring these flows, advising the borrowing countries, reporting on the countries, their borrowing and debt situations, and all the great range of negotiation and surveillance activities in which they participate. They are indispensable to the international economic and financial system.

Such functions cannot be undertaken by anyone else. But as far as concerns aid, the health of the system depends very considerably on the bilaterals as well. Bilateral programmes have close relationships with particular recipients and understanding of their problems. In particular sectors, types of lending, and technologies, as Chapter 5 has illustrated, individual donors have expertise beyond that of the multilaterals. And it is national governments that sustain the multilateral system. If aid did not satisfy the national purposes and humanitarian ideals that motivate governments and public opinion, support for the whole edifice of international cooperation would diminish.

VI Aid-tying

When the world economy slows, governments tend to face pressures to stimulate exports and restrict imports. As far as the development policies of industial countries are concerned, these pressures manifest themselves in increased 'tying' of aid. Strictly speaking, much aid—multilateral and bilateral—has always been tied by end-use: project lending is so tied, by definition. The controversial issue is procurement tying. With multilateral aid, procurement cannot be tied because it is subject to international competitive bidding. With bilateral programmes, that is much less often the case.

DAC aid as a whole became less tied between 1973 and 1983—largely because the share of multilateral aid was rising during most of that period. The average proportion of untied aid rose from 34 per cent in 1973 to 56 per cent in 1983. Even with bilateral aid, the untied element rose from 37 per cent in 1976 to 46 per cent in 1982–3 (see Table 9.8). However, these figures do not tell the whole story. There are many ways in which donors can influence procurement without formal tying. They can choose particular sectors or commodities that are more susceptible to procurement from the donor. More or less subtly, they can indicate that the recipient would be wise to place orders with the donor. Such practices, combined with traditional commercial links which may create inertia in the choice of

TABLE 9.8
Tying status of DAC assistance

	The proportion of each DAC donor's total ODA classified as untied[a]		The proportion of each DAC donor's bilateral ODA classified as untied	
	1973	1982–3	1976[b]	1982–3
Australia	45	71	81	61
Austria	83	23	47	2
Belgium	31	37	24	25
Canada	33	41	15	17
Denmark	53	70	45	64
Finland	56	85	18	80
France	31	39	42	36
Germany	51	68	79	70
Italy[c]	60	61	19	54
Japan	32	67	26	54
Netherlands	33	62	44	57
New Zealand	8	58	96	46
Norway	78	80	60	65
Sweden	85	85	71	81
Switzerland[d]	51	76	29	67
United Kingdom	20	41	21	24
United States	22	58	18	37
DAC average	34	56	37	46

Source: OECD, *Development Cooperation*, various issues, compiled by Jay (1985).

[a]The figures for the UK and New Zealand for 1973 may be understated, since a significant portion of their ODA was listed in this context as "status undetermined".

[b]1976 is the first year in which the data is provided in a bilateral multilateral breakdown.

[c]1982 data.

[d]1983 data.

suppliers, can result in much bigger procurement orders out of aid than formal tying practices alone would produce. Most of France's aid to its former dependencies and the DOM/TOM returns to France regardless of tying conditions; Germany receives orders on a much larger proportion of its aid than it formally ties; the same is true of several donors. Although competitive ability may play a part, other factors are at work as well.

There is abundant evidence that procurement-tying raises costs for the recipient and therefore reduces the real value of its aid receipts. Tied aid limits competition and therefore choice; it may encourage external dependence rather than self-reliance; and it creates opportunities for corruption on both sides of the tied transaction. It transfers specialized equipment and procedures—which often require supplementary training and spare parts costs[33]—and allows suppliers considerable scope to raise prices in the face of an externally set, inelastic demand. It is a significant factor in biasing recipients' investments towards excessive capital intensity.

Procurement-tying also affects a donor's choice of which projects, programmes, and countries to support. Choices among projects and component supplies can be determined by the interests of domestic suppliers, instead of the needs of recipients. Country selection can unduly emphasize those markets of particular export interest to the donor.

Food aid, examined more fully in Chapter 5, is the most common form of commodity aid. Although much of it is supplied multilaterally, bilateral food aid programmes exhibit many of the worst features of tied aid. Most food issues involve the influential farm lobbies in developed countries. Food aid, often a legislative response to donors' surplus production, is thus almost always tied to procurement in the donor country. Often the domestic budetary cost is calculated to include subsidies for the food plus the cost of transport. This often inflated value is the one entered into the aid accounts, reducing the amounts available for other forms of aid.

In varying degrees, bilateral donors acknowledge these criticisms. But most argue that tied aid is a legitimate way of increasing support for the whole aid programme. Tying is increasingly justified as a defensive or retaliatory move, matching what other donors do. These arguments are used to defend other forms of trade protectionism, and all threaten the survival of the post-1945 liberal trading system.

Tying imposes costs on the relatively weak participant, the recipient; its benefits, if any, accrue to the donor. The recipients' capacity to retaliate is limited; they often feel that 'tied aid is better than no aid',[34] if those appear to be the only alternatives. The danger is that, in today's circumstances, each review of a donor's aid programme can produce more aid-tying and less aid—for recipients, a double reduction.

Selected recipients' experiences

Recipients regard tied aid with mixed feelings. Some say its costs are 'not insupportable', especially when it comes from donors with whom they have longstanding and reasonably predictable relations. Others think tying is inevitable, and accept it as such. A few countries object so strongly that they refuse some offers of tied aid.

One of the most notable objectors has been India. Through a determination not to allow aid to distort its priorities, 'India has side-stepped many of the more extreme problems of aid-dependency'.[35] In the 1970s, the Indian government was prepared to reject tenders and offers which seem to involve unduly high prices being charged by donor national firms. In one case, the donor renewed the offer—at half the original quotation.

Faced with India's strong stance, donors have made concessions on the principle of tying. Since 1978, the USA has allowed some of its aid to India to be spent in both India and other developing countries. The Scandinavian countries, the Netherlands, Germany, and Japan impose relatively few procurement restrictions. Where the UK requires procurement-tying, it can be channelled into sectors where the harm is small, and where off shore purchases would in any case be necessary. Even Soviet aid to India, which has always been wholly source-tied, has been confined to heavy industry, such as steel and power, where the Soviet economy's comparative advantage lies. But the India study cites one example of bilateral aid for buying merchant ships from the donor's nationalized industry; the project had low priority: 'the recipient may be doing the donor a favour, rather than the other way round'.

India, however, is far from typical. Few developing countries have its power to affect the restrictive procurement practices of donors. In consequence, if they accept tied aid, they accept its costs. This seems to characterize the attitudes of Kenya, Malawi, and Bangladesh. Kenya's experience[36] shows that bilateral aid tying has raised costs to its government. The requirement to import aid-financed goods in ships of the donor's flag raised the goods' landed costs well above those in the world market. Aid-tying dislocated programmes and imposed inflated costs on departmental budgets for rural water, roads, and agriculture. In the long-term, servicing and spares procurement for a wide range of donor-supplied equipment are viewed as significant problems.

In Malawi,[37] despite helpful instances when donors waived procurement-tying rules, there was evidence of unjustifiably high prices, especially on supplies to the health sector. These bore heavily on a department whose investment and recurrent budgets had already been pared to the bone, partly as a result of government spending priorities but also because of externally imposed adjustment policies. In Bangladesh, 'the increasing commitment of donors to project and import tying' appeared 'likely to work against any tendency to make aid flows more susceptible to market influences'.[38] Such findings are doubly ironic at a time when many donor governments have been forceful advocates of market forces and free enterprise.

Associated financing

Mixed credit and other associated financing schemes are a relatively new form of tying for many donors. They involve two elements, one concessional, one not. Put formally, they create transactions of which the 'main characteristic is that the concessional component is linked in law or in fact to the non-concessional component . . . or the whole financing package is effectively tied to procurement in the donor country'.[39]

These schemes have continued to grow in number, and have significant potential for futher growth. The main reason is the desire of donor governments to help national exporters compete, either 'aggressively' by initiating a mixed credit package, or 'defensively' by enabling them to match the favourable terms offered by competitors' governments.

Such credit competition is a major source of concern. When it is used to soften export credit terms considerably, it may contravene the OECD's 'Guidelines for Officially Supported Export Credits', which aim to ensure that export credit terms approach market terms, and to regulate tied-aid credits. Like aid-tying, credit subsidies are a threat to the whole principle of open international trade.

The scale of associated financing schemes is difficult to assess, in part because they tend to involve large sums of money, so that their total value can shift erratically from year to year. The DAC has identified a significant amount of associated financing transactions in the early 1980s. The share of ODA in such transactions rose from 31 per cent in 1981 to 38 per cent in 1983, and their average grant element from 18 per cent to 25 per cent.[40] For the least developed countries, both the ODA share and the grant element were higher in 1983, at 49 per cent and 35 per cent respectively. Given the plight of the poorest countries, the grant element might appropriately have been much larger.

Like tied aid, mixed credits bias the choice of project towards those in which the content of the donor's exports is larger, and against those where import content is low, or local currency financing high. Such schemes also tend to favour projects where the pay-off is high and prompt, and where the sector or the country is of particular interest to donor country suppliers—often the better-off developing countries.

As with tying, some donors argue that mixed credits result in more lending to recipients because they are a way of 'stretching' aid. This is a matter of controversy—especially about whether, even if this does 'stretch' aid, the resulting quality of the aid is desirable. And while mixed credits may 'stretch' one donor's aid if others do not follow suit, once this sytem becomes competitive its results can be highly deleterious for donors and recipients alike; and, as presently conducted, it actually reduces aid to the poorer countries which need aid most.

Avenues of corrective action

Changes have already begun. In some recipient countries, officials can make informed assessments of the quality and underlying intent of aid offers. But resident aid personnel may be critical in fostering these skills, an area where most of the multilaterals and all but a few bilaterals are still rather weak.

As with aid-tying, the larger recipients can also respond to mixed credit overtures by playing off one package against another, possibly getting the least costly of a sub-optimal set of alternatives. This is already occurring in India and in some Latin American countries. But it cannot be done by the smaller recipients, and is obviously a second-best solution to a problem which can be settled only by the donor governments.

Perhaps the most helpful contribution to reducing the use of mixed credits would be faster growth in the donor economies, which would ease the pressure to promote exports. Recent improvements in aid coordination, particularly at the sectoral level,[41] may also be a hopeful sign. Donor consortia, Consultative Groups, and the UNDP Round-tables all provide fora in which to discuss and arrange untying.

Quite separately, there are key areas—the funding of local and recurrent costs of aid projects and programmes—in which source-tying makes little or no sense. Were donors to recognize this and expand their local cost financing, tying would inevitably be reduced. The DAC has reported that donors have been showing greater flexibility over local cost financing in the past few years.[42] It probably provides the best forum for donors to agree on measures to tackle this aspect of tied aid.

The DAC has also been the first body to address the problem of mixed credits. Although its members did adopt their 'gentleman's agreement' on export credits in June 1983, its negotiation was far from easy. Thus far, it has been possible to raise the established minimum grant element only to 25 per cent.[43] Measures to improve reporting of mixed credits have been agreed, but the likelihood of rigid interpretation of the guidelines and consequent under-reporting remains strong.[44] Moreover, it is doubtful that the guidelines' injunction is being followed: mixed credit arrangements should be reserved for projects and programmes with high developmental priority, selected on the same criteria applied to all ODA. However, a policy measure with two objectives—in this case, commercial and developmental—requires two independently operable instruments if both objectives are to be achieved. With the gentleman's agreement, there is only one instrument. If the initiative for mixed credits can come from domestic suppliers, and their requests are considered on a case-by-case basis, commercial factors will almost inevitably dominate. It would make much more sense to separate the objectives, placing developmental considerations within the donors' aid budgets and commercial considerations in the appropriate commercial departments.

Any donor already using mixed credits is unlikely to take these steps unilaterally.[45] Again, the DAC is the logical forum for multilateral action. But it cannot act without the cooperation and support of its members. The consensus of DAC members on developmental objectives has been eroded. It is their will that is really at issue: on associated financing, tying, local cost financing, and, indeed, the future of the multilateral system.

Notes

1. Pearson 1969, p. 208
2. The discussion of DAC members draws on other data published in OECD DAC 1984*a*, Table II.A.1, and the OECD's press release announcing preliminary data for 1984 (PRESS/A(85)44, 18 June 1985).
3. The income groupings for developing countries are those of the DAC, as defined in footnote *a* of Table 9.2.
4. This study treats India and China as a separate group. As discussed elsewhere, population size alone suffices to distinguish these countries, and, on per capita income and other criteria, both qualify for concessional aid. Yet some donors have advocated speedier 'graduation' of India to harder terms for the development assistance it receives, as one means of conserving scarce ODA resources, on grounds of credit-worthiness and economic performance.
5. See, for example, Friedmann *et al.* 1966, Ohlin 1966, and White 1967.

6. The Goldstein (1984) study of Senegal is relevant in this context: a former French colony, Senegal is a relatively stable and, in key spheres, pro-Western democracy; it also supports a number of Arab political stances. Not surprisingly, its bilateral support from France, the USA and Arab nations is considerable—whether in absolute or relative terms.
7. Sewell *et al.* 1985.
8. Friedmann 1962, p. 37.
9. Friedmann *et al.* 1966 and OECD/DAC 1985*a*.
10. White 1967.
11. Australia, Government of 1984.
12. See particularly Stevens (ed.) 1981, 1983, and 1984.
13. Indeed, Article 108(5) of the Lomé II Agreement states: 'The Community shall be responsible for preparing and taking final decisions on projects and programmes.'
14. See Tables 9.4 and 9.5 above.
15. League of Arab States 1958; Demir 1979. For a general account, see Porter 1986.
16. OPEC Fund 1984; quotation from Demir 1979, p. 47.
17. The Caribbean Development Bank is not treated separately. Established in 1970, its first efforts were largely in technical assistance; it remains a small institution, having disbursed a total of $42 million in 1982, two-thirds of which were on concessional terms.
18. OECD DAC 1984*a*, Ch. VII. See also Chapter 6 above.
19. UNICEF 1985, and internal documents.
20. ADB 1983.
21. The strategy, to be considered in mid-1985, is likely to include an increase in the Bank's own lending and co-financing in the private sector and greater support of member countries' efforts at privatization, including support of changes in policy environment and institutions conducive to private activity.
22. It is worth noting in this context that Japan, like the USA, strongly supports an increased emphasis by the development institutions on the private sector. Japan is likely, therefore, to be appreciative of the quite public stand on that issue of the US Executive Director for the ADB reported in the *International Herald Tribune*, 29 April 1985.
23. OECD DAC 1984*a*, Ch. x.
24. For contrast, recall the generalization in *IDA in Restrospect*: 'Most favor helping poor people in poor countries but feel that current efforts are already sufficient or too large, and that problems at home should take priority. They are sceptical about the effectiveness of official agencies, less sceptical of private ones' World Bank 1982*b*, p. 15.
25. Speaking in July in Philadelphia, preceding and setting a tone for the discussions at the Cancun Summit.
26. Carlucci 1984.
27. Andreas 1984, p. 54.

28. Greene (1983) notes that the government deficit was then being countered with a 'fiscal reconstruction program', under which all programmes but ODA and defence had been restricted to zero growth.

29. 'The Bonn Economic Declaration: Toward Sustained Growth and Higher Employment', 4 May 1985, as reproduced in *The New York Times*, 5 May 1985, p. 16.

30. OECD DAC 1984*a*.

31. The IMF makes extensive use of policy-based conditions in its operations. In cases where the development institutions are also involved, the Fund's participation in policy dialogue and the coordination of resource flows is especially critical. See Chapter 4.

32. OECD 1984*a*, p. 104.

33. This is especially burdensome where several donors are each financing separate but very similar projects, each project having product specifications designed more to fit donor than recipient considerations.

34. Ohlin 1966, p. 94.

35. Lipton *et al*. 1984*a*.

36. Duncan and Mosley 1984.

37. Hewitt and Kydd 1984.

38. Van Arkadie and de Wilde 1984.

39. OECD DAC 1983*a*, p. 169.

40. OECD DAC 1984*a*, ch. viii.

41. *Ibid*., and OECD internal documents.

42. *Ibid*., p. 92.

43. OECD 1984.

44. OECD DAC, 1984*a*, Ch. viii.

45. Governments could, for example, take the initiative away from domestic suppliers, or agree to match only those foreign offers notified by recipient governments if they were acceptable without the foreign aid element; see Toye 1985.

CHAPTER TEN

Summary: Conclusions and Recommendations

I Introduction

Knowledge about the effectiveness of aid is needed both to make judgements about its worthwhileness and to improve its management. Support for aid rests ultimately with public opinion, which has to be convinced that aid is working well. In fact, there is much for aid to take credit for, from its many contributions to raising food production in the South Asian sub-continent, to experimental rural education programmes in Africa; from infrastructure investment — power, roads and railways, ports, communications—to self-help rural development schemes; from widespread support to strengthening developing country institutions, to family planning activities in almost all the countries where they have been assisted. It is not clear what would count as success in the eyes of public opinion. If it is either faster economic progress or visible reductions in mass poverty in the low-income countries, public opinion should be made aware, if it is not already, that aid can and does contribute to both those things; but their achievement depends on many other factors besides: not least recipients' policies — which aid *is* influencing in a positive direction — and the world economy.

It may well be that public opinion cannot easily be swayed by the kinds of careful assessment which appear in this report, of successes and failures, of the learning process that has gone on in aid and of the mistakes that are repeated, of an overall record fallible but creditable. Public opinion seems more easily affected by one or two 'horror stories' of failed projects, or by a polemical diatribe in the fashionable language of the day—or, in a more favourable climate, by a political figure who can make an impassioned plea for his country to stand by the less fortunate, that the haves should help the have-nots.

But observers of aid can take heart from this report. It deals with official aid for long-term development, not with emergency relief or the work of private voluntary organizations. And it considers only the developmental purposes of aid, not any other motives the donors might have. Its basic finding is that *the majority of aid is successful in terms of its own objectives*. Over a wide range of countries and sectors, aid has made positive and valuable contibutions. The report also refutes some of the common criticisms of aid — that it cannot reach the poor, or that it conflicts with development of the private sector.

This does not mean that all is well with aid. A significant proportion does not succeed. The question is, how this should be judged? Suppose it were known that *x* per cent of aid did fail, how would that compare with other kinds of investment—in the private sector in industrial countries or in the public sector? Considering the difficult circumstances in which aid operates, one might conclude that the record compared well with the average for complex human endeavours.

In recent years, aid has not necessarily gone where it is most effective. South Asia, where aid works relatively well, has lost aid almost exactly in proportion as Africa, where it works relatively less well, has gained it. The donors have responded to the political possibilities of a situation in which Africa might be overwhelmed by economic disasters even worse than those already suffered. One option for improving the average effectiveness of aid, namely giving more of it globally to the countries where it is more effective, therefore seems to be at least temporarily ruled out by current aid politics. What is sought is to make it more effective *where the donors want to put it*. But the problem does not reduce to one of making aid to Africa more effective. Other regions are still major aid recipients. And, to a considerable extent, what goes wrong with aid is common to all aid. The things which make development as well as aid-giving difficult are simply more pervasive in Africa.

When aid goes wrong, its failings can be divided into what might be called the more and the less reprehensible. On the donor side, some of the more reprehensible failures come from pursuing commercial or political ends without much regard for the developmental objectives of aid; others, from not learning from past mistakes. Agencies are not all that good at learning from their own mistakes; they are even worse at learning from each other's mistakes, since there is insufficient information exchange among agencies of project experience. The result is that mistakes are repeated with detectable frequency. On the recipient side, the main set of phenomena responsible for aid failure lie in the policy environment within which aid operates. An important set of issues lie here, which recur throughout the report. There is one further cause of failure which is attributable to the behaviour of both sides, namely the lack of coordination of aid.

Less reprehensible are the difficult things which are attempted in adverse circumstances. A good deal of aid takes on complex and innovative investments in the poorest regions of the world. They are risk-prone. But a safety-conscious aid programme would promise little for the poorest people in the poorest countries.

In between the more and the less reprehensible lies a grey area where it is difficult to assign responsibility. If a project is badly designed, or if it goes wrong because it does not sufficiently understand the human and social environment in which it is set, who is at fault? Often the questions are whether sufficient pains have been taken in advance to achieve appropriate understanding as well as technical knowledge, and what counts as sufficient. It is often hard to determine how failure might have been avoided (except with the benefit of hindsight).

Categorization of countries

The discussion of aid, especially its discussion for public opinion would be more satisfactory if developing countries were divided into three groups as far as concerns their financial needs. At one end of the spectrum lie the middle-income, or better-off, developing countries, which need many things from the international economic environment, including in some cases technical assistance, but only exceptionally long-term concessional finance. At the other end of the spectrum lie the 'poorest' countries. They are the countries which will be on the aid list for decades. They lack the fundamental necessities for material development—human skills, sound administration, infrastructure. They often have unstable governments, deteriorating ecological conditions, stagnant or declining agriculture; in some cases, many years of falling per capita income, even falling GNP. In between these two groups of countries lies a large range of low-income and lower middle-income countries. They do not need aid in order to survive; but aid can accelerate their development. However, some of them within the foreseeable future will move out of this middle category into the first category of countries which do not normally require concessional assistance. India and China have to be treated separately, almost as a fourth category: in terms of their poverty, they belong with the poorest countries; but they have a number of developmental advantages not shared by the poorest—capable administrations, considerable industrial development, well-advanced educational systems, and a reasonable spread of human skills. Because of their great size relative to all other developing countries, they inevitably figure as special cases.

A significant conclusion of this report is that the poorest countries require a new approach to aid. Most of the things that need putting right are most needed for these countries. But the requirements of other low-income countries are every bit as important, not least in the sheer volume of avoidable human suffering which aid can help to remedy. They also must receive due attention.

II   Aid and Growth

The relationship between aid and growth has most commonly been studied in international cross-section statistical regressions. They show little relationship between aid and growth when all developing countries are considered together. One or two studies have shown a positive relationship between aid and growth for low-income countries considered alone. Similar analysis has been done for aid and savings. This has in the past been thought to show a negative relationship. But the findings are suspect. The correlations do not distinguish between consumption aid—food aid, for example—and aid intended for investment; if they did, the negative relationship might disappear (as some research findings suggest it does). Further, it is not clear what forces are at work. There may be output changes affecting both savings and aid; and there are year-to-year changes, especially fluctuations in foreign trade, which have a strong influence, particularly on public savings. The main conclusion from this international statistical analysis is that one is better off looking at individual countries.

Consider some of the countries specially studied for this report. In India aid has never exceeded 2 to 3 per cent of GNP; but it has been of macroeconomic importance. In some years it has released a savings or a foreign exchange constraint and been valuable to the economy despite its modest size. One of the most significant macroeconomic contributions of aid to India has been in its contribution to the Green Revolution, and to enlarging food and agricultural output. Before this happened, the Indian economy was grinding to a halt whenever there was a bad harvest; and large foreign exchange expenditures were required for food imports. It can truly be said that the high-yielding grain varieties have helped to transform the Indian economy.

In the poorest countries, aid is a much higher percentage of GNP. In sub-Saharan Africa, aid accounts for some 50 per cent of investment and 40 per cent of imports. It is impossible to say that aid is not macroeconomically important; but one must not look only at these magnitudes. The Malawi study finds that aid made a valuable contribution to growth in the 1970s, paying for most of public investment, and also, through technical cooperation, contributing on a large scale to successful institution-building. The Bangladesh study puts emphasis on the reconstruction assistance which the country received in the aftermath of the 1971 war, without which it is hard to imagine the development of Bangladesh beginning at all in that period. Again, aid today finances 100 per cent of Bangladesh's development budget, and it would be curious to argue that aid is not having very considerable positive macroeconomic effects.

In general, although one would be happier if international statistical analyses did show a stronger relationship between aid and growth, one should not conclude from the absence of a strong statistical relationship that aid is not contributing to growth. On average, aid is relatively small and only one of many factors responsible for growth, and the statistical results are not really surprising. When individual countries are examined, it is easier to show the importance of aid.

III   Aid and Poverty

Poverty is not going down much in the Third World. Progress was being made in the 1970s, but today the proportion of people in poverty is stagnating, possibly rising in some countries; the numbers in poverty are certainly rising. What is at fault? In so far as the relief of poverty is a collaboration between recipient governments and aid, aid is definitely the junior partner. Far more important are the recipient's policies, politics, social structure, and so forth—these are the critical matters. Nevertheless, aid has helped the poor.

In some of the countries studied for this report—Kenya, Malawi, for example—there is no evidence about what is happening to poverty; nor is there any evidence of the donors pursuing consistent policies related to the relief of poverty. In others, the record is somewhat better. For example, in India and other countries there have been considerable consumption gains for the poor (if not gains in improved production and assets), most particularly through the Green Revolution and the increased availability of food. There has also, however, been a considerable amount of 'poverty-oriented assistance' directed towards, for example, small farmers' programmes, cooperatives, health, nutrition, or family planning . . . In Colombia, the poor have benefited both from successful growth and employment policies, assisted by aid, and from poverty-oriented lending.

In general, the evidence shows that poverty-oriented projects do have a high rate of return: there is no necessary trade-off between attempts to reach the poor and economic efficiency, where the attempts have been made. Unfortunately, concern for income distribution only seems to be incorporated in project work when the projects themselves are for rural development, urban informal sectors, housing, or welfare services. Although there are employment and distributional consequences of other projects, and choices to be made which affect those consequences, in the standard case, project preparation and project evaluation for a large range of industrial or infrastructural projects ignore the distributional impact.

The policy dialogue can also be, and has been, valuable for promoting the interests of the poor, both broadly, in promoting growth and efficiency and patterns of growth likely to generate employment and relevant forms of production, and in specific sectors. But the report makes clear that great care is needed to secure the interests of the poor when raising the price of staple foods becomes a necessary element of a new economic strategy.

There have been cases where aid has been harmful to the poor. Tractors provided under some aid-assisted rural credit schemes have adversely affected jobs. Major dam projects have sometimes failed to provide for displaced populations. When cash crops are substituted for food crops it is sometimes found that the nutritional status of people in the area goes down, even though their income rises — markets are just not sufficiently well organized to ensure that additional food arrives to absorb additional demand. Some forms of cost recovery may damage the interests of the poor: in general, the report finds virtue in attempts to makes services self-financing, but not if the interests of poor people are neglected. And some adjustment programmes have called for retrenchment which falls unduly heavily on the poor.

There are also areas where aid has demonstrated an impressive capacity for learning. Basic services provide a clear example, where early aid built metropolitan hospitals or not-so-low-cost housing, and supported forms of education which mainly benefited the better off. Today, support is more likely to go to low-cost and participatory rural health and nutritional schemes, site and service programmes and slum-upgrading, and less elitist education. Similarly for programmes for women—often neglected in the past by recipient governments and aid, today it is well understood (though perhaps still more visible in policy statements than in practical action) that the fight against poverty is often synonymous with fighting subordination of women in society.

An issue becoming steadily more prominent is the role of NGOs. At their best they have an impressive capacity for voicing the needs of the poor, addressing their problems, and eliciting their participation in developmental activities. But their record is variable (and insufficiently evaluated); and there are questions about how much additional public funding they could absorb without compromising their character and independence. NGOs and their potential are increasingly being studied, and they certainly have much promise as channels for increased amounts of official aid.

The report challenges the view that aid cannot help the poor because it sustains the political status quo which underlies poverty: on the contrary, it finds that aid is quite capable of going against that particular grain, if sufficiently determined to do so.

Doing more to combat poverty

Poverty has to be addressed by long-term and short-term actions, from broad and sustained measures to promote economic growth and develop infrastructure and basic services—education and health—to famine relief. But within the constraints under which aid operates, more can still be done.

First, in some countries donors could put a higher proportion of their aid into directly poverty-oriented projects. While these have not always been successful in the past, enough has now been learned that if 'best practice' techniques were pursued on the basis of current knowledge, the percentage of sucess could be very reasonable. One method of doing more for poverty would be by increasing the (matching) funding granted to NGOs of proven capacity.

Second, donors should incorporate income distribution effects and targets in a far wider range of projects—roads, power and so forth — and not just those commonly thought of as a 'poverty-oriented'.

Third, there is scope for intensified concentration on 'self-targeting' commodities: that is to say, productive activities whose outputs are consumed by the poor in particular: certain food staples, legumes, and root vegetables are obvious examples, and the basic services already referred to.

Fourth, donors should continue the trend of increased willingness to cover local and recurrent costs: directly poverty-oriented projects do not usually require a large proportion of imported inputs; but they do make heavy demands on recipients' budgets. At the least, donors should refrain from financing a set of capital-intensive projects whose recurrent costs are so high that the recipients' capacity for carrying labour-intensive and poverty-oriented projects is limited. They should also continue to support food for work and public works projects generally, provided the lessons of past experience are put into practice.

Fifth, the donors could refrain from the range of practices which this report has found to be damaging to the interests of the poor. They are not numerous; nor are they difficult to avoid.

Sixth, the report calls for a new approach to aid for the poorest countries, several of whose provisions would be directly helpful to poor people — at least in those countries making serious efforts to mitigate poverty; these include balance of payments protection and budgetary support, both of which can help maintain government services beneficial to the poor. Further untying of aid would also help.

Seventh, aid-coordinating processes could be used more often to concert anti-poverty programmes with willing recipients. The cooperation of the recipient is essential—such programmes cannot be planted on unwilling countries. But where the country is willing, the donors could do better than pursue, as they do now, a set of activities which have no cohesive focus on poverty; they could make it clear to recipients that the support of public opinion in donor countries depends in part on aid's being seen to reach the poor. This and many other aspects of policy dialogue are important in action against poverty.

Last, the donors could identify and make special efforts to overcome particular obstacles to poverty-oriented development, especially where these do not involve huge resources. It is natural to think particularly of agricultural research in Africa as a subject with a high pay-off for relatively small additional resources; it would have to stress national, adaptive research for poor people's food crops, and the building up of national research cadres, particularly those who could do on-farm work with poor small-holders.

The wider context

All this said, it bears repeating that the recipient must have a commitment to poverty reduction, if aid measures are not to be just a movement against the tide. And both donors and recipients have to be concerned *both* with longer-term development with no immediate poverty impact, *and* with sustaining economic activity generally, especially in a recession period such as the present. Growth and policy reform are also important for the poor. As has been observed, anti-poverty measures will not help much in economies which are running down. The proportion of aid devoted to *directly* poverty-oriented activities cannot be dramatically increased; it must not come at the expense of these other critical goals of aid. Nor must it create premature welfare states.

Donors have in the early 1980s become acutely concerned with the shoring up of entire productive systems endangered by the international crisis and domestic failings, especially in Africa. This may have helped to create an impression that they have lost interest in poverty reduction. The present report does not confirm any such impression. Donors still place a high priority on poverty reduction. Some current changes may be working in the opposite direction: the trend among several donors towards more mixed credits; the cutting off of some population assistance by the USA for reasons unrelated to development; not least, cuts in aid programmes by some governments. But the aid agencies have learned how to help the poor with carefully directed assistance, and are not relinquishing, and cannot afford to relinquish, the task.

They could do more in getting public opinion on their side if they both pursued the measures just summarized, and made clear in their publicity that the poor need other allies in addition to aid: not least their own governments, and a supportive world economy. Aid agencies cannot be blamed for the persistence of world poverty; only for not doing the most they can to mitigate it.

IV   Policy Dialogue

The effectiveness of aid and the success of policy dialogue are intimately related. Donors for a long time have engaged in discussion with recipients about policies at many levels, from macroeconomic policy to details of concern at the project level. But in recent years policy dialogue has taken on a new meaning, especially with the poorest countries. The donors have felt that aid, consisting mainly of projects, did not provide an adequate framework for policy dialogue, while many projects were proving to have disappointing results, in part because of inadequacies of the policy environment in which they operated. At the same time, the recession of the early 1980s and other conditions made it necessary for donors to switch a considerable amount of aid into quickly disbursing forms to support or rehabilitate existing investment — the conditions for large quantities of new investment in many of the poorest countries simply did not exist.

Country studies carried out for this report suggest that policy dialogue is mainly effective when it goes in a direction already favoured by the recipient. When the recipient is in such dire straits that he has little alternative but to move in the suggested directions accompanying an aid package, progress may also be possible. But steps must be taken to avoid alienating the recipient, or reforms may be discontinued when the crisis is past.

The Korean example shows that if the donors' motives are other than primarily developmental, large amounts of aid may have little policy impact. This was true of US aid to Korea in the Synghman Rhee period, when the importance to the USA of sustaining Korea was well known to the Korean regime; there was little developmental impact of aid until the Park government took over and showed willingness to reorient economic policies. From that time on, the policy dialogue, supplemented by the presence in the bureaucracy of US-trained personnel able to articulate policy discussions, began to help move Korea in the favourable directions that led to today's economic successes.

The case of India showed another important feature: that policy dialogue is one thing, leverage another. The attempt of the donors to force a devaluation on India proved to be a turning-point in aid relationships which lasted for many years. The devaluation in 1966 was needed; but its timing was poor, and the aid package which was promised to support it disintegrated within a year. The consequence was a growth of nationalistic and independent-minded sentiment in the government; economic plans and policy statements began to speak much more commonly of moving towards self-reliance and doing without aid. This in turn had a self-fulfilling effect, and aid to India began to shrink. Only in the last few years has the policy dialogue with India and the aid process been restored to a condition of mutual respect and understanding. The results have been gratifying for both sides, with Indian policies moving in useful directions, supported—if to an inadequate extent—by aid.

The greatest concern today is with the countries of sub-Saharan Africa, where there is a growing consensus about certain kinds of policy inadequacy which have hindered development in the past— though not yet a full consensus about how to move from this unsatisfactory state of affairs to a better one. The new willingness of several African countries to consider and implement major reforms is no doubt in large part due to a recent history of economic and social deterioration. But the design of the reforms and the process of implementation are the outcome of policy dialogue and the conditionality which accompanies supporting aid flows. These are making for more effective aid, and also for prospects of improved economic performance in numerous countries which are evolving in this way. The record of this phase of aid dialogue is brief, but it appears to be a promising departure, with some important cases of countries embarking on comprehensive and much-needed reforms—Mali is one such among countries studied for this report.

The IMF

An important feature of the dialogue is the increasing role of the International Monetary Fund. The IMF is not an aid agency, but its connection with the aid process has grown closer as the World Bank's Structural Adjustment Lending has been linked to Fund programmes, with bilateral aid following in their wake. In so far as one is able to judge, the record in low-income countries is encouraging.

Nevertheless, there are some instances in which there are grounds for concern that adjustment measures have not always been sensitive to the situation of certain of the poorest countries, particularly in East Africa. The problem is one of the relationship between short-term adjustment programmes, designed to stabilize the balance of payments, and the requirements of medium- and long-term development. Where this question does arise and macroeconomic retrenchment appears unduly severe, what has given rise to this severity, and what changes might permit a form of short-term adjustment more in keeping with longer-term needs?

In IMF programmes, it is not entirely clear to what extent such problems are due to resource availability, and to what extent to operating practices. Certainly the resource constraint is a major feature in any Fund programme. Countries have to get their balance of payments in order with the amount of foreign borrowing that is available to them. And adjustment must lead, not simply to growth, but to *sustainable* growth. However, questions have been raised of whether, even within existing resources, there have not been cases of adjustment measures imperfectly related to countries' capacities to adjust.

In the 1970s there was a considerable response by the IMF to the problems of the poorer countries after the oil price increase: the oil facility, the Witteveen facility, the Extended Fund Facility (EFF), the Trust Fund, and the Subsidy Account were all put in place in that period; of those, only the EFF is still operative, and in 1984 few of the poorest countries could qualify under its rules. The use of Fund resources has nonetheless expanded greatly since 1979. The problem relevant to aid effectiveness is with the poorest countries—countries with very limited capacity to adjust quickly, whose principal exports are commodities with limited prospects in current circumstances, and which have few possibilities of rapid economic restructuring. Such countries need longer periods to adjust, greater protection than is currently available against swings in foreign currency earnings, and greater attention to supply as opposed to demand issues in their adjustment programmes.

The World Bank

A major initiative of recent years has been the World Bank's programme of Structural Adjustment Loans, designed to equip countries to cope with changed circumstances—particularly in the international economy—by supporting policy reform. The programme has had mixed but many positive results so far. Problems have arisen over the appropriate use of conditions: for example, when most conditions are fulfilled but one is not, the whole loan may be suspended: a procedure that has been criticized. But the report absolves the Bank of other accusations—for example, that it has imposed a unique formula on countries regardless of their circumstances. Reforms in agricultural policies and in public sector management show particular promise.

A strong conclusion of the report is the need for improved collaboration between the Bank and the Fund, to achieve two main purposes: first, a better relationship between policy instruments over which the Fund negotiates, and the actions and policies, normally the province of the Bank, which are complementary to them and necessary for their success; and second, a greater harmony between short-term adjustment and longer-term development. Expanded resources for both organizations, and an improvement of the terms of Fund lending, would assist both to allow low-income countries a more expansionary adjustment path.

Other agencies

Bilateral agencies and the Regional Development Banks also have major roles in policy dialogue. While mostly content to leave macro-economic issues to the World Bank and IMF, the other agencies' experience and skills make them qualified to participate in dialogue, particularly at sectoral and project levels.

Some causes of concern apply to the dialogue as conducted by all agencies, particularly when they are involved in the reform of unsatisfactory policies which have been in place for a long time. The process of reform requires care, not least because of entrenched interests; and it may be easier to say what is wrong than to put it right. Donors must be sensitive to the recipient government's need to compensate or satisfy the interests that suffer under reform.

The issues on which reform has concentrated most include overvalued exchange rates and import restrictions, price regimes (particularly prices for food and other agricultural crops), the management of parastatal organizations, and economic controls on the private sector. While these have all contributed to poor economic performance in the past, changing them is not a simple matter. A more open orientation for an economy is generally desirable, but the timing of opening up must relate with care to each country's export capacity, the state of world markets—including trends in protection—and the ability of domestic producers to benefit from foreign competition. Far greater sensitivity is needed to the adjustment capacities of the poorest countries, which typically need longer periods for liberalizing trade regimes.

When better incentive prices are set for domestic producers, care must be taken that the non-price elements of improved production are in place. While farmers will often respond to increased prices, in other circumstances lack of appropriate plant varieties and related inputs, credit, storage and transport capacity, or marketing facilities, may frustrate an improved price structure. It must be borne in mind, too, that the poor are particularly sensitive to increases in food prices. Different agencies involved in dialogue may all be discussing policy reforms related to agricultural incentives. It is important that their policy advice is harmonized with action to promote all necessary aspects of change.

This point has a more general corollary. The advent of higher levels of programme lending and more 'interventionist' dialogue makes coordination among all agencies more important than ever. If projects proceed under contradictory assumptions, the results may be unsatisfactory, but no worse; however, countries logically cannot pursue contradictory policies.

The recipient side of the dialogue needs attention. Recipients have not always shown strong commitment to adjustment programmes. Part of the problem may lie in their not playing a full part in the elaboration of a programme—which may be equally true of a programme which they do see as generally desirable. This report attaches the greatest importance to the recipients' capacity to engage in dialogue — to discuss policy alternatives, to examine modelling work which leads to important conclusions and be able to pose alternatives, to engage in other parts of analysis important to the working out of policies, and to negotiate. Few of the poorest countries are strong in all these departments. Technical cooperation is already available to support them, but not adequately: it should be given higher priority if dialogue and its effects are to improve. This should help to strengthen recipients' political commitment to reform, which experience has shown to be a key requirement for success.

On balance, the current emphases on policy dialogue in the IMF, the World Bank, and other agencies should prove productive. They can be further refined along lines suggested here. Since deficiencies of the policy environment have been a major cause of past ineffectiveness of aid, aid projects and development generally can be expected to benefit from policy-based lending.

V   Project Aid

The present study has processed a huge number of evaluations of projects, either directly, or through reports which themselves review numbers of evaluations. While most of these are carried out by or for the aid agencies themselves, they are often critical—some might say surprisingly critical—and certainly not necessarily self-serving. This is one of the sources of the conclusion expressed by this report—that the majority of aid does achieve its objectives.

What do these evaluations mean? They mean, most of the time, not only that the roads get built, the dams and irrigation channels are constructed, and the water reaches the farmers' land, but also that there are measurable production benefits (though not necessarily well-distributed benefits). Nevertheless, there are many more things one would wish to know that aid evaluations do not reveal. Not enough impact studies are done showing what is left of a project five years or more after completion. Often, downstream effects are not reported on: there is a well-known phenomenon of 'island' projects which may be successful in themselves but have no influence beyond their boundaries, and do not generate anticipated complementary effects with other investments.

A further problem with evaluations is that they are not comparable. Also, since the lifetime of a project is six or seven years or more from inception to completion and a further two years may be required until evaluation is done, and several more years before impact is fully clear, it may be as much as ten to fifteen years from the time a project has begun to the time when its lessons are understood—and by that time donor policies and practices may have changed.

Nevertheless, there is sufficient evidence that *projects* on average do produce satisfactory results in a very large proportion of cases. Eight major agencies have examined the experience of large numbers of their recent projects, with very similar findings, showing two-thirds to three-quarters of them broadly achieving their objectives. However, contemplation of the unsatisfactory ones suggests areas for improvements. First, some major concerns are discussed that are relevant to evaluation and performance in a range of projects.

Projects and sustainability

A subject requiring much more attention is the life of projects beyond the time of the donors' involvement. This life may depend on the recipient's institutions, on capacities to ensure the payment of recurrent costs, on the novelty and appropriateness of the technology introduced, or on social and cultural factors. Donors should give much more regard to these or other conditions during project design if they are to ensure that projects survive after they withdraw. Perhaps one question above all deserves asking more often about most aid: will this help in the long-run to increase the recipient's self-reliance?

Projects and women

Enough experience has now been gained to show that giving proper weight to women's roles is not only a matter of equity, but very often a condition for projects succeeding at all. The report is encouraged by the number of agencies that have adopted adequate policies for incorporating women more fully in relevant aspects of developmental work, and also by the signs that these policies are beginning to bear fruit. Yet progress in the field is still limited. Donors could do worse than observe the agreed DAC guiding principles which propose taking 'full account of the gender composition of the population at all stages of the [aid] programming cycle'.

Projects and the environment

Something similar can be said of environmental issues. There is clear evidence that some aid has had harmful environmental effects; and also that the agencies are increasingly aware of the fact, and taking steps to ensure that environmental impact is considered at all relevant stages of project preparation and implementation. Yet even here policies are not fully agreed and elaborated; and, in the field, insufficient care for environmental consequences of aid activities is still apparent.

Improving the learning process

A major concern of this report with the proportion of aid projects that go wrong — and they are only a minority of all projects — is the repetition of error. An enormous amount of project experience has been gained and documented, and much aid has benefited in effectiveness as a result. But when known mistakes are repeated, or successes are not followed, there is a strong case for efforts to improve the learning process.

Individual agencies can do that in two main ways: by making information about project experience more accessible; and by ensuring that information is incorporated in work on new projects. Some agencies have gone quite far in these directions. They may prepare brief project summaries on every project, so that officers can quickly discover which past project reports would be relevant to future lending. It is not fanciful to imagine such information being on file in a computer data-base; it is probably more fanciful to imagine aid agencies having terminals accessible to all relevant officers and the officers trained to use them, in the near future at least—though one or two agencies either have moved or are planning to move in that direction.

Agencies also vary in the extent to which they hold systematic reviews of detailed project experience among project staff. It is by no means required in all agencies that officers working on new projects be familiar with past experience on similar projects. It should be. Staff should be called upon, with any new loan, to show how problems encountered in earlier ones will be overcome: this might be termed the 'remedial principle'.

Inter-agency exchange

In some ways, the potential for adding to information by improving its flow *among agencies* is greater, not least because evaluation experience is limited in some agencies, especially the smaller ones. Is an inter-agency project data bank even more fanciful than some of the measures already suggested? It would have to be fairly confidential if agencies were to be frank about their failures; or else projects could be described fully but some aspects of anonymity be preserved. There are, however, useful alternatives to the data bank notion.

Inter-agency conferences or reviews of sector or sub-sector experience, leading to documentation that can be widely shared, have already taken place. The OECD conference which led to its recent publication on aid for irrigation (Carruthers 1983) was an excellent example. More of such activities are planned, and would be highly desirable. This report found distressingly few inter-agency surveys of project experience. Sector summaries by individual agencies are now, however, quite numerous, and their findings could be assembled and integrated. Perhaps the World Bank or the DAC or both, could examine how to deepen the reservoir of comparative aid experience, and also how to do more to ensure that knowledge is put to good use.

The fund-channelling function

Another major problem identified in much evaluation experience is the influence on the quality of aid of the pressure to commit funds. Of course, this pressure has its good as well as its bad sides. It is important that there be pressure to make loans: that is what the agencies are there for, and there must be a sense of urgency as they go about their business. Problems only arise if quantity is the enemy of quality.

At almost every stage in the processing of a loan, staff in donor agencies have incentives to ensure the loan is made. Career incentives from project staff to senior management are on the side of quantity. So is the annual budgetary process, and its requirement that funds in a given department be committed at the end of the fiscal year on pain of facing budget cuts next year. Obviously, these factors are strongest when an agency is going through a period of major and rapid expansion. But they are omnipresent. Quality considerations enter in mainly through the professionalism of staff, and also through pressures from the recipient side (at least from those recipients with developed capacity for judging projects). The evaluations done within the agency normally come too late for this purpose; project staff and country desk officers are highly likely to have moved to other positions by the time projects they have processed are evaluated.

It is unlikely, and not obviously desirable, that agencies will abandon annual budgeting for rolling budgets. Nor will career structures be designed in which promptly discharged responsibilities for making loans will dwindle in their influence on promotion prospects. Nor will officers be kept at the same desks right through evaluation cycles, which may be of ten years or more. Improvements must come within such constraints; some of the prescriptions are the same as those for improving the learning process. Apart from improving the information flow (see above), the problem can be tackled in two ways: weakening the effect of the quantity incentives or strengthening the quality incentives.

Agencies vary in the extent to which they can escape the inflexibility of annual budgeting processes. In some, the scope is considerable. Within budgeted amounts, departments can shift lending among countries and projects, even among years in some cases. It helps in this process to have a 'shelf' of projects to be taken up if obstacles are encountered in parts of a lending programme. 'Accordion' projects, which can be enlarged or take on additional components without loss of quality if funds permit, can also help to use additional funds effectively.

Strengthening the incentives for quality lies in part in applying the 'remedial principle' referred to above, that new loan preparation explains how problems encountered in old loans will be overcome. This should be observed at *all stages* of preparation, beginning with design and appraisal. Monitors and evaluators will then have something additional to monitor and evaluate: whether problem avoidance procedures have been followed, and whether they have been successful. (Of course much new lending is, and should be, for new kinds of projects. Many of them, too, will build on past experience. When there is little past experience as a guide, pilot projects in more than one setting may be a better option than large-scale innovative investments.)

Once again, agencies differ in the extent to which the 'remedial principle' is already embodied in their project work. Some agencies regularly include a section on 'lessons of past projects' in appraisal reports, but they are not always incorporated with great seriousness—just as requirements to cover 'environmental impact' of projects are often ignored. In all agencies there are systems of shared accountability in which peer pressures, management surveillance, and the technical work required on projects all combine in an attempt to ensure quality. (Often the value of cost–benefit analysis is not the rate of return, which is the 'bottom line', but the fact that it forces project staff to be explicit about critical assumptions, which can be questioned by alert management.)

Nethertheless, the variability in quality shows that what is in the rule-book on project preparation is not the whole story. One or two ideas about how to improve 'quality control' can be added. (The analogy with quality control in manufacturing is not very revealing; but it points to one main distinguishing feature — the length of time between preparation of the 'product' and evaluation of its quality.) First, in some agencies the bodies which pass final judgement on new loans contain many of the same people who are responsible for evaluation or to whom evaluators report. This ensures that the experience of evaluation is brought to bear on a crucial stage on loan processing. Second, while there are many reasons not to hold project staff personally responsible for the ultimate fate of projects, they could be rewarded when projects go well. Even if the rewards come several years later, the knowledge that they are to be won could be helpful. Other uses could be found for such 'positive reinforcements', as an alternative to inhibiting disciplines: one of them would be to reward innovation, which deserves greater encouragement in most agencies.

Identification, appraisal, evaluation

There are many common features in unsatisfactory projects. A few of them are examined in this report.

Technical choice.   Projects do not always consider an adequate range of technical specifications, and do not always select the right ones. Some of this may be hard to improve on, especially when the principal harmful influence is the (bilateral) donor's commercial interests. The recipient can refuse, if he indeed knows the technology is unsatisfactory; but he may face a difficult choice if he is offered the aid on a 'take it or leave it' basis. Other reasons may be more remediable: where there are likely to be competitive indigenous technologies, for example, grain storage, donors should investigate the possibilities more thoroughly. Greater clarity in formulating project objectives, more specialized knowledge among project designers, and more careful analysis in advance of the consequences of adoption of particular technologies, seem to be the main requirements.

Appropriate skills in identification and design. The report notes some particular deficiencies among others which could be named. Projects often betray a lack of understanding of the human, social, and physical environment in which they are to be set. Agencies should overcome their reluctance to employ non-economist social scientists who could help to supply this understanding—as could also recipient country personnel. Other examples are marketing and location aspects in industrial projects; personnel with business skills are often lacking in project preparation.

Among common deficiencies at the *appraisal* stage are excessive optimism, against the evidence, over project completion times; poor appreciation of recipient capacity for administration and implementation; over-optimism regarding the time and resources needed by the recipient to take over the project, or for it to become self-reliant; and the lack of proper forecasting of effects on intended beneficiaries. Action can and should be taken on all these points. On the first three, the 'remedial principle' is once more relevant. On the fourth, more attention is needed, not least to base line surveys to determine the pre-project condition of 'target' populations, so that their post-project progress can be assessed.

On how to do *evaluation* there is little to say that donors do not already know. The principal deficiency in several agencies is that it simply is not done fully, or at all, on a sufficient proportion of projects. The report also proposes that agencies which do not already do so make their evaluation findings public, good and bad. More openness and frankness about failed projects would benefit public appreciation of the risks and difficulties of aid, and would be preferable to concealment. That proper note be taken of evaluations in the learning process is the greatest concern of all, already discussed. The report also warns of the dangers of excessive reliance on the rate of return as a criterion for success. While extremely important, its calculation may omit crucial considerations such as sustainability and others mentioned above.

The report contains a discussion of some problems of particular sectors—agriculture, industry, education, population—which will not be repeated here. Some further general features are worth dwelling on. There is a need for *long-term involvement* of donors in some classes of project—in agriculture or eductation for example—where expectations of rapid results have often been excessive, and experience shows that success is greater when the aid relationship is prolonged. *Building project management into recipients' normal administrative structures* and strengthening them, rather than creating new administrative units, is a clear lesson with only a few large projects as exceptions; avoiding 'over-design', or projects which impose too heavy a burden on administrations and which are vulnerable to external events, is another. The role of *management* in projects and the critical *relations between financial and technical assistance* are other particularly important areas. These are just some salient features of a complex discussion, which sound somewhat jejune when baldly repeated; the reader is requested to refer to the full text of Chapters 5 and 6, from which these points emerge.

Three areas of aid were briefly considered in which the main needs are for more resources: agricultural research, population assistance, and education. They are all areas of prime importance to development; they have high pay-offs; a great deal is known about what needs to be done and how to do it; and, in the case of the first two, the requirements for additional resources are modest relative to the demands of other aid-receiving sectors. Education can, of course, absorb very large amounts of aid; both donors and recipients could help by increasing the priority given to primary and basic education at the expense of higher education.

VI Programme Lending

Programme lending in its various forms has two essential purposes—to supply needed imports, and to support policy reforms in so far as it acts as a vehicle for policy dialogue. Both functions became particularly important in the 1980s, when the harsh external climate both made balance of payments support more than usually urgent, and exposed the extent to which a weak policy environment was contributing to lack of progress in development and lack of effectiveness in aid.

The experience of providing programme aid has raised questions about its future. Some of these questions are about the policy dialogue itself, which has already been discussed. For the rest, the donors have really to think through what their policies should be on this type of finance. First, there is a need for all the aid agencies and international financial institutions to collaborate so that non-project assistance (including food aid) is provided at an adequate level to support objectives agreed with recipients—broadly developmental as well as policy reform objectives. Second, as already noted, the greater the volume of programme lending and number of agencies associated with policy dialogue, the greater the need for coordination to ensure consistency among the policies advocated.

Third, there is a need for a greater 'insurance' element in development finance, giving additional support in times of greatest need. When numerous countries are in such need simultaneously, there is little alternative to a widespread move out of project and into programme lending — typically, in such circumstances, large amounts of new project lending cannot be accommodated in any case. In more normal times, greater support should come from improved and expanded compensatory financing mechanisms. A principal aim of such action should be to safeguard long-term investment programmes in the poorest countries, which are otherwise in danger of being sacrificed to short-term exigencies. Of course, such additional support has to be conditional; it will not be forthcoming if countries' difficulties are of their own making, or if they are not taking adequate steps to ensure that resources are being effectively used.

Donors have understandable reasons for preferring project aid to aid in other forms. But a full recognition is overdue of the complementary roles of project and non-project finance, and of the need for their integration into a coherent framework of development finance, but in an uncoordinated manner. Greater systematization of programme lending will help development and also increase the effectiveness of project aid.

(A number of more specific points on improving the effectiveness of programme lending are made in Chapter 5, 153–6. They are not repeated here.)

VII Food Aid

Food aid has gone through a complex history, and has had many areas of failure; but these are now largely well understood and largely avoidable, so that a conclusion of this report is that *programme* food aid has and will continue to have its place in the overall picture of aid, and can achieve valuable results. The main deleterious effects have been in the relationship between programme food aid and agricultural incentives; it is now quite feasible for countries to absorb large amounts of food aid without affecting agricultural production incentives, provided either that food goes to poor people who would not have entered the market for food or, where this is not the case, that market-clearing arrangements are made so that effective demand is maintained.

In *project* food aid, one can only hope that the lessons of failed and successful projects will be heeded. Food aid studies and the literature on nutrition give valuable guidance on how to reach target groups in a population, which has often not been achieved in the past. Perhaps the best way to improve project food aid would be to employ it in support of projects which are within countries' priority investment programmes and subject to all the normal management and evaluation conditions, rather than in projects specially designed to 'absorb' food aid. Many health and nutrition or rural construction programmes being conducted by recipient country ministries could benefit from food aid resources. The trend from project to sector assistance observable in other forms of aid could be and to some extent is being followed in food aid also. (Food subsidy programmes too can be made more efficient, confined more carefully to those really in need, and designed to avoid adverse effects. They can be extended into other areas—such as increasing food-marketing efficiency—helpful to improving nutrition among the poor.) Existing procedures for evaluation of project food aid have been described as casual and neglected. A comprehensive monitoring and impact assessment system is needed, in which key questions are identified at early stages of project preparation, covering at least a selection of food aid interventions in given countries, and with cooperation among major donor agencies.

Finally, questions have been raised of the 'cost-efficiency' of food aid. At least in some cases, recipients would be better off being given in money form the additional costs of delivery of surplus foods from donor countries, than they are with the foods themselves. There should also be more attention to 'triangular transactions'—the purchase with donor financial resources of food from developing countries which have a surplus for delivery to nearby recipients.

Some concluding remarks on 'performance'

The majority of aid projects function well, and improvement is discussed in relation to the less successful activities (or increasing the effctiveness of the already successful). Since so much has been said about the 'learning process', the points that occur through the report will also bear repetition, that a great deal of learning has gone on in whole ranges of project types, for example, roads, irrigation, rural development, health, nutrition, education, and family planning. What is done by aid today has changed radically in the light of experience. Effectiveness has also been increased by activities beyond the parts of the project cycle which are internal to donor agencies, most notably in the policy dialogue, where very considerable strides have been taken in the past five years.

If there is a general weakness in the aid process other than those already dilated upon, it is that understanding of institutional, political, and social constraints to aid effectiveness lags very far behind economic and technical competence in virtually all agencies. The number of people skilled in the latter employed by the agencies outnumber those trained and skilled in the former by several hundred to one.

VIII   Technical Cooperation

Technical cooperation amounts to something like one-fifth of total ODA, althouth it is rarely accorded the treatment it deserves in studies of aid. It includes assistance for education and training and the supply of skilled personnel. The basic findings of the review of TC are similar to those concerning project aid, namely that much the greater proportion has been reasonably successful. The lessons are fairly common, though they are perhaps more difficult to transmit, in part because evaluating TC is a less quantitative matter than evaluating capital aid. (Quite a lot of TC is in fact not evaluated, or evaluated mainly by 'debriefing' returned technical assistance personnel.)

Chapters 5 and 6 also discuss institution-building—a subject on which the record is very varied. It includes many examples of straightforward, successful cooperation with developing countries—from relatively mundane matters, such as improvement of central banking institutions or data collection, to more complex ones, such as setting up and strengthening of rural development agencies, or operations research to promote family planning programmes.

At the same time, there are some areas where institution-building has not been successful. Perhaps the most common of these has been where projects have incorporated their own administrative units outside the line organizations of the recipient country's government and institutions. The lesson appears to be that it is much more important to try to strengthen those agencies and institutions. When aid projects are linked to institution building, there is a high correspondence between the effectiveness of the latter and of the former; both relate in turn to the associated sectoral environment as a whole. Long-term involvement is a condition for success in institutional support.

Some of the recommendations emerging from this study are very similar to those for financial aid. For example, the learning and feedback processes need strengthening, including better communication of evaluation findings between agencies, and systematic mandatory review of relevant findings from past projects during the design and decision procedures for new ones. TC should be provided to help recipient countries build their own evaluation capabilities. In project design, more attention should be paid both to the policy framework and to the institutional and action linkages that will determine the project's effectiveness. And many of the proposals for coordinating capital aid apply equally to coordinating technical cooperation.

The contraction in overseas education has been carried too far for many countries and in many development disciplines. Currently under-utilized capacity in higher education facilities (due to declining school age populations) in some industrialized countries could absorb much larger numbers of Third World students. There is also an unending need for financing in-country *training*, including the strengthening of national and local training capacity in recipient countries.

Cross-cultural problems of TC activities might be reduced if (non-economist) social scientists were employed more regularly in project design. Experts should be trained in cross-cultural communication to raise the success rate of the expert–counterpart relation. The greatest scope for cost reduction in technical cooperation lies in recruiting developing country nationals at competitive local, rather than international, pay scales. This would require bilateral untying for expert recruitment and, in the case of the UN agencies, development of an innovative two-track personnel system.

While financial contributions to the UN system stagnate, the multilateral development banks (MDBs) are devoting more resources and staff thinking to technical cooperation and institution-building. This drift will erode the old distinction between MDBs and capital projects on one hand, and UN agencies and TC on the other. In addition, intellectual and operational leadership in TC may fall to the MDBs by default. Such changes would pose serious issues of staffing and MDB administrative costs, of relationships within the UN system, and of responsibilities and organization for coordination at the field level. This whole set of issues regarding institutional roles and relationships deserves more systematic and higher-level management attention than it has received thus far.

Advanced technologies pose novel problems for the effectiveness of TC, stemming from the rapid change in these technologies, fast obsolescence of hardware, the greater information gap between young technicians and senior supervisors, and the dangers of 'technology-driven' attractions. Aid agencies need to identify the requirements for sustaining their own effectiveness in 'high-tech' subjects, and for meeting the problems peculiar to high-tech TC.

There is a striking weakness in the intellectual underpinnings of institution-building, the development of human capabilities, and associated TC, compared with the theoretical and quantitative tools used to plan physical investment and resource requirements. Work has been done on manpower planning and techniques for development of individual institutions. There is now sufficient experience on which to base historical and comparative analysis of institution-building that might yield methodologies for raising the success rate in this important area. There is quite insufficient guidance for planning institutional requirements at the sector level, for forecasting and matching institutional needs with evolving economic structures, or for systematically defining inter-sectoral and inter-disciplinary institutional linkages (a 'knowledge and technology' analogue to the economic input–output matrix). The basic TC objective of self-reliance has not been defined in terms that would aid the planning of institutional needs and facilitate rational decisions. This report has made suggestions to remedy such deficiencies; the subject really needs a major effort of conceptual development.

IX   Coordination

Some of this report's hardest words are reserved for aid coordination, where it finds donors and recipients sadly wanting, though making belated efforts to improve. Most aid which has been evaluated has looked at individual projects or programmes, or occasionally the involvement of a particular aid agency in a given country. What has only more rarely been studied has been the joint effects of the operations of a multiplicity of donors working in a particular country: a deficiency which the present study attempted to remedy through its country case studies and other investigations.

The principal ill effects which the study finds are as follows. *First*, the collection of aid activities of a variety of donors in a particular country may or may not add up to a coherent contribution to development. The World Bank's most recent Africa report states that the aid activities in a number of countries do not correspond to development priorities—a finding consistent with some of the studies conducted for this report.

Second, what is often referred to as the 'proliferation' of aid projects and of equipment types, is usually the result of too many donor agencies operating in a given sector or sub-sector. A typical low-income country may have twenty or thirty official aid agencies working within its borders, as well as up to twice that number of non-governmental organizations. The results of this are very commonly a large number of projects which the recipient is ill-equipped to manage; and frequently a gross excess of types of equipment creating problems of maintenance, training, etc. (An example given in the report is Kenya's water supply, where eighteen different makes of water pumps were supplied by a variety of donors.) These first two problems produce the principal components of the *third*, the burden on recipient administrations, resulting from the multiplicity of donors, the complexity of their separate procedures, both of contracting for aid and for procurement purposes; and also the procedural and data requirements of project implementation and monitoring. *Fourth*—and most important of all—are the implications of multiple aid activities for the recipients' recurrent budget and foreign exchange requirements related to aid projects.

In a surprisingly large number of (mainly African) countries, the government has no central unit with an overview of all aid flows; donors still negotiate with individual ministries. The first requirement for coordination is that the recipient have such a unit negotiating all aid agreements or having negotiations reported to it. Only then can the government link 'upwards' to the higher-level, donor-coordinating institutions, and outwards to coordination activities within the country. The recipient should also have effective sectoral coordinating bodies to relate aid projects and programmes to each other and to its own development spending.

If the recipient has no inventory of all aid projects, he will not have within his budget expenditure items of domestic budgetary finance related to projects; nor will there be an adequate foreign exchange budget related to aid projects. In such circumstances, the familiar phenomenon of aid projects held up for lack of complementary domestic budgetary or foreign exchange resources is only too likely to be repeated. (It is not ruled out that on occasion the recipient is well aware of this, and is not above using the situation to come back to the donor for additional programme lending to cover these needs; but if the donor is aware of the country's budgetary situation, the blame is shared by both parties.) The report illustrates models of good practices in these regards, even if of fairly recent date. Of course, some of the countries where aid has been operating over a longer period mastered these situations many years ago. Aid coordination is not a major problem in South Asia, except possibly for Bangladesh, but it is a problem in most of the poorest countries.

Strengthening Consultative Groups

Improved coordination is needed both on the ground and at higher levels. To improve overall aid strategy, Consultative Groups (CGs) or other country-level coordinating bodies should move in the direction of reaching broad agreement with each recipient on the recipient's investment priorities and associated aid requirements—project and non-project—and other financing needs. In such a context, dialogue can take place over the policy environment surrounding aid and development. More countries should acquire and use CGs or UNDP Roundtables for these purposes.

CGs could also play a greater part in organizing co-financing of development projects; undertaking sector analysis, discussion, and coordination; analysing recipient public investment programmes; and resolving programme pipeline or project implementation problems. Aid agencies should increase their field representation in order to give further assistance to such work.

Further coordination measures

Further measures to reduce the ill-effects of uncoordinated aid include, in some cases, a 'lead donor' taking on the task of liaison with the recipient government in a particular sector; a reduction of the number of agencies operating in individual sectors; and harmonization of donor procedures in procurement contracting, accounting, management-information requirements and the like. (Such harmonization has been attempted in the past and much discussed in the DAC; there are signs that more progress may be possible in future than has occurred hitherto.)

Bank–Fund coordination

The IMF and World Bank are both currently reviewing their approaches to cooperation. Aid donors in the DAC, and this report, have called for improved cooperation, particularly over the harmonization of short- and long-term adjustment programmes. This is not to be brought about by any redefinition of the functions of the two organizations, but rather by an intensification of existing forms of collaboration. Packages involving exchange rate adjustments and credit controls require consequential redirection of public investment and expenditure programmes—the Fund relies on the Bank over the latter, but does not engage in much discussion over the exchange rate adjustments themselves. The two facets of adjustment could clearly benefit from a more careful relationship to one another.

Similarly, there could be greater efforts at mutual exchange over trade liberalization and price reform measures—on which both institutions do collaborate—and the non-price elements needed to make such measures effective, which are largely the province of the Bank. Such exchanges could be instrumental in producing greater realism about the time-path of successful adjustment, with consequent enhancement of the effectiveness of Fund and Bank programmes.

National Food Strategies

The report has welcomed the initiatives of the WFP and EEC to assist countries in pursuing NFSs, designed to ensure consistency between goals and activities of countries' food, nutritional, and agricultural strategies, and to serve as a focus for donor support and coordination in these areas. But current investigations indicate difficulties in the promotion of these strategies, and suggests that it might be well to watch the progress of some already begun, and to identify possible teething troubles, rather than embark prematurely on large numbers of them in several countries. The strategies have much promise; they should not be allowed to become an aid 'bandwagon' which comes to a halt.

Positive signs

The report is encouraged by current activities in coordination. In particular, the World Bank is pursuing an active leadership role in trying to organize intensified coordination arrangements, with the support of bilateral donors. Many valuable new initiatives can be seen, and are described in the report. However, while there is a good deal of new enthusiasm for coordination as stated at meetings of the various bodies which discuss it, it has yet to be seen whether results in the field will reflect any major improvement.

The reasons why past coordination has failed to get off the ground are fairly well known. On the recipient side, governments have often preferred to be in a position where they can play one donor off against another, and they are apprehensive of the possibility of donors 'ganging up' against them if coordination becomes more effective—they often find the degree of pressure exerted by existing institutions already difficult to accommodate, even without coordination. On the donor side, the bilateral donors are keen to pursue their commercial and political objectives through aid, and there is often a conflict between doing that and concerting their aid with other donors; in addition, the donors sometimes fear that they may not be able to reach agreement with one another over significant policy issues.

Nevertheless, the current concern over coordination is fully justified and has great promise. Strengthening it would add considerably to the effectiveness of aid—particularly in the poorest countries, where the greatest need now lies for redoubled efforts. Both donors and recipients are more and more ready to appreciate that they have far more to gain than to lose if they make such efforts. The present situation is lamentable, and it is high time that it improved.

X Aid and Market Forces

There is a school of aid criticism which holds that aid, consisting most commonly of government-to-government transfers, is *ipso facto* likely to be in conflict with market-oriented developments and therefore unsatisfactory. There are also views based somewhat more carefully on evidence — though not an excess of it — claiming that aid has unduly supported governments pursuing policies inimical to private sector development. There have been suggestions that aid activities have had a 'crowding out' effect on the private sector. This report finds all of these positions wanting, in relation to the recent past, though there was some truth to the second and third arguments in the 1960s and early 1970s. If anything, the opposite is the case: it could be said that aid is, on balance, a good friend of market forces, and has been so for many years.

First, a considerable proportion of aid is on-lent by the recipient government directly to the private sector through such things as rural credit programmes, or through domestic development banks which lend to the private sector. Second, a great deal of aid goes into infrastructure which is the natural domain of public investment, and without which private enterprise would be unable to function. And third, a considerable part of the policy dialogue is occupied with questions of the efficiency of specific forms of economic organization, and has frequently intervened to promote increased use of incentive prices, trade liberalization, and even the conditions for the operation of foreign private companies. Certainly, there is little evidence that aid has systematically supported countries with more rather than less 'dirigiste' economic regimes. Such countries as were dirigiste and supported by aid in fact had their dirigiste regimes implanted in advance of the aid relationship, and the aid relationship has been part of a number of processes which have been leading these countries towards greater liberalization: India, Korea, and Bangladesh are examples studied for this report.

The report also coins a new piece of jargon — 'asymmetrical liberalism'. This is the phenomenon whereby aid donors are putting increasing pressure on recipient countries to make use of market forces, while they are themselves, through aid, distorting the competitive process, not only by the longstanding practices of aid tying, but by the new intensification of the use of mixed credits. There is not always a good match, either, betwen trade policies urged on recipents by donors and the donors' own trade policies.

Promotion of the private sector is a somewhat sensitive subject: it is important that a separation be made between the use of price mechanisms for efficiency purposes—a use which has been insufficiently made in many developing countries in the past—and ideological preference for free market institutions. The report points to the rather obvious recognition that satisfactory development will require promotion both of private and of public sectors, and that aid can and does contribute importantly to both. But aid can and should do more to encourage private sector activities where they have clear advantages, as, in many parts of agriculture and industry, experience shows that they do.

Aid should do more, in the first place, of what it already does — though only to a limited extent: promotion of competitive firms and commercial networks where none exist, development of marketing and its ancillary services (especially for agricultural produce), aid for the central investments in industrial complexes where the downstream units are taken up by the private sector, aid to development banks for on-lending to the private sector, co-financing, and programme lending which supplies inputs to private sector firms and permits fuller capacity utilization.

Aid could also move into areas where it has not been tremendously active: support for development corporations to promote, for example, agribusiness; trading companies and other business-brokering institutions; venture capital; prototype private sector projects with potential for replication; business management training; executive managerial personnel on loan, in a technical assistance capacity, to developing country firms; or joint undertakings between business and private voluntary organizations.

XI   Multilateral–Bilateral Comparisons

The multilateral and bilateral institutions are symbiotic. A large part of the impetus behind the expansion of the multilateral system in the 1970s stemmed from the desire of governments to redress the deficiencies of an aid system which was still, in the 1960s, predominantly bilateral. The main reasons for expanding the multilateral part of aid are as valid today as they were then: to make the inter-country allocation of aid more balanced than it would be if left to the donors' unalloyed self-interest; to carry out policy dialogue on sensitive issues; to avoid duplication of effort in economic reporting and data collection; to assist the coordination of aid; to act as intermediaries between world capital markets and developing countries; and to carry out surveillance over the functioning of the world economy.

The multilateral agencies were set up and are sustained by national governments, which recognized the need for them. But bilateral programmes, which are much the greater part of aid, have important strengths and functions. They have particular knowledge, historical ties, and close relationships with particular recipient countries. They have experience and skills in specific fields of development often superior to those of multilateral agencies. Above all, their serving of national purposes is a key factor in public support for the whole of aid.

The report distinguishes between the part of the multilateral system which mainly provides TC, and that which is principally involved in financial aid. The former needs adequate resources to carry out its work; but it needs streamlining, and determined efforts to remedy its well-documented defects. the latter part of the system is not faultless either; but the report considers its functions as essential to the effectiveness of aid overall. It asks whether these functions could be maintained at lower levels of funding.

In general, the answer to that question is No. The capacity for policy dialogue and aid coordination depends importantly on continuous involvement in recipient countries with active lending programmes. And the budgetary stringency which some agencies face is cutting their resources for evaluation and monitoring, and for overseas representation, at a time when these should be being strengthened. A critical recommendation of this report, that a far greater inter-agency sharing of the results of aid should take place, would be undermined if the agencies which should play a leading role in the process are weakened.

Aid-tying

Questions of aid-tying and 'associated financing' also arise in this context. The report calls for continuation of the longstanding international efforts to curb the effects of traditional tying practices, which impose heavy costs on recipients; and further efforts to address some new practices which have generated an unhealthy form of credit competition. If mixed credits have to continue, their grant elements should be raised, their use confined to equipment tailored to the recipients' developmental needs, and their allocation shifted towards the less well-off countries. When concessional funds are scarce, it is highly regrettable that they are delivered to better-off countries, especially when the process is such that, if each donor would desist, all would be better-off.

A New Approach to Aid for the Poorest Countries

A number of measures of particular interest to the poorest countries have been outlined in this report. Taken together, they would constitute a new approach in attempts to accelerate their development. The main ones are:

Measures to protect these countries more fully against fluctuations in the external environment, so as to provide greater stability to their balance of payments and their budgets. Such measures would involve cooperation among all the agencies engaged in balance of payments lending.

Greater security for long-term investment programmes in these countries, from the above measures, and from multi-year commitments of assistance, most particularly in education, health, family planning, and environmental protection.

Development of a durable and systematic strategy for relating project and non-project aid, including programme loans, maintenance, local and recurrent costs, and food aid.

Far stronger efforts of aid coordination, by donors and recipients, than have been seen hitherto.

More committed attempts, for the benefit of these countries, to mitigate the effects of aid-tying and credit competition.

Of course, major efforts will be required from the countries themselves. Donors and recipients must have confidence in each other, whether it be over the policy dialogue or investment programmes. Technical cooperation to strengthen recipients' capacity for analysis, administration, and evaluation will often be important parts of the relationship. And donors themselves need to strengthen their capacities to understand the institutional, political, and social environment in which their aid activities are set.

This concentration on the poorest countries is needed because their problems are so intractable, and because aid performance there has had disappointing results. But the report must end by reiterating that all the low-income countries face grave difficulties in achieving their development, and need the continued support of official assistance, bilateral and multilateral.

Annex A: List of Studies Undertaken

Country case studies of aid effectiveness

Bangladesh	B. van Arkadie and K. de Wilde
Colombia	B. Bagley
India	M. Lipton and J. Toye with R. Cassen
Kenya	A. Duncan and P. Mosley
Malawi	A. Hewitt and J. Kydd
Mali	G. Bourgoignie
South Korea	D. Steinberg

Project evaluation studies

European agencies:	
Energy and industry[1]	N. Segal and W. Wicksteed
Agriculture	J. Pell and R. Whyte
Transport and communications	G. Ortona
North America-based agencies	C. Gulick

Other studies

Technical cooperation	R. Muscat
Comparison of multilateral and bilateral agencies	E. Sachse
Literature survey	R. Cassen, P. Chaudhuri, and P. Daniel, with S. Griffith-Jones

[1]Including World Bank

Annex B: Synopses of Country Studies

Annex B1: Bangladesh Aid Effectiveness Study

Highlights

In absolute terms, Bangladesh has received large amounts of aid. In the period 1971–1983/4, Bangladesh has been aided by some fifty bilateral and multilateral donors, with cumulative disbursements of US $12 billion, and flows currently running at $1,375 million per annum. However, viewed in per capita terms, aid flows of $15 per annum are modest enough on an international comparative basis.

The initial tasks of the aid programme after independence were relief and reconstruction. Given the circumstances operative in the post-war situation, the restoration of the economy was carried out with some success, to which aid made a significant contribution.

After the initial years, the aid need shifted more to development tasks, although the need to provide food support, particularly in years of poor harvest, remained an important part of the aid programme.

Bangladesh economic performance presents a mixed picture. There has been modest growth in per capita output. Famine has been avoided. The rate of capital formation has been raised. A substantial family planning programme has been organized. In some regards, therefore, in the face of a fast-growing population and a negative external economic environment, performance has not been unsatisfactory. However, growth has been concentrated in the service sector. Growth in agriculture has not kept pace with population. The income distribution has become more unequal; poverty, landlessness, and unemployment have increased, and nutritional levels have deteriorated. In relation to the balance of payments, the most positive development has been the growth of workers' remittances.

For the future, improved performance requires a breakthrough in agriculture, continuing export diversification through a growth in non-traditional exports, an accelerated demographic transition, and progress in relation to the distributional dimensions of development.

The impact of the aid programme on the pattern of development has been a subject of some controversy. Some Bangladeshi critics have argued that the degree of aid dependence has been excessive, and has seriously distorted the development pattern. Among donors, there has been continuing concern regarding the effectiveness of the administration of development and the efficiency of economic policy measures. In some parts of the aid community, frustration is expressed regarding the pattern of development, which is seen as having done little to eradicate poverty or erode the concentration of wealth and power. Quite apart from the large questions about aid and the Bangladesh development strategy, a number of more particular points emerge regarding the effectiveness of the aid programme.

The aid programme has had a number of positive features:

(i) There has been a large degree of flexibility in the balance between food aid, commodity aid, and project aid, although the trend of donors in favour of project aid is likely to reduce flexibility in the future.

(ii) Food aid has supplemented total food supply and helped to avert famine, and parts of the food aid programme (notably Food for Work) have directly increased the incomes of the rural poor. However, much of the food aid has gone to better-off urban groups; there has been some tendency to correct this in recent years.

(iii) The total level of aid provided is probably at about the right level in absolute terms, in that higher levels of aid would exacerbate problems of aid dependency already identified by some aid critics and increase existing management problems.

(iv) Efforts by donors to engage in policy dialogue to improve the efficiency of the Bangladesh policy regime have met with some success in such areas as agricultural input distribution and industrial policy.

(v) After initial difficulties, a fairly successful system of aid coordination has been developed, under the leadership of the World Bank.

(vi) Considerable support has been provided to population programmes.

There are, however, a number of weaknesses:

(i) The allocation of aid has not yet reflected the priority typically accorded to agricultural development in the stated views of donors, nor have sufficiently effective instruments for the chanelling of aid to the rural sector been identified. Given the dependence of the development budget on aid, any bias towards the urban sector or capital-intensive projects will be reflected in the Bangladesh development programme.

(ii) Donors are critical of many aspects of Bangladeshi adminstrative performance, but are insufficiently sensitive to the adminstrative consequences and costs resulting from the complexities of the aid system itself.

(iii) The shift towards an emphasis on project aid will reduce the flexibility of the aid programme.

(iv) Only limited flexibility has been shown in funding local and recurrent costs; greater involvement in rural development may require greater flexibility in this regard.

(v) Those donors concerned with targeting their aid to the poor have yet to devise an effective strategy for achieving that objective.

(vi) The aid programme and Bangladesh development policy have yet to articulate a strategy for providing a boost to labour-intensive, efficient industrial production for export.

The case for concessional aid in relation to Bangladesh will be incontrovertible for a long period ahead. There is no alternative means of funding imports needed for the development programme. Bangladesh is not a plausible candidate for non-concessional private finance. Even on concessional terms, debt-servicing costs are building up to a level of over $200 million in the near future. The only possibility of significant access to private finance is likely to be in relation to direct private investment in the non-traditional export sector.

There is a need for donors to take a long view of the aid commitment to Bangladesh. This suggests the possibilities of increasing the degree of continuity within the donor programmes, of adjusting donor procedures to reduce administrative costs, and of incorporating a more significant element of long-term programme aid.

The impact of aid on poverty has been disappointing. More effective monitoring of the distributional impact of aid is necessary. The formulation of a more coherent strategy for tackling the problems of functional landlessness should be an important focus of attention for those donors who place high priority on meeting the needs of this group.

Annex B2: Colombia Aid Effectiveness Study

Summary

This study examines the contributions of international aid programmes to the social and economic development of Colombia over the last
quarter-century. The Colombian case is a particularly interesting one
for at least three reasons. First, as a 'showcase' for the Alliance for
Progress in the 1960s and early 1970s, Colombia was one of the major
Latin American recipients of international assistance from such
organizations as USAID, the World Bank, and the IDB. Second, as a
result of its impressive growth record during the late 1960s and early
1970s, in 1975 Colombia 'graduated' from USAID concessional programmes. Third, although deeply affected by the 1979–83 global
economic slow-down and recession, Colombia managed to weather
the 1982–4 debt crisis in much better shape than most of its Latin
American neighbours, leading at least some observers to suggest that
Colombia represents a model worthy of emulation by other crisis-
ridden nations in the region.

The principal aid agencies operating in Colombia — the World
Bank, USAID and the IDB — each made major financial contributions to Colombia's development. The World Bank has been the principal international agency functioning in Colombia since the early
1950s, providing the country with $4.6 billion in resources over the
past thirty-five years, versus the IDB's $2.6 billion, and USAID's $1.6
billion for the same period. The World Bank also performed an
important fund-raising function among the Consultative Group
members, beginning in the early 1960s and continuing through the
present. The IDB has been a key member of the Consultative Group
since its inception in 1961, and remained an active member in 1984.
USAID played a prominent role in Colombia during the 1960s — the
halcyon days of the Alliance for Progress — but gradually declined in
importance in the early 1970s and was finally phased out after 1975. It
is no longer an active member of the Consultative Group.

With Colombia's 1975 graduation from USAID programmes, both
the World Bank and IDB became even more important to Colombia as sources of external financing than they had been previously.
During the six years between 1978–83, for example, the World Bank

alone lent as much to Colombia as it had in the previous twenty-nine years of operation in the country. The relative share of the multilateral lending agencies, however, remained about constant, at around a third of total international loans entering the country. The decline of concessional US resources flowing into Colombia was made up by growing reliance on borrowing from the international commercial banks (on shorter terms and at significantly higher interest rates).

Each of the agencies conditioned their project, programme, or sectoral lending on specific steps designed to stabilize the Colombian economy, increase the fiscal soundness of the government, relieve balance of payments problems, and bring prices for government services (for example, water, electricity, transport) or government-regulated prices (for example, petrol, food) into line with real costs of production and delivery. They have sought to strengthen and make more efficient major government spending agencies such as the Ministry of Public Works (Obras Publicas), the Agrarian Reform Agency (INCORA), the National Planning Department (DNP), and a number of decentralised institutes. The annual Memorandum of Understanding between the Colombian government and the World Bank, institutionalized after 1965, and the Projects List prepared annually for the Consultative Group since 1969 have been important levers to pressure Colombia to adopt fiscal and macroeconomic policies in a more timely fashion. While Colombia has from time to time resisted some of these conditions, the resulting availability of foreign credit has enabled the Colombian authorities to expand their development programmes beyond what the country could otherwise have afforded; hence, they have generally been willing to accept them.

The lending provided by the major donor organizations was used primarily for large, individual infrastructure projects (such as railways, highways, airports, electrical power-generating capacity, land irrigation and reclamation, telecommunications facilities, and industrial plant). In the late 1960s and 1970s, considerable effort also went to strengthening the institutional capacity for planning and implementation of development projects. From 1973, there was a growing emphasis, particularly in the World Bank, on addressing the problems of the poorest segments of Colombian society through support of IRDPs, land colonization, rural electrification, and expanded education opportunities for low-income populations in both rural and urban areas. By the late 1970s, these projects began to pay off in terms of significant improvements in the standards of living of Colombia's poor. Even with the financial support and institution-building efforts of the international development agencies, however, Colombia has not been able to escape the economic recession and debt crisis that convulsed Latin America in the 1982–4 period. The crisis arrived later, however, and has not been as severe as those experienced by Mexico, Brazil, Argentina, and Chile. Thus, in comparative perspective, Colombia is relatively better-off than its neighbours. Nevertheless, by late 1984, Colombia was in very difficult economic straits, and seemed likely to adopt an IMF-austerity programme, either formally or informally, in the near future.

International assistance strategies

By the late 1960s (and continuing through the present) relations between Colombia and the international agencies had evolved into a complex and delicately balanced pattern of lending and condition-making. The World Bank, as chairman of the Consultative Group, has played a central role. During crises, the IMF has assumed a leading role. Essentially, conditions have been imposed at three levels. First, the annual Memorandum of Understanding covered major policy issues; initially developed in connection with USAID programme loans, it gradually became the macroeconomic basis for World Bank lending programmes and its advice to Consultative Group members. Second, there were a few broad sectoral policy matters dealt with partly through the memorandum and partly through discussions relating to individual loans. Third, there have been the more traditional project-related conditions, mainly of an institutional and financial nature, taken up with borrowing agencies and the central government in connection with negotiations for each loan. While there have been internal contradictions within this system, over time it has proven to be an effective arrangement for linking Colombia to the international lenders.

Institutional development

The principal international agencies working in Colombia each played major roles in the process of developing the country's public sector institutions over the last quarter-century. The World Bank took the lead in this area in the 1950s and 1960, and remained the major institution builder over the 1970s and early 1980s. With the phasing out of USAID after 1975, both the IDB and UNDP (and such specialized UN agencies as the FAO, UNESCO, and the ILO) have played important complementary roles to the World Bank in the areas of feasibility studies and technical assistance.

Poverty

In 1972, a major World Bank report declared 'the biggest problem in Colombia, to which every major Bank report on the country has pointed, has been and remains widespread, and in places desperate, poverty in the countryside'. By August 1983, however, the World Bank was able to point to major improvements in the conditions of the country's rural and urban poor. 'Over the past two decades, Colombia has achieved significant gains in the standard of living of its people . . . [The country's] economic performance has been especially impressive because a wide cross section of the population, in rural areas and in the urban centres, has been able to share the fruits of development more fully than in many other developing countries.'

Three basic factors explain Colombia's remarkable success in reducing or alleviating poverty over the 1970s. First, sustained economic growth and declining birth rates combined in the 1970s to produce significant rises in per capita income and real wages, especially in the latter half of the decade. Second, many of the redistribution efforts undertaken by Colombia in the late 1960s and early 1970s only came to fruition in the 1975–80 period. Finally, by 1973 the World Bank — led by Bank President Robert McNamara — shifted lending priorities toward greater emphasis on the Third World poor.

Prior to 1973, World Bank lending concentrated primarily on infrastructural development, and systematically emphasized urban over rural areas. Indeed, in the 1960s the Bank was sceptical of land reform, and did not support Colombia's agrarian reform programme. After 1973, the Bank began directing its lending towards the urban and rural poor. Under President Misael Pastrana (1970–4), and subsequently President Alfonso Lopez (1974–8), land reform was essentially abandoned and government policy redirected towards increasing levels of production and productivity in the traditional or peasant sector and nutrition levels among the rural and urban poor. Since 1974, the World Bank has provided substantial assistance to the Colombian government's nutrition programme (PAN), integrated rural development programme, rural electrification, rural secondary schools, and rural roads. Reflecting the shift in the World Bank, IDB lending over the 1970s also focused increasingly on projects like rural electrification to benefit the rural poor. By the early 1980s, these projects had dramatically improved public services in both the rural and urban areas, thereby helping to raise overall standards of living among the poor.

Since 1979, economic slow-down and recession have generated high levels of unemployment, and have reversed the trend toward improvement in real wages. While public services have improved, the prices of these services have also risen and, in the process, become very sensitive political issues. Moreover, the foreign loans used to underwrite these development programmes became increasingly costly as Colombia 'graduated' from concessional loans to commercial bank lending in the second half of the 1970s. In the context of the 1981–5 recession, the servicing of Colombia's mounting foreign debt has become an increasingly serious problem for the country, and has forced major cut-backs on government investment in social and economic development. These cut-backs, in conjunction with price increases for public services, have undermined the gains made by Colombia's poor in the late 1970s to an (as yet) undetermined extent.

Annex B3: India Aid Effectiveness Study

Summary

India's thirty-year encounter with aid and aid agencies makes her experience particularly rich for those in search of lessons on aid effectiveness. Although aid flows have always been small, measured per head of population and as a share in national income, they have made some clear positive contributions to India's economy and society. There have been also mistaken and even wasteful uses of aid; but a learning process in aid management has taken place, and many of the early errors are most unlikely ever to be repeated. India's aid performance is now significantly better than many other aid recipients, a fact which, ironically is now being used as an argument to support switching her *away* from concessional finance. Such a view is most questionable.

In recent years, aid has financed some 8 per cent of Indian investment (20 per cent of *public* investment) and about 15 per cent of imports. These figures fall well below those of the peak period of aid inflows (1955–65). As well as the levels of aid, its economic function has changed over time. In early years, its role was largely that of relaxing macroeconomic constraints – particularly the constraint on the domestic supply of wage goods imposed by bad weather in particular years. More recently, although the harvest cycle has continued, the foreign resources position has been eased by remittances and rising export receipts. Now aid is more concerned with easing sectoral bottlenecks and policy reform at the sectoral level.

Has aid reduced India's poverty? The aid (for agricultural research, fertilizer imports and production and input diffusion mechanisms) which supported the 'green revolution' in northern wheat-growing areas seems to have had the greatest impact on poverty. This impact, made by raising the level and stability of basic food supply, was marred in some areas by the accompanying dispossession of poor tenants and their conversion to landless labourers. Food aid itself had a similar overall positive impact, despite its early (but avoidable) adverse side-effects on domestic food prices. There is no doubt that, in the diffusion of key inputs (rural credit, irrigation water), better-off farmers have been successful in claiming the lion's share from aided schemes. They have tended to benefit most with regard to production, employment, and income. Recently, aid for irrigation has found ways of reaching the poor; but the gains to the rural poor generally have been mainly in terms of extra consumption, or prevention of consumption losses which would otherwise have occurred. But a number of poverty-oriented aid schemes have been implemented successfully, and more could be if the donors supported more actively the anti-poverty programmes mounted by the government.

Many aided schemes are for infrastructure, and the question of who benefits from them is rarely easy to answer but, sadly, even more rarely asked. The other main arena for aid is the 'human resources' sector. Here it is easier to identify success – urban slum upgrading, rural primary health care, and (at last, after many early disappointments) family planning and nutritional assistance. More aid should now be invested in these success areas, and in extending the scope of labour-intensive appropriate technology in both agriculture and industry. In agriculture, more donor support for integrated rural development programmes is recommended, subject to the lessons of past difficulties.

In developing a sensible donor–recipient policy dialogue, India underwent a long series of conflicts related to donors' attempts at macroeconomic aid leverage, especially in the period 1965–71. Since the mid-1970s, under the World Bank's leadership, policy discussions have focused on sectoral rather than macroeconomic issues, and the Indian government has had no difficulty in making sectoral dialogue genuinely two-sided. But obviously its good effects – in supporting trade liberalization, for example – are conditional on continuing concessional flows.

The aid process in India is much more orderly than in other countries. Control of aid receipts is centralized in one department of government, investment planning takes account of anticipated aid receipts, and considerable experience has been built up in the field of international price comparisons. Procedural problems have been different for different types of aid. For multilateral aid, they have centred on international tendering, the payment of local costs, and long delays in the project cycle. For bilateral aid, tying has been the major issue. Discernible progress has, however, been made in ameliorating all of these problems, except project delays and bilateral tying, where 'invisible tying' and 'triple tying' have noticeably surfaced of late. Some further procedural benefits might result from a joint donors' mission to India, giving better coordination and better specialist input to sectoral policy dialogue.

Some sixty evaluations of project aid to India have been examined. But many lack baseline data, calculated rates of return, and a focus on distribution. World Bank projects show good returns, which would have been much better had major delays not occurred. More recent Bank projects show better results than earlier ones, though more focus is still needed on employment/poverty aspects. In many evaluated projects, weaknesses were evident at the appraisal stage. Fuller consideration of alternative projects and alternative (less complex and capital-intensive) designs of the same project are needed. Specific faults can be identified in rural credit projects, especially in the use of such credit for tractor purchases. But more general lessons about the organizational form of successful projects are hard to come by, because some of the successes have used methods that may be unique to their circumstances and that have failed elsewhere. One clear lesson was the need for more and more rigorous project evaluations, especially those which make proper use of baseline data.

Aid to India for TC has been relatively modest (because of India's own very large stock of skilled and trained people), but highly significant in one sector – the development of agricultural research institutes (see above). Other aided TC initiatives in the areas of development, banking, fertilizer, irrigation management, agricultural extension, and the Indian Institutes of Technology have been more recent and varied in their results. Some anxiety has been expressed that donors have not looked sufficiently critically at the conditions for the replication of successful pilot projects, and that agencies' desires to disburse funds rapidly may be connected with this insufficiently critical approach.

TC for training of Indian personnel also has not undergone a sufficiently critical evaluation, and donors' comparative advantages in training, as well as the full range of India's training needs, have not been properly addressed. India still has large needs in low-level and particularly rural skills. TC for training should probably be tied much more closely to the development of sectoral aid programmes, which are themselves now much more rurally focused. USAID is moving in this direction, and other agencies might do well to emulate it.

India's is an economy with many government controls super-imposed on the working of market forces. These controls largely pre-date the setting up of the Aid-India Consortium, and Consortium influence through the policy dialogue has consistently been in favour of greater liberalization. The Indian Government is now more willing to proceed with the relaxation of controls, many of which had, in any case, failed to serve the purpose for which they were originally intended. There is some evidence of possible 'crowding out' by aid of private investment in the 1960s. The effect from multilateral aid was certainly small, the effect from bilateral donors (particularly the classic cases of public sector steel mills) somewhat greater. The changing levels and composition of aid made these effects negligible in the 1970s. Nevertheless, bilateral donors particularly have taken a strong pro-private sector stance for aid in the 1980s; but this in turn brings new contradictions of policy that need resolution.

The multilateral agencies have followed a less fickle approach to the public/private sector question than the bilateral donors. They have maintained a consistent concern for the expansion of infrastructure through efficient forms of organization – regardless of the public/private division. They have coupled this with the view that any form of organization will perform better the more existing controls on trade, investment, and prices are relaxed. This pragmatic approach is hard to fault; but it should be remembered that, for liberalization to succeed, appropriate support through concessional flows must be given. And India, like many developing countries, would embrace trade liberalization more enthusiastically if it could count on liberalization in its industrial country markets.

India's experience of aid, stretching back three decades, is believed to contain useful lessons for aid to other countries today. Many problems now arising in aid to the poorest countries have already been met in India and India's aid history – in aid management, agricultural research, rural credit, sectoral policies, poverty-oriented schemes, and many other areas. Further study from this angle would no doubt prove fruitful.

Annex B4: Kenya Aid Effectiveness Study

Summary of main findings

Statistical evidence

There is no simple correlation between aid inflows and economic growth in Kenya during the period 1966–82; this is at least in part because of the time-lags in the impact of aid programmes, and because at certain periods (for example, 1981 and 1982) aid has increased in response to economic difficulties.

Macroeconomic performance

Kenya's economy is open to the world market (exports plus imports = 70 per cent of GNP in 1980), and therefore heavily influenced by external conditions. It operates a comparatively free market internally, though with heavy government involvement in a wide range of functions, including commercial.

The 1976–7 coffee boom caused the government to undertake an ambitious programme of long-term investment. The 1979–81 oil price rise and recession therefore caused major disruption. By 1980, both the balance of payments deficit and the government's budgetary deficit were over 10 per cent of GNP. Government's response was twofold: heavy external borrowing, and sustained effort to be more efficient in the level and use of its expenditures.

The role of aid has been crucial, rising from 23 per cent of government development expenditure in 1976 to 59 per cent in 1983–4. The current 1984–8 development plan is relying heavily on outside borrowing (to rise from Kpounds 60 million to 123 million) most of it concessional.

The performance of projects was generally satisfactory during much of the 1970s, but had deteriorated in recent years. *Ex post* evaluations of projects recently closed indicate that in several cases internal rates of return have been below the cost of capital.

Concessional flows and donor coordination

There are some forty-eight bilateral and multilateral donors to Kenya, diverse in priorities and procedures. Their motives are the usual mix of commercial, geo-political, bureaucratic, and humanitarian. In addition, Kenya is an important test for the open economy model of development. The multiple objectives of donors have strongly influenced the aid programmes in Kenya, *inter alia* by leading in some sectors to greater capital intensity than is warranted by Kenya's factor endowment.

There has been a large increase in the past four to five years in balance of payments support as part of the aid flows. As far as project aid goes, most donors concentrate on two to three sectors in which they have some comparative advantage or historical association. There is a tendency among some (most strongly the USA) to channel project funds to the private sector. The World Bank is the largest single donor, and is also undertaking a good deal of macro- and sector analysis. Most aid programmes are moving 'upstream', in the sense of giving greater attention to the policy framework and to institutional support.

There is a widely perceived need for improved coordination of aid programmes at the sector level; present arrangements, if they exist at all, tend to be informal. However, a mechanism established this year has begun to set up sector committees (agriculture and energy so far) under the government's chairmanship.

The shift to programme aid and policy dialogue

There has been a marked increase in the proportion of aid funds taking the form of programme aid, among both bilateral and multi-lateral donors. The reasons for this change are perceived weaknesses in absorptive capacity for project funds, and the donors' views that institutional and policy reforms are crucial to sustained economic progress and to effective project implementation.

The major form of programme aid has been two World Bank SALs, both fully disbursed, between 1980 and 1984, with several of the major donors formally linking release of their programme aid to Kenya's meeting World Bank conditionality. The evidence of the two SALs is that comparatively little policy reform of substance has resulted. Moreover, there are disadvantages in linking the macro-funds that the economy needs to specific actions within particular sectors. The evidence from Kenya is that, where conditionality is requiring action that the government would not otherwise have taken, the government will take the minimum necessary steps, and will not take them with the commitment that is needed for sustained policy reform. The danger is that fundamental disagreement between the World Bank and Kenyan decision-makers on a sectoral issue may jeopardize the macro-funds and hence economic recovery.

Absorptive capacity and public sector management

The poor performance of projects in Kenya in recent years has been in good measure ascribed to weak absorptive capacity. We have defined absorptive capacity in terms of three interrelated sets of factors:

(i) *The scale and complexity of the tasks.* This is determined by issues of design and implementation procedures. Many projects, especially in the rural sector, have been too complex in design, especially institutionally. Multi-sector integrated projects have fared particularly badly, with many of those which have relied on inter-sectoral coordination at the level of central ministries running into particular difficulties. Large infrastructure projects have had fewest problems. Implementation procedures, notably for procurement and the release of funds, have been unduly ponderous.

(ii) *The allocation of functions between alternative implementing agents.* The state has a wide range of functions, including commercial activities, which are exacerbating its fiscal and administrative problems. Government has accepted the principle of reducing its responsibilities, and has established a task force to divest itself of parastatals, though progress is likely to be slow. Other actions being taken are to implement a policy of 'district focus', with the aim of increasing the role of local government in planning and management development.

(iii) *The operation of implementing organizations.* Public sector organizations in many cases have performed weakly. A high-level government report has noted a 'crisis of management' and a 'collapse of financial discipline'. The performance of aid-supported projects has inevitably been adversely affected by this. Donor responses have been varied, and include a greater emphasis on strengthening institutions, provision of resources to the private sector, transfer of responsibilities to other organizations, and continuing provision of expatriates in advisory and in some cases in in-line positions. Government is putting considerable emphasis on improving budgetary procedures, with effective support from several donors.

Aid and the private sector

Considerable resources have been provided by donors for the private sector, in part through access to programme aid for priority imports. Care needs to be taken, however, that these resources do not disrupt private sector operations, as has occurred in the case of the provision of some consignments of fertilizer. Resources are also provided to the private sector in the form of loan funds through development and commercial banks. Recovery rates through the development banks are unsatisfactory. A weakness in the system is the continuing low level funds provided to the informal small-scale sector. Despite the difficulties, efforts to increase the share of these borrowers should be sustained.

Sectoral experiences and the learning process

The experience of the aid programme indicates the continuing need for a process of learning on a sectoral basis, to involve both donors and the government. Too little is known about what works effectively, especially in respect of organization and management. Good sector coordination is needed, together with receptivity and flexibility.

(i)   *Agriculture*.   The performance of the agricultural sector has been by and large disappointing in recent years when compared with the 1960s. Many aid projects during the late 1970s and 1980s have fallen well short of targets, the major reasons being those of over-complex design, poor management and, during the 1980s, the acute fiscal crisis. The multi-sector, integrated national projects have been terminated and replaced, actually or in prospect, by single sub-sector projects (for example, extension, dairy). District-level integrated projects continue with varying degrees of effectiveness, although some are encountering a lack of economically sound recommendations for farmers in the drier arable areas. Much remains to be learnt about how to bring about effective sustained development within the agricultural sector.

(ii)   *Transport and energy*.   In respect of transport, the most interesting and valuable experience is provided by the Rural Access Roads Programme, a multi-donor-supported programme which, building on previous experience, devised a labour-intensive method of road construction and maintenance for rural access roads widely through most arable districts of Kenya. Donor coordination has been excellent, and has contributed in good measure to an effective learning process.

In respect of energy, donor assistance has been effective in increasing the capacity of hydro-electric schemes in the country. Over 90 per cent of donor funds for the energy sector have, however, been committed for commercial energy, which contrasts with the fact that 75 per cent of energy used in the country is fuel-wood and other biomass, and that a major fuel-wood crisis is looming, with potentially serious repercussions for standards of living and the economy as a whole. The comparative lack of interest among donors is largely attributable to their pursuit of commercial objectives, reflecting little to their credit. A well-coordinated and large-scale initiative in this sector is needed.

(iii)   *Rural water development*.   Despite a sustained effort over much of the period since independence, involving several donors, to provide protected water sources for the rural population, at least 89 per cent of the rural population still does not enjoy this basic facility. The major reasons appear to be a continuing over-ambitious technology, cumbersome procurement procedures, weak institutional performance, and limited funds for operation and maintenance. Fundamental aspects of policy — the basis for charging for water used, for example — have not been resolved, and donor coordination has been poor. There are significant costs associated with aid-tying (eighteen types of pump in use, and at least one example of pumps of one nationality being removed when another donor undertook support for one large-scale scheme). There is a strong case for a simpler technology with greater local community involvement in planning and maintenance.

(iv)   *Family planning*.   For the past five years, senior political leaders in Kenya have urged the need for reducing the rate of population growth (at 4 per cent per annum, perhaps the fastest in the world). Prior to this the subject was *non grata*, and outside support was at an extremely low level. Since then, several donor programmes have been started and are addressing the issues. This sector, in parallel with the energy sector, requires a sustained and well-coordinated joint approach by donors and government to devise the most effective means of meeting the challenge.

Annex B5: Malawi Aid Effectiveness Study

Summary and conclusions

Malawi's aid relations with donors have gone through three phases: budgetary aid plus project finance to 1971; followed by a decade when almost all aid wás for new development projects; and since the economic crisis starting 1979, a period of macroeconomic restructuring supported by stabilization programmes, with limited scope for new project financing (especially as regards recurrent revenue raising capacity), constraints on an autonomous development strategy, and a stronger need for programme aid and balance of payments support. This phase is likely to continue for another three years, even if the external transport situation improves. Alternatives to aid finance, such as the spurt of commercial borrowing in 1978–80, are no longer possible for Malawi.

Malawi has been relatively under-aided in the past, and has attracted a rather narrow range of donors. Important donor groups – OPEC/Arab funds; 'liberal' European donors – are notable by their absence. Some non-DAC donors are, however, active, but poorly integrated into the planning process. A narrow range of donors (two big bilaterals, two multilateral agencies) has had some advantages for the recipient administration; but prior to the IMF/World Bank SAL operations, there was little coordination among donors, even among European donors within the EEC.

A UNDP-sponsored aid donors' Roundtable was held in 1984. It failed to elicit significant additional pledges (though the Malawi Government was not sanguine about such expectations, and recognized the existing necessarily rigid pledging and programming procedures of its traditional donors), but performed a valuable information function — not just between donors, but within the government's own public spending departments. It set the seal on IMF/World Bank support programmes in determining the direction of economic management — and hence other donor involvement — over the next three to four years.

Although under-aided for a least developed, land-locked country, Malawi's responsiveness to restructuring proposals and generally successful aid utilization record has led most existing donors to sustain and in some cases increase their aid effort — contrary to the case in some other African countries. Some donors are to increase their commitments as a response to perceptions of the government's sensitivity to price signals and further disbandment of public controls over market mechanisms. Dangers of political instability may however be courted if donors press the demolition of established systems of domestic patronage too far.

The stabilization and restructuring programmes required by the IMF and the World Bank have been part of a learning process for both parties. The World Bank's conditionality was initially very mild, and the main thrust of the first SAL (two years from mid-1981) was towards identifying structural problems and studying possible solutions. However, the Bank's conditionality hardened with the second SAL (two years from late 1983). Most of the key conditions of the second SAL (agricultural pricing, management of the parastatals for example) should improve the performance of the economy, while the IMF's credit ceilings should reduce inflation in the medium-term. However, neither the Bank nor the Government appear yet to have developed policies to deal adequately with future pressures on government recurrent spending. The approaches of the early 1980s, increased taxation of individuals, elimination of subsidies in the supply of utilities and housing, and moves towards cost recovery in the provision of social services, carry damaging by-product effects which may become serious if pushed much further. (Increasing the already heavy taxation of individuals may suppress incentives, while cost recovery in the social services will harm the poor.) Thus a radical reconsideration of the government's recurrent spending commitments is necessary. It is likely to be the case that, when compared to the costs of raising further government revenue, certain areas of public sector activity cannot be justified at their current scale. It is probable that some of these less justifiable areas of public sector activity were created or expanded by the capital aid projects of the 1970s. Analysis of Malawi's fiscal problems thus leads to two conclusions, which superficially may appear inconsistent. *First* is that aid donors should support a thorough review of the government's recurrent spending commitments, with the objective of identifying areas where spending may be substantially reduced. A necessary element of donors' participation in this must be a self-critical approach to commitments which have arisen as a result of past capital aid projects. *Second*, in recognition that the severity of the fiscal problem probably precludes rapid expansion in recurrent government support to social services, donors should be prepared to develop schemes for supporting recurrent costs in health and education.

Malawi represents only a small market for Western capital goods, but most of the bilateral donors have responded to the recession by increasing the element of trade orientation in their aid programmes. Normally, procurement-tying to source has not been a major problem – most donors allow derogations to procure from low-cost regional sources in exceptional circumstances – but the emergence of mixed credits and some form of programme aid has shifted donor allocations into non-priority sectors such as telecommunications.

Aid to agriculture has been heavily focused on the peasant sector. The principal vehicle for this aid has been IRDPs, and, at their inception, donors viewed IRDPs as an effective form of 'poverty-focused aid'. The production impact of the IRDPs has been disappointing. Probably the major reason for this was the fact that, over the 1970s, peasant export crop production was subjected to heavy implicit taxation through the government crop marketing board (ADMARC). Other problems were the impact of increasingly severe land pressure in peasant farming areas, an initial under-emphasis on agricultural research on peasant crops and farming systems (with the exception of cotton and tobacco), an over-ambitious and complex management structure (this applies especially to the post-1978 national programme), a weak input distribution system, and the effects of the energy price increases on the viability of the 'technical packages' promoted. IRDPs have already placed a heavy burden on the recurrent budget, leading to considerable difficulties when donor-financed project components end. However, most of this potential burden is still to be felt, but is likely to be a critical problem in the mid-1980s, as more projects come to the end of their donor-funded phases.

In the future, donor support to peasant agriculture must give priority to ensuring a satisfactory macroeconomic climate (this is a key feature of the second SAL), and to improving the efficiency of the marketing system (which received considerable investment funds in the 1970s). Beyond this, capital aid should continue to focus on small farmer credit schemes (based on simple, robust administrative models), on whatever capital aid may be required to improve performance of the marketing system, and on the expansion of agricultural research. Expansion of Malawi's agricultural research system should be at a rate consistent with its continued efficiency, and donors should continue to bear in mind whether, in particular research problems, enhanced support for international crop research organizations might prove a more cost-effective approach to Malawian problems.

Donor interventions in the domestic transport sector were generally very successful. Starting almost from scratch at independence, Malawi now has an almost complete road network, all of it aid-financed. The Ministry of Works has never built a main road with its own budget – it has only carried out patching. One road project (in the Shire Valley) was a conspicuous failure in construction terms, and the Government tended to request roads which duplicated each other for political reasons; but donors generally fended off such approaches. Most of the donor-financed extensions to the rail networks were also viable and, subject to a caveat about Malawi's present external transport links through Mozambique, created a new lifeline for the export economy. Donor-supplied ships for the lake service were sometimes mis-specified (by the donor) but were adapted locally. Emergency or quick-response aid in this sector also proved effective – a donor quickly supplied a road-bridge from Zimbabwe stock when one was washed away, and others responded with alacrity to road construction projects in the north across the Tanzanian border when other export routes became blocked and existing alternatives were imposing undue cost burdens. Regional transport links have however been rather slow to develop – as much due to Malawi Government reluctance as to donors' procedures – but initiatives by the Southern Africa Development Cooperation Council are improving this situation.

Malawi's trade patterns have barely changed as a result of donor involvement. Tobacco has increased its dominance in exports (and hence Malawi's commodity vulnerability), but largely as a result of strong world demand and of directing domestic bank credit to private operators. Sugar expansion has been largely financed by loans and equity investment. European countries still take the bulk of exports (mainly raw commodities), and South Africa remains the leading source of imports. Flagging exports have been less a factor in Malawi's balance of payments difficulties than the debt service burden arising from borrowing at commercial rates. But compensatory finance from the IMF has been used twice, successfully, although drawings on Stabex have been small and always less than the claim submitted. Unfortunately, tobacco, the main export, is not covered under this scheme.

Donors have not been heavily involved in 'basic needs', except in the context of IRDPs – health and primary education in particular. Some donors admit to an undue urban bias in their programmes. Concerted action for the social services is needed, which (as was argued above) must involve donors being prepared to fund recurrent costs.

Administrative and planning capacity is limited. This, together with a tax base for provision of recurrent revenues that cannot easily be expanded, restricts the absorptive capacity for new development projects. Stronger central economic planning is needed – not all the technical assistance supplied here has been effective, and more donor resources should go into training and support. Treasury and Reserve Bank management is relatively strong, but these bodies do not always adequately communicate requirements to sectoral ministries.

There are dangers in seeing Malawi as a 'blend' country in World Bank/IDA terms. Malawi's first SAL was taken on IBRD terms. The Malawi Government has been assured that the scale of SAL lending will not affect its IDA projects, but is justifiably concerned that a smaller seventh replenishment of IDA will affect it adversely, and that it is being forced prematurely to 'graduate'. The economy is not strong enough to borrow on commercial terms (as occurred briefly in 1978–80), and the debt-rescheduling process will sustain an only just manageable debt burden until the end of the 1980s, during which time substantial export diversification cannot be foreseen. Malawi is still in the position of requiring funding to finance its recovery; most of the macroeconomic adjustments are now in train; the external economic environment can be expected to improve, or at least not deteriorate further; so at present it requires quick disbursing forms of aid to sustain the recovery, and to usher in a new generation of development projects.

In general, it can be concluded that Malawi grew steadily and fast over a long period, and most public sector fixed investment over this time was financed or supported by aid. The domestic management of development was strongly assisted by TC. Moreover, Malawi survived the global recession of the early 1980s rather better than many comparable countries, assisted by the flexible aid policies of the traditional donors together with the new sources of World Bank SAL and IMF lending.

Annex B6: Aid in a Sahelian Context – the Case of Mali

The evaluator of aid to Mali is confronted with multiple objectives, different interests, complex and uncertain causation, as well as insufficient and unreliable data. The study attempts to evaluate aid in four dimensions: worthwhileness, efficiency, effectiveness, and impact. Is aid justified? How exactly will development and aid management influence the outputs, given the resources and inputs? What expectations should one have of the degree of fulfilment of objectives? What impact will aid produce?

Worthwhileness of aid

Both the problem of the ecosystem and the prolonged drought in the Sahel are well-known factors affecting the lives of a total population of more than 30 million people inhabiting the eight Sahel countries (Cape Verde Islands, Chad, Gambia, Mali, Mauritania, Niger, Senegal, Upper Volta/Burkina Faso). By the year 2000 they will be 50 million. The whole Sahel region presents a bleak picture. Without international aid, it faces stagnation. Since 1975, aid for the development of the Sahel has more than doubled. Some $11 billion were received between 1975–82, a yearly average of 44 dollars per capita. Nevertheless, to pull through this situation, international aid must still increase and improve. More help must be channelled towards dryland farming, forestry, and village water supplies. In short, aid must focus on established priorities: regional food self-sufficiency and a new ecological balance. Desertification continues to progress.

As Mali's population is estimated to be over 7 million people (doubling every twenty-five years), of which more than half are aged less than twenty, there are serious problems concerning health, schooling, training, and job creation. The urban population is over one million. The urban areas are plagued with poor fuel-wood supplies and general services. Furthermore, the rural exodus towards the cities has worsened since the drought. Health and sanitation conditions in Mali are precarious. Life expectancy is low: thirty-eight years. Infant mortality, morbidity rates, and malnutrition rates are high. River-basin development schemes and water projects are hampered by onchocerciasis. Medical treatment is insufficiently coordinated, and the price of drugs is so high as to constitute a social injustice. In Mali, health is food. The daily food ration is too small and poorly balanced. Education is also precarious. A reform is planned; the number of children attending schools has not progressed since 1970. Most children in rural areas are left out of the school system. Mali's development is tied to the well being and training of its human resources. But because of the costs involved, expensive literacy campaigns and health and school programmes cannot readily be extended. The Malian Government and foreign aid donors must concentrate their efforts on solving this evident dilemma.

For about ten years now, Mali has experienced major economic and financial misfortunes. It has undertaken drastic institutional reforms, in a major economic policy and financial restructuring effort. The donors have warmly welcomed this willingness to improve the situation. Mali's ODA commitments have increased to $1.6 billion for 1975–82. Including the aid from socialist countries, they came to $1.8 billion. Aid disbursements appear to have followed the proposed commitments, falling short by about 20 per cent. Mali also receives direct aid from about fifty foreign non-governmental organizations (NGOs). Foreign aid averages some $200 million annually, namely, around $26 per capita yearly. The major multilateral donors are the World Bank group and the European Development Fund. Bilateral aid comes mostly from European sources, especially France and West Germany. The study gives an exhaustive account of the international aid provided to Mali. Non-project assistance makes up one-third of receipts, covering essentially operational and economic management of the country, 'survival aid' which the Malian Plan for 1981–5 hopes to see increased fourfold.

The donors are involved in giving 'substitution training' technical assistance to Mali, but it seems that training has made much less of an input than substitution. Aid should give more significant consideration to training programmes. Food assistance programmes have become permanent. They represent 8 to 10 per cent of ODA. Every year, food supplies reaching Mali differ from the amount pledged. This hinders greatly any long-term, multi-annual planning – one reason why Mali, along with several donors, is trying to integrate food aid in the broader scope of a coherent Food Strategy. A recent study points out that if the present drought continues, the volume of food needed will be of the order of 500,000 tons yearly by 1990. If such a situation develops, the strengthening of local food production structures will be in jeopardy.

Project aid accounts for more than two-thirds of Mali's ODA, and is essentially aimed at rural development and infrastructure.

There has been a trend for more funding for rural development, but this is not so evident today. In fact, between 1975 and 1982, aid for irrigated agriculture stagnated, aid for livestock and fisheries fell, and there were insufficient funds for reafforestation; but happily, aid has been applied significantly and recently for dryland food and cereal production. Aid to rural development has been in the range of about one-quarter of all aid, or two-fifths of project aid. Infrastructure development, mostly road construction, is still progressing, accounting for 30 per cent of all aid. On the other hand, aid given for human resources development represents a mere 8 per cent of all aid, or 11 per cent of project aid. Better means of communication will improve rural and regional development, but today, in Mali, the priorities are food and clean water. For the future, a better connection is needed between the measures aimed at food production and the infrastructure needed to implement them. Extensive reafforestation and crop protection schemes are also needed. Finally, more consideration should be given to human resource development.

For ten years now, external aid has funded more than 90 per cent of Mali's Development Plans. Needless to say, the major donors' influence weighs heavily on Plan orientation. Dependency grows. External aid represents 80 per cent of the country's external debt.

Aid efficiency

Mali's macroeconomic management, its State-Controlled Corporations (SEE), and Rural Development Offices (ODR) are plagued with lack of funds and qualified personnel. Aid efficiency has been, and still is, crippled by poor general management. The Government intends to apply corrective measures. Current achievements indicate a turning-point in the history and economy of Mali. Nevertheless, for numerous reasons, the reform process will be long and difficult. Political and social risks are obvious. Thus external aid must be dispensed with realistic expectations, understanding dialogue, and with the most appropriate projects.

Several structural and operational factors relate to Mali's absorptive capacity. The desire of a number of donor countries to limit the available funds according to absorptive capacity, itself difficult to assess, should give way to helping Mali's management at the core. Donors can now develop their institutional aid within the current reform strategy. Project planning must be better related to Mali's macroeconomy. The delays between project approval and its implementation must be shortened. But, for a large number of donors, there has been an increase in bureaucratic impediments to efficiency.

Making aid more efficient involves eliminating two bottlenecks. First, donor procedures: project approval, preparation, execution, contracts, technical assistance rotation, etc. Second, projects are often wrongly oriented, badly managed, and making poor use of available equipment. The main objective of any aid programme should not be the bailing out of the country, nor the shipment of sophisticated equipment, but rather a systematic training of Malian employees in management practices, to lead to eventual self-reliance.

Ways to coordinate the different aid programmes have been considered. On the Malian side, there is confusion. On the donors' side, a global formal mechanism has not yet been defined. Nevertheless, the parties are engaged in a structural dialogue using the platform of the Cereals Market Restructuring Project (PRMC), as well as the Sahel Club framework. Aid efficiency is also related to the great problem of recurrent expenses. As aid funds have increased in amount and have become diversified, so have recurrent expenses. Some adjustments have been made; but it seems wise to earmark more resources to maintain and operate exisiting investment rather than press prematurely for new investment.

Aid effectiveness

Regarding health improvements, several measures are needed: health education, decentralized services, more permanent local health workers, village committee participation, plus an operational strategy promoting women's and children's health, as well as providing a good supply of clean water. Less than 40 per cent of the wells dug in the last ten years are still usable. To make educational aid programmes effective, one must tackle the institutional problems, and educational schemes are at present poorly designed for target cliente!es.

Effectiveness in energy (where 90 per cent is provided by firewood) could be increased by developing more agro-silvo-pastoral projects which make a better use of rural and wooded areas, and by encouraging more active population participation; improved stoves are also a priority.

In the livestock sector, better grazing distribution, as well as agro-breeding associations, must be set up. Special awareness is needed in reinforcing marketing and stocking structures. Inland fisheries play an important role in job creation and food production, a fact only recently appreciated. The different relations between crop cultures and export cultures, commercial farming and subsistence farming, irrigated agriculture and rain-fed agriculture, livestock and farming practices, etc., are complex factors affecting the effectiveness of external aid. To increase the output of agricultural projects, certain major restraints must be overcome, some inherent in the established agro-production system, others related to the missing links in the producers' chain of services. The necessary measures are analysed in the study. The dual structure of Malian agriculture in supervised and non-supervised areas must be diversifed. Rain-fed cultures must be much more taken into account by donors.

Aid impact

Joint efforts of both the Sahel people and the donors have been fruitful and have produced some visible advances. The end results, nevertheless, are mixed. Many basic problems are still unsolved. In spite of this, Mali has survived recurrent years of crisis without major disaster. Even today, while Africa suffers from an acute drought, Mali is pulling through better than many of its neighbours.

But the results of the massive development aid the Sahel has received have not been adequately evaluated. In reality, all remains to be done. Aid to Mali has scarcely been evaluated at all, except for a few projects.

Conclusions

There is in Mali a global congruence between the five-year plans, the state budgets (investment), and external aid. All are oriented towards the main objective of food self-sufficiency within a stable ecosystem. In Mali, quite obviously, aid has emphasized rural development. The current reform process will strengthen the policy framework and assist implementation, and should be supported by donors.

Helping Mali to meet basic food needs and to promote economic and social development is aiding it to develop its indigenous financial and human resources. The financial conditions of aid allocation require continuing generosity, but also rigour in project evaluation

Four main priorities stand out in the study. The donors should support the following:

ensure survival to Malians (priority given to food-crop production and stabilization);

ensure Malians increase in their standard of living (priority given to meet the rural population's basic needs);

support Mali's structural institutional reforms (priority given to the rebuilding of the SEE/state enterprises and the ODR/rural development operations);

and finally, increase participation of the people (priority to community-based development, and more support to democratic initiatives).

Annex B7: South Korea Aid Effectiveness Study

Summary

By any standard of performance, South Korea overall is justly considered an economic success. The forces that produced sustained growth are complex; some are rooted in Korea's unique historical and cultural milieu.

Korea emerged from the partition of the World War and the destruction of the Korean war economically devastated, bereft of heavy industries and natural resources – a military and economic ward of its principal donor, the USA. In the long-run, however, its economic disadvantages were offset by non-economic factors – an ethnically homogenous population, linguistic unity, the concept of primacy of mobility through education, and the principle of a meritocratic state. Although mired in abject poverty, its people shared a remarkably equal distribution of the assets that remained because of the land reform inaugurated by the US military government, the material destruction of the war, and the spread of primary education.

Until 1961, the Korean economy followed a policy of import substitution. It was completely dependent on donor support for food and consumption goods, as well as for raw materials and military assistance; Korean policy stressed the maximization of foreign assistance, including maintenance of an unrealistic set of foreign exchange rates that effectively prohibited exports. Charges that donor support was concentrated on consumption goods, and that the PL 480 food import programme retarded realistic agricultural pricing policies, were generally accurate, as the policy goals of donor and recipient were different.

President Park, following the military coup of 1961, internally consolidated and centralized economic and political power, and externally, perhaps in part to distance his government from the USA, shifted economic policy to an export promotion programme. Donor support was diversified, with normalization of relations with Japan a critical element in the introduction of capital and technology. Foreign investment was encouraged, the first IBRD loan signed, and export targets rigorously set and meticulously enforced. President Park's concentration on the economy, which he was able to control through administrative, political and social means, as well as through a government monopoly of institutional credit, was exceedingly effective, as it was his avenue to political legitimacy. Korean growth of GNP, exports, overseas construction earnings, and manufacturing capacity have attracted the admiration of foreign observers, especially in the light of Korea's deft handling of the crises associated with the two oil price increases, a world-wide recession, and an excessive defence burden.

Income distribution, although relatively favourable, worsened as the government until the early 1970s virtually ignored the rural sector. Despite figures on income distribution in Korea that are badly flawed, as they are in many countries, it is evident that, first, the creation of urban employment in manufacturing and, later, subsidies and development in agriculture lowered the percentage of the population in poverty from 40 to 10 per cent. Income disparities are likely to grow with the elimination of pricing subsidies.

Equity in Korean society was greatly enhanced by the creation of employment opportunities, a process in which donor support was an important but unquantifiable factor. There exist, however, important rural and urban income disparities, as well as regional income differentials. Equality of access to the market-place is lacking, as the government has a monopoly on institutional credit, and allocates it in larger part to the successful major industrial and trading conglomerates. Women are denied equal pay and status in the development process.

The importance and effectiveness of the donor role have shifted over time. For the first decade and a half after liberation, donor (essentially US) support was at first essential to the survival of the state and the modest growth that took place. Such support was eminently successful in land reform — although it never reached its full potential — but less so in other fields. Acrimonious disputes between donor and recipient marked economic policy negotiations.

The increasing success of the Korean export drive under President Park encouraged commercial lending and foreign investment, so that concessional assistance is now extremely modest, most of it only considered such by comparison with Korean kerb market rates. The role of multilateral lending to Korea is considered by the government to be an important attraction for commercial lenders.

There is general agreement that since the early 1960s Korea has been an effective user of concessional assistance. Foreign assistance has been of varying importance and impact in differing fields.

Overall, policy advice was followed if it supported the distribution of power and the national directions already determined by government. It was effective in so far as it was viewed as having been internally generated, and was used by one part of the Korean government to strengthen its views in relation to other governmental entities.

Technical assistance personnel, despite problems with language and lack of knowledge of the bureaucratic culture, could be effective if they provided the technical means by which to implement effectively the pre-determined policy directions of the government. Training and human resource development were universally regarded as effective and one of the most important elements of concessional aid.

Donor support has generally followed Korean government policies and priorities. Emphases have changed as governmental priorities have shifted, but (with few exceptions) donors have followed the government's lead. Aid levels in the Korean context have little correlation with the effectiveness of foreign assistance.

Korea is not a model that can be emulated by other nations, but it has been in a very real sense a model user of foreign assistance. Although multilateral aid agencies have an edge in both prestige and flexibility over major bilateral donors, there is need for reform in both camps.

Annex C

Task Force on Concessional Flows

Terms of Reference

Aid Effectiveness Study

Rationale and objectives

At various meetings of the Task Force the issue of aid effectiveness has been emphasized as crucial both in its own right and because of its importance in influencing the mandate for aid and, consequently, prospects for increasing aid volume. Recognizing that considerable effort has been expended in evaluating, at various levels, the effectiveness of aid the Task Force agreed that a study was needed, based mainly on available material, in a form that would: (a) be focused and digestible and (b) draw out the key issues on the effectiveness of aid, for further discussion by Task Force members. It was appreciated that no such effort would be finally conclusive in attributing to every aspect of aid specific results achieved in terms of development. But representatives felt that an attempt should be made to carry out a study which would enable the Task Force to: assess the extent to which conclusions can be reached on the impact of aid on development; express valid and useful opinions on the conditions under which aid is particularly effective; and recommend ways in which effectiveness of aid might be improved.

It was agreed, after considerable discussion of alternative approaches, that experienced consultants should be commissioned by the Task Force to perform this task. They would: (a) undertake an analysis of country experience and of available evaluation/effectiveness materials at various levels, and (b) synthesize for the Task Force valid conclusions and observations on the factors that influence aid effectiveness and suggest approaches and policies for action, on the part of both donors and recipients, which would result in improving the effectiveness of aid. The consultants during their work would seek the views of donors and recipients on the aid process and on means to enhance aid effectiveness.

Work program

The consultants will produce both *survey papers* on a number of topics, based on documentation which already exists or will be submitted to them, and *country studies*. This will result in a number of background documents, which will be synthesized in the consultants' main report to the Task Force.

I. Background documents

(A) *Survey papers*

The consultants will review aid effectiveness in various aspects. including:

1. The experience of aid in countries other than those selected for the 'country studies' outlined below, to extend the generalizability of the findings of those studies.
2. Project evaluation (relying on the work of the DAC evaluation experts' group and other materials).
3. Food aid.
4. Comparisons of bilateral and multilateral aid programs and agencies, covering: the respective contributions of aid from each type of agency based on historical experience; contrasting experiences with policy dialogue; roles in aid coordination, and so forth.
5. Technical cooperation.
6. Submissions by Task Force members and multilateral development banks on their experience of aid, their views on the effectiveness of their aid programs, and documentation they can make available on their aid projects and programs which would be of general interest.

This survey work will result in a set of Survey Papers; their number, the exhaustiveness of their coverage and the number of consultants required to produce them will be determined by timing and budgetary considerations.

(B) *Country studies*

For the purposes of the proposed investigation, the country is an important unit of analysis. It is only in the context of specific countries that the workings of aid and the policy environment can be fully considered. Further, while evaluations of projects or programs of individual donors have been carried out, there are extremely few studies of the composite or 'systemic' effects of the operations of a multiplicity of donors in a given country.

The countries proposed for study are some or all of the following: Bangladesh, India, Kenya, Malawi, South Korea, a francophone least-developed country (Upper Volta or Mali) and a Latin American country (possibly Colombia). The final choice of countries will be made in relation to timing and budgetary considerations, and subject to there being no objections on the part of the countries concerned. (If there are objections such that the representatives of the list of countries becomes unbalanced, alternatives might have to be identified.)

The content of the country study is annexed below.

II.   Synthesis document

The main presentation to the Task Force will be in the form of a synthesis document which will draw together the strands of analysis provided by I (A) and (B) above.

The main paper will be substantial and will attempt to reach generalizations based on the other studies. The country studies will give material for such generalizations. The main paper will summarize what they have found, as supplemented by relevant parts of the survey work.

The synthesis document will present what can be said about effectiveness on the basis of existing knowledge: how effective aid has been, and how it can be improved in future. These findings will be summarized in a shorter 'summary and conclusions' of some 30 pages. The Secretariat will then prepare an issues paper which might form the principal basis of the Task Force's discussions.

Content of country studies

The effectiveness of aid can be considered in relation to a variety of objectives: the Task Force study is confined to its developmental objectives. The criteria by which aid is to be judged are its contribution to improving the productive capacity of a recipient economy (growth) and to the relief of poverty (distribution). The concentration of the studies will go on *measures to improve the effectiveness of aid*; assessment of the past effectiveness of aid will be attempted only in the ways and to the extent required for reaching conclusions on such measures. These measures are understood as potential action on the part of both donors and recipients. Lessons of successes and failures, of a kind which can be drawn upon in a published report, will be of particular value. The Task Force will make available to the consultants a list of particular areas of concern, to which the consultants will pay attention to the fullest extent possible.

The country studies will be conducted under the following main headings:

1. *The Macro-economic contribution of aid resources, past and future*

- How significant is the volume of aid as a contribution to supplementing a country's foreign exchange availability or resources for domestic investment?
- How far has this contribution assisted recipients' development—growth and distribution?
- How important are aid flows relative to other potential sources of external finance, private and official?
- To the extent that countries have opportunities to borrow non-concessional funds, what is the 'trade-off' between the two? (I.e. what volume of non-concessional finance would balance, in its value to a particular economy, a given volume of concessional finance?)

2. *Aid and poverty*

- How far has aid assisted the reduction of poverty, by direct contribution to enhancing the livelihoods of the poor, or through promoting development that enhances their livelihoods?
- To what extent have the benefits of aid been confined to particular groups or classes? Have any groups been made worse off as a result of aid?

3. *The policy dialogue at various levels in project and program aid*

- The policy environment in which aid functions; how effective is the policy dialogue between donors and the recipients at national and sectoral levels?
- Insofar as aid projects incorporate technical assistance and advice, how effective is the project as a vehicle for assisting policy formation?

4. *The systemic effects of aid*

- What problems arise from the operation of a multiplicity of aid programs of various donors in a recipient country? What are the effects on the recipient's budgetary process, on the demand for scarce resources — administrative, managerial, skilled manpower, local or recurrent cost finance?

5.   *Project performance*

- How successful have aid projects been in achieving their objectives and contributing to development?
- What lessons can be learned from successful and unsuccesful projects?
- Have projects had unanticipated side-effects, beneficial or otherwise?

6.   *Donor policies and procedures*

- To what extent do donor preferences for various forms of aid correspond to recipient needs – especially the preference of donors for projects as opposed to programs or local/recurrent cost assistance?
- What is the impact of aid tying?

7.   *Institution building, technical assistance, and resource management*

- What has been the contribution of aid and technical assistance to institution-building and the effective management of resources in public or private sectors at various levels?
- Insofar as administrative and manpower deficiencies set limits to the absorptive capacity for aid, can aid do more to assist the removal of these limitations?

8.   *Aid and market forces*

- What is the distribution of aid, in its final use, as between private and public sectors? Insofar as the final use is in the public sector, what share goes directly to productive enterprises or to infrastructural or other uses beneficial to the private sector?
- To what extent can aid be said to have supported the allocative role of price signals in production in recipient countries?
- How can aid assist the improved functioning of price signals (to move from 'getting prices right' to 'making prices work')?

9.   *Conclusions: improving aid effectiveness*

- What can be said about measures to improve aid effectiveness; measures to be undertaken by donors and recipients? Can conclusions be reached about desirable and feasible new directions for aid coordination?

November 14, 1983

Bibliography

Some frequently cited organizations are listed in the Bibliography under their initials alone. Their names appear in full in the List of Abbreviations on pp. xiv–xv. An asterisk denotes a study commissioned for the present report.

ADB, 1983, *Study of Operational Priorities and Plans for the Asian Development Bank for the 1980s*, Manila, June.
——, 1984*a*, *Annual Report*, Manila.
——, 1984*b*, *Rural Development in Asia and the Pacific*, Manila.
Adelman, I., 1984, 'Beyond Export-Led Growth', *World Development*, vol. 12, 1984.
African Development Bank, *Annual Report*, Abidjan, annual.
African Development Fund, 1983, *African Development Assistance: Background and Prospects*, Abidjan.
Agarwala, R., 1983, *Price Distortions and Growth in Developing Countries*, World Bank Staff Working Paper no. 575, Washington, DC.
Ahluwalia, I. J., 1979, 'An Analysis of Price and Output Behaviour in the Indian Economy: 1951–1973', *Journal of Development Economics*, vol. 6, no. 3.
Ahluwalia, M., 1976, 'Inequality, Poverty and Development', *Journal of Development Studies*, vol. 3.
——, 1978, *Rural Poverty in India: 1956/57 to 1973/74*, World Bank Staff Working Paper no. 279, Washington, DC.
Ahmad, Q. K., and M. Hassain, 1983, *Rural Poverty Alleviation in Bangladesh—Experience and Policies*, Dhaka and Rome (mimeo).
Ahmed, R., 1979, *Foodgrain Supply, Distribution and Consumption Policies within a Dual Pricing Mechanism: A Case Study of Bangladesh*, Washington, DC, IFPRI.
Andreas, D. (Chairman), 1984 *A Report to the President*, The President's Task-Force on International Private Enterprise, USAID, Washington, DC, December.
Appu, P. S., 1974 'The Bamboo Tubewell: A Low Cost Device for Exploiting Ground Water', *Economic and Political Weekly*, June.
Arab Bank for Economic Development in Africa, *Annual Report*, Khartoum, annual.
Arab Fund for Social and Economic Development, 1983, *Financing Operations: Arab National and Regional Development Institutions*, Kuwait, December.
Arndt, H. W., 1979, 'Problems of Aid Recipient Countries' in R. T. Shand and H. V. Richter (eds.) *International Aid: Some Political, Administrative and Technical Realities*, Canberra.
Arndt, T. M., D. G. Dalrymple, and V. W. Ruttan (eds.), 1977, *Resource Allocations and Productivity in National and International Agricultural Research*, Minnesota.

Australia, Government of 1984, *Report of the Committee to Review the Australian Aid Programme*, Canberra.

Ayres, R., 1983, *Banking on the Poor: The World Bank and World Poverty*, Cambridge, Mass., MIT Press.

*Bagley, B. R., 1984, *Aid Effectiveness: Colombia*, Washington, DC, Johns Hopkins SAIS (unpublished).

Balassa, B., 1982a, 'Structural Adjustment Policies in Developing Economies', *World Development*, vol. 10.

——, 1982b, *Development Strategies in Semi-Industrial Economies*, Washington DC, World Bank.

Bale, M. D., and E. Lutz, 1981, 'Price Distortions in Agriculture and their Effects: An International Comparison', *American Journal of Agricultural Economics*, vol. 63.

Baranech, W., and G. Ranis, 1978, *Science and Technology and Economic Development*, New York, Praeger.

Bauer, P. T., 1981, *Equality, the Third World and Economic Delusion*, London, Weidenfeld.

——, 1984, *Reality and Rhetoric*, London, Weidenfeld.

Beijer Institute, 1984, *Energy and Development in Kenya: Opportunities and Constraints*, Stockholm.

Bell, C., R. Hazell, and R. Slade, 1983, *Project Evaluation in Regional Perspective: the Muda Project in Malaysia*, Baltimore, Johns Hopkins University Press.

Bendix, P. J. and H. H. Lembke, 1983, *Nicht-Projektgebundene Finanzierung*, Berlin, German Development Institute.

Berry, R. A., and W. R. Cline, 1979, *Agrarian Structure and Producitivity in Developing Countries*, Baltimore, (ILO) Johns Hopkins.

Bhagwati, J., 1978, *Foreign Trade Regimes and Economic Development: Anatomy and Consequences of Exchange Control Regimes*, New York, NBER.

——, 1981, 'Alternative Estimates of Real Cost of Aid', in P. Streeten (ed.), *Unfashionable Economics*, London, Weidenfeld.

——, and T. N. Srinivasan, 1975, *Foreign Trade Regimes and Economic Development: India*, New York, NBER.

Binswanger, H., 1978, *The Economics of Tractors in South Asia*, New York, Agricultural Development Council and ICRISAT.

Bird, G. and P. Gutman, 'Foreign Aid: the Issue', *National Westminster Quarterly Review*, August.

Bird, R. M., 1982, 'Exercising Policy Leverage Through Aid: A Critical Survey', *Canadian Journal of Development Studies*, vol. 2.

Bol, D., 1984, *Ekonomen en armoede*, Amsterdam; quoted in van Arkadie and de Wilde 1984.

Bornschier, V., C. Chase-Dunn, and R. Robinson, 1978, 'Cross-National Evidence of the Effects of Foreign Investment and Aid on Economic Growth and Poverty: A Survey of Findings and Analysis', *American Journal of Sociology*, vol. 84.

*Bourgoignie, G. 1984, *L'Aide dans un Contexte Sahélien: le Mali*, Ottawa (unpublished).

Brandt Commission, 1983, *Common Crisis: North-South Cooperation for World Recovery*, London, Pan.

Brandt, H., 1984, *The Design and Evaluation of Food Security Programmes*, Berlin, German Development Institute (mimeo).

Burki, J., *et al.*, 1976, *Public Works Programs in Developing Countries: A Comparative Analysis*, World Bank Staff Working Paper no. 224, Washington, DC World Bank. 1976.

Byres, T. J., 1974, 'Land reform, Industrialisation and the Marketed Surplus in India', in D. Lehman (ed.) *Agrarian Reform and Agrarian Reformism*, London Faber.

Cantor, S. M., and Associates, 1973, *The Tamil Nadu Nutrition Study*, Haverford.

Carlucci, F. C. (chairman), 1984, Commission on Economic and Security Assistance, *Report to the Secretary of State*, Washington, DC, US Dept of State.

Carruthers, I. (ed.), 1983, *Aid to Irrigation*, Paris, OECD.

Cassen, R. H., 1976, 'Population and Development: A Survey', *World Development*, vol. 4.

——, 1978, *India: Population, Economy, Society*, London, Macmillan.

*——, P. Chaudhuri, and P. Daniel, with S. Griffith-Jones, 1984, *Aid Effectiveness: Literature Survey*, Sussex, IDS (unpublished).

Chambers, R., 1983, *Rural Development: Putting the 'Last First'*, Harlow, Longman.

——, 1985, 'Putting 'Last' Thinking First: A Professional Revolution', in *Third World Affairs*, London, Third World Foundation.

——, R. Longhurst, and A. Pacey, 1981, *Seasonal Dimensions to Rural Poverty*, London, Frances Pinter.

Chaudhuri, P., 1979, *The Indian Economy: Poverty and Development*, London, Crosby Lockwood.

Chenery, H. B., 1971, *Studies in Developmental Planning*, Cambridge, Mass., Harvard University Press.

——, and A. M. Strout, 1966, 'Foreign Assistance and Economic Development', *American Economic Review*, vol. 56.

CIDA, 1983, *Bilan des évaluations bilatérales 1981—83*, vol. 4 Ottawa.

——, 1984a, *Bilan des évaluations bilatérales 1981——83*, vol.3, Ottawa.

——, 1984b, *Women in Development: Policy Framework*, Ottawa, December.

Clay, E. J., 1985, 'Review of Food Aid Policy Changes since 1978', Occasional Paper no. 1., Public Affairs and Information Unit, World Food Programme, Rome.

Clay, E. J. and M. Mitchell, 1983, 'Is European Community Food Aid in Dairy Products Cost-Effective?', *European Review of Agricultural Economics*, vol. 10, no. 2.

——, and H. W. Singer, 1982, *Food Aid and Development: The Impact and Effectiveness of Bilateral PL 480 Title I-Type Assistance*, AID Program Evaluation Discussion Paper no. 15, Washington, DC, USAID.

——, 1985 'Food Aid and Development: Issues and Evidence', Occasional

Paper no. 3, Rome, Public Affairs and Information Unit, World Food Programme.

Cline, W. R., 1975, 'Distribution and Development: A Survey of Literature', *Journal of Development Economics*, vol. 1.

——, 1982, 'Can the East Asian Model of Development be Generalized?', *World Development*, vol. 10.

Cochrane, S., 1983, *Policies for Strengthening Local Government in Developing Countries*, World Bank Staff Working Paper, no. 582, Washington, DC, World Bank.

Commonwealth Secretariat, 1983, *Towards a New Bretton Woods: Challenges for the World Financial and Trading Systems*, Report by a Commonwealth Study Group, London.

Comptroller General of the US, 1957, *Audit Report to the Congress of the US: US Assistance Program for Korea*, Washington, DC, General Accounting Office.

——, 1972, *US Assistance for the Economic Development of the Republic of Korea*, Washington, DC, General Accounting Office.

Corden, M., 1971, *The Theory of Protection*, Oxford, Clarendon Press.

Crawford, P. R. and A. H. Barclay, 1982, *Aid Experience in Agricultural Research: A Review of Project Evaluation*, Washington, DC USAID.

Dasgupta, B., 1977, *Agrarian Change and the New Technology in India*, Geneva, UNRISD.

De Vylder, S., and D. Asplund, 1979, *Contradictions and Distortions in a Rural Economy: The Case of Bangladesh*, Stockholm, SIDA.

Deboeck, G., and B. Kinsey, 1980, *Managing Information for Rural Development: Lessons from East Africa*, World Bank Staff Working Paper no. 379, March.

Dell, S., 1979, 'Basic Needs or Comprehensive Development: Should the UNDP have a Development Strategy?', *World Development*, vol. 7.

——, 1984, 'A Note on Stabilization and the World Bank', *World Development*, vol. 12, no. 2, February.

Demir, S., 1979, *Arab Development Funds in the Middle East*, New York, Praeger.

Dennison, E. F., 1967, *Why Growth Rates Differ*, Washington, DC, Brookings.

——, 1980, 'The Contribution of Capital to Economic Growth', *American Economic Review*, vol. 70.

Diamand, M., 1978, 'Towards a Change in the Economic Paradigm through the Experience of Developing Countries', *Journal of Development Economics*, vol. 15.

*Duncan, A., and P. Mosley, 1984, *Aid Effectiveness: Kenya*, QEH, Oxford and University of Bath (unpublished).

Dunlop, D. W., 1983, *A Comparative Analysis of Policies and Other Factors which Affect the Role of the Private Sector in Economic Development*, Washington, DC, USAID.

Ehrhardt, R., 1983, *Canadian Development Assistance to Bangladesh*, Ottawa, North-South Institute.

Elliott C., *et al.*, 1982, *Real Aid: A Strategy for Britain*, London, Independent Group on British Aid.

English, E. P., 1984, *Canadian Development Assistance to Haiti*, Ottawa, The North–South Institute.

Eshag, E., 1967, 'Study of Tied Economic Aid Given to Tunisia in 1965', UNCTAD, TD/7/Supp. 81.

——, 1971, 'Foreign Capital, Domestic Savings etc.: A Comment', *Bulletin of Oxford Institute of Economics and Statistics*, vol. 33.

Evenson, R. E., 1982, 'Benefits and Obstacles to Appropriate Agricultural Technology', *Economic Growth Center, Paper no. 313*, New Haven, Yale University.

——, and Y. Kislev, 1975, 'Agricultural Research and Productivity', *Economic Growth Center, Paper no. 225*, New Haven, Yale University.

——, P. Waggoner, and V. Ruttan, 1979, 'Economic Benefits from Research: An Example from Agriculture', *Science*, vol. 205, September.

Faaland, J., 1984, 'Norwegian Aid and Reaching the Poor', *Development Policy Review*, vol. 2, no. 1, May.

FAO, 1975, *Review of Field Programmes, 1974—1975*, C75/4, Rome.

——, 1977, *Review of Field Programmes, 1976—1977*, C77/4, Rome.

——, 1984a, *Review of Forestry Field Programme*, Committee on Forestry, COFO/84/10.

——, 1984b, *The Forestry Field Programme in the Region*, Asia-Pacific Forestry Commission, FO:APFC/84/9.

——, 1984c, 'Training of Manpower for agricultural and Rural Development in Africa', ARC/84/3 (draft).

——/UNDP, 1980, *Agricultural Training*, Rome.

Fei, J. C. H., G. Ranis, and S. W. Y. Kuo, 1979, *Growth with Equity: The Taiwan Case*, New York, Oxford University Press for the World Bank.

Fields, G. S., 1978, *Poverty, Inequality and Development*, Cambridge University Press.

Finland, Government of, *Finnish Development Assistance—Annual Report*, Helsinki, annual.

FINNIDA, 1984, *Women in Development*, Helsinki, October.

Franks, C. R, K. S. Kim, and L. Westphal, 1975, *Foreign Trade Regimes and Economic Development: South Korea*, New York, NBER.

Friedmann, W., 'Methods and Policies of Principal Donor Countries in Public International Development Financing', New York, Columbia University School of Law (mimeo).

——, G. Kalmanoff, and R. F. Meagher, 1966, *International Financial Aid*, New York, Columbia University Press.

Gascoigne, E., 1980 *The Changing Emphasis in Britisih Aid Policies: Towards and Away from more Help for the Poorest* (unpublished MA, Rural Development dissertation, University of East Anglia).

Gavan, J. and I. S. Chandrasekera, 1979, *The Impact of Public Foodgrain Distribution on Food Consumption and Welfare in Sri Lanka*, Washington, DC, IFPRI.

George, P. S., 1979, *Public Distribution of Foodgrains in Kerala: Income Distribution Implications and Effectiveness*, Washington, DC, IFPRI.

Ghosh, A. K., 1983, 'Agrarian Reform in West Bengal: Objectives, Achievements and Limitations', in A. K. Ghosh (ed.), *Agrarian Reform in Contemporary Developing Countries*, London, (ILO) Croom Helm.

Godfrey, M., 1983, 'Export Orientation and Structural Adjustment in Sub-Saharan Africa', *Bulletin*, Sussex, IDS, January.

Goldstein, E. A., 'Making Aid Work: An Analysis of Aid . . . in . . . Senegal, 1981–83', Washington, DC, USAID (mimeo).

Gordon L. E., *et al.*, 1979, *Interim Report: An Assessment of Development Assistance Strategies*, Cambridge, Mass., Harvard Institute for International Development.

Gorman, R. F. (ed.), 1985, *Private Voluntary Organizations as Agents of Development*, Boulder and London, Westview Press.

Greene, J. K., 1983, 'Japan's Aid Administration and Economic Policy-Making Process', Washington, DC, American University (mimeo).

Greene, R. H., 1984, 'Stabilisation in Sub-Saharan African and the IMF: A Critical Review and Prolegomenon—As Illustrated by Tanzania', Sussex, IDS (mimeo).

Griffin, K. B., 1970, 'Foreign Capital, Domestic Savings and Economic Development', *Bulletin of the Oxford Institute of Economics and Statistics*, vol. 32.

——, 1976, *Land Concentration and Rural Poverty*, London, Macmillan.

——, and J. L. Enos, 1970, 'Foreign Assistance: Objectives and Consequences', *Economic Development and Cultural Change*, vol. 18.

——, and A. Ghosh, 1979, 'Growth and Impoverishment in the Rural Areas of Asia', *World Development*, vol 7.

Griffith-Jones, S., and R. H. Green, 1984, *African External Debt and Development: A Review and Analysis*, Report for the African Centre for Monetary Studies, Sussex, IDS.

Grinols, E. and J. Bhagwati, 1976, 'Foreign Capital, Savings and Dependence', *Review of Economics and Statistics*, vol. 58.

Guitian, M., 1981, *Fund Conditionality: Evaluation of Principles and Practices*, Washington, DC, IMF Pamphlet Series no. 38.

*Gulick, C., 1984, *Effectiveness of Aid: Evaluation Findings of the World Bank (and other North America-based agencies)*, Washington, DC (unpublished).

Heller, P. S., 1975, 'A model of Public Fiscal Behaviour in Developing Countries: Aid, Investment and Taxation', *American Economic Review*, vol. 65.

Herz, B., 1985, *Official Development Assistance for Population*, Washington, DC, World Bank Staff Working Paper.

*Hewitt, A., and J. Kydd, 1984, *Aid Effectiveness: Malawi*, Overseas Development Institute, London, and Wye College, Ashford (unpublished).

Hicks, N., 1980, 'Sectoral Priorities in Meeting Basic Needs: Some Statistical Evidence', *World Development*, vol. 10.

Hirschman, A., 1967, *Development Projects Observed*, New York, Twentieth Century Fund.

——, 1970, *Exit, Voice and Loyalty*, Cambridge, Mass., Harvard University Press.

Howell, J. (ed.) 1985, *Recurrent Costs and Agricultural Development*, London, Overseas Development Institute.

Hunt, D., 1984, *Kenya: The Impending Crisis*, London, Gower.

IBRD: *see* World Bank.

IDB, 1981, *The Role of the Bank in Latin America in the 1980s*, Washington, DC, April.

——, 1982a, *Annual Reports on Operations Evaluation*, Washington, DC.

——, 1982b, *Summary of Ex-Post Evaluations of Preinvestment Funds*, GN–1456, Washington, DC.

——, 1982c, *Summary of Ex-Post Evaluations of Technical Cooperation Operations for Institutional Strengthening*, 11/82, Washington, DC.

——, 1983a, *Annual Reports on Operations Evaluation*, Washington, DC.

——, 1983b, *Basic Facts about the IDB*, Washington, DC, August.

——, 1983c, *Summary of Ex-Post Evaluations of Technical Cooperation Operations for Institutional Strengthening*, Washington, DC.

——, 1983d, *8 Highway Projects*, Washington, DC.

IDRC, 1981, *A Decade of Learning*, Ottawa.

ILO, 1970, *Towards Full Employment: A Programme for Colombia*, Geneva.

——, 1971, *Matching Employment Opportunities and Expectations: A Programme of Action for Ceylon*, Geneva.

——, 1984, *The Rural Energy Crisis, Women's Work and Family Welfare*, World Employment Programme Research Working Paper WEP 10/WP35, Geneva.

IMF, 1977, *The Monetary Approach to the Balance of Payments*, Washington, DC.

——, 1982, *World Economic Outlook 1982*, Washington, DC.

——, 1983, *World Economic Outlook 1983*, Washington DC.

——, World Bank, 1981, *Economic Development and the Private Sector*, articles prepared for *Finance and Development*, Washington, DC. September.

India, Government of, Committee on Plan Projects, 1957,—*Report of the Team for the Study for Community Projects and National Extension Service*, 3 vols. New Delhi.

India, Reserve Bank of, 1982, *Capital Formation and Savings in India 1950–51 to 1979—80*, Bombay.

Integrated Development Systems, 1983, *Foreign Aid and Development in Nepal*, Kathmandu.

Inter-American Foundation, 1984, *Report of the Evaluation Group*, Washington, DC, March.

International Trade Commission, 1983, *Trade Promotion: Building National Institutions*, Geneva.

Isaksen, J., 1983, 'Constraints on Rural Production: A Field Impression from Bangladesh', in Parkinson 1983.

Isemman, P., 1980, 'Basic Needs: The Case of Sri Lanka', *World Development*, vol. 8.

——, and H. W. Singer, 1977, 'Food Aid: Disincentive Effects and Their Policy Implications', *Economic Development and Cultural Change*, vol. 25, no. 2.

Islam, N., 1983, 'Lessons of Experience: Development Policy and Practice', in Parkinson 1983.

Jackson, T., 1982, *Against the Grain*, Oxford, Oxfam.

Jay, K., 1985, 'The Use of Foreign Assistance to Promote Commercial Interests', Washington, DC, World Bank (mimeo).

Jennings, A., 1983, 'The Recurrent Cost Problem in the Least Developed Countries', *Journal of Development Studies*, vol. 19.

Jha, S. C., 'ADB Experience with Rural Development Projects', in ADB 1984*b*.

Johnson, B., and R. O. Blake, 1980, *The Environment and Bilateral Development Aid*, London, International Institute for Environment and Development.

Johnson, C., 1982, *MITI and the Japanese Miracle: The Growth of Industrial Policy*, Stanford, Stanford University Press.

Johnson, H. G., 1965, 'Optimal Trade Intervention in the Presence of Domestic Distortions', in R. E. Caves, *et al.* (eds), *Trade Growth and the Balance of Payments*, Amsterdam, North-Holland.

Kenya Government, 1982, *Report and Recommendations of the Working Party on Government Expenditures*, Nairobi, Government Printer.

Khan, A. R., 1983, 'World Bank Assistance Policy: A Case Study of Bangladesh', Washington DC, World Bank (mimeo).

Killick, T., 1978, *Development Economics in Action: A Study of Ghana*, London, Heinemann Educational.

——, (ed.) 1984, *The Quest for Stabilisation: The IMF and the Third World*, London: Heinemann.

Kleemeier, L., 1984, 'Domestic Policies versus Poverty-Oriented Foreign Assistance in Tanzania', *Journal of Development Studies*, vol. 20.

Krueger, A. O., 1978, *Foreign Trade Regimes and Economic Development: Liberalization Attempts and Consequences*, New York, NBER.

——, 1981, 'Loans to Assist the Transition to Outward-Looking Policies', *World Economy*, vol. 4, no. 3, September.

——, 1982, 'Analysing Disequilibrium Exchange-Rate Systems in Developing Countries', *World Development*, vol. 10.

——, and V. W. Ruttan, 1983, *The Development Impact of Economic Assistance to LDCs*, 2 vols., Washington, DC, University of Minnesota for USAID.

Kumar, D., and M. Desai (eds.), 1983, *Cambridge Economic History of India (c. 1757—c. 1970)*, vol. 2, Cambridge University Press.

Kumar, S. K., 1979, *Impact of Subsidised Rice on Food Consumption and Nutrition in Kerala*, Washington, DC, IFPRI.

Kuwait Fund for Arab Economic Development, Al-Humaidhi, B., 1984, *The Role of Arab Gulf States in International Development Assistance*, Kuwait, November.

Ladejinsky, W., 1977, *Agrarian Reform as Unfinished Business, Selected Papers*, ed. L. J. Walinsky, Oxford University Press.

Lal, D., 1983, *The Poverty of 'Development Economics'*, Institute of Economic Affairs, London, Hobart.

Lall, S., 1982, 'The Emergence of Third World Multinationals: Indian Joint Ventures Overseas', *World Development*, vol. 10.

Latin American Railways Association and UN/ECLA, 1976, 'An Appraisal of the Technical Assistance received by the Railways of Latin America', Santiago, UN/ECLA.

Laufer, L., 1984, *Thailand, Country Evaluation Report*, Jerusalem, Israel Association for International Cooperation.

Lavy, V., 1985, *Anticipated Development Assistance, Temporary Relief Aid and Consumption Behaviour of Low Income Countries*, Discussion Paper, Washington, DC, World Bank.

League of Arab States, 1958, *The Arab Financial Institution for Economic Development*, New York, Arab Information Center.

Lecomte, B., and G. Lejeune, 1981, *Evaluation of the Evaluations*, Brussels, EEC, VII/668(81) EN.

Leff, N. H., 1968, 'Marginal Savings Rates in the Development Process: the Brazilian Experience', *Economic Journal*, vol. 1 xxvii.

Lele, U., 1975, *Design of Rural Development: Lessons from Africa*, Washington, DC, World Bank.

——, 1983, 'Growth and Development of Foreign Assistance and the Effect on African Agricultural and Food Production Strategies,' Paper presented to Victoria Falls Conference on Accelerated Growth in Sub-Saharan Africa, Washington, DC, World Bank.

Lethem, F. and L. Cooper, 1983, *Managing Project-Related Technical Assistance*, Washington, DC, World Bank Staff Working Paper no. 586.

Lewis, J. P., 1972, 'The Public Works Approach to Low-end Poverty Problems: The New Potentialities of an Old Answer', *Journal of Development Planning*, no. 5.

——, 1977, 'Designing the Public Works Mode of Anti-Poverty Policy', in C. R. Frank and R. C. Webb (eds.), *Income Distribution and Growth in Less Developed Countries*, Washington, DC, Brookings.

——, 1985, 'Aid, Structural Adjustment and Senegalese Agriculture', Princeton University (mimeo).

Lewis, W. A., 1980, 'The Slowing Down of the Engine of Growth', *American Economic Review*, vol. 70.

Lipton, M., 1972, 'Aid Allocation when Aid is Inadequate', in T. J. Byres (ed.) *Foreign Resources and Economic Development*, London, Cass.

——, 1974, *Why Poor People Stay Poor*, London, Temple Smith.

——, 1976, 'Agricultural Finance and Rural Credit in Developing Countries', *World Development*, vol. 4.

Lipton, M., 1983a, *Demography and Poverty*, Washington, DC, World Bank Staff Working paper no. 623.

——, 1983b, *Labour and Poverty*, Washington, DC, World Bank Staff Working Paper no. 616.

——, 1983c, *Poverty and Undernutrition*, Washington, DC, World Bank Staff Working Paper no. 597.

* ——, and J. Toye with R. H. Cassen, 1984a, *Aid Effectiveness: India*, Sussex IDS and Swansea, Centre for Development Studies (unpublished).

——, *et al.*, 1984b, *National Food Strategies*, Brussels, Centre for European Policy Studies, Working Paper.

Little, I., T. Scitovsky and M. Scott, 1970, *Industry and Trade in Developing Countries*, Oxford, OECD.

Loxley, J., 1984, *The IMF and the Poorest Countries*, Ottawa, North-South Institute.

Luedde-Neurath, R., 1984, 'State Intervention and Foreign Direct Investment in South Korea', Sussex, IDS, *Bulletin*, vol. 15, no. 2, April.

Luisi, H., 1983, 'The Experience of the Inter-American Development Bank', in Carruthers 1983.

McKinnon, R. I., 1964, 'Foreign Exchange Constraints in Economic Development and Efficient Aid Allocation', *Economic Journal*, vol. lxxiv.

——, 1981, 'Financial Repression and the Liberalisation Problem Within Less Developed Countries', in S. Grassman and E. Lundberg (eds.), *The World Economic Order: Past and Prospects*, London, Macmillan.

Magee, S. P., 1973, 'Factor Market Distortions, Production and Trade: A Survey', *Oxford Economic Papers*, vol. 25.

Maizels, A., 1968, *Exports and Economic Growth of Developing Countries*, Cambridge University Press.

——, and M. K. Nissanke, 1984, 'Motivations for Aid to Developing Countries', *World Development*, vol. 12.

Mason, E. S., M. J. Kim, D. H. Perkins, K. S. Kim and D. C. Cole, 1980, *The Economic and Social Modernization of the Republic of Korea*, Cambridge, Mass, Harvard University Press.

Massell, B. F., S. R. Pearson, and J. B Fitch, 1972, 'Foreign Exchange and Economic Development: An Empirical Study of Selected Latin American Countries', *Review of Economics and Statistics*, vol. 54.

Matthews, R. C. O., C. H. Feinstein, and J. C. Odling-Smee, 1982, *British Economic Growth 1856—1973*, Oxford University Press.

Maxwell, S., 1983, 'From Understudy to Leading Star: The Future Role of Impact Assessment in Food Aid Programmes', University of Sussex, IDS, *Bulletin*, vol. 14, no. 3.

Maxwell, S., and H. W. Singer, 1979, 'Food Aid to Developing Countries: A Survey', *World Development*, vol. 14, no. 3.

Minear, L., 1985, 'Reflections on Development Policy: A View from the Private Voluntary Sector,' in Gorman 1985.

Minhas, B. S., 1974, *Planning and the Poor*, New Delhi, S. Chand.

Moore, M. P., 1984, 'Agriculture in Taiwan and South Korea: The Minimalist State?' *IDS Bulletin*, vol. 15, no. 2.

Morris, J., and G. Gwyer, 1983, 'UK Experience with Identifying and Implementing Poverty-Related Aid Projects', *Development Policy Review*, vol. 1, no. 2, November.

Morss, E., 1984, 'Institutional Destruction Resulting from Donor and Project Proliferation in Sub-Saharan African Countries', *World Development*, vol. 12, no 4.

——, *et al*., 1975, *Strategies for Small Farmer Development*, Washington, DC, Development Alternatives Inc.

Mosley, P., 1980. 'Aid, Savings and Growth Revisited', *Bulletin of the Oxford Institute of Economics and Statistics*, vol. 42.

——, 1981, 'Aid for the Poorest: Early Lessons from UK Experience', *Journal of Development Studies*, vol. 17.

——, 1983*a*, 'Can the Poor Benefit from Aid Projects? An Empirical Study of the Trickle Down Hypothesis', University of Bath (mimeo).

——, 1983*b*, 'The Politics of Evaluation: A Comparative Study of World Bank and UK ODA Evaluation Procedures', *Development and Change*, vol. 14, October.

——, and R. P. Dahal, 1984, *Lending to the Poorest: A Case Study of the Small Farmer Development Programme, Nepal*, University of Bath, Papers in Political Economy.

—— and J. Hudson, 1984, *Aid, the Public Sector and the Market in Less Developed Countries*, University of Bath, Papers in Political Economy.

Mujamoto, I., 1973–4, 'Real Value of Tied Aid: The Case of Indonesia in 1967–69', *Economic Development and Cultural Change*, vol. 22.

Muscat, R. J., 1983, *Responding to Changing Nutritional Conditions of the 1980s: Roles for the International Agencies*, New York, UN/ACC/SCN.

*——, 1984*a*, *Aid Effectiveness: Technical Cooperation*, Washington, DC (unpublished).

——, 1984*b*, 'Aid, Private Enterprise and Policy Dialogue: Forms, Experience and Lessons', Washington, DC (mimeo).

——, 1984*c*, *Technical Cooperation Effectiveness: Determinants Scores and Prescriptions*, Washington, DC, USAID.

Nayyar, R., 1984, *Rural Poverty in India: An Analysis of Inter-State Difference*, University of Sussex (unpublished D Phil. thesis).

Nelson, G. O., 1983, 'Food Aid and Agricultural Production in Bangladesh', University of Sussex, *IDS, Bulletin*, vol. 14, no. 2.

Ness, G., 1983, 'The Impact of International Population Assistance', in Krueger and Ruttan 1983.

Netherlands, Ministerie van Buitenlandse Zaken, 1984, *Global Evaluatie*, The Hague, January/April.

Norway, Government of, *Norway's Assistance to Developing Countries*, Norwegian Agency for International Development, Oslo, various years.

OECD, 1984, *Communiqué*, Ministerial Committee Meeting, Paris, May.

—— DAC, 1979, *Guidelines on Local and Recurrent Cost Financing*, Paris Press/A(79) 21.

OECD, DAC, 1982a, *Development Cooperation 1982 Review*, Paris.
——, 1982b, *Evaluation Correspondents' Report on Aid Effectiveness*, Paris.
——, 1982c, *Guidelines on Aid for Maintenance*, Paris, Press A/(82) 74.
——, 1983a, *Development Cooperation 1983 Review*, Paris.
——, 1983b, *Guiding Principles to Aid Agencies for Supporting the Role of Women in Development*, Paris, Press/A(83) 62.
——, 1983c, *Increasing the Effectiveness of Development Cooperation Through Improved Co-ordination at the Country Level*, Paris, Secretariat Note, November.
——, 1983d, *The Role of Non-Governmental Organisations in Development*, Paris, Liaison Bulletin no. 10.
——, 1984a, *Development Cooperation 1984 Review*, Paris.
——, 1984b, *Improving Aid Coordination—A DAC Review*, Paris, Secretariat Note, November.
——, 1984c, *Report of the Expert Group on Aid Evaluation on Lessons of Experience Emerging from Aid Evaluation*, Paris, Secretariat Note.
——, 1985a, *A Chronology of Development Cooperation*, Paris, Working Document, April.
——, 1985b, *Development Cooperation 1985 Review*, Paris.
——, 1985c, *Recommendation of the Council* on environmental assessment of development assistance programmes, Paris, C(85)104, July.
Ohlin, G., 1966, *Foreign Aid Policies Reconsidered*, Paris, OECD Development Centre.
OPEC Fund for International Development, 1984, *OPEC Aid and OPEC Aid Institutions: A Profile*, Vienna.
*Ortona, G., 1984, *Aid for Transport and Communications: European-based agencies*, Turin (unpublished).
Overseas Development Administration: *see* UK ODA.

Papanek, G., 1972, 'The Effects of Aid and Other Resources Transfers on Savings and Growth in Less Developed Countries', *Economic Journal*, vol. 82.
——, 1973, 'Aid, Foreign Private Investment, Savings and Growth in Less Developed Countries', *Journal of Political Economy*, vol. 81.
——, 1983, 'Aid Growth and Equity in Southern Asia', in Parkinson 1983.
Parkinson, J. R. (ed), 1983, *Poverty and Aid*, Oxford, Blackwell.
Patel, I. G., 1971, 'Aid Relationships for the Seventies', in B. Ward (ed.), *The Widening Gap*, New York, Columbia University Press.
Paul, S. and A. Subramanian, 1983, 'Development Programmes for the Poor: Do Strategies Make a Difference?' *Economic and Political Weekly*, March.
Payer, C., 1982, *Tanzania and the World Bank*, DERAP Working Paper A285, Fantoft, Norway, The Christian Michelsen Institute.
Pearson, L. B. (Chairman), 1969, *Partners in Development*, Report of the Commission on International Development, New York, Praeger.
*Pell, J. D. and R. Whyte, 1984, *Agricultural Project Effectiveness: (European-based aid agencies)*, London (unpublished).

Phillips, K., 1984, *Staying on Top: The Business Case for a National Industrial Strategy*, New York, Random House.

Please, S., 1984, *The Hobbled Giant: Essays on the World Bank*, Boulder and London, Westview Press.

Porter, R. S., 1986, 'Arab Economic Aid', *Development Policy Review*, 4 (1) March.

Raj, K. N., 1965, *Indian Economic Growth: Performance and Prospects*, Calcutta, Allied.

Rao, C. H. H., 1975, *Technological Change and the Distribution of Gains from Indian Agriculture*, New Delhi, Macmillan.

Reutlinger, S., 1983, 'Project Food Aid and Equitable Growth: Income Transfer Efficiency First', in WFP/Government of Netherlands 1983.

Reynolds, L. G., 1983, 'The Spread of Economic Growth in the Third World', *Journal of Economic Literature*, vol. xxi.

Rodgers, G. R., 1973, 'Effects of Public Works on Rural Poverty', *Economic and Political Weekly*, February.

Rondinelli, D., 1983, *Development Projects as Policy Experience: An Adaptive Approach to Development Administration*, London, Methuen.

Rose, T., 1984, 'Aid Modalities: A Brief Series of Donor Views, with Special Reference to Sector Aid', Paris, OECD Development Centre (unpublished).

Rubin, B. R., 1982, *Private Power and Public Investment in India*, University of Chicago, (unpublished PhD thesis).

Ruttan, V., 1984, 'Integrated Rural Development Programmes: A Historical Perspective', *World Development*, vol. 12.

*Sachse, E. Y., 1984, *A Comparison of Development Assistance from Bilateral and Multilateral Sources*, Washington, DC (unpublished).

Saith, A., 1981, 'Production, Prices and Poverty in Rural India', *Journal of Development Studies*, vol. 17.

Sandford, S., 1983, *Management of Pastoral Development in the Third World*, London, Wiley.

Saudi Arabia, Government of, 1982/3, *Annual Report*, Riyadh, The Saudi Fund for Economic Development.

Schmitz, H., 1984, 'Industrialization Strategies in Less Developed Countries: Some Lessons of Historical Experience', *Journal of Development Studies*, vol. 21.

Schubert, J. N., 'The Impact of Food Aid on World Malnutrition', *International Organisation*, vol. 35, no. 2, Spring.

Scott, B., *et al.*, 1984, *US Competitiveness in the World Economy*, Cambridge Mass., Harvard Business School.

*Segal, Quince and Associates, 1984, *Aid Effectiveness Study: Review of Four Donors from the Perspective of Industry and Energy Sectors*, Cambridge (unpublished).

Sen, A. K., 1981*a*, 'Family and Food: Sex-Bias in Poverty' (mimeo).

——, 1981*b*, *Poverty and Famines: An Essay on Entitlement and Deprivation*, Oxford University Press.

——, 1981*c*, 'Public Action and the Quality of Life in Developing Countries', *Oxford Bulletin of Economics and Statistics*, vol. 43.

——, 1983, 'Development: Which Way Now?', *Economic Journal*, vol. 93.

——, and S. Sen Gupta, 1983, 'Mulnutrition of Rural Indian Children and the Sex Bias', *Economic and Political Weekly*, Annual no.

Sewell, J. B. *et al.*, 1980, *US Foreign Policy and the Third World—Agenda 1980*, Overseas Development Council (Washington, DC), New York, Praeger.

——, *et al.*, 1985, *Agenda 1985—86*, New Brunswick, Transaction Books.

Shaw, D. J., 1983, 'Triangular Transactions in Food Aid: Concept and Practice—The Example of the Zimbabwe Operations', University of Sussex, IDS, *Bulletin*, vol. 14, no. 2, April.

Shawcross, W., 1984, *The Quality of Mercy*, London, Deutsch.

SIDA, 1982, Review of the Kenya/Sweden Development Programme in the sector of Rural Water Supply, report by a joint review team, Nairobi, Ministry of Water Development, and Stockholm, SIDA.

Singer, H. W. with S. J. Maxwell, 1983, 'Development through Food—Twenty Years' Experience', in WFP/Government of the Netherlands 1983.

Sobhan, R., 1982, *The Crisis of External Dependence: The Political Economy of Foreign Aid to Bangladesh*, Dhaka, University Press.

Stein, R. O. and B. Johnson, 1979, *Banking on the Biosphere*, London International Institute for Environment and Development.

*Steinberg, D. I., 1984, *On Foreign Aid and the Development of the Republic of Korea: The Effectiveness of Concessional Assistance*, Washington, DC, Agency for International Development (unpublished).

Stern, E., 1983, 'World Bank Financing of Structural Adjustment', in J. Williamson (ed.), *IMF Conditionality*, Washington, DC, Institute for International Economics, MIT Press.

Stevens, C., 1979, *Food Aid and the Developing World*, London, Croom Helm.

——, 1983, Review of Jackson 1982, in University of Sussex, IDS, *Bulletin*, vol. 14, no. 2

——, (ed.), *ELC and the Third World—A Survey*, London, Hodder and Stoughton, New York, Holmes and Meier, various years.

Stewart, F., 1971, 'Foreign Capital, Domestic Savings, etc.: A Comment', *Bulletin of the Oxford Institute of Economics and Statistics*, vol. 33.

Streeten, P., 1981, *Development Perspectives*, London, Macmillan.

——, 1985, 'What Price Food? Agricultural Price Policies in Developing Countries', Washington, DC, February (mimeo).

Sukhatme, P., 1978, 'Assessment of Adequacy of Diets at Different Income Levels', *Economic and Political Weekly*, August.

Tait, A. A., W. L. M. Gratz, and B. J. Eichengreen, 1979, *International Comparisons of Taxation for Selected Developing Countries 1972–76*, IMF Staff Papers, vol. 26.

Taylor, G., and S. Moustapha, 1983, 'Strategies for Forestry Development in the Semi-Arid Tropics: Lessons from the Sahel', International Symposium on Strategies and Designs for Afforestation, Reforestation and Tree Planting, Waginer.

Taylor, L., 1983, *Structural Macroeconomics: Applicable Models for the Third World*, New York, Basic Books.

Tendler, J., 1975, *Inside Foreign Aid*, Baltimore, Johns Hopkins University Press.

——, 1979, *New Directions: Rural Roads*, Washington, DC, USAID.

Tendulkar, S., 1971, 'Interaction between Domestic and Foreign Resources . . . Some Experiments for India', in Chenery 1971.

Toye, J., 1985, 'The ATP Scheme—Some General Considerations', Swansea, Centre for Development Studies, May (mimeo).

UK ODA, 1979, *ODA's Training Aid*, EV216, London, ODA.

——, 1981, *Technology to Benefit the Poor: A Review of ODA's Appropriate Technology Programme*, London, ODA.

——, 1983a, *British Overseas Aid 1982*, London, HMSO.

——, 1983b, *The Lessons of Experience: Evaluation Work in ODA*, London, HMSO.

——, 1984a, *Memorandum to the DAC*, London ODA.

——, 1984b, *Renewable Natural Resources Sector Paper*, London ODA.

——, 1984c, 'They Came to Train', London (draft).

——, and Government of Tanzania, 1984, *British and Tanzanian Training Institutions: Collaborative Programmes*, EV315, London, ODA.

UN, 1975, *Poverty, Unemployment and Development Policy*, New York.

——, 1983, *Operational Activities for Development of the UN System*, Note by the Secretary-General, A/38/258, New York, June, Department of International Economic and Social Research.

——, 1983, *Report on the World Social Situation*, E/CN5/1983/3, New York.

UNDP, 1978, *Rural Woman's Participation in Development*, New York 1978.

——, 1979, *Rural Development: Issues and Approaches for Technical Cooperation*, New York.

——, 1984, *Policy Review: Measures to be Taken to Meet the Changing TC Requirements of the Developing Countries*, DP/1984/4, New York, April.

——/FAO, 1984, *National Agricultural Research*, New York.

——/IBRD, 1979, *Comprehensive Development Planning*, New York.

——/UNESCO, 1983, *Education, Innovation and Reform*, Evaluation Study no. 7, New York.

——/UNIDO, 1983, 'Industrial Research and Service Institutions', New York.

UNFPA, 1982, *Evaluation of UNFPA Projects*, Report of the Executive Director to the Governing Council, New York.

UNICEF, 1982, *Programme Cooperation at Intermediate and Local Levels*, E/ICEF/L1439, New York, February.

——, 1985, *Annual Report 1985*, New York.

United States, Government of, 1982, *US Participation in the Multilateral Development Banks in the 1980s*, Washington, DC, US Treasury.

——, 1984, *International Security and Development Cooperation Act of 1984*, Washington, DC, US Govt. Printing Office.

USAID, 1980*a*, *Assessing the Impact of Development Projects on Women*, Washington, DC.

——, 1980*b*, *Program Evaluation Report no. 4*, Washington, DC.

——, 1980*c*, *Rural Water Projects in Tanzania: Technical, Social and Administrative Issues*, AID Evaluation Special Study no. 3, Washington, DC.

——, 1980*d*, *The Workshop on Pastoralism and African Livestock Development*, Washington, DC.

——, 1982*a*, *AID Experience in Agricultural Research: A Review of Project Evaluations*, Washington, DC.

——, 1982*b*, *Approaches to the Policy Dialogue*, AID Policy Paper, Washington DC, December.

——, 1982*c*, *The Economic Development of Korea: Sui Generis or Generic?* Evaluation Special Study no. 6, Washington, DC, January.

——, 1982*d*, *Turning Private Voluntary Organizations into Development Agencies: Questions for Evaluation*, Washington, DC.

——, 1983*a*, *Consultative Groups as Instruments for Donor Coordination*, Discussion Draft, Washington, DC.

——, 1983*b*, *Effective Institution Building*, Program Evaluation Paper no. 11, Washington, DC.

——, 1983*c*, *Evaluation of the Peace Fellowship Program*, Washington, DC.

——, 1983*d*, *Irrigation and AID's Experience: a Consideration Based on Evaluations*, Program Evaluation Report no. 8, Washington, DC, August.

——, 1983*e*, *Strengthening the Agricultural Research Capacity of Less-developed Countries: Lessons from AID Experience*, Program Evaluation Report no.10, Washington, DC, September.

——, 1983*f*, *The Private Sector: Costa Rica*, Evaluation Special Study no. 9, Washington, DC, March.

——, 1983*g*, *The Private Sector—The Tortoise Walk: Public Policy and Private Activity in the Economic Development of Cameroon*, Evaluation Special Study no. 10, Washington, DC, March.

——, 1983*h*, *The Private Sector and the Economic Development of Malawi*, Evaluation Special Study no. 11, Washington, DC, March.

——, 1983*i*, *The Private Sector: The Regulation of Rural Markets in Africa*, Evaluation Special Study no. 14, Washington, DC, June.

——, 1984*a*, *An Economic Evaluation: Zimbabwe's Commodity Import Programmes with Special Reference to US Programs*, Washington, DC (unpublished).

——, 1984*b*, *An Evaluation of the Somalia Commodity Import Program*, Washington, DC (Unpublished).

——, 1985, *Private Enterprise Development*, AID Policy Paper, Washington, DC, May.

Van Arkadie, B., 'The IMF Prescription for Structural Adjustment in Tanzania: A Comment', in K. Jansen (ed.), *Monetarism, Economic Crisis, and the Third World*, London, Cass.

*———, and K. de Wilde, 1984, *Aid Effectiveness in Bangladesh*, The Hague, Institute of Social Studies (unpublished).

Van de Laar, A., 1980, *The World Bank and the Poor*, Boston, the Hague, and London, Nijhoff.

Visaria, P., 1981, 'Poverty and Unemployment in India: An Analysis of Recent Evidence', *World Development*, vol. 9.

Voivodas, C. S., 1973, 'Exports, Foreign Capital Inflow and Economic Growth', *Journal of International Economics*, vol. 3.

Vyas, V., 1979, 'Structural Change in Indian Agriculture', *Indian Journal of Agricultural Economics*, vol. 1.

Wade, R., 1982, 'The World Bank and India's Irrigation Reform', *Journal of Development Studies*, vol. 18.

Weisskopf, T. E., 1972, 'Impact of Foreign Capital Inflows on Domestic Savings in Underdeveloped Countries', *Journal of International Economics*, vol. 2.

Westphal, L. E., and K. S. Kim, 1982, 'Industrial Policy and Development in Korea', in Balassa 1982*b*.

WFP/Government of the Netherlands, 1983, *Report of the Seminar on Food Aid. The Hague, 3–5 October*, Rome, WFP.

Wheeler, D., 1984, 'Sources of Stagnation in Sub-Saharan Africa', *World Development*, vol. 12.

White, G., and R. Wade, (eds.) 1984, *Developmental States in East Asia*, University of Sussex, IDS.

White, J., 1967, *Pledged to Development*, London, Overseas Development Institute.

———, 1972, *Regional Development Banks*, New York, Praeger.

WHO, 1965, *Nutrition and Infection*, Geneva.

———, 1983, *Human Resource Development for Primary Health Care*, Geneva.

Wiggins, S., 1984, 'Integrated Rural Development Revisited: Early Lessons from Kenya's Arid and Semi-arid Lands Programme' (unpublished).

Williamson, J., 1982, *The Lending Policies of the International Monetary Fund*, Washington, DC, Institute for International Economics.

———, 1983*a*, 'On Judging the Success of IMF Policy Advice', in Williamson 1983*b*.

——— (ed.), 1983*b*, *IMF Conditionality*, Washington, DC, Institute for International Econimics Cambridge, Mass, MIT Press.

Wolfson, M., 1983, *Profiles in Population Assistance*, Paris, OECD Development Centre.

Wolgin, J. M., 1983, *The Private Sector, the Public Sector and Donor Assistance in Economic Development: An Interpretive Essay*, Washington, DC, USAID, Program Evaluation Discussion Paper no. 6.

World Bank, 1972, *Review of Bank Technical Assistance to Bangladesh*, Washington, DC.

———, 1975*a*, *Land Reform*, Washington, DC.

———, 1975*b*, *The Assault on World Poverty*, Washington, DC.

———, 1978*a*, *Review of Bank Operations in the Education Sector*, Washington, DC.

World Bank, 1978*b*, *Rural Development Projects: A Retrospective View of Bank Experiences in Sub-Saharan Africa*, Report no. 2242, Washington, DC.

——, 1979*a*, *Operations Evaluation: World Bank Standards and Procedures*, Washington, DC.

——, 1979*b*, *World Development Report 1979*, New York, Oxford University Press.

——, 1980*a*, *The World Bank and Institutional Development Experience and Directions for Future Work*, Washington, DC, Projects Advisory Staff.

——, 1980*b*, *Uttar Pradesh Agricultural Credit: Project Performance Audit Report*, Report no. 3081, Washington, DC.

——, 1981*a*, *Accelerated Development in Sub-Saharan Africa: An Agenda for Action*, Washington, DC.

——, 1981*b*, *Agricultural Research Sector Policy Paper*, Washington, DC.

——, 1981*c*, *Lake Alaotra Project, Madagascar: Impact Evaluation Report*, Report no. 3600, Washington, DC.

——, 1981*d*, *Water Management in Bank-Supported Irrigation Projects*, Washington, DC.

——, 1981*e*, *World Development Report 1981*, New York, Oxford University Press.

——, 1982*a*, *Eighth Annual Review of Project Performance Audit Results*, Washington, DC.

——, 1982*b*, *IDA in Restrospect: The First Two Decades of the International Development Association*, New York, Oxford University Press.

——, 1982*c*, *Report and Recommendation of the President of the IBRD on a Proposed Loan and Credit to the Republic of Kenya for a Second Structural Adjustment Operation*, Report no. P-3322-KE, Washington, DC.

——, 1982*d*, *Review of Training in Bank-Financed Projects*, Washington, DC.

——, 1982*e*, *World Development Report 1982*, New York, Oxford University Press.

——, 1983*a*, *Focus on Poverty*, Washington, DC.

——, 1983*b*, *Learning by Doing; World Bank Lending for Urban Development, 1972—82*, Washington, DC.

——, 1983*c*, *Ninth Annual Review of Project Performance Audit Results*, Report no. 4720, Washington, DC.

——, 1983*d*, *Sub-Saharan Africa: Progress Report on Development Prospects and Programs*, Washington, DC.

——, 1983*e*, *World Development Report 1983*, New York, Oxford University Press.

——, 1984*a*, *Institutional Development in Africa*, Report no. 5085, Washington, DC.

——, 1984*b*, *Ninth Annual Report on Project Implementation and Supervision*, Ch. iv, Technical Assistance, R84–28, Washington, DC, 9 February.

——, 1984*c*, *Nutrition Review*, Washington, DC, Population, Health and Nutrition Department (mimeo).

——, 1984*d*, *Structural Adjustment Lending—Progress Report*, Washington, DC, Country Programmes Department.

——, 1984*e*, *The Bank's Changing Role in Aid Coordination*, Report of the Jaycox Working Group on the Future Role of the World Bank, Washington, DC (mimeo).

——, 1984*f*, *The World Bank Annual Report 1984*, New York, Oxford University Press.

——, 1984*g*, *Tenth Annual Review of Project Performance Audit Results*, Report no. 5248, Washington, DC.

——, 1984*h*, *Towards Sustained Development in Sub-Saharan Africa: A Joint Program of Action*, Washington, DC.

——, 1984*i*, *World Development Report 1984*, New York, Oxford University Press.

——, 1985, *World Development Report 1985*, New York, Oxford University Press.

World Meteorological Organization, 1972, *20 Years of WMO Assistance*, Geneva.

Yates, A. J, 'Development of Industrial Countries', *World Development*, vol. 10.

Yudelman, M., 1984, 'Agricultural Lending by the Bank (1974–84)', *Finance and Development*, vol. 25, no. 4, December.

Zulu, J. B., and S.M. Nsouli, 1980, 'Adjustment Programs in Africa', *Finance and Development*, vol. 21. no. 1, March.